ADOPTION

ADOPTION

A ROAD TO RETRIEVAL

TIM J. R. TRUMPER

Adoption: A Road to Retrieval

Published by:

From His Fullness Ministries
Grand Rapids, Michigan, USA.
www.fromhisfullness.com

ISBN: 978-0-578-38616-4

All Scripture quotations, unless otherwise stated, are taken from the English Standard Version, The Large Print Edition (Wheaton, Illinois: Crossway Bibles, 2004).

IN MEMORIAM

Rev. Dr. Peter R. G. Trumper
July 28, 1934–July 5, 2015
—alias Dad.

Proverbs 17:6
". . . the glory of children is their fathers."

ENDORSEMENTS

Tim Trumper has made tireless efforts to remedy the neglect of adoption's significance for biblical soteriology. Here we have a bountiful collection and pleasing arrangement of the fruit from his theological life's work.

Daniel J. Treier
Gunther H. Knoedler Professor of Theology,
Wheaton College.

J. I. Packer once summed up the gospel in three words: "adoption through propitiation." Once again, however, we see that the first shall be last, for while theologians have lavished attention on the theme of propitiation, adoption has, by contrast, suffered from relative neglect—until now. Tim Trumper here provides a comprehensive biblical, historical, and theological account of this key metaphor for expressing the believer's union with Christ. Here is a scholarly work that preaches!

Kevin J. Vanhoozer
Research Professor of Systematic Theology,
Trinity Evangelical Divinity School.

Tim Trumper offers here a masterly demonstration of the long line of tradition on Adoption as a seam to be mined, even if it be a thin one. That Chrysostom and Augustine had room for it and they in turn provided so much to Calvin (via Oecolampadius?) and a few choice others in the Reformed theological tradition, might well be significant. Adoption does best when it is a little further down the *ordo salutis*, a hinge between justification and union, "prospectively" giving some shape to our understanding of what it is to "become (a) Christian" and know God as Father. The coverage of the history of the theology of Adoption after the Puritan era is most richly informative, with attention in the realm of biblical studies pleasingly becoming the occasion for fresh thinking on the matter, even though not all biblical scholars are happy to pay attention to dogmatic categories. Part II really tries to show how through an exploration of the key metaphor primarily in Paul and John, with Chapter 5 reading Galatians 4 closely, the two worlds can co-exist and collaborate. There is also significant eirenic grace shown to theological opponents!

Mark W. Elliott
Professor of Divinity and Biblical Criticism,
University of Glasgow, Scotland.

I know of no one who has studied the doctrine of adoption in a more comprehensive way or presented the doctrine in a more careful way than my good friend, Tim Trumper. Going forward, I wouldn't dare preach, teach, or write on the subject of adoption without first consulting this decades-in-the-making masterwork.

Mike Honeycutt, Senior Pastor,
Westminster Presbyterian Church (PCA), Rock Hill, SC;
formerly Associate Professor of Historical and Practical Theology,
Covenant Theological Seminary.

I am glad to recommend this marvellous book. Marvellously comprehensive, beautifully written and superbly explained. This is a book for all who love God and His Word.

Tom Holland
Senior Research Fellow,
Union School of Theology, Wales.

Trumper has finally done it! After decades of writing about adoption in various articles, books, and essays, he has now updated, revised, and brought all his thinking together in this one book. In *Adoption: A Retrieval* he takes his readers on a journey that begins with retrieving adoption from its neglect in history, moves into explaining how metaphors work in theology, continues on to provide a fresh exposition of the Pauline texts on adoption, and ends with recommendations on how to retrieve this great doctrine for God's glory and the good of his people. In my view, this is the most thorough and well-researched book on the doctrine of adoption. I highly recommend it!

Barton Priebe
Author, *Adopted by God: Discover the Life-Transforming Joy of a Neglected Truth.*

No one has helped me to study more carefully, think more deeply, understand more fully, and enjoy more devotionally the Bible's teaching on the doctrine of adoption (and its historical neglect and retrieval), than Tim Trumper. Having read his *magnum opus*, "An Historical Study of the Doctrine of Adoption in the Calvinistic Tradition" multiple times for personal encouragement and theological study, I was grateful to learn of *Adoption: A Road to Retrieval.* It is excellent, timely, comprehensive, and challenging. I thank the Lord for Trumper and his scholarly work on adoption.

Michael A. Graham
Author, *Cheer Up! The Life and Ministry of Jack Miller.*

I have long had the impression that in the region of that great truth [the Fatherhood of God and the sonship of His people] there lies a rich field of precious ore yet to be surveyed and explored; and that somewhere in that direction theology has fresh work to bring out of the storehouse of the Divine Word.

Robert S. Candlish, *The Fatherhood of God.*

The Holy Spirit takes truth in portions, and seems sometimes to turn our eye away from one portion of truth on purpose to let us see better some other portion, by keeping our attention for a time fixed on that alone.

Andrew A. Bonar, *A Commentary on Leviticus.*

If at any time I dissent from some divines, I trust they will not put a wrong construction on such a difference. Men have always been allowed to differ without compromising friendship. I ardently desire their sacred friendship: I bow to their learning; I admire their virtues, and I constantly pray to Almighty God, that he would long spare their lives for the good of the schools and churches. I intreat all my readers to give a kind and candid attention to the pages of this work, and if anything is handled rightly, let them give praise to God, if otherwise, let them pardon the writer. And now, farewell indulgent reader, and commend me to God in your prayers.

Benedict Pictet, *Christian Theology.*

If there is one thing more than another which we believers in historic Christianity ought to encourage in the youth of our day it is independence of mind. It is a great mistake . . . to suppose that we who are called "conservatives" desperately hold to certain beliefs merely because they are old and are opposed to the discovery of new facts. On the contrary, we welcome new discoveries with all our hearts, and we believe that our cause will come to its rights again only when youth throws off its present intellectual lethargy, refuses to go thoughtlessly with the anti-intellectual current of the age, and recovers some genuine independence of mind.

J. Gresham Machen, *What is Faith?*

CONTENTS

FIGURES

~~~~

ABBREVIATIONS

A-N F	*Ante-Nicene Fathers* (10 volumes, fourth printing [Peabody, MA: Hendrickson, 2004)
CC	*Calvin's Commentaries*, reprinted from The Calvin Translation Society (Grand Rapids: Baker, 2005)
CD	Karl Barth's *Church Dogmatics*, authorized English translation of *Die Kirchliche Dogmatik*, 1932–1967 (Peabody, MA: Hendrickson, 2010)
CMC	Calvinistic Methodist Confession
CW	John Murray, *Collected Writings* (Edinburgh: The Banner of Truth Trust, 1976–1982)
DG	John M. Frame, *The Doctrine of God.* A Theology of Lordship Series (Phillipsburg, NJ: P&R, 2002)
DKG	John M. Frame, *The Doctrine of the Knowledge of God.* A Theology of Lordship Series (Phillipsburg, NJ: P&R, 1987)
ETS	Evangelical Theological Society
JETS	*Journal of the Evangelical Theological Society*
N and P-N F	*Nicene- and Post-Nicene Fathers* (first series, 14 vols. [Augustine and Chrysostom], and second series, 14 vols. [Peabody, MA: Hendrickson, 1996])
NCC	The New City Catechism
NPP	The New Perspective on Paul
SBET	*Scottish Bulletin of Evangelical Theology*
SJT	*Scottish Journal of Theology*
WCF	Westminster Confession of Faith
WLC	Westminster Larger Catechism
WSC	Westminster Shorter Catechism

~~~~

PREFACE

I believe that one will be much helped in understanding the matter of this book, if he has taken note of the intention, and the method according to which it is discussed. It is my opinion, too, that one who has first seen this preface will not pronounce a rash judgment, if he shall find offered here any thought that is contrary to his own belief.

Anselm, *Monologium*

Over the last thirty years of research, many questions have arisen, some I have been able to answer over time. But among those which may never be fully answerable in this life, is the question as to why, historically, only a minority of pastors and theologians, seeing the doctrine of adoption in Scripture, have made much of it. Ultimately, the answer lies in God's leading and timing. He is the one who chooses when and where to illuminate his revealed truth. But there are also human factors to consider. We come to these in chapter two. But still, the contrast between the glory of our adoption in Christ and the scarcity and sometimes the paucity of what is written on the grace of adoption is most glaring. Supplementing this question is the query as to why those who have written on adoption rarely hint at why they did so, when so many others have not.

We could offer conjecture. Perhaps it was the reticence of pastors and theologians of a former age to speak of their own work. This sounds plausible for there was not in bygone times today's demand to cite sources. Yet, overall, it is more likely that they were oblivious as to how unusual was their interest in adoption, and how helpful a documentation of the influences on them would one day be to the retrieval of the doctrine. As things stand, many figuring in the history of adoption have left us no record of why they wrote about adoption. The narratives of their interest were never penned, are now lost to history, or are yet to be uncovered. Who knows how differently the history of the doctrine may have turned out had those writing on adoption done more to explain why they did so. Even now it would be fascinating to learn how and why the doctrine jumped off the pages of Scripture at them. Was it something domestic, exegetical, theological, spiritual, ecclesiastical, or psychological? Were there sources influencing their understanding? In most cases, we do not know.[1]

It is on account of the intrigue I have felt when gleaning from others that I explain here as best I can why my mind and heart have been so relentlessly taken up with the grace of adoption over the last decades. I seek not to draw excessive attention to myself, thinking more highly of myself than I ought to (Rom. 12:3), but to—

- Thank those who paved the way for this study.
- Shed light on my take on adoption.
- Explain the origin and makeup of this volume.
- Spare researchers the hours I spent tracking down, with little success, influences on the thought of other theologians of adoption.
- Help ensure that adoption does not recede once more into the mists of history. To put the matter another way, the more accounts we have of how the Spirit has led to the truth of adoption, the more difficult it is for the church to continue overlooking the doctrine.

There follows, then, the back story of my particular contribution.

A JOURNEY BEGUN

To make a long story short, it was one day in the early 1990s that the doctrine of adoption came without forewarning to occupy my mind and comfort my heart. That it did is attributable to God alone. Not

---

[1] In another study in progress I include a few notable instances which very clearly identify why some pastors and theologians were taken up with the Fatherhood of God.

only had he, in the mystery of his providence, brought me through to the grace of adoption a decade earlier (August 1981), he called me that day to the intensive and extensive study of the doctrine. I praise God the Father for his call to grapple with it, God the Spirit for illumining, enlivening and sustaining the research, and God the Son for cleansing my endeavors. *Soli Deo gloria!*

It was, however, through Reverend Professor Archibald Boyd (died 2008), erstwhile principal of the Free Church of Scotland College (now Edinburgh Theological Seminary), Edinburgh, that the call came. I cherish his memory, fundamentally for his godliness and his personal kindnesses, but thank God here for his introduction of the student body to the work of Herman Ridderbos.[2]

While not always popular, Principal Boyd's ongoing use of *Paul: An Outline of His Theology* opened our minds to the riches of the apostle's theology and to the emerging international development of Reformed biblical theology. The former was obvious enough at the time, but only with hindsight did the significance of the latter become apparent. In the English-speaking world, Reformed biblical theology has been more associated with the name of Geerhardus Vos. It is he and not Ridderbos who has received from Richard Gaffin the moniker "the father of a Reformed biblical theology."[3] It was Ridderbos, however, who not only introduced me to adoption but who helped me appreciate how fundamental biblical theology is to the understanding of it.

The introduction to Ridderbos occurred through Principal Boyd's yearly assigning of his senior New Testament class the task of summarizing a chapter each of *Paul*, wryly asking us for an "outline of

---

[2] In remarking on Professor Boyd's kindnesses, it would be remiss not to mention Mrs. Doreen Boyd's hosting of us as students. Mrs. Boyd passed to glory in 2019.

[3] Richard B. Gaffin Jr., "The Vitality of Reformed Systematic Theology," Anthony T. Selvaggio, ed., *The Faith Once Delivered: Essays in Honor of Dr. Wayne R. Spear* (Phillipsburg, NJ: P&R, 2007), 6.

an outline of Paul's theology"! It was in running my finger down the list of assigned chapters that the words "The Adoption. The Inheritance" jumped out at me. I vividly recall in that quiet moment in the New Testament classroom the color and warmth of the idea standing in marked contrast to the neutral paintwork surrounding the notice, and can say without exaggeration that that moment in 1991 or 1992, undramatic in itself, forever changed the course of my life.

The moment might not have been so impactful were it not for Ridderbos' take on adoption. Since much of the study is an outworking of his abiding influence, I will forgo saying too much here. Yet, to acknowledge his silhouette, it is fitting to delineate the chief ways in which his chapter on adoption shaped my thinking.

First, I was struck by his recognition of the importance of the motif, all the more so when comparing the quantitative and qualitative neglect of the doctrine in the consecutive volumes of systematic theology.

Second, I learned from Ridderbos that Paul alone uses the term υἱοθεσία. This is the sole term in the Scriptures for adoption. Yet, when I consulted the systematic theologies I often found this crucial hermeneutical key overlooked by those systematicians including adoption in their tomes, and diluted by the admixture of filial or familial terms from outside of Paul's writings.

Third, I could not help but notice Ridderbos' faithfulness to the apostle's salvation-historical approach to adoption, and began to observe that Reformed systematics by contrast focus more narrowly on the order of salvation and the interconnectedness between adoption and neighboring soteric elements such as calling, regeneration, justification, and sanctification, etc.

Fourth, it did not take long, given the preceding, to realize that the full retrieval of adoption requires not simply an understanding of its neglect, and the playing of catch-up in terms of the amount written on the doctrine, but a back-to-Scripture approach highlighting the riches of adoption and suggestive of ways in which the shape and feel of classic Presbyterianism (Westminster Calvinism) can be renewed.

The class assignment quickly passed, but I was left with three impressions that have become unshakable:

- That adoption is a beautiful picture of the grace of God, every bit worthy of further research. The study of the doctrine thus took on the passion of a hobby, yet in that passion lay a growing sense of God's call to commit to the understanding and articulation of his adoptive grace.
- That there is a methodological rift in our Reformed tradition, which, prior, to the assignment, I did not realize existed. Indeed, I was perplexed initially and disturbed by the contrast, new to me, between Ridderbos and the systematicians. No one influenced this perception of the rift. It arose solely from the undeniable tension between the treatment of adoption in the disciplines of biblical and systematic theology.
- That the Reformed faith is central to the retrieval of adoption. This conviction arose not because that is the theology in which I was reared, nor because that was the schooling I was receiving, nor indeed because that is the theology to which I subscribe. It arose on account of the fact that the Reformed did most to expound adoption in the Reformation and post-Reformation eras.

While certain of these discoveries unnerved me initially, they were confirmed by forays into the writings of John Calvin. Not only did his interest in adoption precede Ridderbos', so did his perception of Paul's broad, salvation-historical take on the doctrine. Nevertheless, I was left pondering all the more the differing methodological approaches within the Reformed tradition, and, going by what I had already learned of the biblical data of adoption, was gaining what I later learned is a sympathetic-critical (in that order!) appreciation of Reformed ortho-doxy.

To this we shall return, suffice it to say that it is to Ridderbos that I am indebted for dismantling in my mind the false assumption that Reformed orthodoxy can only be organized by a certain process of ratiocination. Indeed, I took to heart his implicit warning that we may, albeit unwittingly, make idols out of human systems of theology, even Reformed systems of theology. This idolization occurs when systems take precedence over the exegetical specificities of Scripture. The test case of adoption illustrates this, and thus warns that Reformed orthodoxy is not immune from the need to maintain alongside a high view of Scripture a high use of it.

A JOURNEY CONTINUED

Questions of method arose out of consideration as to how best to explain the grace of adoption. Thus, I continued avidly reading around the doctrine. Bit by bit relevant studies, quotes, and arguments came into view. The information they imparted about adoption gradually formed a picture in my mind of its surprising neglect and shed light on its exposition and theology, as also on its devotional, missional, and practical significance.

For the data received early on, I am indebted to an array of theologians, pastors, and historians. Robert Candlish, J. Scott Lidgett, John Murray, James I. Packer, Sinclair B. Ferguson, Douglas F. Kelly, Errol Hulse, Allen Mawhinney, James Scott, Trevor Burke, and Brian A. Gerrish come most easily to mind. They set in motion the desire to sketch the theological history of adoption and to understand the doctrine aright. Friends Murray Linton and the late Rev. Brian Norton (1939–2015) were also a tonic to me, enthusiastically sharing relevant sources they came across.

My informal dabbling with the doctrine became official in 1993. That year I graduated from the Free Church College and entered into the doctoral program of the University of Edinburgh, at New College (today the University's School of Divinity), the next door up from the Free Church College along the city's Presbyterian ridge. There, I was ably mentored by my primary and secondary supervisors, Dr. Gary D. Badcock and the late Professor David F. Wright (1937–2008). To them I am indebted for their holistic concern for my person, and for the freedom they afforded me to follow my passion and what quickly became my instincts. Particularly memorable are three early conversations with Dr. Badcock. Even now, I picture and hear him saying to me over successive meetings:

> "Go and prove to me that adoption has been neglected."
>
> "Now go and prove to me why adoption should not have been neglected."
>
> "I think the time has come to investigate what Calvin says of adoption."

As one of the last of the dinosaurs at New College (those under less pressure to finish the doctorate in three years), I had the luxury over the coming years of developing the research along two tracks. The one led through fields of biblical, metaphorical, and systematic theology, satiating my thirst for general knowledge of adoption and informing my assessment of the contribution of prior theologians and scholars already at work in the field. The other led through the field of historical theology and served the dissertation. Both tracks emerged as two shoots from a common stem, namely, an increasing awareness of the historic neglect of adoption and a growing passion to help rectify it.

This endeavor was made possible by funding from a variety of sources, but especially helpful were those grants accompanied by opportunities for articulating fresh ideas and obtaining feedback. Throughout, the times with Dr. David Cook and (now Professor) Mark Elliott of UCCF's Whitefield Institute, were most welcome. Yet, the second year of the doctoral research, 1994–95, was spent as an Erasmus scholar at the Eberhard Karls Universität, Tübingen, Germany. In that bastion of Lutheranism I continued to plod away on the historical track, but not discovering much in its annals (which included an interview with freshly retired professor Jürgen Moltmann), I spent the year away from Edinburgh focusing on the relevant biblical data.

This turned out to be a Godsend, for it afforded the opportunity to satisfy a growing conviction that I could not evaluate the thought of the various theologians of adoption without obtaining a settled understanding of adoption. In this pursuit, Professor Otto Betz (1917–2005) gave generously of his time and expertise in the University's *Kolloquium für Graduerte* and encouraged me in delineating the increasingly apparent differences between Johannine and Pauline thought.

On returning to Edinburgh, David Wright suggested that I begin submitting the preliminary findings of the research to the *Scottish Bulletin of Evangelical Theology (SBET)*. Thus, there began the intermittent publication of six articles in three couplets which appeared between 1996 and 2005. In them I began to plot, in summary fashion, a path toward the retrieval of adoption. This volume is built on their spadework, more of which is below.

Meanwhile, the historical track continued to develop. In 1997 Professor Wright sent me to Dr. Kevin Vanhoozer, who was serving at the time on faculty at New College and was chair of Rutherford House's 1997 Edinburgh Dogmatics Conference. The conference that year focused on the Westminster Standards since it was the 350th anniversary of their publication. Responding to Professor Wright's suggestion of delivering a paper on adoption, Dr. Vanhoozer expressed the hope that it would address the metaphorical issues germane to adoption. His request was appropriate, for, observes John Frame, consideration of the nature of religious language is one of the "many tasks waiting to be done" in systematic theology, with few taking on the work.[4] Traditional treatments of adoption bear this out. Yet, given the celebratory nature of the conference and that I was still feeling my way in understanding the nature of biblical language, I remained within the sphere of historical theology. In time, the paper was published, and the

---

[4] Frame, *DKG*, 213–14.

doctoral dissertation was finished (2001).[5] More on these in chapter one.

These decades later, I have continued to investigate adoption along both tracks of research, pondering further the loss of adoption from the everyday theology of Westminster Calvinism. This led to the publication of *When History Teaches Us Nothing: The Recent Reformed Sonship Debate in Context* in 2008.

But I have also used the intervening years to share what has been taught me from Scripture and the annals of church history. While studiously avoiding turning adoption into a homiletical hobby horse, preferring to preach representatively the whole counsel of God (Acts 20:27; 2 Tim. 3:16), I have periodically preached series on adoption, early on at Grove Chapel, Camberwell, London, and at Seventh Reformed Church, Grand Rapids. Besides realizing that it is very difficult to preach sermons so close to one's area of research, these series also alerted me to how alien has been a salvation-historical approach to the doctrine. We are greatly affected by Western individualism, and yet winds of change are beginning to blow. These are helping us to balance the individual and communal facets of Christian doctrine (for more see ch. 6).

Additionally, it has been a privilege to share the research with seminarians, congregants, and conference attendees as far afield as the U.K., the U.S.A., Zambia, Indonesia, the Philippines, Turkey, and

---

[5] Titled "Adoption: The Forgotten Doctrine of Westminster Soteriology," the paper was published in Lynn Quigley, ed., *Reformed Theology in Contemporary Perspective (Westminster: Yesterday, Today—and Tomorrow?)*, Edinburgh Dogmatic Conference Papers (Edinburgh: Rutherford House, 2006), 87–123. Although published later, the chapter constitutes an earlier treatment of adoption in the Westminster Standards than its counterpart in the doctoral dissertation (Tim J. R. Trumper, "An Historical Study of the Doctrine of Adoption in the Calvinistic Tradition" [University of Edinburgh: Ph.D. Diss., 2001], 217–46). The dissertation is now accessible through the Edinburgh Research Archive (www.era.lib.ed.ac.uk/handle/ 1842/6803).

Ethiopia. In particular, my thanks go to radio and online hosts Lindsay Brooks (apologetics.com), Chris Arnzen (ironsharpensironradio.com), and Dan Cruver (Together for Adoption) for their respective interviews about the doctrine. Together for Adoption also invited blogs on adoption which afforded the opportunity to probe the church fathers' interest in adoption. Such invitations afforded welcome outlets for the public discussion of the internal workings of the mind.

Now, at last, the time has come to pull together a summary of both tracks of research. I do so to strategize a way of retrieving adoption. Although the current study builds on the original *SBET* articles, it is so much more than their modestly enhanced collection.[6]

First, there is the value of bringing together in one place the material covered in the articles. Their use by different scholars and pastors, while gratifying, has not infrequently been partial and resulted in hasty deductions. This monograph thus encourages a fuller and more accurate reading of the case offered for the retrieval of adoption.[7]

---

[6] Four of the six articles are available online. For links to them, go to https://fromhisfullness.com/adoption, accessed August 12, 2019, clicking on the associated tabs Doctrinal History of Adoption, Exposition of Adoption, and Implications of Adoption.

[7] One scholar to have made use of all the articles is Isomi Saito, "Divine Adoption in the Confessions of the Reformation Period" (Amsterdam: Vrije Universitaet, 2016). Less admirable in quality and *ad hominem* tone is Robert Letham's critique of the sixth article, "A Fresh Exposition of Adoption: II. Some Implications" in *The Westminster Assembly: Reading Its Theology in Historical Context* (Phillipsburg, NJ: P&R, 2009), 109–111. I have foregone a point-for-point rebuttal, believing a fair-minded consideration of the said article and my chapter "John Frame's Methodology: A Case Study in Constructive Calvinism" (in John Hughes, ed., *Speaking the Truth in Love: The Theology of John M. Frame* [Phillipsburg, NJ: P&R, 2009], 145–72) suffices to negate Dr. Letham's criticism. Idiosyncratic, this criticism nevertheless reminds us of the variant methodological and attitudinal tendencies among today's Reformed. For more on these, see the Appendix.

Second, the republication of the articles affords the opportunity to improve their sequence. Those published first on the metaphorical import of adoption—"The Metaphorical Import of Adoption: A Plea for Realisation I. The Adoption Metaphor in Biblical Usage" 14 no. 2 (Autumn 1996) and "The Metaphorical Import of Adoption: A Plea for Realisation II. The Adoption Metaphor in Theological Usage" 15 no. 2 (Autumn 1997)—reappear here as the basis of part two (chs. 3 and 4). The second couplet—"The Theological History of Adoption: I. An Account" 20 no. 1 (Spring 2002) and "The Theological History of Adoption: II. A *Rationale*" 20 no. 2 (Autumn 2002)—are the origins of part one (chs. 1 and 2). The most recent couplet—"A Fresh Exposition of Adoption: I. An Outline" 23 no. 1 (Spring 2005) and "A Fresh Exposition of Adoption: II. Its Implications" 23 no. 2 (Autumn 2005)— are now developed in part three (chs. 5 and 6). A cursory glance at the table of contents shows clearly enough the benefits of this rearrangement. Accordingly, we here journey in three coordinated movements from the history of adoption to its importance, ending with a preliminary exposition of the doctrine and its ramifications for the method, balance, and feel of systematic theology.

Third, the collection of articles has occasioned their thorough revision. This is based on additional research that has not seen the light of day before, except in draft forays into the writings of the Fathers. The research now includes:

- More interaction with the defense of Protestant scholasticism, especially that of Richard Muller.
- A reading of the entire Hendrickson collection (10 vols.) of Ante-Nicene Fathers for references to adoption.
- A selective reading of the Hendrickson collection of Nicene and

post-Nicene Fathers for references to adoption.[8]

- An extension of the theological history of adoption up to the present, thereby offering a latest progress report on how far the retrieval has advanced to date.
- An expanded explanation of the neglect of adoption.
- An advancement of the discussion of metaphor, distinguishing metaphors from models, and models from the supramodel of the Fatherhood of God. My aim has been to help pull the oars (a reference to John Frame's description of the labor needed), seeking here to fulfill belatedly Dr. Vanhoozer's request for more on adoption as a metaphor. Note in this regard, my inclusion of Erin Heim as a latest dialogue partner.

- A more detailed discussion of the ramifications of the retrieval of adoption for the defense of Protestant scholasticism and the discipline of systematic theology.

In the grand scope of theology, these may be described as modest advances, but they are significant in regards to the doctrine of adoption. Some of them are firsts, and some are gathered in a single volume for the first time.

The current volume ought not, then, to be considered money for old rope. Rather, the monograph constitutes:

- An entire rewriting and elaboration of each article.
- An updating of the references. Key improvements are found in the pre-Reformation awareness of the theological history of adoption (ch. 1), the layout and elaboration of the reasons for the doctrine's

---

[8] Since reliance on substantive, exegetically reliable studies of adoption in the Fathers has not been an option, the review constitutes but a series of preliminary observations. As inadequate as they are, I prefer to make them, than to leave a gaping lacuna in the theological history of adoption. If such observations stir Patristic scholars to take up the study of adoption, resting their studies on informed exegesis of adoption, then my brief remarks will have served their purpose.

neglect (ch. 1), the discussion of adoption as a model rather than as a metaphor (chs. 3 and 4, and the theological benefits of the retrieval of adoption (ch. 6).

- An enhancement of the overall argument where necessary, notably in the discussion of perspectivalism, the *ordo salutis* (the order of salvation), union with Christ, and the necessity of a new biblical dogmatic for the full retrieval of adoption.

Fourth, the collection provides an opportunity to publish a couple of hymns. Although neither a poet nor the son of one, these are included as a reminder of the dearth of hymns on adoption and as a corrective to their perpetuation of commonplace exegetical fallacies. My hope is to inspire the more lyrical to compose fresh compilations that avoid the theologians' authorial and metaphorical conflations. More immediately, the hymns serve to ensure a seamless garment of doctrine and doxology. Ronald Wallace's description of Calvin's approach to theology is also true of praise: "Theology, always near to prayer, passes into it."[9] Also memorable and relevant is a sermon preached in the 1990s by Professor Donald Macleod at Buccleuch and Greyfriars Free Church of Scotland, Edinburgh. His lament, "Who is writing poems to Christ today?" is likely less relevant than it was then. Nevertheless, my fledgling efforts have borne in mind his call to shed from our hearts the lackluster moderatism which negatively impacted eighteenth-century Scottish Presbyterian history.

Everything considered, these changes to the original articles are akin to a major house remodeling. The holding walls are the same, but they are largely unrecognizable. Here we discern fresh paintwork, significant restructuring, a reconfiguration of the old furniture, and the presence of new pieces. While I now live in this remodeled house and

---

[9] Ronald S. Wallace, "A Christian Theologian: Calvin's Approach to Theology," in Nigel M. De S. Cameron, ed., *The Challenge of Evangelical Theology: Essays in Approach and Method* (Edinburgh: Rutherford House Books, 1987), 143.

ought to be contacted here rather than at the original *SBET* addresses, I remain grateful to the staff of Rutherford House Evangelical Research Trust, Scotland (now the Rutherford Centre for Reformed Theology), for the initial publication of the articles.

A JOURNEY UPCOMING

As we get ready to set off, looking down the road before us, a number of explanatory remarks are in order.

Our aims.

Within our overall aim to retrieve adoption are a number of subsidiary aims; the provision of—

- *A comprehensive theological history of adoption.* While it is less than ideal to open with a chapter of such length, it is important that we have on record as full a narrative as possible of the doctrine's history. Chapter one, although inexhaustive, enlarges significantly our knowledge of the fortunes of adoption over the last two millennia. The account is subdivided into different eras to make the chapter more manageable. It is put forth with the prayer that it will not only inform but encourage yet fuller histories of the doctrine in time to come.

- *A thorough rationale for the foregoing history.* The more we know of the history of adoption the better the opportunity to explain it. Building, then, on the helpful insights of others, there is assembled in chapter two the most robust explanation to date of the treatment of the doctrine.

- *A rigorous back-to-Scripture investigation of the doctrine.* We return to the original wording of Scripture, gleaning the structure of adoption from within the Pauline corpus. We then follow up with an investigation of the metaphorical character and function of the language of adoption. This investigation is typically forgone in theological treatments of adoption but is very revealing of what Paul seeks to accomplish by referring to adoption in his theology.

- *An attesting of Protestant scholasticism, its methodology, rejection, and defense, by the test case of adoption.*
- *A probing of a fresh approach to the systematizing of the truths of Scripture.* Since the unqualified retrieval of adoption looks impossible without an overhaul of the discipline of systematic theology, we consider in the final chapter why we cannot go all the way with the defense of Protestant scholasticism, why concerns repeatedly arise from within the ranks of the Reformed orthodox about the classic way in which biblical truth has been systematized, and what it will take to slot the doctrine into a system of theology without truncating, coercing, or manipulating the model.

Our approach.

Fundamentally, we shall follow the historical and biblical data where it leads. While I come, as guide, from an historic Protestant, Reformed, and Evangelical hue, it is first and foremost as a Christian that I lay out the historical narrative and distinctive structures of adoption. My aim, then, is not tribal but the pursuit of the overall good of the church. Even the discussion of classic Reformed distinctives has in view the enhancement of the understanding of the church universal.

Catholicity, though, is a two-way street, requiring not only the Reformed orthodox to show interest in the universal church, but the universal church to consider the Reformed orthodox contribution to the history and understanding of the doctrine of adoption. After all, Reformed orthodoxy is not a narrow swathe of Christian theology. The Reformed orthodox were related theologically to the reformers who, in turn, stood on the shoulders of the church fathers. Furthermore, the work of the Westminster Assembly began as a revision of the thirty-nine articles (Anglican/Episcopalian), and became the foundation of the Savoy Declaration of 1658 (Congregational) and of the Second London Baptist Confession of 1689. To engage discussions of the

Westminster Standards (a classic statement of Reformed orthodoxy) is, then, to enter into the historic belief of most of Protestantism.

The ecumenical interest in adoption and its fraternal overtones thus combine to create a treatment of the subject that is catholic in spirit. Inevitably, there will be occasion to contend for the faith against errors that are clearly unbiblical and a threat to Christian orthodoxy, but we shall seek to address them non-contentiously.

In this spirit of catholicity, I have forgone overall my previous use of the term *recovery* for that of *retrieval.* Derek Rishmawy remarks, "the theological hills are alive with the sound of 'retrieval'"! Retrieval, he notes, bespeaks:

- An ecumenical endeavor across Catholic and Protestant traditions (but omitting, to date, Eastern Orthodoxy).
- Diversely borne fruits, depending on the nature and location of the engagement with the past.
- Creative breaking of modern, interpretative molds.
- A practical and present-day concern for church renewal. The engagement of the past seeks not simply its preservation but its use in the battles of the present.

Since, then, the language of recovery and retrieval is to my mind equivalent, there are no insurmountable challenges in the primary use of the latter term. But I do not make the transfer to be what Rishmawy calls "a cool kid." There are few things quite so "cringeworthy" as someone now longer-in-the-tooth attempting to be cool![10]

Our stance.

Ironically, given the breadth of Christian theology, one of the biggest discussion points our study touches on is the appraisal of

---

[10] Derek Rishmawy, "Retrieval—It's What All the Hip Reformed Catholic Kids Do," *Reformdish* (https://derekzrishmawy.com/tag/retrieval-theology/, accessed Dec. 29, 2017).

Protestant scholasticism. Since I have not come out previously with an all-in-one statement of what I see are the implications of the history and exposition of adoption for the criticism and especially the defense of Protestant scholasticism, I am sorely tempted to do so here. I actually drew up a point-for-point interaction with Richard Muller's case for the reappraisal as a means of clarifying my stance, and hope to return to that again, but have opted here for a briefer statement instead.[11]

My reasoning is twofold. First, I feared that forays into the discussion of Protestant scholasticism would take us too far into the discussion of in-house Reformed issues. These are necessary in retrieving adoption since the Reformed have had a particular interest in the theology of adoption, but to focus here so heavily on the Reformed tradition would detract too much from the catholic scope of the study.

Second, the discussion belongs more naturally to what I am trusting God will be an updating and publication of the doctoral dissertation. I look forward, then, to engaging there in greater detail the cases for and against Protestant scholasticism.

In the meantime, for the sake of those whose curiosity is piqued or who have a vested interest in where I stand as regards the debate, the following points, boiled down, may suffice:

First, that the doctrine of adoption is a significant but hitherto untried test case in the evaluation of Protestant scholasticism. In my view, the history and biblical data of adoption reveal strengths and weaknesses in both the scholastic influence on Reformed orthodoxy and evaluations of it.

---

[11] See Richard A. Muller, "The Problem of Protestant Scholasticism—A Review and Definition," in Willem J. Van Asselt and Eef Dekker, *Reformation and Scholasticism: An Ecumenical Enterprise* (Grand Rapids: Baker Academic, 2001); *After Calvin: Studies in the Development of a Theological Tradition*, Oxford Studies in Historical Theology (Oxford, New York, *et al.*: Oxford University Press, 2003), 63–102.

Second, that the history of adoption supports the broadening out of the discussion of the origin of Reformed scholasticism from Calvin to Theodore Beza and Peter Martyr Vermigli, leading us to concur that individual reformers or treatises are not *the* measures of the entire Reformation era or of the character of the Reformed orthodox. That said, the neglect of adoption forces us to focus on select figures. This can be misleading for those whose primary attention is the defense of Protestant scholasticism.

Third, that the history of adoption supports a *methodological* hiatus within Protestant scholasticism (specifically Reformed orthodoxy) but not a *theological* fissure. It comports, then, with the defense's plea that we distinguish method and content in the evaluation of continuities and discontinuities traceable from Medieval scholasticism, through the Reformation, to the post-Reformation.

Fourth, that the retrieval of adoption not be understood as an endeavor to resurrect the case for a central dogma in Reformed thought. Therein, the doctrines of Scripture and of God have been considered the *principia theologiae*, but they were understood to be foundational rather than central.

Fifth, that the history and doctrine of adoption support, at least in principle, a full reappraisal of Protestant scholasticism based on scholarship that is objective and current.

Sixth, the test case of adoption, built on a back-to Scripture approach, agrees with cautions against:

A. Explaining the form, structure, *loci communes*, *disputationes*, *institutiones*, or systems in terms of 'tensions" or "problems" in theology.

B. Personal antagonisms entering into the assessment of the reformers, the scholastics, and, we may add, to be even handed, the neoorthodox.

C. Sweeping, typically pejorative generalizations aimed against Protestant scholasticism. That said, we distance ourselves from this caution in cases where it is used to invalidate objective, verifiable critiques of Protestant scholasticism.

Seventh, the biblical data relevant to adoption does not support the assumption that because the scholastics belonged to an age of great philological expertise and were conversant with and reliant on exegetical tradition that they are therefore free of the charge of proof-texting and excessive ratiocination of the biblical text.

Eighth, the history of adoption does not assume that criticisms of Reformed orthodox theologians such as Francis Turretin, Charles Hodge, and Louis Berkhof arise from personal antagonism or neoorthodox tendencies. As the narrative of adoption unfolds, we cannot avoid concluding that some theologians aided interest in adoption in the everyday theology and life of God's people, while others either contributed unwittingly or gave actual expression to it.

In summary, the test case of adoption supports, in my view, the classic Reformed-orthodox critique of both theological liberalism (especially) and neoorthodoxy, while helping to explain why their protests against Protestant and Reformed orthodoxy arose. In other words, the test case concurs with the defense of Protestant scholasticism, but discerns reasons in history and in biblical exegesis for a less than absolutist defense. Specifically, the defense lacks the benefit of the inter-disciplinary engagement of classic Protestant and Reformed scholars in Old- and New-Testament studies. It is only in such an engagement, I posit, that we heed Muller's advice:

> [A]bove all, the theological biases that would remake either Reformation or post-Reformation theology for the sake of arguing a [twenty-first] century position should be avoided and the documents allowed to speak for themselves.[11]

That is, indeed, my intent in all that follows.

---

[11] Muller, *After Calvin*, 100–101.

Our terms.

More briefly, I have opted to use, first, the *history of salvation* and the *salvation-historical* rather than for the *history of redemption* and the *redemptive-historical.* Although they are equivalent, the former serves to circumnavigate confusion when later distinguishing the models of redemption and adoption.

Second, there is the matter of androcentric terminology. Terms such as *Father, Son, sons,* and *brothers* are essential to Paul's teaching of adoption and are therefore unavoidable. Nevertheless, Paul tempers his use of male terminology by referring in certain instances to "children" and to "daughters." While these terms may not acquit Paul of misogyny in the eyes of some, the observation of female scholar Erin Heim suffices for me: "This metaphor [read model] is not intending to make a statement about the superior ontological status of one gender over the other, but rather is borrowing an image from the surrounding culture to structure the shape and perception of what it means for a believer to be ἐν Χριστῷ."[12] I, therefore, follow the terminology of Paul, not to support male domination, but to accurately unpack his imagery and the theology it contains. Under the inspiration of the Holy Spirit, such terms help males and females alike.

Our thanks.

In addition to the long-standing thanks of those already mentioned, I acknowledge Dr. Vanhoozer and Dr. Dan Treier for their feedback on this manuscript. I have implemented with gratitude those comments that were agreeable and feasible, and believe that their input has benefitted this study of adoption.

In preparing the manuscript for publication I am more than ever grateful to my friend Marilyn Van Dyke of Grand Rapids. My debt

---

[12] Erin Heim, "Light through a Prism: New Avenues of Inquiry for the Pauline Υἱοθεσία Metaphors," (Ph.D. Diss.: University of Otago, Dunedin, New Zealand, 2014), 80.

for her painstaking copyediting grows with every succeeding manuscript she edits, as does my admiration for her selfless service to her Lord and to me. To say "Thank you!" is so inadequate.

Naturally, the responsibility for the book is all mine. It has been a joy to wrestle through the material in prayer, knowing that whether by the positions taken or by their shortcomings, the task of theology will proceed.

Jürgen Moltmann reminds us, however, that theology is to become "not just a scholarly study which teaches, but also a *wisdom* which makes wise out of the experience of God":

> True theologians must have addressed and worked through their struggles with God, their experiences of God, their fears of God, and their joy in God. They must have laid themselves open personally to the things they maintain, and must neither suppress their negative experiences of their own selves before God, nor hide their positive delight in God (Ps. 37:4). It is good if we can perceive the theologian in his or her theology—good, if in those who have "the cure of souls" we can sense the soul that itself has been touched.[13]

I pray this may be true of the study before you.

Finally, sincere thanks go to those who have helped indirectly— the donors to From His Fullness ministries whose generosity has afforded the completion of the manuscript amid international travels and, more recently, the coronavirus. Specifically, I thank my wife, Brenda, for her love, prayers, kindnesses, companionship, and sacrifices. How precious it is to be equally yoked in the gospel and service of Christ! I am as thankful for her sake as for mine to hand off this study. Along the way, I have drawn encouragement from the general support of my pastor, Rev. Bob Van Manen (Little Farms Chapel, Orthodox Presbyterian Church), and of our board of directors, notably Doug Brink who read the manuscript in its entirety and gave thoughtful feedback.

---

[13] Jürgen Moltmann, *Experiences in Theology: Ways and Forms of Christian Theology*, transl. Margaret Kohl (Minneapolis: Fortress Press, 2000), 24.

The volume is dedicated to my father, Rev. Dr. Peter Trumper, for he did more than he knew to inspire my interest in the Fatherhood of God and his adoptive grace. Although I was born to him (and to Margaret Trumper, his best carer), his patriarchal status in our family combined as the years went by with his multiple sclerosis and accumulated ailments to point powerfully to the paternal grace of God and to the adoption, defined by Paul in Romans 8:23 as the redemption of the body.

We shall return at the end to my father's inspiration. But in remembrance of his twenty-five years homebound, it is fitting to quote Tertullian's words to those imprisoned for the faith:

> Let us drop the name of prison; let us call it a place of retirement. Though the body is shut in, though the flesh is confined, all things are open to the spirit [sic?]. In spirit, then, roam abroad; in spirit walk about, not setting before you shady paths or long colonnades, but the way which leads to God. As often as in spirit you know your footsteps are there, so often you will not be in bonds. The leg does not feel the chain when the mind is in the heavens. The mind compasses the whole man about, and whither it wills it carries him. But where thy heart shall be, there shall be thy treasure. Be there our heart, then, where we would have our treasure.[14]

Those who saw my father homebound will recognize in Tertullian's words Dad's theocentricity. It was very evident both in his response to his ministry and to his sufferings, but also in his interest in this research. Discussing it periodically over the years of visiting home, I still hear his probing questions. He would have especially appreciated the irony, that a book such as this, which argues for ongoing reform according to God's Word, was written during and after the 500th anniversary of the start of the Protestant Reformation (and was edited earlier on over Reformation weekend in Wittenberg!). After all, as a student of the Reformation and an advocate of its theological principles, Dad spent his ministry passionately stoking the fires of church reform.

---

[14] *A-N F* 3:694.

He was, however, a rare combination of a brave reformer, cultured gentleman, and meek sufferer. I remember him as a father whose fathering commended the Father, whose ministry commended the Son, whose life commended the Spirit, and whose long road in illness commended the adoption (Rom. 8:23). It is a delight to dedicate the volume to his memory.

Our reminder.

As theological as is this volume, Dad would certainly want me to remember that it is a study of the gospel. While I have assumed throughout that most readers are already adopted by their heavenly Father and seek more knowledge of his grace in Christ, I would indeed be guilty of theorizing the gospel were I not to implore you to rest in Christ if you are yet to do so. Know that God, entirely of his grace, promises you through Christ's shed blood both redemption from enslavement to sin (whether of religious traditionalism or of sinful license) and adoption into his family. The empty hands that receive Christ's redemption receive also the Father's adoption. May the Spirit grant you this saving faith.

Without it, this study will be of no eternal value to you. As Herman Bavinck lay dying a century ago (1921), he made this very point, testifying, "My dogmatics doesn't [*sic?*] help me now; it is faith that counts."[15] Bavinck knew this all along. I trust you will from here on out, too, for the road we now travel is no substitute for faith in Christ. Rather, the vistas about to enter our sight serve to point us to Christ. Through him alone do we become God's sons and daughters.

With this in mind, we now hit the road.

~~~~

---

[15] Gordon J. Spykman, *Reformational Theology: A New Paradigm for Doing Dogmatics* (Grand Rapids: William B. Eerdmans, 1992), 111.

PART ONE

THE THEOLOGICAL HISTORY OF ADOPTION

For you did not receive the spirit of slavery to fall back into fear, but you have received the Spirit of adoption as sons, by whom we cry, "Abba! Father!"

Romans 8:15

For we know that the whole creation has been groaning together in the pains of childbirth until now. And not only the creation, but we ourselves, who have the firstfruits of the Spirit, groan inwardly as we wait eagerly for adoption as sons, the redemption of our bodies.

Romans 8:22-23

They are Israelites, and to them belong the adoption, the glory, the covenants, the giving of the law, the worship, and the promises.

Romans 9:4

But when the fullness of the time had come, God sent forth his Son, born of woman, born under the law, to redeem those who were under the law, so that we might receive adoption as sons. And because you are sons, God has sent the Spirit of his Son into our hearts, crying, "Abba! Father!" So you are no longer a slave, but a son, and if a son, then an heir through God.

Galatians 4: 4-7

In love he predestined us for adoption as sons through Jesus Christ, according to the purpose of his will, to the praise of his glorious grace, with which he has blessed us in the Beloved.

Ephesians 1:4-5

1.

ADOPTION IN HISTORY
A Narrative

> The word adoption is of great importance in the system of our faith, as is seen from the apostolic writings . . . adoption is a significant symbol.
>
> Augustine, *Reply to Faustus the Manichaean*

> The evangelical doctrine of Adoption—succinctly described as "an act of God's free grace, whereby we are received into the number, and have a right to all the privileges, of the sons of God" [WCF 12]—has received but slender treatment at the hands of theologians. It has been handled with a meagerness entirely out of proportion to its intrinsic importance, and with a subordination which allows it only a parenthetical place in the system of evangelical truth.
>
> Robert A. Webb,
> *The Reformed Doctrine of Adoption.*

Welcome to a road less traveled. We have a significant journey ahead of us. Our destination is the city of Adoption. Many travel to the worthy municipalities of Regeneration, Justification, and Sanctification in the fashionable county of Essential, but few visit Adoption. The route is often overlooked, the signposts vary in reliability, and depictions of the city differ. Adoption lies close to Regeneration, Justification, and Sanctification, but is located across the border in the county of Retrieval.

A route has been chosen. Many are the sights to take in. Some are familiar, others are little known, and a few are unknown. Naturally, you want to know that I drive safely and can get us to the heart of Adoption. Admittedly, absolute assurances come from God alone, but the route is mapped, and the best travel guides have been consulted.

So, with map in hand, the best advisors to understand it, and fresh signposts erected, we are ready to go. We aim not only to get to Adoption, but to depict its beauty and to trigger its reallotment to the county of Essential.

First, we must get onto the highway. To do so, we take "a Michigan left"—heading in the opposite direction to the one in which we want to go, so as to make a safe U-turn toward Adoption. The maneuver is slow but worth it.

~~~~

To fully retrieve adoption, we first head back into history. There we learn the importance of pursuing the retrieval of adoption. Sketching the history of adoption will take some time, yet three benefits accrue from beginning with the past.

First, we gain a better knowledge of the overall history of the doctrine. This is no small accomplishment. A century ago Thornton Whaling lamented that "the history of the doctrine of adoption is yet to be fully and adequately written." Many church historians and theologians have overlooked the doctrine and thereby minimized its history. Others, without a thorough acquaintance with the history, have made overly bold claims concerning it.[1]

For example, Scottish pastor-theologian John Dick (1764–1833) claimed that "a place is commonly assigned to [adoption] in systems of Theology." Other theologians beg to differ but put the state of affairs down to the lesser importance of adoption compared to neighboring soteric elements such as regeneration, justification, and sanctification. Later, another Scottish pastor-theologian Hugh Martin (1822–85) wrote that "in Dr. Cunningham's Lectures on Historical Theology [to these we shall come], the doctrine [of adoption] is not even broached—for the simple reason that it has no history to present." Knowledge of the history teaches us, however, that while the neglect of adoption is real, Martin's claim is excessive. We learn from the history that while James Packer's assessment is less sweeping, it is closer to the truth: "It is a strange fact that the truth of adoption has been little regarded in Christian history." "There is," he asserts, again with some

---

[1] Thornton Whaling, "Adoption," *Princeton Theological Review* 21 (1923), 234; John Dick, *Lectures on Theology*, 2 vols. in 1 (New York: Robert Carter and Brothers, 1851), 224.

overstatement, "no evangelical writing on [adoption], nor has there been at any time since the Reformation, any more than there was before."[2]

In drawing together the most detailed narrative of adoption to date, we are able to muster authority in speaking of its history. We shall find, for instance, a dearth of serious theological monographs on adoption. Generally, the creeds and writings of the pre- and post-Reformation eras make but fleeting allusions to it. Statements here and there found hidden amid the discussions of other doctrines make for serendipitous discoveries. On rare instances, adoption is granted its own section, but these do not appear, so far as we have found to date, until the second millennium and are too brief to have attracted much attention.

This presents us with a practical difficulty: whether to document those who have written on adoption, or those who have not. There are advantages and disadvantages either way.

The listing of those overlooking adoption, playing it down, or significantly misunderstanding the biblical data by dint of its neglect, certainly constitutes the most dramatic case for its retrieval. While useful for shock effect, the compilation of such a record is neither feasible nor scintillating, nor does it bring to light the resources relevant to the stimulation of creative thinking about adoption in the years to come. In the statement, for example, that apostolic fathers such as Clement (Phil. 4:3), Mathetes, Polycarp, Ignatius, Barnabas, Papias, or Justin Martyr are silent about adoption, we learn very little other than that we need not go to them for help in its exposition. In fairness, the authors of early documents such as *The Gospel of Peter* and *The Diatessaron of Tatian* (a harmony of the four gospels), various apocalypses and romances, *The Epistles of Clement*, *The Apology of Aristides the Philosopher*, and *The Passion of the Scillitan Martyrs*, likely

---

[2] Hugh Martin, "Candlish's Cunningham Lectures," *British and Foreign Evangelical Review* 14 (Oct. 1865), 728; James I. Packer, *Knowing God*, 1975 ed. (London: Hodder and Stoughton, 1988), 255.

had no need to refer to the doctrine. More recent theologians, such as Adolf von Harnack, Isaak August Dorner, Karl Rudolph Hagenbach, Charles Hodge, Robert J. Breckinridge, W. G. T. Shedd, Thomas Chalmers, George Hill, and William Cunningham (to list a few), did have need. Yet, the shock value of these revelations quickly fades, leaving us with little else to ponder, other than our anticlimactic feelings. What is needed is a record of those theologians supplying resources to aid the retrieval.[3]

Second, the history of adoption helps us to balance out Protestant perspectives on church history and historical theology. Donald Fairburn rightly reminds us that we cannot truly comprehend our Reformation heritage without appreciating the heritage of the reformers. When we view them as standing on the shoulders of the church fathers, we gain not only a longer historical view of their work, but also the broader theological setting of their doctrine. Specifically, we shall perceive that those reformers who referenced adoption took their lead in understanding it, at least in part, from the significant Trinitarianism, "biblical-theological" method, and prior interest of the church fathers.[4] The reformers did not typically pinpoint those fathers who influenced their theologizing, nevertheless the general influences to which they were subject suggest that those who wrote of adoption were influenced to some degree by the fathers to do so.

Third, the history of adoption reveals that it was only comparatively recently that the church began awakening to her protracted neglect of adoption. Scottish pastor-theologian Robert S. Candlish (1806–73) is the first we know of presently to have

---

[3] *A-N F* 9:1–285. Edward McKinlay, "The relation of incarnation to atonement in the Christology of R. S. Candlish and its contribution to the development of Scottish Theology" (Ph.D. Diss.: University of Edinburgh, 1966), 110; Robert A. Webb, *The Reformed Doctrine of Adoption* (Grand Rapids: Eerdmans, 1947), 17.

[4] Donald Fairbairn, *Life in the Trinity: An Introduction to Theology with the Help of the Church Fathers* (Downers Grove, IL: IVP Academic, 2009), 11.

commented on the neglect in print. I refer to his inaugural series of Cunningham Lectures (March 1864), established in honor of Free Church of Scotland historical-theologian William Cunningham (1805–61).

Accordingly, we begin our journey with the longest of its stretches, outlining as much as we know currently of the history of adoption. Admittedly, there is a danger, in identifying relevant sources from the last two millennia, of creating a superficial impression that the doctrine has not been so neglected after all. That, however, is a risk worth taking, for our aim is to fill in the history's remaining lacunae, to unearth the most relevant resources, and, ultimately, to retrieve the doctrine.

1. THE APOSTOLIC FATHERS

The apostolic fathers are designated as such because of their personal knowledge of the apostles and their teaching. All the same, we need not detain ourselves long with them. Writes Edward McKinlay, "The failure to consider, and adequately to develop along satisfactory lines, the doctrine of adoption, can be traced back to the early Fathers of the Church." Theirs, says A. Cleveland Coxe, "were times of heroism, not of words; an age, not of writers, but of soldiers; not of talkers, but of sufferers." They were called not to plumb the depths of biblical teaching so much as to ensure its survival amid the fires of persecution.[5]

Nevertheless, the apostolic fathers refer frequently in their writings to the Fatherhood of God, at least from *The Epistle of Mathetes to Diognetus* onward. They focus on the Father's role in creation, his relationship to the Son, his will in the Son's incarnation, his obedience unto the death of the cross, and his resurrection. This is not to say that the apostolic fathers had no theological knowledge of adoption. Their allusions to related themes such as eternal calling, sonship, and the household of God, although rare and scattered, suggest otherwise. At no

---

[5]McKinlay, "The relation of incarnation to atonement," 106; *A-N F* 1:vii.

point, though, in their extant writings do they come close to expounding adoption. Their concerns lay elsewhere than with Christ's redemptive work and the Father's adoption. The specifics of soteriology were assumed rather than expounded.

2. THE ANTE-NICENE GREEK FATHERS

With the possible exception of the corrupted *Excerpts of Theodotus* (150–80), the first extant reference to adoption currently known to us is found in the writings of Irenaeus (130–202), Bishop of Lugdunum, Gaul (Lyons, France).[6] Whereas the early apologists defended Christianity philosophically from the Gnostics, Irenaeus countered them by developing the exposition of the biblical revelation. This he undertook by juxtaposing the Hebrew Scriptures, the four Gospels, and the apostolic writings (although not the full set we use), highlighting the use of both Testaments as the church's supreme rule of faith and conduct.

According to the translation, Irenaeus refers to adoption but once in *The Demonstration of the Apostolic Preaching*. There are, however, thirteen uses of the noun in his best-known work *Adversus Haereses* (175–85). Especially relevant therein is Irenaeus' pervasive focus on the Fatherhood of God. Consistently, he draws on the paternal language of the New Testament to stress, contra the Gnostics, "faith in one God, the Father Almighty, and in one Lord Jesus Christ, the Son of God." Adoption is significant since it proves "that there is none other called God by the Scriptures except the Father of all, and the Son, and those who possess the adoption." From the Father, the sons of God receive a general or creational portion of the Spirit, and in Christ an adoptive portion. All receiving the grace of adoption are enabled to cry

---

[6] The two mentions of adoption in the *Excerpts of Theodotus* allude, via Rom. 8:15 and Gal. 4:6, to the freedom of believers from enslaving fear. "Advanc[ing] by love to adoption" believers, as erstwhile slaves, love the God we once feared. We are, then, emancipated to adoption (*A-N F* 8:45, 47).

"Abba, Father" and make up the church.[7]

It is significant that as the first figure in church history to accord adoption a functional role in his theology, Irenaeus understood, in part at least, Paul's salvation-historical unfolding of adoption. Stated alternatively, the first church father to make anything significant of adoption was also the father of biblical theology. It is important that this sink in, for the connection is, I argue, fundamental to the retrieval of adoption.

From Galatians 4:4-6 Irenaeus perceived that the believer's adoption is grounded in Christ's coming for our redemption in the "fullness of the time." The sufficiency of Christ's redeeming work explains why we simply "receive" adoption; why the old covenant laws of bondage are now canceled; and why the sons of God have greater freedom in this new covenant era to know, to love, and to revere the Father (book four, chapter sixteen; see Gal. 3:23–4:7).[8]

Irenaeus' emphasis on the incarnational union of the Son of God with us in our humanity serves to underline the necessary precondition of the believer's spiritual union with him in his Sonship. Asks Irenaeus, "In what way could we be partakers of the adoption of sons, unless we had received from Him [God] through the Son that fellowship which refers to Himself, unless His Word, having been made flesh, had entered into communion with us?" And, again, in words typically attributed to John Calvin, "He who was the Son of God became the Son of man, that man, having been taken into the Word, and receiving the adoption, might become the son of God."[9]

In reflecting on Irenaeus' contribution to the Fatherhood of God, J. Scott Lidgett goes too far when claiming that "nowhere can we find more emphatic and constant reference to the 'adoption of sons' as the characteristic gift to believers in Christ than in Irenaeus." Nevertheless, Irenaeus' references to adoption justify the more general claim of Hans

---

[7] *A-N F* 1:320, 463, 546, 419.

[8] *A-N F* 1:441.

[9] *A-N F* 1:448.

von Campenhausen that, "Everything in [Irenaeus'] thought is concerned with the new relationship of sonship which Christ has established." Nevertheless, his "writings fell remarkably quickly into the background and were almost completely forgotten by his fellow countrymen. His written style failed to connect, and fresh challenges to the church inspired a return among the emerging Greek Fathers to the early apologists and their philosophical defense of Christian orthodoxy.[10]

Illustrative of this trend is Theophilus of Antioch. In *Theophilus to Autolycus* he primarily references God's existence and attributes, the inspiration of the prophets, creation, and providence. He names God "the Father," "the Father of the universe," and "the Father and Creator of the universe" on several occasions but goes no further. Similarly, Athenagoras, a little-known converted Athenian philosopher, credited, ironically as we shall see, with instigating the Alexandrian School of Christian thought, says nothing of adoption in his works *A Plea* [*Apology* or, literally, *Embassy*] *for the Christians* and *The Treatise of Athenagoras*—a defense of the resurrection of the dead (cf., Rom. 8:22-23). Like the early apologists, Athenagoras focused more narrowly on the case for Christ's resurrection (Acts 17:31-32).

Together, Theophilus and Athenagoras formed a bridge between Irenaeus and the leading lights of the School of Alexandria: Clement of Alexandria (150–215), Origen (185–254), and Athanasius (296–373).

While it is said that Clement was not a public teacher of the faith, he nevertheless became the illustrious head of the catechetical school at Alexandria and the ethicist of the Christian church. He wrote much,

---

[10] J. Scott Lidgett, *The Fatherhood of God in Christian Truth and Life* (Edinburgh: T&T Clark, 1902), 160. Lidgett claims that Irenaeus "is the teacher, above all others, of the Fatherhood of God" (ibid. Cf., 153 and 156). For the reasons underlying Irenaeus' emphasis, ibid., 156–157. Hans von Campenhausen, *The Fathers of the Church: The Fathers of the Greek Church* (Peabody, MA: Hendrickson Publishers, 1998), 21, 24.

but few of his writings are extant: *The Exhortation to the Heathen, The Instructor, The Stromata,* and the tract *Who is the Rich Man That Shall Be Saved?* These reveal Clement's concern to depict the Christian as the perfect gnostic—someone completely at one with God in knowledge and love. In developing this theme, Clement sees a role for the theme of adoption. The first three of these extant sources contain seven references to the doctrine plus discussion of other relevant texts of Scripture.

Clement, too, perceives the relevance of adoption to the various phases of salvation history. God not only foreordained his people to the highest adoption before the foundation of the world, he created them for it. Adoption, then, is the utmost of that divine utterance, "Let Us make man in Our own image and likeness." Although humankind fell in Adam, God pursues his adoptive purposes. In old covenant times, his people were as a child under the education of a schoolmaster, the law instilling discipline and the knowledge of the coming Christ. Under the new covenant, Christ, the just, true, and good, and sole possessor of the image and likeness of the Father, shares with us for our adoption his natural Sonship and what he has beheld in his Father. His Sonship remains of more substance than the adoptive sonship of the Christian, nevertheless our "childhood which is in Christ is maturity, as compared with the law" (cf., Gal. 3:23–4:6).[11]

It is essential that a person believes in Christ. "For us, yea us," writes Clement, "He has adopted, and wishes to be called the Father of us alone, not of the unbelieving." To elaborate: "The Father of the universe cherishes affection towards those who have fled to Him; and having begotten them again by His Spirit to the adoption of children, knows them as gentle, and loves those alone, and aids and fights for them; and therefore he bestows on them the name of child." Note Clement's connecting of the new birth (regeneration) and adoption. God the Spirit begets those whom God the Father adopts. The one action

---

[11] *A-N F* 2:218 (cf., 2:364), 234.

grants the child of God his new nature, the other his new standing. The child of God is privileged to enjoy the particular love of God, his help, and protection; and is responsible to obey the Father, fulfilling irreproachably and intelligently his commands to the extent they are known. This obedience is possible through the Son—"the great High Priest who has deigned to call us brethren and fellow-heirs." The "perfect inheritance belongs," says Clement, "to those who attain to 'a perfect man'." That is to say, to the person reflecting the image of his Lord. While we cannot be virtuous as God is virtuous, there must be a similitude of virtue. The true child of God becomes like God. To this end God's people are "introduced into adoption and the friendship of God, [and] to the just inheritance of the lords and gods is brought."[12]

Next up is Origen. Possessing prodigious talent, purity of character, and capacity for learning, Origen became president of the catechetical school at the tender age of eighteen. A strict ascetic, he grew into the most prolific of the ante-Nicene Fathers, guiding seekers from non–Christian philosophies and heretical Gnostics into the Christian faith. His estimated 6,000 publications, described as "fertile thought, keen penetration, and glowing imagination," emphasizing catholic or universal theology, and influencing the exegesis of Scripture, raises the question as to his interest in adoption.

It is said that the Fatherhood of God "has a perceptible prominence for [Origen] that it did not have for earlier Christian writers." Indeed, Peter Widdicombe believes Origen's notion of the spiritual journey from fear and servanthood to sonship was "mainly shaped by the Pauline imagery of adoption and the Johannine imagery of the rebirth."[13]

---

[12] *A-N F* 2:206, 214, 376, and 506.

[13] Peter Widdicombe, *The Fatherhood of God from Origen to Athanasius*, Oxford Theological Monographs (Oxford: Clarendon Press, 1994), 7 (contrast Lidgett, *The Fatherhood of God*, 152–153), 43.

Allowing for the fact that the Hendrickson series of the ante-Nicene fathers includes but representative samples of Origen's writing—namely, the theological treatise *De Principiis* on the fundamental doctrines of Christianity, sample commentaries such as on the Gospels of Matthew and John, and his apologetic treatise *Against Celsus*—it is nevertheless surprising to find but three mentions of adoption in 760 pages of Origen's writings. The general neglect of soteriology plus Origen's allegorizing approach to biblical exposition (which took him away from the context and exegesis of the text), may largely explain why he did not say more. Despite traversing a wider array of sources, Widdicombe seems either to have markedly overstated the place of adoption in Origen's writings (Widdicombe's direct quotes of Origen do not often mention the doctrine), or to have read into his use of the New Testament's filial terms more of adoption than Origen intended. Origen, he writes, "wove Johannine and Pauline themes together and gave them a central place in his theology." But as we shall see from the relevant biblical data, the admixture of Johannine and Pauline thought does not guarantee the presence of adoption, at least not a clear picture of it.

An accurate picture of adoption in Origen requires, then, both an understanding of the biblical data and a survey of Origen's broader corpus. Those taking up the investigation are perhaps best beginning with his *Commentary on the Epistle to the Ephesians* and his treatise *On Prayer*.[14]

Following Origen and immediately preceding the Council of Nicaea (254–325), the Greek Fathers almost entirely ceased to mention adoption. Only six references are found among the extant writings of Gregory Thaumaturgus and Dionysius of Alexander (Origen's two most distinguished students in the School of Alexandria); Julius Africanus; Anatolius; the minor contributions of Alexander of Cappadocia, Theognostus of Alexandria, Pierius of Alexandria, Theonas of Alexan-

---

[14] *A-N F* 4:379, 421, and 642; Widdicombe, *The Fatherhood of God*, 116.

dria, Phileas, Pamphilus, and Malchion; Archelaus; Alexander of Lycopolis; Peter of Alexandria; Alexander of Alexandria; and Methodius. The aforesaid references are found in the writings of but two: Gregory Thaumaturgus and Bishop Alexander of Alexandria.

Gregory's references occur in *A Sectional Confession of Faith*, but his authorship of the Confession is doubted and one of the references is a quotation of Romans 8:15-16. The other two help distinguish the Sonship of Christ "who is in nature God" from the sonship of angels and of men.[15]

The references of Bishop Alexander, the last figure of note in the School of Alexandria, are in a similar vein but possess an interesting context. Alexander's predecessor, Achillas, had allowed Arius (256–336), known for his denial of the Son's coequality with the Father, to become presbyter of the oldest and most influential church in Alexandria. Initially, Arius influenced some deacons, which led Alexander to call a meeting of the presbytery. Failing to defeat the error, a synodical meeting was arranged, until at last a council of the entire church, meeting at Nicaea, rejected Arius' teaching. Although Alexander is sometimes said to have moved too slowly against Arius, he prevented Arius' views from becoming accepted orthodoxy by means of his treatise *Epistles on the Arian Heresy and The Disruption and the Deposition of Arius* and became the patron of the young Athanasius who went with him to the Council of Nicaea as his deacon.

In Alexander's writings, there is a thrice-repeated distinction between the Sonship of Christ and that of believers. Christ's Sonship, "which is according to the nature of the Godhead of the Father, transcends, by an ineffable excellence, the sonship of those who have been adopted by Him." In effect, Alexander warns, somewhat ironically, against the believer's privilege of adoptive sonship obscuring the ever unique and divine Sonship of Christ. The very Lord who is "by nature the Son of the Father," possesses a Sonship that is "proper and peculiar,

---

[15] *A-N F* 6:1-43, especially 43 and 45.

natural and excellent," and "is by all adored." Yet, the Lord blesses those he makes sons by adoption, granting them "the spirit of adoption." Alexander's distinguishing of the Son from the sons grates, however, on Protestant ears: "The only-begotten Son of the Father . . . possesses an indefectible Sonship; but the adoption of rational sons belongs not to them by nature, but is prepared for them by the probity [integrity] of their life, and by the free gift of God."[16]

3. THE ANTE-NICENE LATIN FATHERS[17]

Tertullian broke onto the scene in Carthage, North Africa, in 197 with the publication of his *Apology*. His "angrier imitation of Justin Martyr's [*Apology*]" began "a spate of eloquent, witty[,] and argumentative tracts on doctrines and morals."[18] Known for his seminal systematic treatment of the Trinity, Tertullian expressed in his tracts— especially *Apology, Against Praxeas, The Shows, On Repentance, Against Marcion, Against Hermogenes*, and *On the Flesh of Christ*—the apologetic significance of the Fatherhood of God, but mentions adoption, according to the translation, on but three occasions.[19] Still, these refer-

---

[16] *A-N F* 6:293, 294.

[17] The distinction between the Greek and Latin Fathers is rarely explained. It contains, first, an irony of language. In ante–Nicene times the language of Rome was predominantly Greek. Not until a century after the origination of Greek theological literature (at the end of the second century and the beginning of the third [i.e., prior to the Council of Nicea]) did Municius and Tertullian begin the trend of theologizing in Latin. Second, the distinction has a certain irony of origin. Municius and Tertullian were likely Africans rather than Romans. Tertullian knew Rome and Roman law but is mostly linked with Carthage in North Africa. Greek-speaking Irenaeus hailed from the East (modern day Turkey), but is remembered as the Bishop of Lyons in the West. Such ironies are explained in part by the fact that the Empire was not firmly split into East and West until 395.

[18] Williston Walker et al., *A History of the Christian Church*, Fourth Ed. (Edinburgh: T&T Clark, 1985), 80.

[19] *A-N F* 3:378, 436; 4:81. There is a reference to adoption added in 3:94fn4. The reference to adoption in 3:265 refers to Christ and requires interpretation.

ences combine with related themes to suggest a coherent understanding of the doctrine, one sensitive to the exegesis of Scripture.

Fundamentally, adoption explains how God, initially our Judge, becomes Father to his people. The Jews were first to be adopted—a point Tertullian gleans from the elder brother in the parable of the prodigal son. Yet, believing Jews and Gentiles now share the same adoption, experiencing by it a changed relationship to God. This occurs through the revelation of the truth, confession of error, and pardon for sin. The price of pardon is personal repentance, the result of which is redemption. Although this implies that repentance is meritorious, there is no doubting Tertullian's belief that Christ came to redeem us. It is redemption, then, which is the basis of adoption (Gal. 4:5). Adoption, though, grants the penitent not only Christ but the Holy Spirit. He enables the adopted to cry out, "*Abba*, Father," and indicates thereby that the adopted are no longer slaves, for they are freed from charging themselves with "past thefts and desertions."[20]

Not all claims to have been adopted are authentic. Those truly adopted, however, become "worthier" relations of Jesus than the unbelieving relatives of his earthly family (Matt. 12:46-50), for adoption entails the forming of a spiritual family, as was prophesied under the old covenant (Is. 43:6). "We are," says Tertullian, "a body knit together as such by a common religious profession, by unity of discipline, and by the bond of a common hope." Although fear of God, joy, grief, and suffering are also common, we share as brothers "a common Spirit from a common Lord and Father."[21]

The adopted, though, not only have God for their heavenly Father, they have an earthly mother. She is the church who cares for God's family. Arising from baptism into her house, it is therein that the adopted call on the Father for his grace and gifts. These come to

---

[20] *A-N F* 3:661.

[21] *A-N F* 3:46, 168, 528, 613, 664.

us through lady mother—"from her bountiful breasts and each brother out of his private means." Tertullian especially in mind the bodily needs of the imprisoned "martyrs designate." Yet, through mother's provisions all the adopted eventually arrive in heaven, our Father's permanent home.[22]

Next of relevance is Hippolytus (170–235). With Greek name and Roman location, he epitomizes the difficulties of distinguishing the church fathers along Greek and Latin lines. Likely born in Rome, becoming a presbyter and bishop of the church there, Hippolytus became a pupil of the Greek father Irenaeus, and wrote in Greek. Naturally, then, we wonder about his interest in adoption. In Hippolytus' extant works—*The Refutation of All Heresies;* the exegetical fragments, the dogmatic and historical fragments; and "the dubious and spurious pieces"—there are three mentions of adoption. These appear on two consecutive pages of his *Discourse on Holy Theophany.* We cannot be sure of the degree to which Irenaeus impacted these references, but we do know that Hippolytus' development of a related doctrine of participation in Christ (deification) is attributed to Irenaeus' influence.[23]

The importance of deification for Hippolytus explains his contribution to the early but growing trend of admixing adoption and the new birth. The two images come together in Hippolytus' view of Christ's baptism. In the Father's affirmation "This is my beloved son," Hippolytus detects the pattern of the renewal of the old man and the committing to him again of "the sceptre of adoption." Yet, the baptism also demonstrates the way the Father washes his people through Christ with the water and the Spirit. Thereby, we are begotten again to incorruption of soul and body. Hippolytus reminds us of Paul's phrase "the washing of regeneration" (Tit. 3:5), while his bold claim that the

---

[22] *A-N F* 3:693.

[23] *A-N F* 5:9–259. For more on deification, see Dietrich Ritschl, "Hippolytus' Conception of Deification: Remarks on the Interpretation of Refutation X," *SJT* 12 [1959]), 388.

washed "will also be God" echoes hyperbolically 2 Peter 1:4 ("partaking of the divine nature").

Through deification the newborn are made joint-heirs with Christ. The language of joint-heirship is naturally allied in Paul to his doctrine of adoption (Rom. 8:12-17). It is this which begs the question as to whether Hippolytus' warm invitation to deification (or mystical union) constitutes a juxtaposition or a conflation of the new birth and adoption: "Come then, be begotten again, O man, into the adoption of God." The same question emerges from Hippolytus' explanation of the process of deification:

> He who comes down in faith to the laver of regeneration, and enounces the devil, and joins himself to Christ; who denies the enemy, and makes the confession that Christ is God; who puts off the bondage, and puts on the adoption,—he comes up from the baptism brilliant as the sun, flashing forth the beams of righteousness, and, which is indeed the chief thing, he returns a son of God and joint-heir with Christ.[24]

Moving on to Cyprian (200–258), the spiritual son and pupil of Tertullian and Bishop of Carthage, we find the greatest potential for adoption. The subject of the first Christian biography and a martyr under the persecution of Roman Emperor Decius, Cyprian's biographer Pontius the Deacon surmised following his execution that "he will probably never cease to speak even to the end of the world." Cyprian's translators have claimed in turn that "nobody can understand the history of Latin Christianity without mastering [his] system." Today, Cyprian is best known for his saying, "He can no longer have God for his Father, who has not the church for his mother." While the sentiment was not new to Cyprian (cf., Tertullian), its frequent attribution to Cyprian is likely due to John Calvin (*Inst.* 4:1:1).[25]

Certainly, Cyprian's writings are rich in expressions of God's Fatherhood, the exchange of the Son for the sons, brotherhood and joint

---

[24] *A-N F* 5:237.

[25] *A-N F* 5:267, 264, 423.

heirship with Christ, and the church's motherhood. These themes recur amid Cyprian's apologetic and pastoral emphasis on the oneness of God, the unity of the church universal, and the treatment of returning heretics and the lapsed. While genuine repentance is requisite, it is for shepherds of Christ whose pastoring reflects God's "medicine of paternal affection" to encourage it.

For all such familial expressions, Cyprian says nothing of adoption. Despite the somewhat Pauline feel of his familial references, he chose the Johannine language of the new birth to describe how we obtain a filial relationship to God (see Jn. 1:12-13, 3:1-21; 1 Jn 2:29–3:3). Regeneration and/or the new birth is mentioned in Cyprian's testimony (*Epistle to Donatus*), his biography (both in Pontius' narrative and in the citing of Cyprian), and other epistles and treatises. In his treatise *On the Lord's Prayer* it is the language of the new birth that Cyprian injects: "The new man, born again and restored to his God by his grace, says 'The Father,' in the first place because he has now begun to be a son."[26] Nowhere does Cyprian explain either his preference for the new birth or his omission of adoption, though his choice comports with his view of the church as mother. While we laud him for capturing the relational (explicitly familial) atmosphere of the New Testament, and for underlining the church's maternal privileges and responsibilities, his overlooking of adoption sets the course of the decline of interest among the early Latin Fathers. In the remaining Hendrickson collection of ante-Nicene Latin Fathers there is no hint of adoption.

Those following Cyprian—Novatian, Lactantius, Venantius, Asterius Urbanus, Victorinus, and Dionysius of Rome[27]—may not have

---

[26] *A-N F* 5:449.

[27] The *Ante-Nicene Fathers* also includes other miscellaneous writings, chiefly the *Early Liturgies*, the Pseudo-Clementine Literature, the *Apocrypha of the New Testament*, *The* [Papal] *Decretals*, and ancient Syriac Documents (*A-N F* 7:509–8:785). Some are of uncertain origin, some are apocryphal, and some are forgeries. They do not alter the overall profile of adoption in the early centuries.

taken their lead from him. In the list from Venantius onward the usual occurrences of terms related to adoption appear, namely "Father," "sons of God," "children of God," "brothers," and "heirs." However, I have found but three references to adoption—the two in the *Excerpts of Theodotus* mentioned earlier, and another in the *Recognitions of Clement*, what the translator Thomas Smith calls "a kind of philosophical and theological romance": "When God had made man after His own image and likeness, He grafted into His work a certain breathing and odour of His divinity that so men, being made partakers of His Only begotten, might through Him be also friends of God and sons of adoption."[28] While the counting of references is not everything, as the New Testament's uses of υἱοθεσία indicate, few references in the ante-Nicene Fathers carry theological freight. That said, our judgments are based solely on known *extant* writings.[29] In miscellaneous documents such as *Acts and Records of the Famous Controversy about the Baptism of Heretics*, *A Treatise Against the Heretic Novation*, and *A Treatise on Re-Baptism*, we find, as with *The Seven Books of Arnobius Against the Heathen*, some passing references to the Fatherhood of God and a few to those born "the children of the Lord," but that is all.

4. THE NICENE AND POST-NICENE GREEK FATHERS

The search of the Nicene and post-Nicene Fathers entails a journey through successive subdivisions of history: the Constantinian and Athanasian (or the Nicene and Trinitarian) age to the First Council of Constantinople of 381; the post-Nicene or Christological and Augustinian age extending to the Council of Chalcedon in 451; and the rise of the Papacy in the West ending with the close of the Roman Empire in 476. We offer here but a first word concerning the place of adoption in the Nicene and post-Nicene Fathers. The period warrants

---

[28] *A-N F* 8:136.

[29] *A-N F* 5:601ff.; 6:413ff.; 7:1–368. For instance, we only have fragments of the writings of Caius (Gaius) of Rome.

further research for Schaff avers that the age is second only in productiveness to those of the apostles and the Reformation.[30]

We would not expect to find much of relevance in the writings of the first church historians. Certainly, in Eusebius of Caesarea (263–339) we do not. When covering in his *Church History* the various *Epistles of Dionysius*, he uses a plethora of phrases including "the adoption of God," but does so in regard to Dionysius' treatment of the Gospel and Apocalypse of John. Likewise, it is most doubtful that the church histories of Socrates (379–450?), Theodoret (393–c.457), or Sozomenus (400–c.450) contribute anything significant to the theological history of adoption.[31]

As for the theologians of the period, there are differing opinions as to the degree to which adoption figures in the thought of Athanasius. At the outset of the twentieth century, Lidgett opined that in Athanasius "The Father is insufficiently manifested in and through the Son to men; and men are insufficiently brought, in the Son, to the Father." By the century's end, however, Widdicombe claimed that "it was not until the fourth century with Athanasius [c.297–373] that the fatherhood of God became an issue of sustained and systematic analysis." These views are not necessarily contradictory. However, Widdicombe goes further, "The idea of sonship is central to Athanasius' soteriology." He points us to Athanasius' works *Contra Arianos*, *Contra Gentes*, and *De Incarnatione*, although there is no reference to adoptive sonship in the third study. Nevertheless, the anthropology in the first two works informs the soteriology in the third. Commenting on *Contra Arianos*, Widdicombe remarks, "The idea of sonship by adoption runs as a

---

[30] Philip Schaff, *History of the Christian Church*, Volume 3: *Nicene and Post-Nicene Christianity From Constantine the Great to Gregory the Great A.D. 311–590* (Peabody, MA: Hendrickson Publishers, 2006), 6–7, 9.

[31] E.g., *N and P-N F* (second series), 1:311. For the church histories see *N and P-N F* (second series), vols. 2 and 3. Theodoret does, however, reference three adoption texts in a letter to John the Oeconomus: Rom 8:14-17; Gal 4:6, 7; and Eph 1:4-5 (3:319).

leitmotif throughout."[32]

Athanasius believed adoption is implied in creation, the description of Christ as the Firstborn "prov[ing] the framing and adoption of all things through the Son."[33] Following Paul in Romans 9:4, he also read the history of Israel in terms of adoption. The children of Israel knew adoption, however, only through the Son.[34] Widdicombe writes, "As Son of God by nature who becomes Son of Man, and bestows upon us the Holy Spirit, the Son enables us to become sons of the Father by adoption." The Son can do so because he alone fully knows God on the one hand, and because his identification with human need is complete on the other. Christ's fullness of both deity and humanity is thus essential to the believer's adoption. As Son of God, Christ bestows grace, but as Son of Man he receives it. In a process of divinization man receives from Christ incorruptibility and communion with God and is exalted and brought into the presence of God, yet without dehumanization.

This divinization is the Christian's adoption. It entails a transformation from the sole status of creature into that of adopted son and participant in the knowledge and love of the Father. Ephesians 1:3-5 and Galatians 4:6 are crucial in this regard. The particular vehicle by which we receive the Spirit and enter into adoption is baptism. Baptism marks the transition from a condition of death in Adam to that of life in Christ. Whereas Christ's Sonship is natural, the believer's is transferred. It is real, of grace, but secondary to the Sonship of the Son. We may lose this sonship by the making of evil or immoral choices, and yet, curiously, remain within the church and the grace of God. "We may," expounds Widdicombe, "fall away from the Spirit, but the enduring grace of the Father and the Son, made present to us by the Spirit, means

---

[32] Lidgett, *The Fatherhood of God*, 180; Widdicombe, *The Fatherhood of God*, 1, 223.

[33] *N and P-N F* (second series), 4:398; cf., 4:383.

[34] *N and P-N F* (second series), 4:441, 445; cf., 4:380. In what follows, I chiefly summarize Widdicombe, *The Fatherhood of God*, 223–50.

that our participation in the divine life, and in the life of the community, is guaranteed, provided that we are willing to repent." In short, the Christian may fall from sonship, but the penitent may gain it back.

Athanasius aided the Alexandrian School in reflecting more persistently John's teaching of the new birth and Paul's of adoption. Although they are fundamental to "Athanasian soteriology," we are not to assume that Athanasius understood them to be distinctively structured teachings. In his *Four Discourses Against the Arians*, for example, he writes: "we are made sons through [Jesus Christ] by adoption and grace, as partaking of His Spirit (for 'as many as received Him,' he says, 'to them gave He power to become children of God, even to them that believe on His Name').[35] Although Athanasius erringly assumes that John refers to adoption in John 1:12, he stands out as at least including adoption in his theologizing. Contrast what we know of the Cappadocian fathers:

Basil the Great (329–79). In a less contentious age the Archbishop of Caesarea, may have taken up the theme of adoption in his treatise *De Spiritu Sanctu*. At the time, though, he was concerned for the fundamental reality of the distinct and coequal personhood of the Holy Spirit within the Godhead.[36]

Gregory of Nazianzen (329–90). The discovery of adoption in his oratians and letters is unlikely.

Gregory of Nyssa (335–95). Among his writings, *The Great Catechism* is the best test of the place of adoption in his thought. Yet the categorization of the *Catechism* suggests the work is more apologetical than theological. It contains a modicum of soteriology, but in the little relevant that he writes he focuses on regeneration (the new birth).[37] Elsewhere, in his dogmatic treatise *Against Eunomius*,

---

[35] *N and P-N F* (second series), 4:404.

[36] *N and P-N F* (second series), 8:1–50.

[37] *N and P-N F* (second series), 5:471–509 (especially 500, 504, and 506–8).

Gregory mentions adoption a couple of times. He does so in defending the recently deceased Basil from Eunomius' "laboriously-written abuse of our father in God" and in seeking to overturn his controversion of Basil's sound doctrine of the eternal Sonship of Christ. The burden of proof, Gregory insists, lay with Eunomius to prove that the church has believed in vain that "the Only-begotten Son truly exists, not adopted by a Father falsely so-called, but existing according to nature, by generation from Him Who is."[38] This belief the church obtained from Scripture. Reflecting on Paul's words in Romans 8:32, "He spared not His own Son," Gregory writes: "He contrasts the true Son with other sons, begotten, or exalted, or adopted (those, I mean, who were brought into being at His command) marking the specialty of nature by the addition of 'own.'"[39] Although, according to the footnote, Gregory's use of "adopted" is doubtful,' his rebuttal of Eunomius stands. Amid his argumentation, it is clear that his references to adoption are intended to set apart the way believers are sons from the Sonship of Christ. We are adopted, but Christ was eternally the Son of God.

In Cyril of Jerusalem (313–86) we find four mentions of adoption, in the most obvious place of his *Catechetical Lectures*—his seventh lecture, on "The Father, Ephesians 3:14, 15." There Cyril teaches that although God is, strictly speaking, the Father of One-only, the Only-begotten Son, our Lord Jesus Christ, and has been eternally so, by the gift of our Father's loving-kindness, those "transferred from servitude to sonship by the grace of the Father, through the Son and Holy Spirit . . . are permitted so to speak." This grace is not according to nature, but by adoption. Whereas Paul writes of the believer's predestination to adoption (Eph. 1:5), Cyril places the accent on our choice: "The adoption is in our own power." Judas chose to be a son of the devil (for he was not one by nature), but Paul chose to turn from

---

[38] *N and P-N F* (second series), 5:33, 163.

[39] *N and P-N F* (second series), 183–84; cf., 109.

persecuting to preaching. Reminiscent of Athanasius, Cyril rests his thinking on John 1:12: *"But as many as received Him, to them he gave the power to become the children of God, even to them that believe in His name.* For not before their believing, but from their believing they were counted worthy to become of their own choice the children of God."[40]

The writings of other Nicene and post-Nicene Fathers such as Dydimus of Alexandria (313–98), Epiphanius (310–403), and Cyril of Alexandria (376–404) are omitted from the Hendrickson edition. Naturally, those of John Chrysostom (347–407) are included. Although Chrysostom appears to say little of adoption, he is aware of the doctrine. In *The Gospel of Matthew* he states generally but fulsomely that, "he who calls God Father, by him both remission of sins, and taking away of punishment, and righteousness, and sanctification, and redemption, and adoption, and inheritance, and brotherhood with the Only-Begotten, and the supply of the Spirit, are acknowledged in this single title."[41] That said, Chrysostom does not typically read adoption into his commentary. The few passing comments he makes on adoption, as we might expect from one of the great expositors of the Christian church, are found in his sermons, especially on the relevant adoption texts. This largely explains their salvation-historical flavor, as will become apparent from our later exegesis of the New Testament references (ch. 5).

In his *Homilies on Ephesians*, Chrysostom describes adoption as a high privilege granted to those who draw near to God. God brings us at once from a state of enmity to the adoption of children by the work of a "really transcendant love." In this work, nothing is done without the Father and the Son. The one predestines us, the other brings us near. Yet, the greatness of the blessing is found not in the blessing *in se* but in

---

[40] *N and P-N F* (second series), 7:44–48.

[41] *N and P-N F* (first series), 10:134. The singularity of the title *Father* explains our later reference to the Fatherhood of God as a supramodel. It is the umbrella covering the expanse of the multifaceted aspects of our salvation.

the Christ through whom we receive it. God sent not a servant to accomplish our adoption, but his Only-begotten Son. It follows, so says his *Commentary on Galatians*, that the privilege of sonship comes through faith rather than through law. Through faith we put on Christ, are delivered from the curse of the broken law, and are promoted to sonship. Hence Paul's idea of "receiving" the adoption (Gal. 4:5).[42]

Chrysostom underlines mainly the application of salvation. Its complementary pillars are the believer's union with Christ and possession of the Spirit of adoption: "How does it appear that we have become sons? He [Paul] has told us one mode, in that we have put on Christ who is the Son; and now he mentions another, in that we have received the Spirit of adoption." In his commentary *The Epistle to the Romans*, Chrysostom writes that while the Spirit is to those in the state of grace the Spirit of Wisdom, of Power, of healing, of prophecy, and of tongues, so he is also the Spirit of adoption. It is the Spirit who enables us to call God "Father"; not only "Father" but "Abba, Father"—the "Hebrew" (*sic*) indicating "a most true descent" and serving as "a special sign of true-born children to their fathers." The Spirit is also the Comforter who bears witness with our spirits that we are God's children (Rom 8:16). He takes away any doubt as to our dignity.[43]

To be a child of God is, then, "a grace unspeakable." It is a greater privilege still to be a joint-heir with Christ. Although we suffer before entering the inheritance, the suffering aids us in our waiting for the adoption (Rom. 8:22-23). Chrysostom thereby acknowledges that the salvation-historical trajectory which has revealed God's adoptive purposes to the present, continues into the future until the consummation of adoption at the return of Christ. Anticipating his hearers'

---

[42] *N and P-N F* (first series), 13:52. The Jews of the old covenant era enjoyed a high birth as sons of God (*N and P-N F* [first series], 10:59–60), but from Chrysostom's comments on Rom 8:17 we learn that he did not consider them to have the same adoption as new covenant believers (*N and P-N F* [first series], 11:442).

[43] *N and P-N F* (first series), 13:30; 11:442.

struggle with what we now call the "now" but "not yet" eschatological tension, Chrysostom writes:

> What dost thou say, let me hear? Thou didst insist on it at every turn and didst cry aloud, that we were already made sons, and now dost thou place this good thing among hopes, writing that we must needs wait for it? Now it is to set this right by the sequel [the consummation of adoption] that he says, "to wit, the redemption of our body." That is, the perfect glory.[44]

5. THE NICENE AND POST-NICENE LATIN FATHERS[45]

The Council of Nicea (325) did not do much to raise the profile of adoption in the West. News of the Council became common knowledge only after Constantine took control of the empire in the West in 353. Trinitarian and christological concerns continued to dominate. In his treatise, *De Trinitate*, Bishop Hilary of Poitiers (310–67), a Nicean, mentions adoption but more as a negation of a false view of God the Son than as a positive view of the believer's sonship: "The son of God is not false God, nor God by adoption, nor God by gift of the name, but true God."[46]

Similarly, Ambrose of Milan (340–97) rarely refers to the grace of adoption, although his treatise *Of the Christian Faith* contrasts the Son by generation and sons of God by grace. The editorial footnote explains that this is the grace of adoption. This becomes clearer a few pages later: "Now a son is so called either by means of adoption or by nature, as we are called sons by means of adoption. Christ is the Son of God by virtue of His real and abiding nature." Ambrose's treatise *Of the Holy Spirit* notes further a contrast within the believer. Once we were servants, now we are sons, sons awaiting the full freedom of our filial status in the age to come. Curiously, Ambrose attributes our adoption

---

[44] *N and P-N F* (first series), 11:445.

[45] Fitting neatly into neither the Greek nor Latin Fathers are Aphrahat (280–345) the Persian sage and Ephraim Syrus (306–373). Neither appears to be relevant.

[46] *N and P-N F* (second series), 9:86.

to the Spirit: "The Spirit made us children by adoption." He witnesses thereafter to us that we are adopted.[47]

To date, no comparable comments on adoption have been found in the writings of Jerome (c.342–420). Serving the church as translator and historian, he was a propagandist for Greek education, imparting a knowledge of Greek commentaries and homilies, although his friends remained Latin. He was, says von Campenhausen, "a typical and conscious representative of Latin Christianity." In urging the church in the West to catch up intellectually with her Eastern counterparts, Jerome exercised a greater influence on Western biblical philology than on her methodological and theological principles or doctrines.[48]

It was not given to Sulpitius Severus (363–425), a friend of Jerome, to expound adoption in his *Life of St. Martin*, *Letters*, *Dialogues*, or *Sacred History*, nor to Vincent of Lérins (died 445). In *A Commonitory* he distinguishes universal truth from heresy, indicting Photinus for advocating that we worship only the Father as God, honoring Christ as only a man, and Nestorius for perpetrating a Quarternity, including two Sons of God, the one divine and the other human. However, in the spiritual and practical Conferences of John Cassian (360–435) we come across a couple of references to adoption. In "The First Conference of Abbot Isaac; On Prayer," he introduces Pauline thought in treating the "Our Father" of the Lord's Prayer: "When . . . we confess with our mouths that the God and Lord of the universe is our Father, we profess forthwith that we have been called from our condition as slaves to the adoption as sons." In "The First Conference of Abbot Chaeremon; On Perfection" he writes regarding Romans 8:15 of the fear overcome by the inflaming of the Father's perfect love, for "the Divine adoption has

---

[47] *N and P-N F* (second series), 9:101 (cf., 127, 458), 144, 216fn., and 221. Interestingly, Peter Martyr Vermigli later references Ambrose on adoption in his *Loci Communes*.

[48] von Campenhausen, *The Fathers of the Church: The Fathers of the Latin Church*, 179–81.

already made sons [of them] instead of servants."[49]

Of greater interest is the place of adoption in the thought of Augustine (354–430), and not only because of his massive influence on the Christian church. In his *Reply to Faustus the Manichaean*, Augustine offers for the first time, so far as we know, an evaluation of adoption: "The word adoption is of great importance in the system of our faith, as is seen from the apostolic writings." He offers as proof Paul's talk of adoption in Romans 9:4, 8:23, and Gal. 4:5, stating that "These passages show clearly that adoption is a significant symbol." Yet, a preliminary search of Augustine's other writings suggests a deficit between what he thought of adoption and how much attention he gave to it. Augustine scholars can check on this, but adoption seems to crop up in didactic or apologetic pieces, such as in his *Reply to Faustus the Manichaean* and his *Sermons on New Testament Lessons*.[50]

Naturally, Christ is relevant to adoption as Augustine's comments in *On Faith and Creed* indicate. As the only-begotten, Christ had no brethren, yet as the first begotten he gives the name of brethren to those "born again into the grace of God through the adoption as sons." The third day after his crucifixion he rose from the dead, "the first begotten for brethren destined to come after Him, whom He has called into the adoption of the sons of God." These he makes joint-partners and joint-heirs. Slavish fear has no place in the lives of those possessing the Spirit of adoption (he returns to Rom. 8:15-16 repeatedly), for we are reconciled to God through love. Having the Spirit, the adopted groan with the remainder of the creation for the adoption (Rom. 8:22-23)—a text to which Augustine fittingly returns in his tract *On Patience*.[51]

John Rist states that Augustine uses the idea of adoption to explain the quasi-divine condition reached through divinization. This, though, is not clear from Augustine's specific references to adoption.

---

[49] *N and P-N F* (second series) 11:1, 139–40, 393, and 421.

[50] *N and P-F* (first series), 4:160 and 6:256.

[51] *N and P-F* (first series), 3:324, 326, 330, 331, 431, 432, 529, 535.

Nevertheless, Gerald Bonner agrees, claiming that Augustine's neo-platonically influenced view of deification equates with the New Testament's use of υἱοθεσία. As proof of this, he points to Augustine's *Epistulae ad Galatas expositio* (24.8) and his *Tractates on St John's Gospel*, stating that Augustine's references to deification are in full agreement with the Greek concepts espoused by Irenaeus and Athanasius. On this understanding, there is in Augustine's view of deification a point of connection between the Greek and Latin fathers. Not all, however, are so positive about his contribution. H. P. C. Lyons argues that Augustine failed to grasp either the richness of the implications of adoption or the opportunity to integrate it into his teaching on grace. As challenging as is this assessment, it is certainly more nuanced than Lidgett's claim that, "With the theology of Augustine[,] the Fatherhood of God . . . passed entirely out of sight. It had been replaced by the conception of His sovereignty."[52]

Leo the Great (400–461) read Paul's thought on adoption into Matthew's Gospel in "A Homily on the Beatitudes" (Matt. 5:1-9). In the "gentleness and grace of 'the Spirit of adoption'" Leo sees a contrast with the harshness of the law and the terrors of bondage.[53]

As Protestants, we may immediately assume of Leo that this grace is to be mixed with works and our faith with merit. In one Whitsuntide sermon, for instance, he proclaims that our salvation is accomplished by the Son's propitiation of the Father *and* our act of faith: "It was necessary that those who are to be saved should also do something on their part, and by the turning of the hearts to the Redeemer should quit the dominion of the enemy, even as the Apostle

---

[52] John Rist, "Augustine of Hippo," in *The Medieval Theologians: An Introduction to Theology in the Medieval Period*, G. R. Evans, ed. (Malden, MA: Blackwell, 2001), 15–16; Gerald Bonner, "Augustine's Conception of Deification," *Journal of Theological Studies*, NS, 37 pt. 2 (Oct. 1986), 377, 378, 381, 384; H. P. C. Lyons, *A Catholic Dictionary of Theology*, s.v. "Adoption of sons" (New York: Nelson, 1962); Lidgett, *The Fatherhood of God*, 200.

[53] *N and P-N F* (second series), 12:203.

says, 'God sent the Spirit of his Son into our hearts crying Abba, Father,' 'And where the Spirit of the Lord is, there is liberty,' and 'no one can call Jesus LORD except in the Holy Spirit.'"[54] Since Protestants also believe that a person is not saved without faith and repentance, the question arises whether Leo understood the doing part to be meritorious. We ask in effect, whether he saw faith and repentance as contributing to our salvation, or, as in Protestantism, as merely the occasion on which we are saved.

Another sermon suggests we pause before reading later Roman Catholic soteriology back into Leo. Christians, "born of corruptible flesh," may be freed from slavery and promoted to sonship through a rebirth by the Spirit of God. In it, we "obtain through grace what [we] hadst not by nature" and, as a consequence, "acknowledge" ourselves to be sons of God "by the spirit of adoption" and "dare to call God Father." Likewise, in an additional sermon *On the Feast of the Nativity*, Leo attributes our sonship to the power of God. Our Savior "became the Son of man in order that we might have the power to be the sons of God." Again, that power is found in the new birth.[55]

The next century, Gregory the Great (540–604) doubtless held to the same soteriology, shorn, apparently, of Pope Leo's passing references to adoption.[56]

6. THE MIDDLE AGES

The Middle Ages (or Medieval period), typically dated from the fall of the Roman Empire in 476 until the rise of the Modern period at the end of the fifteenth century, entails some overlap in their early

---

[54] *N and P-N F* (second series), 12:192.

[55] *N and P-N F* (second series), 12:131, 137.

[56] See *The Book of Pastoral Rule, and Selected Epistles, of Gregory the Great, Bishop of Rome* (*N and P-N F* [second series], 12:1–243.

centuries with Schaff's subdivisions of the post-Nicene Fathers.[57] Even more so than the Nicene and post-Nicene eras, the Medieval period awaits further study of the fortunes of adoption. At this point, I can only offer some leads. These pertain not only to those who wrote of adoption but how they did so, for whereas the references by the fathers to adoption had a salvation-historical feel, the rise of Medieval scholasticism in the Middle Ages gradually altered the method by which the doctrine was expounded and thus its resultant feel.

Some logical works, says L. M. de Rijk, are found as early as in the writings of Boethius (477–524) a sixth-century Roman Senator and philosopher. The scholastic method, however, went on to straddle the Middle Ages and early Modernity, first in the church, then, after 1200, in differing genres of discourse in the emerging universities in Bologne, Paris, and Oxford.[58] By that time, the last of the Greek Fathers, John of Damascus (676–749), was long gone. More of an encyclopedist of prior thought than an original thinker, John is regarded as an early if not the earliest systematician. His *Exposition of the Orthodox Faith* offered a plan to systematize the truths of Scripture which influenced the later Schoolmen and, ironically, the Western discipline of systematic theology. Although John allots adoption neither a section nor discussion, he mentions it in a familiar vein: "He who is by nature Son of God became first-born amongst us who were by adoption and grace sons of God, and stand to Him in the relation of brothers."[59]

We may state in general, then, that whereas the Fathers developed the mind of the church and created her theological materials

---

[57] Two were omitted earlier: the Justinian age and the despotism of the state church (527–65), and the Gregorian age (590–604).

[58] W. J. van Asselt and Eef Dekker, "Introduction," in *Reformation and Scholasticism: An Ecumenical Enterprise*, Willem J. van Asselt and Eef Dekker, eds., [Grand Rapids: Baker Academic, 2001]), 14–21, 38 (cf. 230); Antonie Vos, "Scholasticism and Reformation," in *Reformation and Scholasticism*, 106.

[59] Michael F. Bird, *Jesus The Eternal Son: Answering Adoptionist Christology* (Grand Rapids: Eerdmans, 2017), 23.

in their most straightforward forms (e.g., doctrinal formulae), the scholastic doctors presupposed the materials and sought a union of doctrine and mind. In this, they were influenced by:

- Boethius' translation of Aristotle, which created the philosophical terminology of the Middle Ages.
- Tenth- and eleventh-century developments in Latin grammar (the function of words in their sentences).
- Twelfth-century linguistics (mature syntactical and semantical theory, and the terminist logic relating to the properties of terms and their uses in propositions).
- The confluence of developments in language (*grammatica*) and logic (*dialectica*) producing a flow of analytical (precise and critical) thinking.

The resultant scholasticism, although mistaken as a regurgitation of Aristotle, may more accurately be described as Aristotelist. Medieval logic (e.g., syllogistic reasoning) surpassed Aristotelian syllogisms, and Christian thought differed from Aristotelian philosophy (with its espousal of the eternality of the world and the finitude of God).[60]

Scholasticism produced a surge in academia in the interpreting of Scripture (*sacra pagina*) and took the ratiocination of exegesis (the logical analysis of language) to a new level. Now regarded as a science, theology probed Scripture's constitutive parts, as also the relation with other spheres of knowledge, notably in the confessional-Christian universities spread over Europe by the eighteenth century. By developing the basis for systematic theology, Scholasticism anticipated the later Protestant use of Scripture. Its research and teaching methods

---

[60] Cf. William J. Townsend, *The Great Schoolmen of the Middle Ages: An Account of their Lives, and the Services they Rendered to the Church and the World* (London: Hodder and Stoughton, 1881), 161; von Campenhausen, *The Fathers of the Church: The Fathers of the Latin Church*, 278–79, 288; van Asselt and Dekker, "Introduction," 34–35; Vos, "Scholasticism and Reformation," 107–8; Wolfhart Pannenberg, *Systematic Theology*, vol. 1, transl. Geoffrey W. Bromiley, reprinted (Grand Rapids: Eerdmans, 1998), 23.

utilized, in the words of de Rijk, "an ever and ever recurring system of concepts, distinctions, propositional analyses, argumentational techniques, and disputational methods."[61]

Theology was not deemed scientific merely because it was studied in university. Rather, at the university, the battle was fought between the theology of Christianity and the philosophy of Aristotelianism. While Christianity predominated, it nevertheless did so amid (and thereby in contact with) the presence of logic and the philosophy of language. With its theology of creation and its dismantling of the errors of ancient philosophy, Christian influence over education spawned science after science from the thirteenth century (but especially from the fifteenth).

John Duns Scotus (1265–1308), possessing, says Townsend, "special aptitude for gathering knowledge from many sources, and then constructing systems and theories," prepared the way for the great Schoolmen. It was, however, Albert the Great who first reproduced Aristotelian philosophy on a systematic basis, molding it thereby to meet the Church's requirements in dogma. Thus, there arose among the Schoolmen, beginning with Alexander of Hales (1452) and rising to Aquinas' "literary wonder of the Middle Ages," the *Summa Theologiae*. States Townsend, it is "the ripest fruit of his genius and of Scholasticism and, indeed, of the entire literature of the Latin Church."[62]

Against this methodological backdrop, we ponder the interest in adoption. According to M. M. Loughran, the church in the West did not follow (catch-up is better) the adoptive interest of the East. In the millennium following the fathers, Western interest in God's Fatherhood waned as issues of divine sovereignty and justice came to dominate dogmatic concerns. Yet, this claim awaits a full survey of Medieval

---

[61] Vos, "Scholasticism and Reformation," 103, 106–7. Cf., Luco van den Brom "Scholasticism and Contemporary Systematic Theology," in *Reformation and Scholasticism*, 282.

[62] Townsend, *The Great Schoolmen of the Middle Ages*, 57, 83, 165, 205, and 207.

soteriology.[63] Presently, we know that:

- Martin Luther drew on Bernard of Clairvaux (1090–1153), specifically his *Sermon on the Feast of the Annunciation of the Blessed Mary*, concerning how the "witness of the Spirit is the filial trust of our heart in God" (Rom. 8:16).

- Karl Barth interacted with Peter Lombard (1100–1160), stating that the threefold nature of God's presence *ad extra*—God's presence in all nature (omnipresence), in indwelling grace, and in Christ—was recognized in Scholasticism from Lombard onward due to the protracted use of his *Sentences*. Whereas Christ's sense of God's presence (*gratia unionis*) is unique, Israel and the church receive their sense of it (*gratia adoptionis*) from the fullness of Christ's *gratia unionis*, which is to say, in him and for his sake. Indeed, their acceptance in him constitutes the *gratia adoptionis*.

- Edwin Palmer alludes to the theories of adoption of Bonaventura (1221–74) and Duns Scotus. The former compares adoption to the relation between a bride and a groom, for adoption is based not on a new nature (birth) but on a new status. The latter understood adoption in terms of friendship, for it is based on love. Such theories raise important theological issues about grace and need to be attested exegetically.

Jeff Fisher remarks that in the medieval exegetes "there is a strong ecclesiastical and meritorious reading of adoption." But this he states rather than demonstrates. Thus, his suggestion of a survey of the *Glossa Ordinaria*—a multivolume work produced in twelfth-century France containing the entire biblical text with commentary by patristic and medieval authors—plus a study of medieval exegetes such as Nicholas of Lyra [1270–1349] and Denis the Carthusian [1402–71]), is

---

[63] *New Catholic Encyclopaedia*, s.v. "Adoption, Supernatural" by M. M. Loughran. Not all Catholic scholars agree with Loughran. Lyons asserts that "adoptive sonship is no less clearly taught by the Latin fathers" ("Adoption of sons"). Lidgett, *The Fatherhood of God*, 198–200; *contra* Whaling, "Adoption," 234.

well taken.[64]

The uncertainty of the place of adoption in Medieval theology is seen in the two greatest Schoolmen: Anselm (1093–1109) and Thomas Aquinas (1225–74). In fairness to Anselm, his best known writings—*Monologium, Proslogium,* and *Cur Deus Homo*—are not chiefly soteriological. In *Monologium* he raises the interesting question as to the names of the Trinity, given God lacks gender (ch. 42). Anticipating today's discussion of metaphor, he argues that the Father is called the Father because he is the "principal cause of offspring," and the Son is called the Son because he reflects the Father. This leads to a discussion of God's love. Excepting a few comments, Anselm focuses on how love plays out within the Godhead. When he mentions the relationship between God and his rational creatures, he does so in terms of the creature's love of God's essence. For this love, we are created, and in it we are blessed and overcome fear and suffering.[65]

In *Proslogion*, a discourse on God's existence, Anselm takes further the relationship between God and man, setting out the importance of the prior satisfaction of God's justice for such a relationship. Yet, the establishment of this relationship is not Anselm's chief concern. It becomes such, however, in *Cur Deus Homo.* God cannot, he argues, put away sins by compassion alone. There must be payment for the honor taken from God by our sins. In the gospel, then, there is a meeting of the love and justice of God. In love, God provides a Savior to satisfy his justice. He does so by suffering the just penalty of our sin. This supplication of the Father on our behalf excites "a wondrous depth

---

[64] Martin Luther, *Commentary on the Epistle to the Romans,* abridged transl. J. Theodore Mueller (Grand Rapids: Zondervan, 1960), 106; Edwin H. Palmer, *Scheeben's Doctrine of Divine Adoption* (Kampen: J. H. Kok N.V., 1953), 16; Karl Barth, *CD,* II.1, 485; Jeff Fisher, "The Reformation of Adoption: Calvin and Oecolampadius on Roman 8," (drive google.com/file/d/0B1uICU_BoP_bWXhvZUFfYkNJbjA/view, accessed on October 27, 2016).

[65] *Saint Anselm: Basic Writings,* transl. S. N. Deane with an introduction by Charles Hartshorne, 2nd ed. (La Salle, IL: Open Court, 1974), 105, 116 (cf., *Proslogion,* 28–29), and 134.

of devotion . . . in the hearts of the hearers," but that is the closest Anselm comes to the application of salvation.[66]

Distaste for Anselm's theory of satisfaction hinders balanced assessments of his view of the atonement. Loughran argues that Anselm's juridical view of redemption, rooted in God's sovereignty, inevitably downplays God's love. Anselm, though, was very interested in God's Fatherhood, but understood the Father to be holy and just as well as loving. Charles Hartshorne is likely more accurate, stating that Anselm's "central failure"—"his only radical one"— was "that he never relates the necessary, and therefore abstract, to anything which is more than abstract in God." This Hartshorne puts down to the Neoplatonic worship of the necessary or the eternally immutable, over against the contingent or the noneternal." Thus, Anselm focused more on God as he is in himself than on the sinner's relationship to God.[67]

Turning to Aquinas, it is said that he not only ignored God's Fatherhood but consciously dispensed with it. To quote Lidgett, "Every line of the theology of Aquinas has . . . gone, not only to make the Divine sovereignty the only conceivable relationship between God and man, but also to externalise and harden it." But is this true? The answer requires a full survey of Aquinas' writings, including his commentaries on different parts of Scripture, Lombard's *Four Books of Sentences*, the tracts of Boethius, the treatise *On the Divine Names*, and on that of Dionysius the Pseudo-Areopagite, the *Book of Causes*, almost all the works of Aristotle, and *The Disputed Questions*.

We comment here on but two representative series: *Summa Contra Gentiles*, Aquinas' classic Christian manual published between 1259 and 1264 for use by missionaries in Spain, and his unfinished *Summa Theologica* published between 1265 and 1272.

---

[66] *Saint Anselm*, 18, 283, 285.

[67] Loughran, "Adoption, Supernatural," 139; Hartshorne, Introduction to *Saint Anselm*, 15.

The *Summa Contra Gentiles* seems to corroborate the view that prior to the Reformation the gospel had become couched in thoroughly juridical terms. Hopes are slim of finding much interest in the Fatherhood of God or the sonship of believers. The relationship between the Father and the Son is not discussed until Book Four ("Salvation"), nor is the relationship between the three persons. There is no consideration of the constitutive elements of the doctrine of salvation, for soteriology was yet to come into its own during the Reformation and post-Reformation eras. Instead, Aquinas focuses on the Roman sacraments and the redemption of the body. He quotes Romans 8:21 but omits our bodily redemption as the adoption (Rom. 8:22-23). His interest lay rather in the metaphysics of resurrection.[68]

Note, though, some interesting twists in the *Summa Theologica*. First, Aquinas' *Summa* contain more of a familial or filial feel in the discussion of God and the creature. Aquinas, for example, distinguishes the eternal and the temporal: "The eternal comes before the temporal. But God is the Father of the Son from eternity; while He is the Father of the creature in time. Therefore, paternity in God is taken in a personal sense as regards the Son, before it is so taken as regards the creature." The personal sense, taken by the creature, arises from a similitude of grace in adoptive sonship and a certain likeness to the image of the Father.[69]

Second, Aquinas includes what is, currently, the earliest known chapter or section on adoption.[70] Titled "Of Adoption as Befitting to Christ," it amounts to under three of 3,000 pages, but, true to Scholasticism, asks four questions. Namely, whether:

---

[68] Thomas Aquinas, *Summa Contra Gentiles, Book Four: Salvation*, transl. Charles J. O'Neil (Notre Dame: University of Notre Dame Press, 1975), 40–42, 143–146, and 297–349.

[69] *St. Thomas Aquinas Summa Theologica*, Complete Edition in Five Volumes (Allen, Texas: Christian Classics, 1948), 1:175.

[70] *St. Thomas Aquinas Summa Theologica*, 4:2141–43.

- It is fitting that God should adopt sons? Just because divine adoption exceeds human adoption it does not follow that we must be strangers to be adopted by God, as is the case in human adoption.
- It is fitting that the whole Trinity should adopt? In divine adoption, it befits the three persons to adopt by dint of the oneness of the Godhead. Through an admixture of New Testament texts Aquinas deduces that adoption is appropriated to the Father as its author, to the Son as exemplar of sonship, and to the Spirit as imprinter on us of Christ's likeness as exemplar.
- It is proper to the rational nature to be adopted? Although divine adoption is not proper to the human nature, being received rather by grace, the rational creature is nevertheless capable of being adopted.
- Christ as man is the adopted Son of God? Whereas Hilary and Augustine understood that Christ, as man, was adopted by God, Ambrose denies this, arguing that a natural son cannot also be an adopted son. Aquinas weighs in on the side of Ambrose, reasoning that since sonship belongs to the uncreated person and not to the created nature, the Son of God, as natural Son in his divinity prior to the hypostatic union of the two natures, must remain a natural rather than an adopted son.

Aquinas' comments not only whet the appetite for further studies, notably of Hilary, Augustine, and Ambrose, but of the Medieval period. As they stand, they have a significance out of all proportion to their brevity for present-day discussions of whether Christ was, as the God-man, adopted.

7. THE PROTESTANT REFORMATION

The burden for the reform of the one, holy, catholic, and apostolic church, while traceable back to such forerunners as John Wycliffe and Jan Hus, became unstoppable by the sixteenth century. The reformers' identification of marks (*signa*) of the true church of the Lord Jesus Christ were intended not to create a new church, but to purify the existing one. In the backdrop of such reforms were the influences of Medieval Scholasticism and the more recent Renaissance.[71]

The reformers maintained Medieval scholasticism's commitment to objective, immutable, unified truth, the pursuit of freedom from the traditionalism of church authority, and the belief that truth can be accessed by faith. Constituting a method rather than a theology, scholasticism rode the waves of the Reformation, and was used alike by Roman Catholic, Lutheran, and Reformed schools of theology. Those positive about the scholastic method were not obliged to endorse every theological position stated amid its use, nor were those positive about a given theology obliged to agree with everything about the scholastic use of Scripture. Although the scholastic method was static (depending on its definition), the content of Scholastic theology was dynamic. Thus, we acknowledge the scholastic elements in Protestant thought without confusing the reformers with the Medieval scholastics.[72]

Reformed scholasticism is thought to have gained momentum early in the movement for reform, in Italy (in and around Padua) under the influence of erstwhile Augustinian monks Peter Martyr Vermigli (1500–1562) and Girolamo Zanchi (1516–90). Additionally, scholars have long observed Scotistic elements in Calvin's thought. Certainly, Calvin lectured in a scholastic style, and trained his *scholastici* in the Academy of Geneva in logic and the method of disputation. Richard Muller also observes a methodological continuity between Calvin's teaching and the scholastics' extended to his preaching. Following T. H. L. Parker and David Steinmetz, he mentions, whether felicitously described or not, their shared practice of "glossing the entire text of Scripture in a running commentary as the basic course in the theolo-

---

[71] Van Asselt and Dekker, "Introduction," 22–24.

[72] Bert Loonstra, "Scholasticism and Hermeneutics" in *Reformation and Scholasticism*, 304; van Asselt and Dekker, "Introduction," 34; van den Brom, "Scholasticism and Contemporary Systematic Theology," 279.

gical curriculum."[73]

Yet, the reformers' use of Scholasticism was neither wholly continuous nor wholly discontinuous with the Medieval period. While they used logic, they did not necessarily utilize the *quaestio* technique, which, in Muller's definition of [Protestant] scholasticism, stood, in some form of the following structure, as a *sine qua non* "in every period":

1. The presentation of a thesis or *quaestio* (thematic question);
2. The indication of the subject(s) to be discussed in relation to the *quaestio* (i.e., the *status quaestionis*);
3. The treatment of a series of objections (*objectiones*) against the accepted position;
4. The formulation of a comprehensible answer (*responsio*) in which account is taken of all the available sources of information, and the rules of rational discourse are upheld.[74]

Thus, there developed out of Medieval scholasticism a scholasticism of the Reformation era differing from its Medieval equivalent; an Aristotelianism, too, although, according to Luther, one differing from Aquinas and the Medieval scholastics. The reformers maintained, for instance, the Aristotelian fourfold causality, but amalgamated it with additional emphases:

- The place-logic of Rudolf Agricola (1443–85). Modified by Melanchthon, it examined texts, supremely the text of Scripture, to identify topics or central issues.
- The technique of Peter Ramist (1515–72) which challenged the use of Aristotelian logic by the use of dichotomous divisions intended to simplify subjects, later influencing Amandus Polanus' *Syntagma* and William Perkins' *Golden Chaine*.

Alongside this evolving scholasticism (and Aristotelianism) there emerged the influence of Renaissance humanism. While it is too

---

[73] Muller, "The Problem of Protestant Scholasticism—A Review and Definition," 52.

[74] Van Asselt and Dekker, "Introduction," 25–26.

simplistic to claim that the scholastics' method emanated from the universities but the reformers' more kerygmatic or rhetorical style from the pulpits, we cannot ignore how differences in the handling of adoption began opening up around this time.[75]

Of particular significance is the influence of Erasmus (1467–1536), especially on the likes of Lefèvre d'Étaples (c.1450–1536). In turn, Lefèvre influenced the reformers at large, notably through his humanist interest in the Pauline writings, mediated via his massive *Commentary on the Epistles of Paul* (1512). Calvin, for instance, used his humanist teachers to counter scholastic speculative tendencies in theology and philosophy and to challenge the academic use of language. Seeking the reform of the curriculum in the church, *l'ecole de Dieu*, he believed a new curriculum would serve as a springboard for yet broader reforms. While not opposed to the use of reason in theologizing, Calvin was more sensitive than the earlier Medieval and later Protestant scholastics to the humanness of Scripture, the salvation-historical unfolding of its doctrine, and the feel of the Scriptures. His approach reflected more the best fathers.

Against the backdrop of such methodological developments we now consider the fortunes of adoption in the Reformation era. Certainly, the humanist interest in Paul led to the recognition of adoption in his theology. This is seen, for example, in the *Commentary upon St. Paul's Epistle to the Romans* (1556) by Juan de Valdes (c.1490–1541). Yet, during the Reformation, opines Robert Candlish, "the subject of adoption, or the sonship of Christ's disciples, did not . . . occupy the place and receive the prominence to which it is on scriptural grounds entitled." Let us consider the evidence.

For all the impact on Martin Luther (1483–1546) of Paul's Roman and Galatian epistles (containing four of the five biblical uses of υἱοθεσία), the German reformer did not, says Lidgett, generally express "the graciousness—and indeed fatherliness—of God in Christ . . . strictly

---

[75] Van den Brom, "Scholasticism and Contemporary Systematic Theology," 285.

in terms of Fatherhood." Brigit Stolt avers that only once Luther became a father did he realize the loving, comforting, and joy-affording character of fatherhood. Hitherto, his appreciation of it had been hindered by his austere childhood.[76]

Luther's theology of the cross and his following of the Christian calendar ensured that his sermons were very largely taken up with the Gospels. Few drew from the *corpus Paulinum*, and fewer still from the apostle's adoption texts. Luther, though, does not overlook that God is Father to his children, but it was not a thought he unpacked. He focused rather on the question of how an individual can be right with God. In other words, his concern lay more with the justification of sinners than the adoption of sons.

Over the years, Luther preached on the entire pericope of Galatians 3:15–4:7, in three sermons: 3:15-22 on the thirteenth Sunday after Trinity, 4:1-7 on the Sunday after Christmas, and 3:23-29 on New Year's Day.[77] On 3:15-22, Luther begins by pointing us to his commentary on Galatians for a fuller treatment, explaining that Paul is at length to distinguish between the righteousness of faith (which justifies) and the righteousness of works or the law (which does not). Specifically, the apostle underlines the vanity of the Jews' boastful delusion that they were justified and became God's children through law. Rather, states his sermon on Galatians 3:23-29, since "Christ is the child of God . . . he who clothes himself in Christ, God's son, must be the child of God. He is [therefore] clothed with divine adoption, which

---

[76] Robert S. Candlish, *The Fatherhood of God: Being the First Course of the Cunningham Lectures*, 5th ed. (Edinburgh: Adam and Charles Black, 1869), 192; 240–47; cf., McKinlay, "The relation of incarnation to atonement," 105–6. Martin Luther, *Works,* vol. 25; ed., H. C. Oswald (Saint Louis: Concordia Publishing House, 1972), 71–73; and vol. 27, ed., J. Pelikan (Saint Louis: Concordia Publishing House, 1964), 288–91; Lidgett, *The Fatherhood of God*, 251; Brigit Stolt, "Martin Luther on God as a Father," *Lutheran Quarterly*, New Series, 8 (Spring 1994), 389–90.

[77] *The Complete Sermons of Martin Luther* (Grand Rapids: Baker, 2000), 4.2:248–54; 3.2:224–310.

unquestionably must constitute him a child of God."[78] Luther, however, was less concerned with the adoptive act (the process of adoption) than with the adoptive state (the life of sonship or childhood [*Kindschaft*]). He fails, therefore, to do justice to the unfolding in Galatians 3:15–4:7 of God's adoptive dealings with his people, from the minority adoptive sonship of Israel under the old covenant to the majority sonship of believing Jews and Gentiles under the new. He contrasts instead the servant (under the Law and working unwillingly) and the child (possessing faith and working cheerfully). Accordingly, his sermon on 4:1-7, which he believed was greatly needed, was as much about justification as adoption.

Among Luther's sermons are also three deliverances on Romans 8—one on 8:12-17 and two on 8:18-22. Once more, the adoptive state is to the fore, only more naturally so given the content of the chapter. Distinguishing the true and the false Christian, the child of God has the comfort of possessing the Holy Spirit, of being led by him, and of receiving eternal life and glory. In this context, Luther describes Romans 8:15 as worthy of letters of gold and provides a winsome and roughly accurate interpretation of the application of adoption. He defers, however, to his sermon on Galatians 4:1-7 (v. 6) for a greater explanation of the Spirit of adoption, merely stating that possession of the Spirit distinguishes God's children from the devil's. The former are heirs of God. This privilege Luther unpacks in his two sermons on Romans 8:18-22.

Yet, when dealing in Romans 8:18-22 with Paul's declaration concerning the eager expectation of the revelation of the children of God, he strangely ends both sermons without getting to the adoption,

---

[78] *The Complete Sermons of Martin Luther*, 3.2:287. Likewise, he comments on Rom. 8:15 that the contrast between the spirit of bondage and Spirit of adoption is intended to show how we become God's children: "We are not children by nature (as alone in Christ), nor by descent, nor because of our merits (as the Jews boasted), but alone because of our gracious adoption by God as children (in Christ)" (Luther, *Commentary on the Epistle to the Romans*, 105).

the redemption of our bodies (8:23). This is the consummation of the adoptive act, for when God adopts us, he adopts the whole person, their bodies as well as their souls. Likewise, in his Romans commentary (using, admittedly, an abridged translation to hand), he says nothing of either the adoption or the redemption of the body mentioned in the verse. If this is consistent with the unabridged original, then Luther overlooks in adoption the earlier milestones of salvation history and confirms his primary interest in the present individualized appropriation of salvation. He ignores, then, the adoptive act, whether occasioned by faith or consummated by the return of Christ.[79]

Not so the second-generation reformer, John Calvin. Although he includes no distinct chapter or section on adoption in his *Institutes*, we may fairly claim, contrary to his austere reputation, that he is, after Paul, the church's theologian of adoption *par excellence*. From the comments strewn throughout his corpus, we detect his very fine grasp of the contours of Paul's thought. This is now available in a comprehensive but nonexhaustive exposition.[80]

Anthony Lane rightly recommends a hermeneutic of suspicion when assessing which church fathers influenced Calvin's interest. Neither Calvin's mention of a church father nor similarity of thought equates to influence. Under the citation rules of the day, Calvin may well have been impacted by those not cited and could have come to a fondness of adoption before encountering a church father confirming

---

[79] *The Complete Sermons of Martin Luther*, 4:96–118, 168-79; cf., Luther, *Commentary on the Epistle to the Romans*, 110.

[80] Tim J. R. Trumper, "An Historical Study of the Doctrine of Adoption in the Calvinistic Tradition" (Ph.D. Diss., University of Edinburgh, 2001), 38–214. See also Nigel Westhead, "Adoption in the Thought of John Calvin" *SBET* 13 (1995), 102–15; Howard Griffith, "'The First Title of the Spirit': Adoption in Calvin's Soteriology" *EQ* 73:2 (2001), 135–53. I am unclear as to the basis of Isomi Saito's claim that my exposition of Calvin fails to capture cohesively the salvation-historical tapestry (election to consummation) and theological framework of Calvin's view of adoption ("Divine Adoption in the Confessions of the Reformation Period," [Amsterdam: Vrije Universitaet, 2016], 88).

his interest. Without solid evidence, Lane argues, parallels must be distinguished from influences. In this light, it may prove impossible to determine precisely who, if any, particular Greek or Latin father(s) shaped Calvin's interest in adoption.

That said, we can be confident of two details. First, Calvin's initial reference to adoption occurs in his 1535 Preface to Olivetan's Bible translation, published according to some estimates just a year after his conversion. Second, that besides quoting Eusebius in the Preface, Calvin also quotes Chrysostom three times. Indeed, Calvin cites Chysostom more than any other father except Augustine and Jerome. Although Jerome's influence is unlikely, Lane's hermeneutic of suspicion precludes us presently from explaining Calvin's interest in adoption by either the influence of Chrysostom or Augustine.[81]

As regards the influence of Medieval theologians on Calvin, we need a much clearer picture of the place of adoption in their thought before we can identify parallels or influences.[82] The same may be said of the influence of earlier reformers of the Reformation era. Nevertheless, a couple of connections merit comment.

Consider Calvin's connection to Johannes Oecolampadius (1482–1531). Although Oecolampadius died in Basel shortly before Calvin took refuge there, the two men pursued studies of Romans, about a decade apart. Fisher quotes Akira Demura to the effect that Calvin doubtless "had Oecolampadius' exegetical works beside him and consulted them with reasonable frequency."[83] Bearing in mind Lane's

---

[81] Consider Anthony N. S. Lane's eleven theses in weighing the influence of the church fathers, in *John Calvin: Student of the Church Fathers* (Grand Rapids: Baker, 1999), xi, 1–13 (cf., 54–61), 70 and 72.

[82] For Lane's investigation of Calvin's use of the Medievals, see *John Calvin*, 15–66.

[83] Jeff Fisher, "The Reformation of Adoption: The Exegesis of John Calvin and Johannes Oecolampadius on the Doctrine from Romans 8," a paper delivered at the Midwest meeting of the ETS, March 11, 2016. Fisher references Alkira Demura's chapter "Two Commentaries on the Epistle to the Romans: Calvin and Oecolampadius" in *Calvinus*

hermeneutic of suspicion, Fisher's comparison of their respective studies in Romans are nevertheless intriguing: "the most noticeable differences in their commentaries is that Calvin's comments [on adoption] are, for the most part, more extensive than Oecolampadius's." Unless, then, Calvin was directly influenced by Oecolampadius, it seems unlikely that the scope of his interest in adoption is solely due to Oecolampadius. Consider also, then, Calvin's connection to his older friend and correspondent, Peter Martyr Vermigli (1500–1562). Vermigli relates adoption in his *Loci Communes* to the old and new covenants, the differences between the Son and the sons, and union with Christ.[84]

Regardless of whose influence determined Calvin's interest in adoption, Lidgett claims, with merit so far as we know presently, that, "no other writer of the Reformation makes such use of the Fatherhood of God [or, we may add, of adoption] as does Calvin." Certainly, he took interest in adoption to a new level. In the *Institutes*, for instance, he asserts that the authority of the entire gospel is embraced in adoption and the effecting of salvation. This assertion he returns to time and again throughout most if not all his works. [85]

In his tract, *The True Method of Giving Peace to Christendom, and of Reforming the Church*, Calvin boldly describes the grace of adoption

---

Sincerioris religionis vindex: Calvin as Protector of the Purer Religion, ed. Wilhelm H. Neuser and Brian G. Armstrong (Kirksville, MO: Sixteenth Century Journal Publishers, 1997), 165–168.

[84] For Vermigli on adoption, see "De adoptione Dei. Ex Rom. 8. cap. ver. 15" in *Loci Commvnes D. Petri Martyris Vermilii, florentini, Sacrarvm Literarvm in Schola Tigvrina* (Londini: Excudebat Thomas Vautrollerius typographus, 1583), 502–4. *The Common Places of the Most Famous and Renowmed [sic?] Diuine Doctor Peter Martyr, diuided into foure principall parts: with a large addition of Manie Theological and Necessarie discourses, some never extant before*, transl. Anthonie Marten, 1583, Pts. 2:16, 18 and 3:3.

[85] Lidgett, *The Fatherhood of God*, 253. See Marc Lienhard, "Luther et Calvin: Commentateurs du notre Père," *Revue D'Histoire et de Philosphie Religieuses* 72

as "not the cause merely of a partial salvation, but [that which] bestows salvation entire[,] which is afterwards ratified by baptism." In the preamble to his commentary on Ephesians, he explains that in the letter there "occurs a striking display of God's wonderful mercy, when the salvation of men is traced to its true and native source, the free act of adoption." Also significant is his assertion, in his commentary on 2 Corinthians 1:20, that chief of all the promises, which, in Christ, are "yea" and "amen," is that "by which God adopts us to himself as his sons." In the same context, he describes Christ as "the cause and root of adoption." In his testimony, written just prior to his death, Calvin acknowledged that he had "no other defence or refuge for salvation than [God's] gratuitous adoption, on which alone [his] salvation depend[ed]."[86]

Although we can only surmise what exactly Calvin's statements mean, we may deduce with Garret Wilterdink, that, "for Calvin, adoption into the family of God is synonymous with salvation." Writes Sinclair Ferguson, "while there is no separate chapter on sonship in the *Institutes*, *adoptio* (sonship) is one of the expressions by which he most frequently designates the idea of being a Christian. He does not treat sonship as a separate *locus* of theology precisely because it is a concept which undergirds everything he writes."[87]

(1992/1), 73-88; *Inst.* 3:25:3 (*CO* 2 [30]:730); cf., T. H. L. Parker, *Calvin: An Introduction to His Thought* (London: Geoffrey Chapman, 1995), 123.

[86] *Calvin's Tracts and Treatises*, transl. Henry Beveridge. Historical Notes and Introduction to the current edition by T. F. Torrance (Edinburgh and London: Oliver and Boyd, 1958), 3:275. In Latin Cavin's sentence from *The True Method* reads: "Baptismum ergo praecedat adoptionis gratia, necesse est: quae non dimidiae tantum salutis causa est, sed eam ipsam salutem in solidum affert, quae baptismo deinde sancitur" (*CO* 7 [35]:619). For the succeeding quotes, see *CC* XXI, 191 (*CO* 51[79]:141); *CC* XX, 137–38 (*CO* 50 [78]:23); "Life of John Calvin" (*Tracts*, 1:cxxiv [*CO* 21 {49}:162]).

[87] Garret A. Wilterdink, "The Fatherhood of God in Calvin's Thought," in Richard C. Gamble, ed., *Articles on Calvin and Calvinism*, vol. 9, *Calvin's Theology, Theology Proper,*

Certainly, Calvin traces the historical scope of God's grace from the first things to the last things through the motif of adoption, discerning along the way the relevance of such themes as the Father's predestination of his people, the loss of Adam's pre-Fall knowledge of God as Father, the covenant which God graciously made with his people under the old covenant, and the wonderful exchange in which God's Son by nature becomes the son of man in order that the sons of men may, by adoption, become the sons of God. The three moments constituting the wonderful exchange—the incarnation; the anointing of Christ to his offices of prophet, priest, and king; and his death and resurrection— pave the way for the granting of the Spirit who, in applying the work of Christ, unites the Son and the sons. By working faith in the elect, the Spirit becomes the bond of union between the firstborn and the adopted. Two gifts are granted in this union: justification and sanctification. Since Calvin speaks of these gifts in filial terms, it is uncertain how he views adoption—whether as a strong metaphor of union with Christ or as a blessing of it. According to this paradigm, adoption either undergirds or overarches justification and sanctification. Whichever, we know the adoptive act was determined in the mind of God before the world began, was guaranteed by the redemptive work of Christ, and is occasioned by the receiving of it. In resting in Christ, we enter the adoptive state—a life of sonship characterized by liberty, prayer, assurance, providence, obedience, and the inheritance.

Calvin, though, was not, as defenders of Protestant scholasticism are keen to point out, the sole fountainhead of Reformed theology. Yet, this caution should not be permitted to diminish Calvin's influence on the inclusion of adoption in the development of Reformed theology.

Eschatology (New York & London: Garland Publishing Inc., 1992), 185; see also *Tyrant or Father? A Study of Calvin's Doctrine of God*, vol. 1, Scholastic Monograph Series (Bristol, IN: Wyndham Hall Press, 1985), 21. Sinclair B. Ferguson, "The Reformed Doctrine of Sonship," in *Pulpit and People: Essays in Honour of William Still*, ed. Nigel M. De S. Cameron and Sinclair B. Ferguson (Edinburgh: Rutherford House, 1986), 82.

Consider, in this regard, the thought of John Knox (c.1515–72), who, for a few years, was a refugee in Calvin's Geneva. Although his writings are less prodigious than those of Calvin's, he resonates the familial strands of Calvin's theology.[88] Particularly relevant is his lengthy tract *On Predestination in Answer to the Cavillations by an Anabaptist, 1560*. Predestination, he says, is "the eternall and immutable decree of God, by which he hath once determined with himself what He will have to be done with everie man." Those God loved in Christ from everlasting he called. These enjoy an assurance of adoption by dint of their justification through faith. Divine predestination proves, then, the freeness and certainty of salvation. "We affirm, those whom he [God] judgeth worthie of participation of salvation to be adoptate and chosen of his free mercie for no respect of their own dignitie."[89]

Aside from the interest of individual theologians, the church's creeds and confessions are a good gauge of intensive and extensive interest in adoption. Since "a creed," to quote Phillip Schaff, "may cover the whole ground of Christian doctrine and practice, or contain only such points as are deemed *fundamental* and *sufficient*," the profile of adoption in formal or official statements of the faith reveals the degree

---

[88] See Knox's *Works*, vol. 5, ed., David Laing. (Edinburgh: James Thin, 1895), 7-468. In the tract *On Predestination* Knox's more notable statements relate to: the Fatherhood of God (27, 35, 50, 56, 82, 130, 204–205, 231, 241, 254, 376–77, 394–95, 412); the children of God (21, 23, 28, 52, 58, 81, 87, 92, 96, 210, 235, 236, 237, 249, 250, 257, 273, 285, 301, 338, 340, 356, 376-377, 383, 394–95, 403, 414, 415, 417); the sons of God (310 [cf., 312], 413, 417, 418); adoption (26, 36, 38, 44, 169); and the children of the devil (131, 136).

[89] Note Knox's use of Eph. 1:4-5: "In love the Father predested us for adoption through Jesus Christ" (*On Predestination, Works* 5:44; cf. 5:36, 26 [cf., 169], and 38).

to which adoption is deemed "fundamental."[90] Since they are compiled in community, they also reveal the extent of the interest.

There had been some discussion of adoption at the Council of Toledo (675) and the Synod of Frankfurt (792), but it was not until the creed-making age of the sixteenth century that allusions to adoption begin to appear with some regularity:

- The first creed of the Reformed churches—The Sixty–Seven Articles or Conclusions of Ulrich Zwingli (1523)—lacks specific references to adoption, but two articles allude to the believer's relationship to his or her heavenly Father.[91]

- Zwingli's *Fidei Ratio* (1530) possesses a relational tone consistent with Paul's doctrine of adoption. There is a glimpse of it in Article Two on God's eternal counsel, but direct or indirect references to adoption are found in Articles Three (on soteriology), Four (on original sin), and Six (on ecclesiology). In Article Three, in relation to Ephesians 1:4, Zwingli refers to the elect being received unto God—code language for adoption. More explicit still, are Zwingli's words: "It is his goodness that he has elected whom he will, but it is of his justice to adopt [*adoptare*] and unite the elect to himself through his Son."[92]

- In the First Helvetic Confession (Latin 1536) there is a general relational tone and in Article Eleven a possible reference to adop-

---

[90] Philip Schaff, *The Creeds of Christendom: With a History and Critical Notes*, 3 vols., ed., P. Schaff, rev. D. S. Schaff. Sixth ed. (reprinted from the 1931 ed.; Grand Rapids: Baker Books, 1990), 1:4 (italics inserted). My assessment of the place of adoption in Christian creeds and confessions is based foundationally on a thorough review of Schaff's three volumes.

[91] Article 8: "From this follows, first, that all who live in the Head are members [*Glieder*] and are children of God [*Kinder Gottes*], and that is the Church or communion [*Gemeinschaft*] of the saints, a housewife of Christ, the catholic church"; Article 27: "That all Christian men are the brothers of Christ and are subject to one another. Therefore, no one shall *be* named Father. For this reason orders and sects[,] *etc.* decline" (Schaff, *Creeds of Christendom*, 3:198 and 201).

[92] Saito, "Divine Adoption in the Confessions of the Reformation Period," 124.

tion in Christ's brotherhood (although the reference could also be to Hebrews' teaching of sonship (2:10-18; 12:3-11). The Confession unmistakably refers to baptism in Article Twelve in terms of both regeneration and adoption.[93]

- The Genevan Confession (1536), variously attributed to Farel and Calvin, alludes to adoption in Article Fifteen ("Baptism"): "Baptism is an external sign by which our Lord testifies that he desires to receive us for his children, as members of his Son Jesus."[94]

- In the Genevan Catechism (1541/42) there is a clear emphasis on the Fatherhood of God (Q and A 12 and 22) and the believer's filial consciousness (Q and A 250), as well as on correlative themes such as union with Christ as portrayed (at least) in the sacraments. Yet, in Question and Answer 323 the Catechism speaks tantamount to adoption in relation to the sacraments when mentioning that "God receives us as members of his family." Only in Q and A 46 does the Catechism mention adoption explicitly. We call Christ the Son of God although believers are also called God's children because we are children of God by adoption and by grace (*par adoption et par grace*).[95]

- The *Consensus Genevensis* (1552), more a defense of the doctrine of election during the Bolsec controversy than a creed, confession, or catechism, naturally focuses on Ephesians 1:3-6 and the election of believers to adoption in God's Son. Adoption is wrapped up in the meaning of election, election guaranteeing in turn the believer's possession of the Spirit of adoption.

- The Confession of the English Congregation at Geneva (1556) contains no direct reference to adoption but defines salvation as

---

[93] Saito's "Divine Adoption in the Confessions of the Reformation Period," 128–37.

[94] "The Confession of Faith—Confession de la Foy" (creeds.net/reformed/gnvconf.htm, accessed October 16, 2017).

[95] Saito, "Divine Adoption in the Confessions of the Reformation Period," 166–83.

a change of status from "children of perdition" to "children of God," alluding to related christological, pneumatological, ecclesiological, and eschatological implications of adoption.[96]

- Unsurprisingly, The French Confession of Faith or Gallic Confession (*La Confession de foi de 1559*), prepared by Calvin, both mentions and alludes to adoption.[97]

- The Scots Confession of Faith (1560) makes no mention of adoption but speaks of sonship.[98]

- The Canons and Dogmatic Decrees of the Council of Trent (1563) mention adoption in the Decree on Justification, chapter two. In chapter four justification is said to involve "a translation, from that state wherein man is born a child of the first Adam, to the state of grace, and of *the adoption of the sons of God*, through the second Adam, Jesus Christ, our Saviour." Adoption is clearly implied in chapter eight. Moreover, in chapters seven, eleven, and sixteen there are references to the closely related themes of inheritance and eternal life.[99]

---

[96] Saito, "Divine Adoption in the Confessions of the Reformation Period," 184–96.

[97] Articles 17, 19, and 22 (*Creeds of Christendom*, 3:369-372; cf., the translations in *Reformed Confessions of the 16th and 17th Centuries in English Translation, Volume 3,1567–99*, compiled with an Intro., James T. Dennison, Jr., [Grand Rapids: Reformation Heritage Books, 2012], 313–16).

[98] Article 13, "Of the Cause of Good Works" (*Creeds of Christendom*, 3:452–53). For more on the Scots Confession, see Tim J. R. Trumper, "Adoption: The Forgotten Doctrine of Westminster Soteriology," Lynn Quigley, ed., *Reformed Theology in Contemporary Perspective (Westminster: Yesterday, Today—and Tomorrow?)*, Edinburgh Dogmatic Conference Papers (Edinburgh: Rutherford House, 2006), 87–123, or Trumper, "An Historical Study," chap. five.

[99] *Creeds of Christendom*, 2:91, 94–95, 97, 101, and 107.

- The Heidelberg Catechism (1563) uses *adoptati* in the original Latin of Answer Thirty-Three, which reference to adoption is sometimes lost in translation.[100]
- The Second Helvetic Confession (1566), which Schaff describes as "the last and best of the Zwinglian family," states in chapter twenty ("Of Holy Baptism") that, "there is only one baptism in the Church; it lasts for life, and is a perpetual seal of our adoption."[101]
- The Thirty-Nine Articles of the Church of England (1566; English 1571) mentions adoption in at least two articles. Article Seventeen ("Of Predestination and Election") reads:

  > Wherefore *such as have* so excellent a benefit of God *given unto them*, to be called according to God's purpose by his Spirit working in due season: they through grace obey the calling: they be justified freely: they be made sons by adoption: they be made like unto the image of *God's* only begotten Son Jesus Christ: they walk religiously in good works and at length, by God's mercy, they attain to everlasting felicity.

  Additionally, Article Twenty-Seven ("Of Baptism") states:

  > Baptism is not only a sign of profession, and mark of difference, whereby Christian men are discerned from others that be not christened: but is also a sign of regeneration or new birth,

---

[100] Cf., T. F. Torrance's preference for "adopted" in *The School of Faith: The Catechisms of the Reformed Church*, transl. and ed., Thomas F. Torrance (London: James Clarke & Co., 1959), 75, with *The 400th Anniversary Edition of the Heidelberg Catechism* (Cleveland, OH: United Church Press, 1962), 39, which opts for "accepted." Question and Answer 33 read: "*Quam ob causam Christus vocatur* FILIUS DEI UNIGENITUS, *cum nos quoque simus filii Dei? Quia solus Christus est coaeternus et naturalis aeterni Patris Filius; nos autem propter eum ex gratia a Patre adoptati sumus*" (*Catechesis Christiane Religionis* in *The Heidelberg Catechism in German, Latin, and English with an Historical Introduction Prepared and Published by the Direction of the German Reformed Church in the United States of America*, Tercentenary edition [New York: Charles Scribner, 1863], 166). The German translation in *Der Heidelberger Katechismus* translates *adoptati* as *angenommen* which can mean either "accepted" or "adopted" (*Creeds of Christendom*, 3:318). For further consideration, see Question and Answer 120 (*Creeds of Christendom*, 3:351).

[101] *Creeds of Christendom*, 1:390, 414.

> whereby as by an instrument, they that receive baptism rightly, are grafted into the Church: the promises of the forgiveness of sin, and of our adoption to be the sons of God, by the Holy Ghost, are visibly signed and sealed: faith is confirmed: and grace increased by virtue of the prayer unto God.[102]

- The Formula Concordiae (1576 [Latin 1584]) lists the Schwenkfeldian errors. The fourth complains that "the water of baptism is not a means whereby the Lord seals adoption in the children of God and effects regeneration."[103]

- Craig's Catechism (1581) contains two sections on adoption—"The Certainty of Our Adoption" and "The Trial of our Adoption" with nine and twelve questions apiece, each with the briefest of one-line answers. Nevertheless, Craig's Catechism, named after John Craig (c. 1512–1600), evinces the early influence of Calvin's *Institutes* and was a Scottish staple in instruction until the production of the WLC and WSC.[104] It is the first Catechism we know of to include distinct sections on adoption.

- In The Saxon Visitation Articles, 1592, Article 3.4 states that "baptism is the bath of regeneration, because in it we are born again, and sealed by the Spirit of adoption [*Kindheit/adoptionis*] through grace."[105]

Much of the list above contains but the briefest and faintest allusions to adoption. Whereas distinctive treatments afford a clearer idea of the quality of understanding, the allusions and sporadic references to adoption are useful for establishing the tone of a document and

---

[102] On Article 17 see *Creeds of Christendom*, 1:633 (cf., The Forty-Two Articles of the Church of England [1553] in Oliver O'Donovan's *On the 39 Articles: A Conversation with Tudor Christianity*, A Latimer Monograph [reprint ed.; Carlisle: The Paternoster Press, 1993], 142). On Article 27 see *Creeds of Christendom*, 3:504–5 (cf., O'Donovan, *On the 39 Articles*, 148).

[103] *Creeds of Christendom*, 3:178.

[104] *Reformed Confessions of the 16th and 17th Centuries in English Translation*, 3:603–5.

[105] *Creeds of Christendom*, 3:184.

for highlighting the way Paul discerned the connection between adoption and other doctrines.

Saito and I arrive at variant perspectives on the place of adoption in the Reformation confessions. Typically, I do not regard summaries of biblical truth as relevant merely because they mention the Fatherhood of God. Divine paternity has relevance to regeneration as well as to adoption, sometimes relating only to the former (e.g., The Anglican Catechism, 1549). Second, the presence of union with Christ does not guarantee reference to adoption either, for an image of it may be generally relational rather than specifically familial. In any case, the imaging of union with Christ as an adoption makes no guarantee of the inclusion of the broader salvation-historical scope of adoption. Whereas Saito, then, offers an uncritical defense of the Protestant orthodoxy of the past, for me its best defense lies in overcoming its areas of weakness.[106]

8. THE POST-REFORMATION ERA

Following the Reformation, there occurred two significant developments germane to the history of adoption.

First, the continued evolution of scholasticism birthed a methodological shift within Protestantism. Initially, the *Quaestio* method of earlier scholasticism continued:

> In the seventeenth century, a theological work was identified as "scholastic" when it belonged to the classroom, echoed the patterns of disputation then typical of education, and employed a refined method of argument to define the terms of debate, the *status questionis*, and the resolution of debate with various clearly identified opponents.

Now scholasticism went further. Continues Muller: "The Protestant scholasticism of the seventeenth century involved 'ratiocination' in order to formulate [quoting Hans Emil Weber's *Reformation, Orthodoxie, und Rationalismus*] 'a logically coherent and defensible system of

---

[106] *Creeds of Christendom*, 3:517, 521; Saito, "Divine Adoption in the Confessions of the Reformation Period," 45–59 and 91–274 (95 especially).

belief.'" The ratiocination did not supplant Scripture, but reasoned on the basis of the Scriptures as the foremost authority. The method entailed drawing out of Scripture the *principia* or *axiomata* from which deductions could be drawn. The logic utilized factored in exegesis and aimed at the construction of a system of theology, but resisted the use of logic for its own sake, and looked beyond the system to the best way, utilizing the foremost exegetical results considered in the light of catholic tradition, to express and defend the theology in view.[107]

Distinguishing ratiocination from the philosophy of rationalism, Muller notes how the Medieval *Questio* technique gave way, from Melanchthon on, to the *locus* method. This method would prove most useful in the systematization of biblical truth. In discussing each *locus*, scholastics could make use of syllogistic reasoning—that is to say, a series of three propositions wherein, if the first two are true (the major and minor premises), the third (the conclusion) must be true. And yet, the term *scholasticism* could be regarded more pejoratively in disputations to refer to theologies submerged under burdens of logic and speculation. Since, however, adoption was not subject to rigorous and protracted debate, the use of *scholasticism* in this regard is irrelevant.

Second, there occurred the stultifying of the creative orthodoxy of the Reformation era. The flow of theological writings continued unabated, but aimed more at the consolidation of the gains of the Reformation. In contemporary soccer terms, once ahead the Protestant and Reformed orthodox preferred to "park the bus in front of their own goal," than to push forward in hope of scoring further goals. In effect, whereas the Reformation "swelled the treasury of the creeds of

---

[107] Muller, "The Problem of Protestant Scholasticism—A Review and Definition," 54; Muller, *After Calvin*, 76. I have not gone as far as James Payton Jr, either here or throughout the study, to claim that the methodological shift altered the teaching of the Reformation (supposing he refers to its content), but shall concur with Payton that attempts to defend Protestant scholasticism absolutely do not succeed (*Getting the Reformation Wrong: Correcting Some Misunderstandings* [Downers Grove, Illinois: IVP Academic, 2010]), 195, 202, 209).

Christendom,"[108] the post-Reformation era witnessed by the end of the seventeenth century more of a settled orthodoxy.

Lidgett places the responsibility for this settlement in the lap of the reformers. He claims they remained too wedded to Augustine's view of the gospel which was more a divine condescension than as a fellowship through grace. Lidgett posits multiple reasons for this, yet his perspective seems not a little influenced by the atmosphere of the Victorian liberalism of his day. Nevertheless, it is true to say that Protestant theologians fell short overall in balancing the juridical and familial aspects of the gospel. While the Reformed did more over subsequent centuries than most, if not all, of the children of the Reformation to afford attention to adoption, its place in the everyday theology of the church remained uncertain.[109]

On the continent, a furor erupted over the Remonstrance (1610), published by the followers of Jacobus Arminius (1560–1609). *The Counter Remonstrance* authored by Festus Hommius of Leiden the next year, underlines the inextricable connection between predestination and adoption. Whereas Arminius rejected the predestination learned in Geneva under Calvin's successor Theodore Beza (1519–1605), Hommius writes in paragraph six of the preservation of the elect in terms of the Spirit wrestling on their behalf not only as the Spirit of sanctification but of adoption. The definitive response to the Remonstrance came, however, from the Synod of Dort (1618–19), fleetingly referring to adoption in relation to election (quoting Eph. 1:4-6), assurance (a reference to the children of God), and perseverance:

> For God, who is rich in mercy, according to his unchangeable purpose of election does not take his Holy Spirit from his own completely, even when they fall grievously. Neither does he let them fall down so far that they forfeit the grace of adoption and the state of justification, or commit the sin which leads to death (the sin

---

[108] B. A. Gerrish, *Saving and Secular Faith: An Invitation to Systematic Theology* (Minneapolis: Fortress, 1999), 49.

[109] Lidgett, *The Fatherhood of God*, 240–47.

against the Holy Spirit), and plunge themselves, entirely forsaken by him, into eternal ruin.[110]

Neither fleeting nor limited references to adoption could, however, do justice to the doctrine. In his *Reformed Dogmatics*, Heinrich Heppe alludes to adoption in reference to but three sixteenth- and seventeenth-century theologians: Andreas Hyperius (1511–64), Franciscus Burman (1628–79), and Johann Heinrich Heidegger (1633–98).[111] It will take further research of the period to determine whether Heppe's few allusions to adoption reflect the negligable interest among post-Reformation theologians or Heppe's own oversight of the doctrine. Either way, the neglect of adoption is glaring.

From what we can tell, interest in adoption was more promising in England. There, Separatists of Calvinistic persuasion drew up the First London Confession of Faith (1644), borrowing partially from the Second Confession of the London-Amsterdam

---

[110] *Reformed Confessions of the 16th and 17th Centuries in English Translation: Volume 4, 1600–1693*, Compiled with Intros., James T. Dennison, Jr. (Grand Rapids: Reformation Heritage Books, 2014), 47; *Canons of Synod of Dort*, The First Main Point of Doctrine, Art. 7 (cf., The Second Main Point of Doctrine, Art. 8); The First Main Point of Doctrine, Articles 10 and 13 (cf., Art. 12) (*Creeds of Christendom*, 3:573 and 594); The Fifth Main Point of Doctrine, Art. 6 (*Creeds of Christendom*, 3:572 and 593). The same Main Point also connects perseverance and assurance. Art. 10 ("The Ground of This Assurance") explains that the assurance of the believer's preservation arises not from some private revelation beyond or outside of the Word, but from faith in the promises of God revealed in his Word; from "the testimony of the Holy Spirit testifying with our spirit that we are God's children and heirs (Rom. 8:16-17)"; as well as from a serious and holy pursuit of a clear conscience and good works (The Fifth Main Point of Doctrine, Art. 10) The next Article, "Doubts Concerning This Assurance," speaks of God as "the Father of all comfort" and Art. 13 of his "fatherly goodness."

[111] Heinrich Heppe, *Reformed Dogmatics: Set out and Illustrated from the Sources*, transl. G. T. Thomson (reprint ed.; Grand Rapids: Baker Books, 1978), 552. For further biographical details, see *Die Religion in Geschichte und Gegenwart: Handwörterbuch für Theologie und Religionswissenschaft*, Herausgegeben von Kurt Galling (Tübingen: J. C. B. Mohr [Paul Siebeck], 1957), s.v. "Hyperius, Andreas Gerhart (1511–64)" (H. W. Weißgerber), "Burman, Franciscus (1628–79)" (W. F. Dankbaar), and "Heidegger, Johann Heinrich (1633–98)" (J. F. G. Goeters).

Church (1596). The latter refers to the power of Christ in applying to believers the benefits of his prophethood and priesthood, and includes the adoption of sons. The former speaks of the oneness between our triune God and believers, by dint of which we "are the adopted sons of God, and heirs of Christ, co-heirs and joint-heirs with him of the inheritance of all the promises of this life, and that which is to come."

Remaining in the 1640s, the Puritans, who had influenced the development of Dutch Puritanism through the work of Willem Teellinck (1579–1629), took a step that was to have a lasting influence on the subsequent history of adoption. The commissioners of the Westminster Assembly, building on the Irish Articles of 1615 which connect adoption and predestination,[112] compiled the first known *confessional* chapter on adoption (cf., Craig's Catechism, 1581). The twelfth chapter, "Of Adoption," took the formal summarizing of the doctrine to an unprecedented level, becoming thereafter the single most influential confessional statement on adoption.

Yet, at 101 words, "Of Adoption" is the WCF's shortest chapter:

All those that are justified, God vouchsafeth, in and for his only Son Jesus Christ, to make partakers of the grace of adoption: by which they are taken into the number, and enjoy the liberties and privileges of the children of God; have his name put upon them, receive the Spirit of adoption; have access to the throne of grace with boldness; are enabled to cry, Abba, Father; are pitied, protected; provided for; and chastened by him as by a father; yet never cast off, but sealed to the day of redemption, and inherit the promises, as heirs of eternal salvation.

A couple of reasons explain the commissioners' brevity. First, the Westminster commissioners had no historical errors to refute. Second, while generally retaining the *historica series ordo* from *locus* to *locus*, within the *locus* of salvation, the relevance of adoption to the

---

[112] The section entitled "Of God's Eternal Decree and Predestination" (Art. 15) reads: "Such as are predestined unto life be called according unto God's purpose (his spirit working in due season), and through grace they obey the calling, they be justified freely; they be made sons of God by adoption; they be made like the image of his only-begotten Son Jesus Christ" (*Creeds of Christendom*, 3:529).

entire history of salvation was cropped, limiting overall the significance of adoption to the application of salvation. Thus, the commissioners, while including adoption in Westminster theology, cut the biblical teaching to fit their highly ratiocinated method of laying out biblical doctrine. Nevertheless, when we consider that the chapter was written at a time in which the legal systems of the British Isles had no adoption process, we marvel that it was included at all and that it is supported by answers in the Westminister catechisms to the question "What is Adoption?": [113]

> *WSC Answer 34*
> Adoption is an act of God's free grace, whereby we are received into the number, and have a right to all the privileges of the sons of God.
>
> *WLC Answer 74*
> Adoption is an act of the free grace of God, in and for his only Son Jesus Christ, whereby all those that are justified are received into the number of his children, have his name put upon them, the Spirit of his Son given to them, are under his fatherly care and dispensations, admitted to all the liberties and privileges of the sons of God, made heirs of all the promises, and fellow-heirs with Christ in glory.

That said, it is doubtful that the Westminster commissioners would have envisioned their statement being treated as if it were the last word on adoption. Muller rightly claims that the Reformed orthodox drew on exegetical tradition, yet, in the case of adoption, we may question its reliability. The neglect of adoption had limited the maturity of expositions of adoption, seen most clearly in the admixture of Pauline and non-Pauline thought. We shall corroborate this in part two, when considering the relevant biblical data. This objectivity concerning the Westminster Standards does not imply that what the commissioners taught of adoption was erroneous, but it does mean to say that the texts relied on to explicate adoption are not necessarily germane to the doctrine. Citations of Scripture are true to the Bible overall, but not necessarily to the doctrine under discussion.

---

[113] Francis Lyall, *Slaves, Citizens, Sons: Legal Metaphors in the Epistles* (Grand Rapids: Academie Books [Zondervan], 1984), 67–68.

We may understand in part, then, Candlish's less defensive assessment of WCF 12, WSC 34, and WLC 74: "I never have had any scruple to affirm that their [Westminster] statements on the subject of adoption are by no means satisfactory. No doubt all that they say is true; but it amounts to very little."[114] In fairness, though, to the Westminister commissioners, there is more in their standards on adoption than Candlish admits.

What is not in doubt is their protracted influence. This was aided no end by the replication of WCF 12 in The Savoy Declaration (1658) and The London Baptist Confession of Faith (1677, reprinted in 1689 with a third edition in 1699), respectively. Likewise, the Baptist Catechism (1693) heavily relied on the WSC, as is clear from Questions and Answers 34 and 37.[115]

Individual Puritans also took interest in adoption. John Downame (1571–1652) comments periodically on adoption in connection with the Spirit's ministry in the believer's life in *The Christian Warfare* (1634). Thomas Goodwin (1600–1679) and John Owen (1616–83) refer to the doctrine in relation to predestination and communion with God, the latter regarding adoption as the highest privilege of grace, subsuming it under communion with Christ.[116] Others, however, dedicated entire chapters to adoption:

---

[114] Candlish, *The Fatherhood of God*, 194.

[115] *Reformed Confessions of the 16th and 17th Centuries in English Translation*, 4:471, 547–48, 577–78.

[116] *The Works of Thomas Goodwin, D.D.*, vol. 1, containing an exposition of the first chapter of the Epistle to the Ephesians (Edinburgh and London: James Nichol and James Nesbit, 1861), 83–102. *The Works of John Owen*, vol. 2, ed. W. H. Goold; facsimile reprint ed. (Carlisle, PA: The Banner of Truth Trust, 1966), 5–274 (notably 207–22). Owen also has a short treatment of Gal. 4:6 in his treatise "A Discourse of the Work of the Holy Spirit in Prayer" (*Works*, vol. 4 [facsimile reprint ed.; Carlisle, PA: The Banner of Truth Trust, 1967], 265–70). For a nineteenth-century comparison of Owen and Goodwin on adoption in relation to Christ's Sonship, see Hugh Martin, "Candlish's Cunningham Lectures," *British and Foreign Evangelical Review* 14 (1865), 780. Sinclair B. Ferguson, *John Owen on the Christian Life* (Edinburgh: The Banner of Truth Trust, 1987), 89.

- William Ames (1576–1633) lists twenty-seven characteristics of adoption in his *The Marrow of Theology* (1629).
- David Dickson (c.1583–1663) expounds on the WCF's chapter on adoption in *Truths Victory over Error, or, The True Principles of the Christian Religion*—a series of lectures delivered to divinity students at Edinburgh University in the 1650s.
- Edward Leigh (1602–71) has a chapter titled "Of the Communion and Fellowship Believers have with Christ, and their Benefits by him, and specially of Adoption" (*A Treatise of Divinity* [1646]). Leigh was unusual in that he treated adoption as logically prior to justification in his treatment of union with Christ: effectual calling, conversion, faith, adoption, justification, and sanctification.
- Thomas Watson (1620–86) includes a chapter in his *A Body of Divinity* (1692).
- Herman Witsius (1636–1708) includes two chapters in his *The Economy of the Covenants between God and Man* (1677).[117]

Then there are the "entire treatises on adoption." Joel Beeke has helpfully gathered seven of them:

- Thomas Granger, *A Looking-Glasse for Christians. Or, The Comfortable Doctrine of Adoption* (1622).
- M. G., *The Glorious Excellencies of the Spirit of Adoption* (1645).
- Samuel Petto, *The Voice of the Spirit. Or, An Essay towards a Discoverie of the witnessings of the Spirit* (1654).
- Simon Ford, *The Spirit of Bondage and Adoption: Largely and Practically handled, with reference to the way and manner of working both those Effects; and the proper Cases of Conscience belonging to them both* (1655).

---

[117] I am indebted to J. V. Fesko for the pointers to Dickson and Leigh (*The Theology of the Westminster Standards: Historical Contests and Theological Insights* (Wheaton, IL: Crossway, 2014), 235 and 236.

- John Crabb, *A Testimony concerning the Works of the Living God. Shewing how the mysteries of his workings hath worked many ways in and amongst mankind. Or, The knowledge of God revealed, which shews the way from the bondage of darkness into the liberty of the Sons of God* (1682).
- Samuel Willard, *The Child's Portion: Or the unseen Glory of the Children of God, Asserted, and Proved: Together with several other Sermons Occasionally Preached* (1684).
- Cotton Matther, *The Sealed Servants of our God, Appearing with Two Witnesses, to produce a Well-Established Assurance of their being the Children of the Lord Almighty or, the witness of the Holy Spirit, with the Spirit of the Believer, to his Adoption of God; briefly and plainly Described* (1727).[118]

Puritan sermons also convey, not infrequently, a filial or familial tenor. Thomas Hooker's sermon *The Privilege of Adoption, and Tryall thereof by Regeneration* closes out his study *The Christians Two Chiefe Lessons* (London, 1640). The volume *Puritan Sermons 1659–1689: Being the Morning Exercises at Cripplegate, St. Giles in the Fields, and in Southwark by Seventy-five Ministers of the Gospel* (London, 1660) includes relevant messages by William Cooper, William Bates, Richard Mayo, and Roger Drake. Gordon Cooke notes that although Jeremiah Burroughs wrote no treatise on adoption, deep within his forty-one sermons on the Beatitudes are two on the subject, based on Matthew 5:9: "Blessed are the peacemakers for they shall be called children of God." The verse, writes Cooke, is "perhaps not the first verse from which we would preach adoption," yet he falls prey to today's trend in conservative Reformed circles to exonerate the Puritans at every turn, defending their eisegesis with the remark that, "the Puritans didn't

---

[118] Joel R. Beeke, *Heirs with Christ: The Puritans on Adoption* (Grand Rapids: Reformation Heritage Books, 2008), 11 (with dates added, and reordered accordingly).

preach in the exegetical straightjackets we impose upon ourselves!"[119]

The evidence of adoption in the Puritans supports in part Beeke's rebuttal of the charge that they neglected the doctrine. They wrote, he calculates, 1,200 pages on adoption between the years 1622 and 1727. That exceeds, from what we know, the output of others of their day and perhaps of any other day. Yet, the amount appears very slight when compared with what the Puritans wrote on other themes. Reliant on Thomas M'Crie, the younger, Iain Murray notes: "Questions about Church Unity, Schism, Episcopacy, Church and State, etc., bulk large in seventeenth-century works. Between 1640 and 1662 it is estimated that 30,000 books and pamphlets were written on matters relating to the Church." He adds, "H. M. Dexter records how his research into sixteenth-century Puritanism led him to draw up a bibliography of works on church government and related themes which contained some 1,800 titles for that century alone!" Clearly, then, there is a seismic quantitative difference in the output of the Puritans on adoption and church government.[120]

While Beeke, then, is correct to revise Packer's claim that there has been no more evangelical writing on adoption since the Reformation than there was before, there remains truth in Packer's view that Puritanism suffered from a comparative neglect of adoption: "The Puritan teaching on the Christian life, so strong in other ways, was

---

[119] Thomas Hooker, *The Christians Two Chiefe Lessons* (London: TB for P. Stephens and C. Meredith, 1640), http://digitalpuritan.net/thomas-hooker/, accessed December 29, 2017; *Puritan Sermons 1659–1689: Being the Morning Exercises at Cripplegate, St. Giles in the Fields, and in Southwark by Seventy-five Ministers of the Gospel*, originally published London, 1660 (Wheaton, IL: Richard Owen Roberts, Publishers, 1981), 3:129–53, 368–77, 4:253–63, and 5:328–44, respectively; Gordon Cooke, "The Doctrine of Adoption and the Preaching of Jeremiah Burroughs," *Eternal Light, Adoption and Livingstone.* Congregational Studies Conference Papers (Evangelical Fellowship of Evangelical Churches, 1998), 25.

[120] *The Reformation of the Church: A Collection of Reformed and Puritan Documents on Church Issues*, Selected with introductory notes by Iain H. Murray, reprint ed. (Edinburgh: The Banner of Truth Trust, 1987), 7.

notably deficient here [on adoption], which is one reason why legalistic misunderstandings of it [the Christian life] so easily arise."[121] The deficit was both quantitative and qualitative. Whereas Puritan publications on church government represent their mature reflection and have influenced many Reformed churches and denominations down to the present, Puritan treatments of adoption lack accurate reflection of the biblical data. Admits Beeke, adoption was "not developed as thoroughly as several closely-knit doctrines such as justification, sanctification, and assurance."[122]

While their expositions of adoption did greater justice to the divineness of Scripture than to its humanness, we nevertheless remain grateful for their attention to adoption. Adolf von Harnack, lamenting how every renewal of religious experience of sin and grace since Augustine's day has been "levered" by the idea of predestination, surprisingly remarks: "How much enthusiasm was inspired in Cromwell's troops. And how greatly were the Puritans on both sides of the ocean strengthened by *the consciousness of adoption*, although this consciousness, too, was only a coefficient [of predestination]."[123]

Yet, the Puritans, Reformed theologically, were not alone at that time in their interest in adoption. The Orthodox Confession of the Eastern Church (1643), as we might expect, reads the grace of adoption into John's Gospel. Question thirty-five states: "This grace of adoption [τῆς υἱοθεσίας] is given freely through Christ, as the Scripture says (John 1:12), as many as received him to them he gave the authority to become the children of God." The Confession, written for the Russian church, was later given new sanction by the Synod of Jerusalem, thus making the Confession the creed of the entire Greek and Russian

---

[121] Packer, *Knowing God*, 255–56; cf., Errol Hulse, "Recovering the Doctrine of Adoption" (*Reformation Today* 105 [1988], 10).

[122] Beeke, *Heirs of Christ*, 7 (cf., Dan Cruver's comment in the Foreword, xii).

[123] Adolf von Harnack, *What is Christianity?* Transl. Thomas Bailey Saunders (New York and Evanston: Harper and Row, Publishers, 1957), 172.

Church. The Confession of Dositheus, or The Eighteen Decrees of the Synod of Jerusalem (1672), speaks at the end of Decree 16 of the receipt (ἀναλαμβάνει) of adoption (υἱοθεσία) upon return to the Lord through the mystery of repentance. Meanwhile, The Confession of the Waldenses (1655) mentions adoption in the context of baptism in Article twenty-nine: "That Christ has instituted the sacrament of Baptism to be a testimony of our adoption, and that therein we are cleansed from our sins by the blood of Jesus Christ, and renewed in holiness of life."[124]

9. THE LATE SEVENTEENTH THROUGH EARLY NINETEENTH CENTURIES

The promise of the Reformation and post-Reformation eras, as patchy and exegetically unreliable as were some of their treatments of adoption, did not materialize. There was no guaranteed focus on adoption to supplement that on justification, and among those retaining the inclusion of adoption in their theology, there was the belief that adoption ought to be subsumed under justification.

This trend can be traced back at least as far as Zwingli's successor in Zurich, Heinrich Bullinger (1504–75), but is most connected with the name of Francis Turretin (1623–87) and the protracted influence of his *Institutio Elencticae Theologiae.* Writing in the late nineteenth century, Robert Duff noted that "the doctrines he [Turretin] defined and upheld are those which distinguish much of the evangelical theology of the present time." [125]

The furtherance of Turretin's influence is attributable in part to his nephew Benedict Pictet (1655–1724), Pastor and Professor of Divinity in the Church and University of Geneva. Responding to his "studious youth" for a system of didactic theology that would supplement the elenctic theology of his "revered uncle, and most

---

[124] *Creeds of Christendom*, 2:316–17, 427; 3:766.

[125] Robert Duff, "Theologians of the Past—Francis Turretin," *Catholic Presbyterian* v (Jan.-Jun. 1881), 372. Cf., *Reformed Theology in America*, ed. David F. Wells, vol. 3; first published 1985 (Grand Rapids: Eerdmans, 1989), 19–20.

beloved father in Christ, the illustrious Turretine," Pictet took the same line. Although he dedicated a separate chapter in his *Christian Theology* to adoption, "Of Adoption" appears in his eighth section, "Of Justification and Sanctification," beginning with the words, "The other part of justification is *adoption*." [126]

Meanwhile, the doctrine figured in the theological writings of the Dutch Second Reformation. The *Nadere Reformatie*, as it is better known, developed within the Dutch Reformed Church and ran from c.1600–1750. Putting spiritual meat on theological backbone developed by the Synod of Dort of 1618–19, the *Nadere Reformatie* sought to balance doctrine and piety, applying the Reformation more closely to the lives of God's people, the worship of the church, and the transformation of society. Influenced by English Puritanism through Willem Teellinck's (1579–1629) firsthand experience of it, we cannot be certain of the degree to which the Dutch Reformed took an interest in adoption. Such an interest would embellish the little interest there is in the Three Forms of Unity (the Belgic Confession [1561], the Heidelberg Catechism [1563], and the Decrees of the Synod of Dordt [1618–19]).

We know that prominent pastor-theologian Wilhelmus à Brakel (1635–1711) of Rotterdam wrote a comparative lengthy chapter on adoption. Nevertheless, he, too, claimed that "justification includes spiritual sonship" before, ironically, going on to extol the excellencies of the origin of, translation into, and privileges of spiritual sonship. We also know of the interest in adoption of Alexander Comrie (1706–74), a native of Scotland. In the twilight of the *Nadere Reformatie*, Comrie distinguished an assurance of the uprightness of faith from the assurance of adoption. The prior is contingent on an indirect work of the Spirit which aids the believer's reasoning, the latter is divinely reserved for a minority of believers and constitutes a direct and

---

[126] Benedict Pictet, *Christian Theology*, transl. From the Latin by Frederick Reyroux (London: R. B. Seeley and W. Burnside, 1834), viii and 373–75.

immediate sealing of the Spirit.[127]

The Dutch-speaking were not alone in their inclusion of adoption. In 1749 there appeared The Easter Litany of the Moravian Church. It contains the following:

> I believe in God, the Father of our Lord Jesus Christ, who hath . . . made us meet to be partakers of the inheritance of the saints in light: having predestined us unto the adoption of children [*zur Kindschaft*] by Jesus Christ to himself, according to the good pleasure of his will, to the praise of the glory of his grace, wherein he hath made us accepted in the Beloved.[128]

In the British Isles, meanwhile, the Presbyterians who inherited Westminster's confessional inclusion of adoption began, ironically, to lose sight of the doctrine. The loss can be explained variously, largely by the successive threats of Rationalism, Deism, Arianism and Socinianism, Neonomianism and Arminianism, the Enlightenment, Romanticism, and industrialization. Under pressure, Presbyterians did more to defend orthodoxy than to enhance it.[129] Yet, the orthodoxy Presbyterians defended became increasingly lopsided, resulting eventually in the early-nineteenth century protest for paternal grace.

---

[127] Joel R. Beeke and Randall J. Pederson, *Meet the Puritans: With a Guide to Modern Reprints* (Grand Rapids: Reformation Heritage Books, 2006), 741–44; Wilhelmus à Brakel, *The Christian's Reasonable Service in which Divine Truths concerning the Covenant of Grace are Expounded, Defended against Opposing Parties, and their Practice Advocated as well as the Administration of this Covenant in the Old and New Testaments*, vol. 2 transl. Bartel Elshout based on the 3rd ed. of the original Dutch work entitled *Redelijke Godsdienst* published by D. Bolle, Rotterdam, The Netherlands (Ligonier, PA: Soli Deo Gloria Publications, 1993), 415–38; Joel R. Beeke, *Assurance of Faith: Calvin, English Puritanism, and the Dutch Second Reformation*, American University Studies (Series 7 Theology and Religion) vol. 89 (New York: Peter Lang, 1991), 281–320, especially 298–99.

[128] *Creeds of Christendom*, 3:799. See also the passing reference to adoption in Question 35 (*ibid.*, 802).

[129] For an unpacking of these reasons, see Tim J. R. Trumper, *When History Teaches Us Nothing: The Recent Reformed Sonship Debate in Context* (Eugene, OR: Wipf and Stock, 2008), 1–32.

Although heightening attention to the filial and familial in the New Testament, the protest, influenced by both the Enlightenment and Romanticism and channeled through Christian consciousness (receiving only from Scripture that which is personally agreeable), proved to be erroneous and unhelpful.

Amid the Reformed-orthodox loss of adoption and the Victorian protest for paternal grace to which it eventually led, it was, writes Ferguson, "perhaps more than anything else . . . the presence of [WCF 12] which . . . kept alive within Presbyterianism (particularly in Scotland and the Southern Presbyterian Church in the U.S.A.) the significance of Sonship in the life of Faith."[130] That said, the exceptions to the Presbyterian neglect of adoption included the formidable pastor of Ettrick, Scotland, Thomas Boston (1676–1732).

In his *Complete Body of Divinity*, Boston refers to adoption as a distinct benefit of effectual calling. Specifically, his *View of the Covenant of Grace*, deals, among other things, with the promissory aspects of the covenant. It pledges a new and saving relationship to God, built on reconciliation, adoption, and Jehovah's commitment to be the God of his people.[131] While Boston could have said more of adoption, he said enough to expose exaggerated criticisms of federal theology which fail to distinguish the everyday versions of it from the attempt in the Westminster Standards to balance the juridical and relational (familial). James B. Torrance claims, for instance, that "the federal scheme has substituted a *legal* understanding of man for a *filial*. That is, God's prime purpose for man is legal, not filial, but this yields an impersonal view of man as the object of justice, rather than as primarily

---

[130] Ferguson, "The Reformed Doctrine of Sonship," 83.

[131] *The Complete Works of the Late Reverend Thomas Boston, Ettrick*, Rev. Samuel McMillan, ed., reprinted ed. (Wheaton, IL: Richard Owen Roberts, Publishers, 1980), 1:612–53; 2:15–36; and 8:483–86. In his otherwise fine study of Boston, A. T. B. McGowan curiously defers to Stephen Charnock when he comes to Boston on adoption (*The Federal Theology of Thomas Boston*, Rutherford Studies in Historical Theology [Edinburgh: Rutherford House Books, 1997], 108 and 109; cf., 100).

the object of love. We can give people their 'legal rights' but not see them as our brothers."[132] This would have been more difficult to claim had theologians of the period developed further the Westminster Standards inclusion of both the juridical and familial.

Meanwhile, a similar but largely unknown understanding of adoption is found in the trans-Atlantic corpus of Jonathan Edwards (1703–58), especially in his *Miscellanies*. In the second year following his conversion, while preparing to defend in his Master's *Quaestio* the proposition "a sinner is not justified in the sight of God except through the righteousness obtained by faith," Edwards put his concern for public acceptance down to a "want of the spirit of adoption." While "Spirit of adoption" is a title of the Holy Spirit, Edwards uses "spirit" here to speak of the Holy Spirit's indwelling by which his own spirit could sense his adoption. Argues Dave Schutter, this emphasis on adoption remained with Edwards throughout the next three decades of his life and ministry.

Edwards understood adoption to be grounded in the pretemporal covenant of redemption, and to be a part of the one gospel running throughout Old and New Testament times. As such, adoption is an objective blessing of the covenant of grace. Contra Turretin and his progeny, Edwards believed adoption to supersede justification in importance. It not only brings believers into a relationship with God that surpasses Adam's in Eden, it entails a special union with the Only-begotten Son of God and results in a new sense of status through the Spirit of adoption and membership of God's family. The sealing of the Spirit is the highest kind of evidence of our adoption to which we can attain, although obedience is a necessary characteristic of the adopted son. Thus, Edwards, like the Puritans before him and the Methodists

---

[132] James B. Torrance, "The Concept of Federal Theology—Was Calvin a Federal Theologian?" in *Calvinus Sacrae Scripturae Professor*, International Congress on Calvin Research; ed. Wilhelm H. Neuser (Grand Rapids: Eerdmans, 1994), 35.

who had begun to emerge by the time of his death, emphasized the experience of adoption.[133]

James MacDonald insists that the leading Methodist, John Wesley (1703–91), held to the doctrine of adoption as firmly as any other Christian theologian.[134] He points as evidence to his sermons *The Spirit of Bondage and Adoption* and *The Witness of the Spirit*: "By the testimony of the Spirit I mean, an inward impression of the soul, whereby the Spirit of God immediately and directly witnesses to my spirit that I am a child of God, that Jesus Christ has loved me and given Himself for me; and that my sins are blotted out, and I, even I, am reconciled to God."[135] Given the number of sermons Wesley preached, this is scant evidence, but clearly indicates his experiential interest in the "Spirit of adoption"—a theme traceable throughout Wesleyan and Calvinistic Methodist homiletics, hymnody, and devotion. The testimony of Welsh Calvinistic-Methodist exhorter Howell Harris is indicative:

> June 18th 1735, being in secret prayer, I felt suddenly my heart melting within me like wax before the fire with love to God my Saviour; and also felt not only love, peace, etc., but longing to be dissolved, and to be with Christ. Then was a cry in my inmost soul, which I was totally unacquainted with before, Abba, Father! Abba,

---

[133] David H. Schutter, "Adoption, Doctrine Of," *The Jonathan Edwards Encyclopedia*, ed., Harry S. Stout (Grand Rapids: Eerdmans, 2017); unpublished paper, "The Place of the Doctrine of Adoption in the Ministry of Jonathan Edwards" (Philadelphia, PA: Westminster Theological Seminary, 2012). For more, see his "Jonathan Edwards's Preaching of Romans 8: Presenting and Evaluating Two Previously Unpublished Sermons" (Th.M. thesis: Westminster Theological Seminary, 2017).

[134] James A. MacDonald, *Wesley's Revision of the Shorter Catechism* (Edinburgh: Geo. A. Morton, 1906), 57–58.

[135] Cited by John Stoughton in *History of Religion in England, from the Opening of the Long Parliament to the End of the Eighteenth Century*, Vol. 6 *The Church in the Georgian Era.* New and revised ed. [London: Hodder and Stoughton, 1881], 119); J. Scott Lidgett, *The Victorian Transformation of Theology: The Second Series of Maurice Lectures delivered at King's College, London, Lent Term, 1934* (London, Epworth Press, 1934), 52–53.

> Father! I could not help calling God my Father; I knew that I was
> His child, and that He loved me and heard me.[136]

Whereas Wesley was troubled by the Westminster Assembly's use of adoption to highlight predestination, other Calvinists of the period saw in adoption a defense of Calvinistic theology. The Baptist John Gill (1697–1771) understood the indissoluble connection between predestination and adoption to vindicate the free and sovereign grace of God. In his *Body of Doctrinal Divinity*, Gill includes a separate section on adoption in Book Six (chs. 9 and 10). There he grounds it in an internal act of God. Such acts are accomplished in eternity past and include the union of the elect with God, their justification and adoption. In considering their arrangement, Gill reasons:

> I know not where better to place them, and take them into
> consideration, than next to the decree of God, and particularly the
> decree of election: since as that flows from the love of God, and is
> in Christ from everlasting, there must of course be an union to him
> so early: and since predestination to the adoption of children, and
> acceptance in the beloved are parts and branches of it, Eph. I. 4, 5,
> 6, they must be of the same date.

At conversion, the elect but awaken to the fact that their adoption into the family of God occurred in eternity past.[137]

Not so, taught Gill's peer, John Brown of Haddington (1722–87), another Presbyterian exception. In *A Compendious View of Natural and*

---

[136] Cited by Eifion Evans, *Daniel Rowland and the Great Evangelical Awakening in Wales* (Edinburgh: The Banner of Truth Trust, 1985), 53. Cf., George Whitefield's testimony, cited by John Stoughton, *History of Religion in England*, 6:125–126.

[137] Peter Toon, *The Emergence of Hyper-Calvinism in English Nonconformity 1689–1765* (London: The Olive Tree, 1967), 98, 124; Gill's *Body of Doctrinal Divinity* is part of his *Body of Divinity* (reprinted from the London ed. of 1839; Atlanta, GA: Turner Lassetter, 1950), 518–28. See also Book Two (*ibid.*, 172, 201). According to Toon, the distinction between the internal and external acts of God was common to hyper-Calvinists of the first half of the eighteenth century (*The Emergence of Hyper-Calvinism*, 108–11). Toon mentions eternal adoption, though, only in reference to Gill's *Body of Divinity* and John Brine's *Motives to Love and Unity*.

Revealed Religion, Brown includes a brief treatment of adoption, suffused with nuggets of truth amid a tidal wave of eisegesis. Yet, his comment that the elect "are *actually adopted* in the moment of their union to Christ" reveals, biblically, that one does not have to locate the adoption of the believer in eternity past to safeguard the inextricable connection between predestination and adoption.[138]

Such exceptions as Boston and Brown (Presbyterian), Edwards (Congregationalist), the Calvinistic Methodists, and Gill (Baptist) cannot eradicate the impression that the Fatherhood of God and the adoption of sons had little place in the everyday theology of the Reformed Protestantism of the period. The problem with the accepted orthodoxy lay not with its two predominant foci—the sovereignty of God and the doctrine of justification—although these remain easy targets for critics, but with the juridical shorn of the familial.

While the legal elements of the gospel are essential, they are not absolute. The gospel is more than a legal transaction. It is initiated by divine love and issues, through repentance and faith in Christ, in privileges that are both legal and filial (or familial). Yet, once Reformed orthodoxy ceased to capture in large measure this balance, appreciation for the Reformed faith began to suffer. Over the period from c.1650 there developed a pressure for revolt against an ossified Calvinism which combusted in the early decades of the nineteenth century. The revolt forever altered the theological landscape of mainstream Protestantism.

The protest began with the familial emphases of Thomas Erskine of Linlathen (1788–1870) and John McLeod Campbell (1800–1872). Independently, they set about recasting the theology of the period. Substituting the authority of Scripture for their "Christian consciousness," they replaced, to varying degrees, the exegesis of Scripture with their own romantically driven schemas of what

---

[138] *The Systematic Theology of John Brown of Haddington* (Fearn, Ross-shire, Scotland: Christian Focus Publications and Grand Rapids: Reformation Heritage Books, 2002), 397.

Scripture teaches. Abandoning the self-authenticating controls of Scripture, Erskine turned Universalist over the course of seventeen years, and McLeod Campbell, deposed from the Church of Scotland in 1831, jettisoned a penal view of the atonement, as is clear from his later work *The Nature of the Atonement* (1856). Instead, however, of discerning the kernel of truth in their protest, the Reformed beat the drum of the orthodoxy they had inherited, oblivious to how lopsided it had become.

10. THE EARLY NINETEENTH THROUGH THE EARLY TWENTIETH CENTURIES

The standoff between the historic Protestant orthodoxy and the post-Enlightenment Romanticism appears to have been a fixture throughout the remainder of the nineteenth century. Again, there were exceptions. The eighteenth-century Methodist emphasis on the Spirit of adoption was replicated in nineteenth-century Brethrenism. While J. N. Darby (1800–1882) says little explicitly of adoption in his thirty-four volumes of *Collected Writings*, his theology nevertheless retains something of the familial imagery and tenor of Scripture and found a distinctive outlet in Brethren hymnody.[139] The preface to *Hymns of the Little Flock* (1881) states for instance that "the great principle in selecting and correcting" is "that there should be nothing in the hymns for the assembly but what was the expression of, or at least consistent with the Christian's conscious place in Christ before the Father."

Not until Robert Candlish's Cunningham Lectures on the Fatherhood of God (March 1864), was a high-profile attempt made to

---

[139] J. N. Darby, *Collected Writings*, 34 vols; ed. William Kelly (Lancing, Sussex: Kingston Bible Trust, 1964[?]–67), especially his treatment of "The Prodigal with the Father," "Notes on Romans—Ch. 8," "Notes on the Epistle to the Ephesians," "Fellowship with the Father and with the Son," and "On Sealing with the Holy Ghost" (*Collected Writings*, vols. 12, 26, 27, 28, and 31, respectively). As for Brethren hymns, see *Hymns and Spiritual Songs for the Little Flock*, selected 1856 (revised ed.; Kingston-on-Thames: Stow Hill Bible and Tract Depot, 1962).

address the protest for the familial. Candlish evoked, though, but a short-lived debate with his fellow Calvinist Thomas J. Crawford, professor of Divinity at the University of Edinburgh. At issue was the nature of Adam's standing before God in Eden (son, subject, or both), and the nature of the union between Christ's Sonship and the believer's (identical or analogical). Candlish's fellow ministers in the Free Church of Scotland weighed in on the debate. In 1865, Scottish pastor-theologian Hugh Martin (1821–85) published a lengthy review of the debate, and in 1869 the renowned Free Churchman, John Kennedy of Dingwall (1819–84), published *Man's Relations to God* to cut through its dense arguments. That said, Candlish's seminal comments about the historic neglect of adoption have borne more fruit posthumously than in his day:

> The more I think of it, the more I am disposed to regret that the subject of adoption, or the sonship of believers, has been so little made account of in our Reformation theology. It seems to me to be the appropriate crown of Calvinism, and the best safeguard at the same time against by far the most formidable line of attack to which in these days it is exposed.[140]

As the Candlish/Crawford debate rumbled on through successive editions of their volumes titled *The Fatherhood of God*, others began to comment on the familial side of the faith. Daniel Dewar (1788–1867), Principal of Marischal College, Aberdeen, published his three–volume *Elements of Systematic Divinity*. The fact that his chapter

---

[140] Candlish, *The Fatherhood of God*, xxxi; cf., 167, 192, and *The Fatherhood of God: Being the First Course of Cunningham Lectures Delivered before the New College, Edinburgh, in March 1864*. Supplementary volume to the 5th ed. (Edinburgh: Adam and Charles Black), 1870; Thomas J. Crawford, *The Fatherhood of God considered in its general and special aspects and particularly in relation to the atonement with a review of recent speculations on the subject*. 2nd ed. revised and enlarged with a reply to the strictures of Dr Candlish (Edinburgh and London: William Blackwood and Sons), 1867. For a summary of the debate see John Kennedy, *Man's Relations to God: Traced in the Light of "the Present Truth"* (reprint of 1869 ed.; The James Begg Society, 1995); Martin, "Candlish's Cunningham Lectures," 720–87; Trumper, "An Historical Study," 337–97.

on adoption is silent about the Candlish/Crawford debate likely indicates its limited impact at the time.[141]

That said, the very year of Candlish's Cunningham Lectures, evangelical Anglican, Hugh M'Neile, of St. Paul's. Prince Park, Liverpool, published sermons on adoption preached at Chester Cathedral. In the Preface, he laments that amid "the battle of criticism" his peers were reading more about the Bible, than the Bible itself; also, that there was not the acquaintance with the Scriptures that there ought to have been. M'Neile, thus, set about preaching and publishing sermons that were expository rather than evidentiary or defensive, calling hearers back to an intellectual reliance on the Word and a moral application of it. Significantly, the first three (of sixteen) sermons are on adoption (Rom. 9:4; 8:15, 23). Refreshingly, they follow the flow of salvation history: salvation past (national adoption), present (personal adoption), and future. Rather uniquely in treatments of adoption, M'Neile applies the adoption of Israel to the adoption of Great Britain, "a nation in covenant with God."[142]

In a similar vein, prominent Irish Reformed Presbyterian, Thomas Houston (1803–82), published in 1872 his detailed work of practical and experimental theology, *The Adoption of Sons, Its Nature, Spirit, Privileges and Effects*. Although Houston's rare treatise on adoption is hardly coincidental, there is about it an air of abstraction from the cut and thrust of the Victorian debate, preferring a straight-forward expositional and theological approach. Its loss to history was unwarranted and is more of a commentary on the history of adoption than on the quality of the work (which is among the best of its kind).[143]

---

[141] Daniel Dewar, *Elements of Systematic Divinity*, vol. 2 (Glasgow: Thomas Murray and Son, 1867), 488–503.

[142] Hugh M'Neile, *The Adoption and other Sermons* (London: James Nisbet and Co., 1864), iii–51.

[143] Thomas Houston, *The Adoption of Sons, Its Nature, Spirit, Privileges and Effects: A*

Across the Atlantic, the esteemed Southern preacher Benjamin Morgan Palmer (1818–1902), addressing the Alumni Association of Columbia Seminary, South Carolina, in 1881, used the fiftieth anniversary of the founding of the seminary to suggest that Dr. John L. Girardeau (1825–98), Professor of Didactic and Polemical theology, complete the system of theology begun by his illustrious predecessor, the late James Henley Thornwell (1812–62). Palmer seems to have had in mind a theological textbook conveying the particular brand of Reformed theology emanating from Columbia Seminary—one comparable to the systematic theologies of Robert Dabney (1871) and Charles Hodge (1880) of Union and Princeton seminaries, respectively, but doing greater justice to such issues as adoption.[144]

More immediately, Girardeau chose to use his shorter incumbency as a professor to explore particular areas of theology stimulated by his mentor, Thornwell. Contra Thornwell, Girardeau preferred the idea of federal representation to justification as the central principle of theology and differed on the question of whether Adam was a son of God in Eden. Thornton Whaling claims excessively that adoption was supreme and regulative in Thornwell's theology, yet, as editor of Thornwell's works, Girardeau would have noted Thornwell's fleeting references to the doctrine, especially in connection with the covenant of works and the nature of salvation. Accordingly, his interaction with Thornwell, Robert J. Breckinridge (1800–1871), and the chatter from the Candlish/Crawford debate, led Girardeau to take an interest in adoption. His treatment, consisting of an assemblance of

---

Practical and Experimental Treatise (Paisley, UK: Alex. Gardner, 1872). Houston's work is now republished, with biographical sketch added (Brighton, UK: Ettrick Press, 2021).

[144] On adoption, see especially volume 3 of Hodge's *Systematic Theology* (London and Edinburgh: Thomas Nelson and Sons, 1880), 128–29 and 164, and Robert L. Dabney, *Systematic Theology*. First published 1871 (Edinburgh: The Banner of Truth Trust, 1985, 627).

papers, is weighted heavily toward the discussion of Adam's original standing, and is published in his *Discussions of Theological Questions*.[145]

Of greater significance at the time, was Girardeau's influencing of his erstwhile student and son-in-law Robert A. Webb (1856–1919), who went on to export the Columbia interest in adoption to Southwestern and Louisville Seminaries. His class lectures were published posthumously in *The Reformed Doctrine of Adoption* (1947). To this day the volume ranks as a rare serious theological monograph on adoption. Webb's volume, when promoted to Eerdmans, was said to foreshadow the defeat of theological liberalism. Now largely lost to history, the volume is, ironically, best known for its early *faux pas* in claiming that Calvin "makes no allusion whatever to adoption." Although now debunked, the claim nevertheless reveals the extent to which the Reformed lost sight of the importance Calvin especially placed on the doctrine of adoption.

That said, Girardeau and Webb not only helped to shape Columbia theology, they supplemented Candlish's endeavors in seeking to reintroduce adoption into the everyday theology of the Reformed faith. According to Douglas Kelly, "it was the Presbyterian theologians of the American south who most fully developed and applied the implications of the Westminster and biblical teaching on adoption in

---

[145] James H. Thornwell, *Collected Writings*. vol. 1, first published 1875. Facsimile reprint ed., (Edinburgh: The Banner of Truth Trust, 1986), Lectures xi and xii, 252–300. In addition, one could include the last fourteen pages of Thornwell's piece entitled "Theology, its Proper Method and Central Principle. A Review of Breckinridge's Theology" (*ibid.*, 474–88); Robert J. Breckinridge, *The Knowledge of God, Subjectively considered. Being the Second Part of Theology considered as a Science of Positive Truth, both Inductive and Deductive* (New York: Robert Carter & Brothers and Louisville: A Davidson, 1859), 178–202; *Thornwell Centennial Addresses* (Spartanburg: Band & White), 1913, 28–29 (cf., John L. Girardeau, *Discussions of Theological Questions* [Harrisonburg, VA: Sprinkle Publications, 1986], 64–72, 428–521; Trumper, "An Historical Study," 406–11).

the nineteenth century."[146]

Presbyterians were not alone in recovering awareness of adoption. In his *Manual of Theology* (1857), Southern Baptist John L. Dagg (1794–1884) lists adoption as a blessing of grace, although his exposition covers just its privileges. His peer, James Petigru Boyce (1827–88), a founder and first president of Southern Baptist Seminary, includes a brief chapter in his *Abstract of Systematic Theology* (1887). Very much along the lines of the ratiocinated approach of the Westminster Standards, Boyce ends with reasons for which adoption ought not to be included in justification: The Bible speaks of them distinctly and does not include adoption to any degree in justification; justification is ascribed to the righteousness of God, adoption to his love; justification constitutes a change of relation to the law, adoption a change of relation to the family of God; saving faith in justification precedes a forensic act, but in adoption it precedes the receiving of Christ; justification is ascribed to the Father, adoption to the Father and the Son (Jn. 1:12). Thus, Boyce concludes that adoption ought no more to be subsumed under justification than ought sanctification. Justification and adoption "are separate effects which flow from the union with Christ attained through faith; because of which we are made partakers of all the benefits of his meritorious work."[147]

Across the Atlantic, renowned Baptist Charles Haddon Spurgeon (1834–92) preached a number of sermons on adoption. Leaving it to others to trawl his entire corpus, we know of his exposition of adoption from his *Expository Encyclopedia*. Included under "Adoption" are five sermons: "Adoption—The Spirit and the Cry—

---

[146] Robert A. Webb, *The Reformed Doctrine of Adoption* (Grand Rapids: Eerdmans), 1947, 17; Trumper, "An Historical Study," 436–38. Morton H. Smith, *Studies in Southern Presbyterian Theology,* first published 1962; (Phillipsburg, NJ: P&R, 1987), 258; Douglas F. Kelly, "Adoption: An Underdeveloped Heritage of the Westminster Standards" *Reformed Theological Review* (Australia) 52 (1993), 113.

[147] James Petigru Boyce, *Abstract of Systematic Theology,* reprint ed. (Lexington, Kentucky: publisher not given, 2012), 305–6.

Gal. 4:6"; "The Spirit of Bondage and Adoption—Rom. 8:15, 16"; "The Great Birthday and Our Coming of Age—Gal. 4:3-6"; "What Christians Were and Are—Eph. 2:3; Rom. 8:16, 17"; and, less relevant, "Exposition of Ephesians 2." Known as a Puritan preacher, it follows that Spurgeon's sermons, rich in detail, are very much in the vein of Puritan systematics: deficient on the salvation-historical contours of adoption but strong on the adoptive act and its application.[148]

Meanwhile, contemporaneous with the Candlish/Crawford debate of the 1860s there ran a contention in the Roman Catholic Church over the formal cause of adoption between Matthias Joseph Scheeben (1835–1888) and Theodore Granderath (1839–1902). "Never before in the history of Roman Catholic theology," writes Edwin Palmer, "was there such an extensive discussion of the formal cause of adoption as in the Granderath-Scheeben debate."[149] All told, such developments indicate that even where the aberrations of the Victorian protest for paternal grace did not take hold, there began to develop across the spectrum of Christianity a greater orientation toward the familial.

Two evidences of this are apparent.

Note, first, the glut of studies of the Fatherhood of God and related themes. These began appearing from the second half of the nineteenth century across differing traditions, schools of thought, and approaches. They include George Gilfillan's *The Grand Discovery; or, The Fatherhood of God* (1854); Robert Mitchell's *The Fatherhood of God* (1879); Edward Dennett's *The Children of God: Being an Exposition of the Fatherhood of God and the Relationship of His Children* (1883); Thomas Erskine's posthumously published *The Fatherhood of God Revealed in Christ: The Comfort and Hope of Man* (1888); John Watson,

---

[148] John L. Dagg, *A Manual of Theology*, first published 1857 (Harrisonburg, VA: Gano Books, 1982), 274–77; Charles H. Spurgeon, *Expository Encyclopedia: Sermons by Charles H. Spurgeon*, Volume 1 (Grand Rapids: Baker Book House, 1951). 73–118.

[149] Palmer, *Scheeben's Doctrine of Divine Adoption*, xi.

The Fatherhood of God: Being the Second Hartley Lecture Delivered in Leeds, June 1898 (1899); J. Scott Lidgett's influential *The Fatherhood of God in Christian Truth and Life* (1902), followed up in 1921 with *Sonship and Salvation: A Study of the Epistle to the Hebrews*; C. H. v. Bogatzky's *Edifying Thoughts on God's Paternal Heart: A Devotional Commentary on the Lord's Prayer* (1903); Julius Kögel's *Der Sohn und die Söhne: Eine exegetische Studie zu Hebräer 2,5–18* (1904); Archibald Thomas Robertson's *The Teaching of Jesus Concerning God the Father* (1904).

Second, a fresh but brief creed-making era opened up, expressing a more relational (but not necessarily a less juridical) understanding of the gospel. The Articles of Religion of the Reformed Episcopal Church in America (1875) do not mention adoption explicitly but resonate a relational tone.[150] A Commission of the National Council of the Congregational Churches of the US' statement of doctrine (1883) is somewhat general. Article seven merely acknowledges that "through the person and work of Jesus Christ as mediator and redeemer and sender of the Holy Spirit, those trusting in him are made the children of God."[151] More importantly, three distinctive statements on adoption or related themes are added to those of the seventeenth century. Article fourteen of the XXIV Articles of the Presbyterian Synod of England (1890), although entitled "Of Sonship in Christ," closely follows the biblical contours of adoption:

> We believe that those who receive Christ by faith are united to Him, so that they are partakers in His life, and receive His fulness; and that they are adopted into the family of God, are made heirs with Christ, and have His Spirit abiding in them, the witness to their sonship, and the earnest of their inheritance.[152]

---

[150] The closest to a specific reference is found in Art. 14 ("Of the Sonship of Believers"), although the article alludes to regeneration as much as to adoption (*Creeds of Christendom*, 3:819; cf., Art. 10, 817).

[151] *Creeds of Christendom*, 3:914.

[152] *Creeds of Christendom*, 3:918. The New Testament includes other filial models. This

The Confessional Statement of the United Presbyterian Church of North America (1925)—described by Schaff as "the boldest official attempt within the Presbyterian family of Churches to restate the Reformed theology of the sixteenth century"—also contains an article on adoption. Article eleven of The Basis of Union of the United Church of Canada (1925), while titled "Of Justification and Sonship," reads:

> We believe that God, on the sole ground of the perfect obedience and sacrifice of Christ, pardons those who by faith receive Him as their Saviour and Lord, accepts them as righteous, and bestows upon them the adoption of sons, with a right to all the privileges therein implied, including a conscious assurance of their sonship.[153]

For all these developments, neither the liberal protest for paternal grace nor the conservative reaction succeeded in retrieving adoption. Writing following the close of the Victorian era, James Lindsay remarked:

> Strange that nothing like full justice has yet been done in modern theology to the sovereign and absoluteness of God—so emphasised in Reformed theology—by adequately setting forth of that sovereignty, not on a monarchical basis, but as interpreted in terms of Fatherhood. I say strange because—though it seems often unknown or forgotten—Calvin had the high merit to be the first theologian for ages to give Fatherhood its rightful place in Christian experience.[154]

We find Samuel King lamenting similarly four years later: "Adoption has not come into its own in the teaching and discussion of our [Reformed] doctrines."[155] Whereas the liberal protest proved exegetically unaccountable, the conservative reaction typically defended the traditional lopsidedness. The standoff between the

---

is reflected, for example, in Art. 11 ("Of the New Birth and the New Life") of a "Brief Statement of the Reformed Faith" (1902), prepared by a committee of the Presbyterian Church in the USA (*Creeds of Christendom*, 3:923).

[153] Schaff, *Creeds of Christendom*, 3:924, 936.

[154] James Lindsay, "The Development of Scotch Theology", *Princeton Theological Review* vol. 4 no. 3 (1906), 343.

[155] Samuel A. King, "The Grace of Adoption" *Union Seminary Magazine* 22 (1910), 30.

emergent theological liberalism and classic evangelical orthodoxy became enshrined in texts such as Adolf von Harnack's *What is Christianity?* (1901) and J. Gresham Machen's *Christianity and Liberalism* (1923).

While von Harnack (1851–1930) observed God's paternity to be rooted in the Gospels, his notion of an inner yearning for the familial struggling to the surface of Christian consciousness and theological expression, proved to be a poor substitute for the rigors of historical investigation and theological exegesis.[156] Machen, by contrast, ably defended classic orthodoxy, boldly asserting that theological liberalism constituted a different faith from orthodox Christianity. As a Princetonian, however, he inherited the Turretinian neglect of adoption (as mediated by Charles Hodge), and was thus poorly positioned to concede how lopsidedly juridical classic orthodoxy had become. This is not to invalidate his central concern that liberalism had undermined the ontological and moral gulf between God and man and limited thereby the necessity of an accomplished and applied atonement (redemption by incarnation rather than by atonement). It is to say, however, that Machen represented an apologetic, which, underplaying the significance of adoption, was inadequately equipped to challenge effectively the liberal protest for paternal grace.

The difficulty that Presbyterians had in realizing the devotional and apologetic appeal of adoption was not exclusive to them. Whereas they had lost sight of adoption, the continental Reformed (thinking here especially of the Germans and the Dutch) had rarely made much of it. After all, there is little of it in the Three Forms of Unity.

Whereas Abraham Kuyper (1837–1920) dedicated forty-five pages of *The Work of the Holy Spirit* to regeneration, surprisingly as few as twenty-four to justification, and eighty-two to sanctification, he allots neither chapter nor section to adoption, although, contra Calvin,

---

[156] Harnack, *What Is Christianity?* 299.

he mentions it but periodically.[157]

Kuyper's younger colleague in the Free University of Amsterdam, Herman Bavinck (1854–1921), mentions adoption but took a similar line to Turretin. The prioritization "is due to justification, for by it we understand that gracious judicial act of God by which he acquits humans of all guilt and punishment of sin and confers on them the right to eternal life." True enough, but Bavinck illustrates the difficulty the Reformed have in according justification the attention that Scripture and Reformation history allot it without ignoring or downplaying the adoption of God's sons. He says very little of adoption in either *Our Reasonable Faith* or his *Reformed Dogmatics*. In the fourth volume, on soteriology and the church, he has a section of sixty-six pages on calling and regeneration, fifty-three on justification, but apparently only six pages containing references to adoption, in a volume running to 730 pages! Bavinck equates adoption and its benefits with the right to eternal life, helpfully distinguishing the Johannine and Pauline uses of filial language (the former emphasizing the ethical and the latter the juridical), noting Paul's unique and salvation-historical use of υἱοθεσία, while nevertheless reading adoption into the Johannine corpus.[158]

Across the Atlantic, however, Dutch émigré Geerhardus Vos (1862–1949) began breaking the continental mold. Known, as we shall see in chapter six, for fathering a renaissance in Reformed biblical theology, it is perhaps not so surprising that Vos did more to include adoption in his theology than many from his European background. What is more, whether wittingly or not, he contributed modestly to the

---

[157] Abraham Kuyper, *The Work of the Holy Spirit*, originally published 1900; transl. Henri De Vries (Chattanooga, TN: AMG Publishers, 1995).

[158] Herman Bavinck, *Reformed Dogmatics*, Volume 4: *Holy Spirit, Church and New Creation*, ed. John Bolt and transl. John Vriend (Grand Rapids: Baker Academic, 2008), 89 and 227, 179 (Cf., Herman Bavinck, *Our Reasonable Faith: A Survey of Christian Doctrine*, transl. Henry Zylstra [Grand Rapids: Baker, 1977], 464); and 226 (cf., 494).

reversal of the influence of his Princetonian forebear, Charles Hodge, on the neglect of adoption.

We ought not to make too much of this since, in his *Reformed Dogmatics*, Vos resonates Turretin and Pictet of the seventeenth century and Dabney of the nineteenth in subsuming adoption under justification: "The first aspect [of justification] is generally called *forgiveness of sins*, the second *adoption as children*." As such, adoption bespeaks a legal act. Yet, Vos qualifies this view by stating that adoption is also of ethical significance. Whereas judicial adoption belongs to justification, ethical adoption belongs to regeneration, conversion, and sanctification. Judicial and ethical adoption are not two adoptions but two facets of a singular adoption. These we refer to nowadays as the adoptive act and the adoptive state. However, in perpetuating the admixture of Pauline and Johannine thought and in proposing the subsuming of adoption under justification, Vos overlooked the coherence of Paul's adoption model.[159]

The neglect of adoption in the Dutch enclave of the Midwest of America proved, however, to be resistant. The *Systematic Theology* (1939) of Louis Berkhof (1873–1957) contains but one extended paragraph on adoption plus some isolated references to it. Berkhof depicts adoption as but the positive side of justification and refers, rightly but ironically, to its apologetic significance in countering liberal views of the Fatherhood of God. "Believers," he writes, "are first of all children of God by adoption. This implies, of course, that they are not children of God by nature, as modern liberals would have us believe, for one cannot well adopt his own children."[160]

---

[159] Geerhardus Vos, *Reformed Dogmatics*, volume four: *Soteriology*, first published in 1896 (handwritten) and printed in 1910; transl. and edited by Richard B. Gaffin Jr., *et al.* (Bellingham, Washington: Lexham Press, 2015), 152, 155–56.

[160] Louis Berkhof, *Systematic Theology*, first British ed., 1958; reprint ed. (Carlisle, PA: The Banner of Truth Trust, 1974), 515–16; cf., the equivalent in Berkhof's *A Summary of Christian Doctrine*, first published 1938 (Carlisle, PA: The Banner of Truth Trust, 1993), 131.

Likewise, the *Studies in Dogmatics* (1949–72; in English, 1952–76) of G. C. Berkouwer (1903–96) generally omit adoption, most strikingly so from the volumes *Faith and Justification* and *Faith and Sanctification*. Berkouwer denies the existence of an *ordo salutis* in Romans 8:30, due, ironically, to the omission of sanctification, but not of adoption. The same trend is found in the writings of continental Reformed ministers. Erstwhile professor at Western Seminary, Holland, Evert J. Blekkink published in 1942 *The Fatherhood of God: Considered from Six Inter-related Standpoints*. Focusing on the Fatherhood of God in God, creation, the incarnation, redemption, prayer, and the Father's House forever, the study is faithful and accessible but more theological than expositional. It has little to say about the most germane texts of the New Testament on adoption. More typical of the continental Reformed neglect of the doctrine is Gordon H. Girod's *The Way of Salvation* (1960) and *The Deeper Faith* (1978).

11. THE EARLY THROUGH THE LATE TWENTIETH CENTURY

In the intervening decades, a neoorthodoxy had arisen along a trajectory situated between classic orthodoxy (aka classic fundamentalism) to the right and theological liberalism to the left. Theologians such as Peter T. Forsyth (1848–1921) came to reject the latter without returning to the former. His book *God the Holy Father* opens with a tracing of God's Fatherhood from Old Testament times into the New, distinguishing the feel and content of his thought from the prevailing lopsidedness of the orthodox.

Forsyth anticipated Karl Barth (1886–1968). Repulsed by the overweening confidence of liberal rationalism and the extortionate life-costs of World War I, Barth offered an indictment in his *Der Römerbrief*, the second edition of which (1922) began a lifetime of theological publishing. His *Church Dogmatics* (1932–67) reveal an interest in the familial, including adoption.[161]

How Barth's comments should be interpreted in light of his views of natural theology, election, and history (*Historie, Geschichte*), etc., I leave it to others to determine. Suffice it to say that Barth denies natural theology and with it the general Fatherhood of God. God is known as Father solely by his revelation of himself in Christ. In him we are reconciled to God. This reconciliation has two parts: justification and sanctification. Writes Barth: "'I will be your God' is the justification of man. 'Ye shall be my people' is his sanctification." Adoption, by contrast, results from union with Christ, as per Peter Lombard. Compared to Calvin, Barth says little in detail of sonship (or childhood), although, clearly, he believed that Christian sonship means nothing in the present unless it is utilized in the service of God and of the brethren. Where our sonship is authentic there is accompanied a groaning for redemption from the bondage of corruption into the glory of the children of God (Rom. 8:19-23). This service and these groanings are connected, for God's children serve in the present by the promise of God's unmerited adoption at the Consummation.[162]

To this day, the Reformed orthodox wish that Barth had less "neo" and more "orthodoxy." Notwithstanding the limitations of his breach with liberalism, he did more to draw the sting from the Victorian protest for paternal grace than had the Reformed orthodox. What was needed in answer to the Victorian protest was not less of the familial,

---

[161] For use of the adoption texts, see Karl Barth, *CD* V.1, 135, 136, 154, 155–56, and 206. References to "Children of God" are included in the Index (210), but, given the translation of υἱοθεσία as *Kindschaft*, these can be of uncertain meaning. For the relevant sections, see especially those titled "God the Father" and "God the Father as Lord of His Creature" in *CD* I.1, 384–98; III.3, 58–288. All references to the "Children of God" in the Index refer to this section, pages 243, 250, 260, and 269.

[162] *CD* IV.2, 499. Clearly conscious of his Protestantism, Barth writes: "Justification is not sanctification and does not merge into it. Sanctification is not justification and does not merge into it" (*CD* IV. 2, 503). *CD* IV.1,499–840, especially 506, 529, and 608, 705, and 750; IV.2, 505.

but more of it biblically grounded and expounded. Barth understood this in principle, as had Candlish earlier. By the time of Barth's death in 1968, the Reformed orthodox had begun waking to the beauty and strategic significance of God's adoptive grace.

Numerous factors influenced this development: a renewed interest in the writings of the apostle Paul, the emergence of a Reformed biblical theology, a mid-twentieth-century renaissance in the study of John Calvin, the republication of vintage Reformed writings, and with it the reminder of the unfulfilled potential of the nineteenth-century Scottish and Southern Presbyterian interest in adoption. These developments are traceable along two streams of influence.

The first issues from D. Martyn Lloyd-Jones' Friday evening lectures at Westminster Chapel, London, delivered between 1952 and 1955. Combining the influences of Welsh Calvinistic Methodism (Presbyterianism) and English Congregationalism/Independency, Lloyd-Jones (1899–1981) laments that,

> for some inexplicable reason it [adoption] is a doctrine about which we rarely hear. How often have you heard addresses or sermons on it? Why is it that, even as evangelical people, we neglect, and indeed seem to be unaware of, some of these most comforting and encouraging doctrines which are to be found in the Scriptures?[163]

Treading the well-worn path of running together the Pauline term "adoption" and the more general term "sonship," Lloyd-Jones' exposition is nevertheless unusually fresh.

Without diminishing the role of subordinate standards, Lloyd-Jones' exerted a freedom from the obligation, too prevalent in Reformed circles, of reading biblical doctrine through the Westminster Standards (rather than the Standards through Scripture). He thus distinguished more clearly than the Puritans whose writings he did so much to resurrect, the Johannine language of regeneration from the Pauline language of adoption. He notes the υἱοθεσία texts, affording more

---

[163] Martyn Lloyd-Jones, *Great Doctrines of the Bible*, Volume 2: *God The Holy Spirit* (Wheaton, IL: Crossway, 1997), 179; cf., 189.

attention than the Puritans to their salvation-historical setting, before considering the place of adoption in the *ordo salutis*.

Lloyd-Jones repeats, in effect, A. A. Hodge's (re)interpretation of the WCF, published in *The Confession of Faith: A Handbook of Christian Doctrine Expounding The Westminster Confession* (1869). Therein, Hodge argues that adoption is to be understood as a capstone sitting astride justification and regeneration. "Adoption," he writes, "is a combination of justification and regeneration. It is the new creature in a new relationship to God—as a child of God." [164]

Lloyd-Jones' promising but initially unpublished interest in adoption has gone largely unnoticed. Worth investigating, however, is his influence on his younger Puritan aficionado, Anglican James I. Packer (1926–2020). By the time of their separation in 1970 (over Packer's involvement in the book *Growing into Union*), they had worked together on the annual Puritan Conference for twenty years. Interestingly, Packer had given a paper at the conference in the early years on "The Witness of the Spirit: The Puritan Teaching" (1956).[165] Yet, in 1973 he published what is now considered his classic, *Knowing God*. No chapter has done more than "Sons of God" since then to raise the present-day awareness of adoption in evangelical thought.

It was needed. James Oliver Buswell's *Systematic Theology* (1962) recalled the place of adoption in the Westminster Standards, but has just a single page on the doctrine. Titled "The Full Status of Mature Sonship," the section downplays the necessity of translating υἱοθεσία as "adoption." In 1966 Presbyterian-turned-Episcopalian, John Macquarrie published his *Principles of Christian Theology* (1966)

---

[164] Cf., Lloyd-Jones' chapters "A Child of God in Christ" and "Adoption," (*Great Doctrines of the Bible*, 2:95–105 and 179–89. Note his comment on 97). The quotation is from *Great Doctrines of the Bible*, 2:184.

[165] Iain H. Murray, "The End of the Puritan Conference," banneroftruth. org/us/resources/articles/2010/the-end-of-the-puritan-conference/, accessed June 29, 2017; *Puritan Papers: Volume 1, 1956–1959*, ed. D. Martyn Lloyd-Jones (Phillipsburg, NJ: P&R, 2000).

omitting all reference to adoption, transitioning without pause from justification to sanctification in his section, "The Holy Spirit and Salvation." Not so Scottish Presbyterian minister Wallace B. Nicholson. His little-known study *A Defence of Evangelical Theology* (1969) has several pages on adoption.

By then, however, a second stream of Reformed thought had begun which was traceable to Presbyterian theologian John Murray (1898–1975). Murray is particularly significant in that he sat, under the influence of Calvin and of Geerhardus Vos, astride contemporaneous developments in theological method and the history of adoption. To the former development we shall return in chapter six, showing how both developments have merged to make the full retrieval of adoption a real possibility in our day.

It is not certain, though, how much of adoption Murray saw in Calvin. His point of reference in this regard was not so much the reformer as the Westminister Standards. Consistent with them, but contrary to Vos' advocacy of judicial adoption, Murray understood the doctrine to be distinct but inseparable from justification. Yet, as in the case of Vos, his exposition of adoption is hampered by his conflation of Johannine and Pauline thought.

These observations are drawn from Murray's *Redemption: Accomplished and Applied* (1955) and his posthumously published *Collected Writings* (1977). The latter indicates awareness of the Candlish/Crawford debate, John Kennedy's reaction to it, Webb's *The Reformed Doctrine of Adoption*, and Lidgett's important work *The Fatherhood of God*. Significantly, Murray remarks that, "too infrequently [adoption] has been regarded as simply an aspect of justification or as another way of stating the privilege conferred by regeneration. It is much more than either or both of these acts of grace."[166] Adoption is rather, he claims, "the apex of redemptive grace and privilege." While

---

[166] John Murray, *CW*, 2:223fn; *Redemption: Accomplished and Applied*, reprint ed. (Edinburgh: The Banner of Truth Trust, 1979), 132.

we may question along methodological lines how Murray, in his early attempts to modify traditional systematics, arrived at his high estimate of adoption, he, like Lloyd-Jones, supported the trend of introducing salvation-historical considerations into the discussion of biblical doctrine. When considering God's adoptive Fatherhood, for instance, he traces the development of sonship from the preparatory sonship of Israel under God's theocratic Fatherhood to the consummative sonship of the New Testament era.

This salvation-historical perspective on adoption was given a considerable boost by the translation of Herman Ridderbos' (1909–2007) *Paul: An Outline of His Theology* (1977). His exposition—significantly, of continental Reformed origin—recognized uninhibitedly the salvation-historical contours of the apostle's thought on adoption and set apart his understanding from the Puritans' primary interest in adoption as an element of the *ordo salutis*. Some years were to pass, though, before Ridderbos' influence on the retrieval of adoption took root.

In the meantime, Sinclair Ferguson, reared like Murray in the Puritans and Scottish Presbyterianism, had become aware of his Scottish compatriot in 1966 as a student in Aberdeen, Scotland. He traces his interest in adoption back to the reading of *Redemption: Accomplished and Applied*. In 1981 Ferguson published *The Christian Life* to which Packer wrote the Foreword. In it, Ferguson included a chapter titled "Sons of God." Like Murray, Ferguson treats justification and adoption prior to union with Christ and draws from Candlish's Cunningham Lectures on *The Fatherhood of God* and his sermon series *The Sonship and Brotherhood of Believers*. He rightly comments, "since those days [the 1860s] all too little has been written on the subject."[167]

Ferguson's appointment to Westminster Theological Seminary undoubtedly exposed him further to the legacy of Murray's hybrid

---

[167] Sinclair B. Ferguson's testimony at the 2012 National Pastors' Conference of *Together for Adoption*; *The Christian Life: A Doctrinal Introduction*, first published 1981, reprint ed. (Edinburgh: The Banner of Truth Trust, 2009), ix–xii, 80–114.

methodology. The Calvinian-Vosian approach to systematics combined with the heavily ratiocinated structure of Puritan dogmatics, was, by that time, mediated and subjected to further reform by Murray's former students, Richard Gaffin and John Frame (see ch. 6).

Ferguson brought to the mix his interest in adoption, publishing in 1986 a very helpful chapter, "The Reformed Doctrine of Sonship" (*op. cit.*). Contradicting Packer, he has traced the prior demise of interest in adoption to Luther, more recently to Francis Turretin, and most recently to the Victorian liberal emphasis on the universal Fatherhood of God and brotherhood of man. Although Victorian liberalism "seemed to sound the death-knell of the doctrine of adoption," Ferguson notes that voices had begun calling for its recovery. He then offers a somewhat prophetic assessment of what the retrieval of adoption requires:

> Perhaps more than any other influence, the impact of biblical theology on systematic theology has demanded a reorientation of soteriology towards the concept of sonship. The doctrine may therefore be on the verge of a long-awaited reinstatement to the position it occupied in Calvin's thought, one which pervades the whole ethos of the Christian life.

Three years later Ferguson published *Children of the Living God* (1989). Appearing sixteen years after Packer's *Knowing God*, Ferguson's awareness of Packer's chapter is clear. There is also discernible some movement toward the disentangling of the new birth and adoption in that they are allotted separate chapters. This frees him to accord a measure of justice to the salvation-historical contours of adoption, although he continues the Puritan oversight of how the filial and familial terms function metaphorically.

Despite raising popular awareness of the filial elements of biblical soteriology, *Children of the Living God*, Ferguson has publicly stated, has sold the fewest copies of all his books. Nevertheless, it aids his desire "to begin to recommunicate to the living church the privileges and responsibilities of being able to call God 'Father.'" These Ferguson returned to in passing in *The Holy Spirit* (1996).[168]

What Ferguson does not mention, to my knowledge, is whether fellow Scotsman Francis Lyall, Professor of Public Law in the University of Aberdeen, also influenced his interest in adoption. Lyall published on the Roman impact of the legal metaphors of adoption, aliens and citizens, and the slave and the freedman in *The Journal of Biblical Literature, New Testament Studies* (1970), and *Evangelical Quarterly* (1976), respectively. He also published other related and frequently cited pieces from December 1975 to June 1976, in 1979 and 1981. He brought the collection together in his study *Citizens, Slaves, Sons: Legal Metaphors in the Epistles* (1984), offering there a sociocultural approach to adoption which has been more popular than the salvation-historical approach. Intriguingly, *Citizens, Slaves, Sons* originated in the same year, same city, and likely the same church as the birth of Ferguson's interest, from a class Lyall taught at his home church of Gilcomston South Church of Scotland, Aberdeen.

Although the Reformed have been prominent in laying a foundation for today's retrieval of adoption, they have not been alone in awakening to the significance of the Fatherhood of God and adoption. Throughout the twentieth century, the Pentecostal movement grew phenomenally, offering a theologically conservative alternative to the relational emphases of Victorian liberalism. By the 1960s Charismatics came to prominence, differing from the former in the evaluation of the extraordinary *vis-à-vis* Scripture and in their range of ecumenical relations. Within the Charismatic movement, theologian Tom Smail published *The Forgotten Father* (1980) to lament the movement's

---

[168] Sinclair B. Ferguson, *Children of the Living God* (Edinburgh: The Banner of Truth Trust, 1989), xii, 5; *The Holy Spirit.* Contours of Christian Theology, ed. Gerald Bray (Leicester, England: Inter-Varsity Press, 1996), 102–3. Along the way, Errol Hulse, a Baptist of Reformed hue, published a brief article titled "Recovering the Doctrine of Adoption" (*op. cit.*, 5–14). Written for pastors and interested laity, Hulse affirmed the neglect of adoption, drawing on Murray, Packer, and Ferguson to make the case for the doctrine's recovery.

spiritual immaturity and self-absorption. Whether consequent or not, Charismatics have come some way since then to recover the Fatherhood of God, as is evident in such books as Mark Stibbe's *From Orphans to Heirs: Celebrating Our Spiritual Adoption* (2001), Jack and Trisha Frost's *Spiritual Slavery to Spiritual Sonship: Your Destiny Awaits You* (2006), and James Jordan's *Sonship: The Journey into the Father's Heart* (2012).[169]

12. THE LATE TWENTIETH CENTURY TO THE PRESENT

By the 1980s interest in the Fatherhood of God and the adoption of sons began trending, at least in evangelical and Reformed circles. While the prior history warns us against making too much of this, the amount and breadth of literature now being published on adoption suggest the interest has become more than a fad. Interest has spread across both denominational lines and disciplines of theology. A generation has arisen, influenced by the wilderness voices, to contribute to the history and grasp of the doctrine some deeper studies offering fresher perspectives and more information. This augurs well for the future of adoption.

Already, a chronological tracing of the remainder of the history has been complicated by the array of theological disciplines now taking an interest in adoption. We thus trace the most recent developments along the lines of juxtaposed disciplines of theology.

Developments in Biblical Studies.

Current Biblical studies of adoption have benefited greatly from a number of prior studies. Willi Twisselmann's *Die Gotteskindschaft der Christen nach dem Neuen Testament* (1939) traces the theme of the children of God along the authorially distinctive lines of the Old Testament and Judaism; the synoptic Gospels; Paul; Hebrews, James, and I Peter; and John. Witold Marchel's dissertation *"Abba, Père! La*

---

[169] Thomas A. Smail, *The Forgotten Father*, reprint ed. (London et al.: Hodder and Stoughton, 1990), 16–17.

Prière du Christ et des Chrétiens (1961), published as a summarized German edition *Abba, Vater! Die Vaterbotschaft des Neuen Testaments* (1963) and republished in full in a new French edition in 1971, follows the same authorially diverse approach to the Fatherhood of God as did Twisselmann's to the children of God. This method needs to be brought into relevant studies in English.

Interestingly, some of the most prominent studies of adoption or related themes have been either written or published by Roman Catholics (notably by the publisher Analecta Biblica): S. I. Dockx's *Fils De Dieu Par Grâce* (1948); Silverio Zeddas' comprehensive history of the exegesis of Galatians 4:6 in *L'Adozione A Figli Di Dio E Lo Spirito Santo: Storia Dell'Interpretazione E Teologia Mistica Di Gal.4:6* (1952); Matthew Vellanickal's *The Divine Sonship of Christians in the Johannine Writings* (1977), which is often cited in treatments of adoption on account of its setting of the Johannine corpus in the context of the Old Testament sonship tradition, the writings of later Judaism and Hellenism, the Synoptic Gospels, and Paul; and Brendan Byrne's *"Sons of God"—"Seed of Abraham": A Study of the Idea of the Sonship of God of All Christians in Paul Against the Jewish Background* (1979).

In the 1980s, however, pertinent Protestant studies began appearing. Allen Mawhinney's Baylor University doctorate, titled "υἱοθεσία in the Pauline Epistles: Its Background, Use and Implications" (1982), lent weight to the case for a Roman background to Paul's use of υἱοθεσία. Mawhinney followed it up the next year with an audio book titled "Adoption," thereafter delving into cognate themes such as Christian sonship, the Fatherhood of God, and the church as family. In his article "God as Father: Two Popular Theories Reconsidered," he sought the recovery of an evangelical view of God's Fatherhood, yet in a way resonating a more salvation-historical take on adoption. His later comment that "Calvin displays the incredible breadth of the Bible in a way that the Westminster Confession does not," comports with this observation.[170]

Then in 1992 came James M. Scott's influential study, *Adoption as Sons of God: An Exegetical Investigation into the Background of ΥΙΟΘΕΣΙΑ in the Pauline Corpus*. Especially useful is his concentrated focus on Paul, his in-depth study of the background of υἱοθεσία which upholds the specific translation *adoption as son*, and his demonstration of Paul's filling of the Hellenistic term with Old Testament content. Scott's work has thus done much to promote a clear perception of the distinctive Pauline, salvation-historical structure of the adoption model.

In the early 1990s Trevor Burke began publishing articles on adoption culminating in two significant monographs: *Adopted into God's Family: Exploring a Pauline Metaphor* (2006) and *The Message of Sonship* (2011). "I am convinced," he writes, "that one cannot understand the Scriptures without due consideration of the importance which familial language has to play. Unlike our twenty-first century fragmented society, the family in both Testaments was the basic building block of ancient society." Specifically, Burke confirms the uniqueness of Paul's use of υἱοθεσία and the authorial diversity of the New Testament, raising its profile as a metaphor, distinguishing adoption from both justification and regeneration. In *Adopted into God's Family* Burke contrasts Paul's use of υἱοθεσία with the language of John (new birth/regeneration). In *The Message of Sonship* he outlines the theme of sonship in the synoptic Gospels and the writings of John and Paul (also Hebrews), respectively, breaking with the practice of reading

---

[170] Allen Mawhinney, "Baptism, Servanthood, and Sonship," *Westminster Theological Journal* 49:1 (Spring 1987), 35–54; "God as Father: Two Popular Theories Reconsidered," *JETS* 31:2 (Jun. 1988), 181–89. For the practical application of adoption, see Mawhinney's 1992 ETS paper titled, "The family of God: one model for the church of the 90's."

adoption into John 1:12-13 and 1 John 3:1.[171]

Soon after Burke's contributions began appearing, my *SBET* started seeing the light of day (from 1996 onward). Whereas Burke expounds the exegetical fundamentals of adoption chiefly in terms of the sociocultural background of υἱοθεσία, I have done so more in terms of the Old Testament/ salvation-historical context. Yet, in parts two and three of our study we seek to correlate these two approaches by means of the more recent scholarship of Erin Heim.[172] In the meantime, more could be done to include in the discussion of the origin of Paul's adoption modelEdward Watson's lesser-known study, *Paul, His Roman Audience, and the Adopted People of God* (2008).

Developments in Historical Theology.

Douglas Kelly's article "Adoption: An Underdeveloped Heritage of the Westminster Standards" (1993) added to Ferguson's preliminary comments about the fathers, medievals, and the reformers, reflecting on the Puritans and thereafter. He notes the strengths and weaknesses of the Westminster Standards' treatment of adoption. The weaknesses, he argues, would have been less pronounced had the followers of the Westminster Tradition, by neglecting adoption, not given grounds for other Christians to think that the Westminster Standards have an insufficient grasp of familial themes so central to Scripture. "Those in the official Westminster Tradition," Kelly laments, "have far less excuse for this omission than others, for their Confession of Faith is unique

---

[171] Trevor J. Burke, *Adopted into God's Family: Exploring a Pauline Metaphor* (Downers Grove, IL: InterVarsity Press, 2006), 22, 23, 25, 26, 28, 32–45, 120, 141, 194, and 203–4; *The Message of Sonship* (Downers Grove, IL: InterVarsity Press, 2011), 18fn4, 120–38, 140, and 206–30. Burke's articles include "The Characteristics of Paul's Adoptive-Sonship (Huiothesia) Motif," *Irish Biblical Studies* 17, January 1995, 62–74; "Adoption and the Spirit in Romans 8" *EQ* 70:4 (1998), 311–24; "Pauline Adoption: A Sociological Approach" *EQ* 73:2 (2001), 119–34.

[172] Erin Heim, "Light through a Prism: New Avenues of Inquiry for the Pauline Ὑιοθεσία Metaphors," (Ph.D. Diss.: University of Otago, 2014).

among other historical confessions in granting an entire chapter to this significant Biblical doctrine." [173]

This neglect was supported in large measure by the want of awareness of the place of adoption in the Reformed tradition, notably in Calvin. This I sought to remedy throughout the 1990s, sketching in my doctoral dissertation (2001) the history of the doctrine among Calvinists (classically Reformed and otherwise) from Calvin through the Southern Presbyterianism of Robert A. Webb.

Since then, J. Todd Billings has published *Calvin, Participation, and the Gift: The Activity of Believers in Union with Christ* (2007). His reading of Calvin strews references to adoption throughout. Additionally, he has a chapter on the *duplex gratia Dei* and on prayer as participation in adoption. He also perceives how relevant adoption is for Calvin's understanding of the sacraments. Billings' work on Calvin became more accessible in 2011 with the publication of *Union with Christ: Reframing Theology and Ministry for the Church*. He sees in Calvin the opportunity to overturn the neglect of union with Christ, for the "images of union with Christ, ingrafting into Christ, partaking of Christ, and adoption were drawn from Paul and Johannine writings in the New Testament and were deeply woven into the fabric of his soteriology."

Billings chooses Paul's metaphor of adoption as the medium through which to discuss union, because it, too, is often neglected. He deals, accordingly, in his opening chapter with "Salvation as Adoption in Christ: An Antidote to Today's Distant Yet Convenient Deity," drawing from Burke's observation of the uniqueness of Paul's language of adoption. Given Burke's sociocultural approach, it is unsurprising that Billings' referencing of "the drama of adoption" lacks the breadth of the salvation-historical context of either Paul or Calvin. For them, incarnational union helps secure the centrality of adoption in Christ within the history of salvation (cf., Gal. 4:4-6). Nevertheless, Billings' weighing in on an area requiring further study is welcome, his reading

---

[173] Kelly, "Adoption," 111.

of orphanhood into adoption in his remarks on "Salvation as Adoption in Christ" less so.[174]

The following year, 2008, Joel Beeke published *Heirs with Christ: The Puritans on Adoption*. The book followed up on his 2007 chapter "Transforming Power and Comfort: The Puritans on Adoption." By very helpfully filling in the details of the Puritan interest, he raised further adoption's profile among the Reformed but stopped short of offering a critical analysis of their treatments in the light of Scripture.[175]

More recently, specific historical studies have begun to appear. Earlier, we made use of the 2016 contributions of Jeff Fisher on Calvin and Oecolampadius and drew from Isomi Saito's Free University of Amsterdam doctoral dissertation, "Divine Adoption in the Confessions of the Reformation Period."

Developments in Systematic Theology.

Independent of the foregoing trajectory is Wolfhart Pannenberg's Lutheran *Systematic Theology* (1991–93). In his section titled "Adoption as God's Children and Justification," he refers to the history of adoption in German theology (mentioning chiefly Schleiermacher, Barth, and Ritschl), pointing to the distinctiveness of justification and adoption in the theology of Paul, also the connection of the two doctrines in Romans and Galatians. Running somewhat contrary to the post-Reformation history of adoption, Pannenberg remarks that there is no reason why adoption should be subordinate to

---

[174] J. Todd Billings, *Union with Christ: Reframing Theology and Ministry for the Church* (Grand Rapids: Baker Academic, 2011), 2–3, 15–16, 18-21, 65.

[175] Joel R. Beeke, "Transforming Power and Comfort: The Puritans on Adoption," *2006–2007 Yearbook: Heritage Reformed Congregations* (Grand Rapids: Reformation Heritage Books), 79–119. Since *Heirs with Christ* Beeke has published two other pieces in familiar vein: "The Puritans on Adoption" in *A Puritan Theology: Doctrine for Life* (Grand Rapids: Reformation Heritage Books, 2012), 537–54, and "The Apostle John and the Puritans on the Father's Adopting, Transforming Love (1 John 3)," (*The Beauty and Glory of the Father*, ed. Joel R. Beeke [Grand Rapids: Reformation Heritage Books, 2013], 79–105).

justification, since Paul presupposes both in a faith fellowship with Christ.

In the English-speaking world, there have appeared a number of relevant evangelical or Reformed systematic theologies. Consider James Montgomery Boice's *Foundations of the Christian Faith* (1986); Wayne Grudem's *Systematic Theology* (1994); Morton Smith's *Systematic Theology* (1994); Robert Reymond's *Systematic Theology* (1998); Robert Culver's *Systematic Theology* (2005); Gerald Bray's *God Is Love: A Biblical and Systematic Theology* (2012); John Frame's *Salvation Belongs to the Lord* (2006), later enlarged in *Systematic Theology: An Introduction to Christian Belief* (2013); Michael Horton's *The Christian Faith* (2011), later abridged in *Pilgrim Theology: Core Doctrines for Christian Disciples* (2013); Michael Bird's *Evangelical Theology* (2013); and Robert Letham's *Systematic Theology* (2019).[176] Grudem notes, contra John Dick's assessment, that, "many systematic theologies do not treat adoption as a separate topic, but include a discussion of its privileges in a discussion of justification and its results." These volumes, coming in quick succession, demonstrate to one degree and another a welcome wind of change.

That said, the treatments remain brief and tend to repeat the exegetical fallacies of history. Robert Reymond commits just four of his 1,093 pages to adoption. Nevertheless, his thought is fresh, independent, and worth noting, as also is his tome *Paul: Missionary Theologian* (2000). Similarly, Culver dedicates but three of the 1,256 pages of the main text to adoption. Frame deals with justification and adoption in the same chapter, not to subsume the latter under the former as had the likes of Turretin and Dabney, but because they both meet needs—the need for legal status and family, respectively. Similarly, he distinguishes adoption and regeneration (new birth),

---

[176] Cf., Morton Smith's interest of a decade earlier in *Studies in Southern Presbyterian Theology*, first published 1962 (Phillipsburg, NJ: P&R, 1987), 266–67.

rightly observing that they are different metaphors conveying varying lessons.

Horton injects salvation-historical considerations into his treatment of adoption but, like Frame, considers adoption in the same chapter as justification. This is either incidental or because he regards both as forensic aspects of union with Christ. The uneven length-and-depth of Horton's respective treatments highlight the contrasting history of the two doctrines. Similarly, Bird brings together biblical and systematic considerations, interweaving the voices of the past with his own innovations. His brief discussion of adoption occurs in his section, "The Gospel of Salvation," and is set against the backdrop of redemptive history and the order of salvation. His innovative approach to the arrangement of soteriology we shall return to in chapter six.

Fittingly, Letham includes adoption in his seventh section, "On the Spirit of God and the People of God." It occurs, significantly, subsequent to union with Christ, not though in the sections on the beginning of the Christian life (calling, regeneration, repentance and faith, justification, and baptism), but in the sections on the progress of the Christian life (assurance, adoption, and sanctification). Given what we shall encounter of the scope of adoption (inclusive of both the adoptive act and adoptive state), it is questionable whether the choice was necessary.

Clearly, the close connection between assurance and adoption is once more under consideration. Found in Paul, Calvin (the theologian of the Holy Spirit), the Puritans, and the Methodists, Chun Tse has recently published *Assurance of Adoption: A New Paradigm for Assurance of Salvation* (2020). Understandably, the rise of theological interest in the grace of adoption is accompanied by the need to know personally that we are adopted by God.

In the meantime, there has appeared David Garner's in-depth and warmhearted monograph, *Sons in the Son* (2016). Based on his doctoral dissertation "Adopted in Christ" (2002), the study highlights the ongoing renaissance of interest in adoption and confirms the solid case for a salvation-historical approach to the exposition of the apostle's unique use of υἱοθεσία. The volume is, then, a most welcome addition to the rare monographs on adoption and raises the overall level of their quality. Yet, in chapter five we shall consider how and why Garner's fixation with the idea of the resurrection-adoption of Christ sabotage's the volume's reliability as an exposition of the doctrine.

Despite such advances in the profile of, and approach to adoption, its place in the creedal, confessional, and catechetical statements of the church remains uncertain. When we recall Schaff's defining of a confession as that which contains what is "necessary for salvation, or at least for the well-being of the Christian Church,"[177] we can ascertain the distance we have to go in retrieving adoption. Neither maximalist nor minimalist creeds automatically include the doctrine. Typically, it receives but passing comment related to subjects such as predestination, assurance, and the sacrament of baptism. This supporting role does not reflect the biblical data. In Scripture, adoption is more often than not introduced climactically, topping off the discussion of other doctrines such as predestination (Eph. 1), justification (Gal. 4), and justification and sanctification (Rom. 8).

This uncertainty is easily demonstrated. Readings of the Reformation continue to overlook adoption, with commemorations of Calvin's birth, for instance, largely omitting his significant contribution to the understanding of the doctrine.[178] Consider also recent confessional and catechetical statements. The Statement of Faith of the World Reformed Fellowship (2011) includes in its fifth article, "God's work of salvation," a ninth section, "The adoption of believers in Christ."

---

[177] *Creeds of Christendom*, 1:3–4 (italics inserted).

[178] *Tributes to John Calvin: A Celebration of His Quincentenary*, edited by David W. Hall, The Calvin 500 Series (Phillipsburg, NJ: P&R, 2010). In the same series there is a brief section by Derek Thomas in "The Mediator of the Covenant" on "Adoption and the Fatherhood of God" in *A Theological Guide to Calvin's Institutes: Essays and Analysis*, edited by David W. Hall and Peter A. Lillback (Phillipsburg, NJ: P&R, 2008), 209–10. Thomas concludes his section, "The metaphor of God's fatherly care will eventually dominate in the *Institutes*."

It is the longest confessional statement on adoption that we know of in the history of the church:

> The position of the Lord Jesus Christ as the eternal uncreated Son of God by nature is unique. Nevertheless he is not ashamed to call those he has saved his brothers and sisters. These adopted children of God are heirs of the inheritance which Christ has secured for them, the full measure of the blessings of redemption, and so they are described as "heirs of God and fellow heirs with Christ."
>
> As children of God, believers share in all the blessings provided by God for his family and by the internal witness of the Holy Spirit, they recognise and address God as Father. They are the objects of the love of God, of his compassion, and of his care for their needs. The children of God also have the privilege of sharing in the sufferings of Christ and his subsequent glorification. A further privilege of God's children, which confirms their adoption, is their experience of the fatherly chastening of God. They are assured that: "God is treating you as sons. For what son is there whom his father does not discipline?" The unity of the children of God in one body is also a privilege to be enjoyed and a responsibility that requires mutual love and ministry.
>
> The full blessings of adoption will not be enjoyed until the glorious return of the Lord Jesus Christ. Adoption has a present dimension but also an eschatological dimension, which is an element of Christian hope. Thus "we ourselves, who have the firstfruits of the Spirit, groan inwardly as we wait eagerly for adoption as sons, the redemption of our bodies." Adoption will not be complete until Christ gives his people new bodies at the resurrection, when believers will enjoy "the freedom of the glory of the children of God" along with the renewed creation.

Although the Statement does not avoid entirely the mixture of different images of sonship or childhood in the New Testament and reflects the historic overshadowing by justification (on which there are three sections), the inclusion, theology, and feel of the article combine to form another marker on the road to the retrieval of adoption.

The following year, though, The New City Catechism (NCC) was released as an app. Since 2017 a print edition has been available. While the catechism is intentionally shorter than its Heidelberg and Westminster equivalents, in introducing it Timothy Keller affirms that the first purpose of catechisms is to expound the gospel, explaining what it is and laying out the biblical doctrines on which it is founded. The NCC is based on and adapted from Calvin's Genevan Catechism, the WSC, WLC, and especially the Heidelberg Catechism. In this light, it is regrettable and surprising that the NCC asks "What do justification and sanctification mean?" (Q. 32) but drops the questions "What is Adoption?" (WSC 34 and WLC 74) and "Why is he [Jesus] called God's 'only begotten Son' when we also are God's children? Because Christ alone is the eternal, natural Son of God. We, however, are adopted children of God—adopted by grace through Christ" (HC 33). The NCC falls short in this regard of a full (prospective as well as retrospective) exposition of the gospel, and undoes confessionally one of the notable advances in the history of adoption. Conversely, *A Reforming Catholic Confession* (2017), brief as it is, acknowledges adoption in its section on "The Gospel."[179]

Developments in Practical Theology.

In the field of counseling, we cannot be sure what gave rise to Michael Bobick's *From Slavery to Sonship* (1998). There, he discusses a little of the linguistic category of the term *adoption*, dealing, like Calvin, with the motif exegetically and in the context of God's covenantal dealings with his people. He purposes to show, in contrast to secular counseling, that man is a covenant breaker (i.e., an idolater) and, as such, is in slavery to fear. "A major goal of counseling, then," writes Bobick, "is for counselees [adopted] in Christ to view themselves as sons by believing God's Word and obeying it." Those doing so gain fresh confidence and freedom.[180]

Whether Bobick influenced Jack Miller's emphasis on sonship is

---

[179] The New City Catechism, Introduction by Timothy Keller (www.newcitycatechism. com/introduction-timothy-keller/ and "A Reforming Catholic Confession" (www. reformingcatholicconfession.com/explanation/), both accessed September 18, 2017.

[180] Michael W. Bobick, *From Slavery to Sonship: A Biblical Psychology for Pastoral Counseling* (D. Min.: Westminster Theological Seminary, 1988), 95, 212, 220–24.

unclear. As a professor of practical theology at Westminster Theological Seminary, Miller had become enamored with the central adoption text, Galatians 4:4-7. He discerned from its context and content a way out of what Ron Lutz and John Yenchko call "the deadly dance of legalism, formalism, and moralism." This dance, Jack and his wife, Rose Marie, observed, produces folk who, though genuinely Christian, fall into the trap of building their own record of personal righteousness. Justified through faith alone in Christ alone, they nevertheless live as if justified by works. Hence, the jadedness and joylessness of their worship and service.[181]

To correct this, the Millers drew up a Sonship Discipleship Course.[182] Many undergoing it have testified to a fresh sense of freedom in Christ, yet the course is criticized for being excessively experiential, confusing the *ordo salutis*, marring the doctrine of sanctification, perpetuating a crisis or revivalist theology, and for constituting a program. When, however, we view *Sonship* within the all-important context of the historical neglect of adoption, we perceive how God has used it despite some of its exegesis and theologizing. In effect, the program repeats the early nineteenth-century protest for paternal grace, since Presbyterians had, in the meantime, continued to miss its kernel of truth. The critics of *Sonship* are proof of this. Left

---

[181] Ronald E. Lutz and John Yenchko, "Practical Calvinism: Grace, Sonship and Mission," *The Practical Calvinist: An Introduction to the Presbyterian and Reformed Heritage (In Honor of Clair Davis' Thirty Years at Westminster Theological Seminary)*, ed. Peter A. Lillback (Fearn, Ross-shire: Mentor [Christian Focus Publications]), 2002, 464. For a fascinating and thorough account of the life and ministry of C. John ("Jack") Miller, see Michael A. Graham's "Cheer Up! A Biographical Study of the Life and Ministry of C. John ("Jack") Miller: A Twentieth Century Pioneer of Grace (Ph.D., Diss.: Southeastern Baptist Theological Seminary, Wake Forest, North Carolina, May 2019). A published version is now available titled *Cheer Up! The Life and Ministry of Jack Miller* (Phillipsburg, NJ: P&R, 2021).

[182] The basic story of the origins of the course are told by Rose Marie Miller in *From Fear to Freedom: Living as Sons and Daughters of God* (Wheaton, IL: Harold Shaw Publishers, 1994).

unchallenged, they simply repeat the mistakes of history.[183]

In the area of mission, today's interest in adoption has done much to increase orphan care. There is historic precedence for this. Although of dubious authenticity, authorship, and date, the likely fourth-century *Constitutions of the Holy Apostles*—a practical manual of church order—speaks of two kinds of adoption: one that is spiritual or saving, and another that is practical or diaconal. Whereas the former describes the relationship of deacons to bishops, as also the meaning of the baptism of catechumens,[184] the latter expresses the social conscience of the church in her opposition to abortion and infanticide and her care of orphans. "Those who have no children," reads the first title of Book IV, "should adopt orphans, and treat them as their own children":

> When any Christian becomes an orphan, whether it be a young man or a maid, it is good that some one of the brethren who is without a child should take the young man, and esteem him in the place of a son; and he that has a son about the same age, and that is marriageable, should marry the maid to him: for they which do so perform a great work, and become fathers to the orphans, and shall receive the reward of this charity from the Lord God. But if anyone

---

[183] For more on the brief analysis offered here, see Trumper, *When History Teaches Us Nothing*, 33–88.

[184] Describing the work of a bishop, the *Constitutions* states that he "is the minister of the word, the keeper of knowledge, the mediator between God and you in several parts of your divine worship. He is the teacher of piety; and, next after God, he is your father, who has begotten you again to the adoption of sons by water and the Spirit." The deacon must revere the bishop as father. "By thy bishop, O man, God adopts thee for His child. Acknowledge, O son, that right hand which was a mother to thee. Love him who, after God, is become a father to thee, and honour him." As for catechumens, they are to "hate every way of iniquity, and walk in the way of truth, that [they] might be thought worthy of the laver of regeneration, to the adoption of sons, which is in Christ." The bishop for his part must bless the baptized and sanctify them, preparing them to become worthy of the Lord's spiritual gifts and of "the true adoption of [God's] spiritual mysteries." They will, for instance, pray three times a day, "preparing themselves beforehand, that [they] may be worthy of the adoption of the Father" (*A-N F* 7:410, 412, 470, 476, and 484).

who walks in the way of man-pleasing is rich, and therefore is ashamed of orphans, the Father of orphans and Judge of widows will make provision for the orphans, but himself will have such an heir as will send what he has spared; and it shall happen to him according as it is said: "What things the holy people have not eaten, those shall the Assyrians eat." As also Isaiah says: "Your land, strangers devour it in your presence."[185]

Independent of this history, Jeanne Stevenson-Moessner interacts with the church fathers (notably Irenaeus, Clement of Alexandria, Tertullian, and Augustine) in *The Spirit of Adoption: At Home in God's Family* (2003). She also draws from the Westminster Standards and Webb's *The Reformed Doctrine of Adoption* (citing as authoritative his flawed claim that Calvin wrote nothing on adoption!). She does so to "support families in adoption and to formulate a theology of adoption . . . applicable to Christian churches." Although Stevenson-Moessner does not expound adoption, she seeks as an adoptive mother to:

- Embolden Christians to rely on the biblical anthropological mirror, to see themselves as adopted sons and daughters of God.
- Encourage the church as the family or household of faith to acknowledge and accept the differences seen in adoptive families.
- Place the doctrine of adoption alongside justification and sanctification.
- Redirect attention to the earlier theologians on adoption.
- Extend our images of God to include adoptive as well as birthing parents.
- Offer supportive insight to families involved in the adoption of children.
- Hope that more clergy, adoptive parents, grandparents, neighbors, and friends are drawn into God's womb-love.

"When, as Christians," she explains, "we take the name of 'adopted children of God,' we also intentionally identify with those who have been marginalized by our society. We become emboldened to say

---

[185] *A-N F* 7:433.

to those who have no home and no birthright in society, 'I will add your name to my name so that we can be seen to belong together, with Christ the Firstborn, at home in God's family." Adoption is, for the church then, a theologically driven humanitarian cause. It takes the church family and not simply the nuclear family to raise the adopted child. [186]

A more expository case for the use of adoption in orphan care is laid out by Russell Moore in his *Adopted for Life: The Priority of Adoption for Christian Families and Churches* (2009), but his admission of slavery as the context of adoption jars with his use of the doctrine to promote orphan care.

It is Dan Cruver, erstwhile president and cofounder of Together for Adoption, however, who has been particularly adept at bringing together by means of interviews and conferences those interested in recovering adoption. He has also edited *Reclaiming Adoption: Missional Living through the Rediscovery of Abba Father* (2011) and authored half of its eight chapters. "We believe," states Cruver, "that:

- The doctrine of adoption has been widely neglected within the church historically;
- It remains neglected within much of the evangelical church today;
- A proper theological grounding of horizontal adoption *within* vertical adoption has profound implications for our understanding of both aspects, and therefore;
- To the extent we can recapture theological balance regarding adoption, the church will be transformed and our witness to the world will be radically redefined."[187]

Those new to the study of the doctrine will find help from Cruver's expository comments, not least because they perceive more

---

[186] Jeanne Stevenson-Moessner, *The Spirit of Adoption: At Home in God's Family* (Louisville: Westminster John Knox Press, 2003), 6, 8, 9 (cf., 85 and 116), 40, 45, 68, 86, 114, 127.

[187] *Reclaiming Adoption: Missional Living through the Rediscovery of Abba Father*, ed. Dan Cruver (Adelphi, MD: Cruciform Press, 2011), 8.

than other popular/quasi-popular treatments the uniquely Pauline use of the term "adoption" and the salvation-historical layout of its content.

It will be interesting to see where evangelical orphan care goes from here. Notwithstanding the movement's laudable ministry to orphans, the doctrine of adoption is not the best theological model to substantiate the ministry. This we shall demonstrate in later chapters, indicating thereby that a fresh appeal to Scripture is needed for the biblical justification of the heart-warming work of orphan care.[188]

John MacArthur's *Slave: The Hidden Truth About Your Identity in Christ* (2010), while somewhat conspiratorial in claiming without substantiation the "perpetual hiding of an essential element of New Testament revelation," and overdone in claiming that "no one had pulled the hidden jewel [of slavery] all the way into the sunlight," nevertheless includes two chapters titled "From Slaves to Sons" which help debunk the popular "adopted from orphanhood" narrative, and could help the orphan care movement in its reworking of its biblical support.[189] Meanwhile, Cruver has had to respond to criticism of the movement's accepted adoption practices by Canadian lawyer David Smolin. Whether Cruver's response lays to rest the concerns or stimulates further discussion, time will tell.[190]

Finally, there is the figuring of adoption in devotion or piety. Despite the dearth of substantial theological monographs on adoption, a spate of cross-denominational books on God's Fatherhood has appeared reminiscent of the glut published in the late nineteenth and

---

[188] See, for instance, Brady Boyd's *Sons and Daughters: Spiritual Orphans Finding Our Way Home* (Grand Rapids: Zondervan, 2012).

[189] John MacArthur, *Slave: The Hidden Truth About Your Identity in Christ* (Nashville, et al.: Thomas Nelson, 2010), 2, 3, *passim*, 163–68, 214–15.

[190] David Smolin, "Of Orphans and Adoption, Parents and the Poor, Exploitation and Rescue: A Scriptural and theological critique of the evangelical Christian adoption and orphan care movement," *Regent International Law Review* 8:2 [Spring 2012]); Dan Cruver, "The First Step in the Way Forward: A Response to David M. Molin's 'Of Orphans and Adoption,'" *Journal of Christian Legal Thought* 2:1 (Spring 2012), 11–13.

early twentieth centuries. It includes Clifford Pond's *Our Father: Enjoying the Fatherhood of God!* (1996), John Koessler's *God Our Father* (1999), John W. Miller's *Calling God "Father": Essays on the Bible Fatherhood & Culture* (1999), Marianne Meye Thompson's *The Promise of the Father: Jesus and God in the New Testament* (2000), and Joel R. Beeke's edited *The Beauty and Glory of the Father* (2013). Although these are not quite the same as studies dedicated to adoption, they do reflect the rising interest in the familial.

One popular phenomenon in this regard is the anomalous work of Brennan Manning (1934–2013). By 1982 he had left the Franciscan Order to marry, ministering freelance out of New Orleans. Publishing with Protestant publishers and citing Roman Catholic and evangelical authors, he stirred an avid interest among Evangelical and Reformed pastors in the Fatherhood of God. Best known for *The Ragamuffin Gospel: Good News for the Bedraggled, Beat-Up, and Burnt Out* (1990)— a book intended to "revive lost hope and lift readers into the majestic, awesome, and yet furiously loving presence of God our Father"— Manning thereafter made the theme of God's Fatherhood prominent, such as in *Abba's Child: The Cry of the Heart for Intimate Belonging* (1994); *The Boy Who Cried Abba: A Parable of Trust and Acceptance* (1996); *Reflections for Ragamuffins: Daily Devotions from the Writings of Brennan Manning* (1998); *The Journey of the Prodigal: A Parable of Sin and Redemption* (2002); *The Furious Longing of God* (2009); and *Souvenirs of Solitude: Finding Rest in Abba's Embrace* (second ed., 2009).

Although his treatments of the Fatherhood of God are non-exegetical, their readership among the Evangelical and Reformed serves to compensate for the loss of the Fatherhood of God nearer home.[191] That loss is gradually being remedied. Further popular treatments of the Fatherhood of God and adoption have appeared to supplement the influence of Murray, Packer, and Ferguson, such as

---

[191] Cf., Roman Catholic reactions to Brennan Manning at the website "Catholic Answers: To Explain and Defend the Faith" (forums.catholic.com/showthread. php?t=15167, accessed March 15, 2014).

Mark Johnston's *Child of a King: The Biblical Doctrine of Sonship* (1997), Robert Peterson's *Adopted by God* (2001), and Michael Milton's brief primer *What is the Doctrine of Adoption?* (2012).

Besides books, more sermons are being preached on adoption. Note Barton Priebe's "Belonging to God's Family: Measuring the Effect of Sermons on Paul's doctrine of Adoption in the Lives of Believers" (2020). He has now published *Adopted by God: Discover the Life-Transforming Joy of a Neglected Truth* (2021). How far the retrieval of adoption has come that studies such as these now grasp Paul's exclusive reference to adoption, setting the relevant texts in the context of salvation history. These advancements augur well for the enhancement of popular treatments of adoption in time to come.[192]

Clearly, history marches on. What this means for the doctrine of adoption we await to see. Nevertheless, we end in upbeat mood our sketch of the history of adoption (Pentecost to the present [fall 2021]). How thrilling it is to discern the Spirit of God leading the people of God to retrieve the truth of God. The retrieval of adoption is now within reach.

~~~~

---

[192] Barton D. Priebe, *Belonging to God's Family: Measuring the Effect of Sermons on Paul's Doctrine of Adoption in the Lives of Believers* (D.Min. diss.: Associated Canadian Theological Schools [Northwest Baptist Seminary and Trinity Western University], Langley, British Columbia, 2020).

ADOPTION IN REVIEW
An Analysis

> Why has the subject of Adoption—so rich and
> fertile in fine thought and feeling, so susceptible
> also of beautiful theological treatment—been so
> little investigated and illustrated? . . . Certain it is
> . . . that a good treatise on Adoption—such as
> should at once do justice to the fine theology of
> the question, and to the precious import of the
> privilege—is a desideratum.
>
> Hugh Martin,
> *Christ's Presence in the Gospel History* (1865).

We are nearing the intersection to make the U-turn for Adoption, and now prepare to make the turn. Mirror, signal, maneuvre, and then, I promise you, it will be full speed ahead to Adoption and Retrieval!

~~~~

Although the opening chapter contains the fullest history of the doctrine of adoption to date, it echoes the truth of Ernest Cushing Richardson's introduction to Jerome's *Lives of Illustrious Men*: "In such work absolute exhaustiveness is all but impossible."[1] Despite the digging yet to be done, we have at least arrived at a point at which we can make some preliminary observations:

- The neglect of adoption is protracted and widespread. The unearthing of adoption in hitherto unknown places does not change this.
- The Pauline, salvation-historical approach to the doctrine dates back to the church fathers in piecemeal references. Thus, today's challenging of the more ratiocinated treatments of adoption of the

---

[1] *N and P-N F* (second series), 3:353, 359.

Medieval era and of Protestant Scholasticism has historical precedence as also, we shall see, biblical warrant.

- The running together of the filial and familial terms of the New Testament, while mitigated somewhat by those understanding most the salvation-historical flow of Paul's thought, has featured throughout the history of adoption, muddling the clarity of his doctrine of adoption. Thus, reliance on exegetical tradition is an inadequate defense of the scholastics, for, notwithstanding their undoubted philological and exegetical abilities, they fed off and perpetrated long-standing conflations of Johannine and Pauline thought. This is largely explained by the want of serious investigation of adoption.[2]

- The retrieval of adoption requires a qualitative as well as a quantitative improvement of attention to the doctrine. Not only is there room for more to be written on adoption, the study of it requires a back-to-Scripture approach that attests both historic and contemporary exegesis and aids the fresh formulation of the doctrine.

In what follows, we probe further the first observation (the neglect of adoption), returning in parts two and three to the others.

In part, the neglect of adoption needs no confirmation. After all, awareness of it is one of the successes of the current upturn of interest in adoption. So much so that the *pro forma* acknowledgment of its neglect has, remarks David Garner, "become almost annoyingly habitual."[3] Yet, for so long as the theological history of adoption retains

---

[2] See, for example, Richard A. Muller, "The Problem of Protestant Scholasticism—A Review and Definition," in Willem J. Van Asselt and Eef Dekker, *Reformation and Scholasticism: An Ecumenical Enterprise* (Grand Rapids: Baker Academic, 2001), 60, 63; and *After Calvin: Studies in the Development of a Theological Tradition*, Oxford Studies in Historical Theology (Oxford, New York, et al.: Oxford University Press, 2003), 10, 21, 42, 46, 59, 71, 85, and so on.

[3] David B. Garner, *Sons in the Son: The Riches and Reach of Adoption in Christ* (Phillipsburg, NJ: P&R, 2016), 32.

seismic lacunae, we shall have cause to look back, not least to ensure that the doctrine does not recede once more into the shadows of theological discourse.

So, to double down on ensuring that does not happen, we now follow up our account of the theological history of adoption with an investigation of the reasons why it has unfolded as it has. These serve to:

- Confirm the reality of the historical neglect of adoption.
- Mature our understanding of the history of adoption.
- Explain why the call to retrieve adoption has previously gone unheeded.
- Dissuade the church from falling back into the neglect.
- Supply fresh insights into the development of doctrine in general.
- Shed clearer light on debates past and present.
- Encourage fresh analysis of how the church has treated other doctrines.

While Garner is likely correct to say that the reasons for the neglect remain mysterious to an extent, the falling back on mystery more appropriately concludes a review of the theological history than opens it. Thus, we now glean from the prior history those reasons for the neglect that are identifiable and verifiable.

1. NEGLECT THROUGH OVERSIGHT

In the annals of history, the church has witnessed time and again, and accumulatively throughout the course of the last millennia, the fulfillment of the Lord's promise that the coming Spirit would guide his people into all truth. (Jn. 16:12). In consequence of both the Spirit's energizing of Christ's followers and the illumination of their minds, theology is a growth subject.

This means several things. First, that each follower, on coming to Christ, becomes a theologian. Second, that to some are given a specific call and giftedness to serve as pastors, theologians, or pastor-theologians (Eph. 4:11-12). Third, that as the church engages inscripturated revelation, so, through the presence of the Spirit in the church, the church's attention to biblical doctrine increases and matures.

How the church's maturing occurs is a matter decided by the will and providence of God. Certainly, God's will is that his church grows in comprehending his revealed counsel (Acts 20:27; 2 Tim. 3:16), and yet it is also within his sovereign determination as to when the church enters into a fuller understanding of each respective doctrine of Scripture.

The most fundamental explanation of the neglect of adoption is, then, that the doctrine, for reasons known only to God, has yet to come into its own. And yet, within the mystery of God's will, we may discern subsidiary reasons for the neglect.

2. NEGLECT THROUGH PREOCCUPATION

The church has gone through long and hard seasons contending for the faith. As discouraging as such contentions can be, God has an impressive track record in overruling controversy to develop our understanding of important truths. Southern Presbyterian John Girardeau expressed this well:

> [The] subjective apprehension of objective truth may be increased in intensity, in scope and in adequacy. It is needless to observe that its growth, in the history of the church, has largely depended upon the challenge of acknowledged truth by errorists, by the conflict of theological views, and by the thorough-going discussion which has for these reasons been necessitated. In this way the church's knowledge of the doctrine of the Trinity, of sin, and of justification has been cleared up, matured and crystallized. To the precisely formulated statements of these truths it is not to be expected that much that is either novel or important will be added.[4]

Yet, the church's attention to certain doctrines has come at a cost to others, not least to the Fatherhood of God and of adoption.

---

[4] John L. Girardeau, *Discussions of Theological Questions* (Harrisonburg, VA: Sprinkle Publications, 1986), 428.

Neither has been controverted. Explains Thomas Crawford:

> The Fatherhood of God, whether in relation to all men as His intelligent and moral creatures, or more particularly in relation to those who are "the children of God by faith in Christ Jesus," has hitherto been in a remarkable degree exempted from the speculations and controversies of theology. No heresies of any note have ever arisen with respect to it. No schisms or bitter contentions have been occasioned by it. A comparatively small space has ordinarily been allotted to it in our articles of faith and systems of divinity.[5]

The same goes for the doctrine of adoption. States Girardeau:

> [Adoption] has not been made the subject of much controversy, nor has it received the didactic exposition which has been devoted to most of the other topics included in the theology of redemption. Its importance has been to a large extent overlooked, its place in a distinct and independent treatment of the covenant of grace has been refused, while leading theologians have differed in regard even to its nature and its office.[6]

While it is fitting that adoption, so redolent of God's love and grace, has escaped the acrimony that has characterized the discussion of other doctrines, it should not take the staging of a drama to ensure its retrieval. The retrieval is better pursued by means of the wider recognition and maturer discussion of the doctrine.[7]

---

[5] Thomas J. Crawford, *The Fatherhood of God considered in its general and special aspects and particularly in relation to the atonement with a review of recent speculations on the subject*, second ed. revised and enlarged with a reply to the strictures of Dr. Candlish (Edinburgh: William Blackwood and sons, 1867), 1; cf., 2.

[6] John L. Girardeau, *Discussions of Theological Questions* (Harrisonburg, VA: Sprinkle Publications, 1986), 428–29.

[7] The theological history of adoption suggests, contra The Reformed Forum podcast, "Adoption: Accomplished and Applied" (https://www. facebook.com/reformedforum/videos/270556298144566, accessed June 3, 2021), that the retrieval of adoption should, for the present, take priority over the contention with Rome that adoption, like justification, is by grace alone, in Christ alone, and through faith alone. The rush to defend adoption *sola gratia* arises more from the Reformation and post-Reformation defense of justification *sola gratia* than from the specific history of adoption. Of more pressing need is the extolling of the intrinsic beauty of God's adopting grace.

All this said, we learn much from a consideration of how the church's preoccupation with other doctrines precluded the consideration of adoption.

The preoccupation with Adoptionism.

The first example takes us back to the Medieval period, to the later seventh and eighth centuries. The Medieval theologians, following the church fathers both chronologically and theologically, "were preoccupied with questions of greater weight—questions of *real* grace, rather than questions about *relative* grace—questions such as the true nature of the Word made flesh, or the relations of the Trinity within the Godhead."[8] The Adoptionist controversy is a case in point.

The controversy began when Elipandus, Archbishop of Toledo, claimed Jesus was the adoptive Son of God. According to Willemien Otten, he had meant neither that Christ was adopted by the Father (as in Arianism) nor that Christ had adopted a human body, but that by assuming flesh Christ became the firstborn in adoption and grace (along the lines of Christ's self-emptying in Phil. 2:7). In this view, Elipandus was supported by Felix, Bishop of Urgella. Felix posited that Christ's two natures must imply two different modes of sonship, the one divine or natural as the Only-begotten Son of God and the other human or adoptive. At the same time, writes Berkhof, "he sought to preserve the unity of the Person by stressing the fact that, from the time of his conception, the Son of Man was taken up into the unity of the Person of the Son of God."[9]

While the critics of Felix stopped short of claiming he taught that Christ had a dual personality, they felt his talk of two modes of sonship would resurrect Nestorianism. Alcuin, an English monk and a

---

[8] Edward McKinlay, "The relation of incarnation to atonement in the Christology of R. S. Candlish and its contribution to the development of Scottish Theology" (Ph. D. Diss.: University of Edinburgh, 1966), 106.

[9] Louis Berkhof, *The History of Christian Doctrines*, reprint ed. (Carlisle, PA: The Banner of Truth Trust, 1985), 111.

prominent advisor to Charlemagne, following Pope Hadrian I, charged him with dividing Christ into two sons, arguing effectively that no father could have a son by both nature and adoption. "Undoubtedly," writes Berkhof, "the Adoptionists were in error, when they assigned to the human nature of Christ a sort of alien position until He was made to partake of divine sonship by a special act of adoption." The relation of sonship pertains not to one or to either of the natures of Christ but to his person. Accordingly, the Council of Toledo (675) rejected the idea of the two modes of Sonship and declared that Christ is the Son of God by nature and not by adoption. The Synod of Frankfurt thought likewise and rejected Adoptionism in 794. The Council and the Synod thus became the first bodies we know of to introduce the language of adoption.[10]

Without following the debate further, note how ironic it is that the term *adoption* came into vogue in a controversy about the Son rather than the sons of God. Also relevant is the fact that the victors went no further than to settle the Sonship of the Son. The history of adoption could have turned out very differently had the church gone on to consider the believer's sonship. In the centuries which have since passed, like issues have arisen in—

- The Candlish/Crawford debate of the 1860s, in which the soteriological discussion of adoption led, in reverse, to the discussion of Christ's Sonship.[11]

---

[10] Berkhof, *The History of Christian Doctrines*, 111–12; Robert S. Candlish, *The Fatherhood of God: Being the First Course of the Cunningham Lectures*. Fifth ed. (Edinburgh: Adam and Charles Black, 1869), 65–66; Willemien Otten, "Carolingian Theology" in *The Medieval Theologians: An Introduction to the Theology of the Medieval Period*, ed. G. R. Evans (Malden, MA: Blackwell Publishing, 2001), 66–69.

[11] For their respective arguments, see Tim J. R. Trumper, "An Historical Study of the Doctrine of Adoption in the Calvinistic Tradition" (University of Edinburgh: Ph.D. Diss., 2001), 337–97.

- Today's use of Romans 1:3-4 as support of the resurrection-adoption of Christ, notably in Garner's promotion of the two dimensions of Christ's sonship (for more, see ch. 5).

The preoccupation with justification.

The second example brings us to the Protestant Reformation. Brevard Childs fittingly remarks that "The importance of soteriology for the intellectual and spiritual life of the church is too obvious to belabor." Yet, through the church's distraction, the divine timing of the Holy Spirit, or both, soteriology did not develop until the Anselmic era of the eleventh and early twelfth centuries. Since Anselm focused more on the accomplishment than the application of salvation, only at the Reformation did the application of salvation become front and center of theological inquiry.[12]

It was the contention over the grace of justification that occasioned the rise of soteric interest. Over against Rome the Protestant reformers were united on three essential principles of justification, namely, that:

- Justification is a forensic doctrine teaching a change of status brought about by God's declaration of the sinner as righteous in his sight.
- "Justifying righteousness" is the alien righteousness of Christ imputed to those who can do naught else but receive it through faith.
- God's external act of justification must be distinguished from sanctification or regeneration (the internal process of renewal within man).[13]

---

[12] Brevard S. Childs, *Biblical Theology of the Old and New Testaments: Theological Reflection on the Christian Bible* (Minneapolis: Fortress, 1992), 523; John McIntyre, *The Shape of Soteriology: Studies in the Doctrine of the Death of Christ* (Edinburgh: T&T Clark, 1992), 15–25.

[13] Alister E. McGrath, *Iustitia Dei: A History of the Christian Doctrine of Justification—*

Thus, according to the reformers, justification is a free gift of God's grace (Rom. 5:15-17). It speaks of how we may each be right with God, enter eternal life, and escape eternal death.

While affirming the vital importance of justification, the evidence suggests that there developed in Protestantism such a preoccupation with it that the profile of adoption came to suffer significantly. This preoccupation is traceable through several phases of history.

We begin with the Reformation and with a pertinent observation by Herman Ridderbos:

> It may seem ungrateful to speak critically about Reformation preaching. For if the truth of God was ever adequately maintained in the face of the destructive inroads of human legalism, it was in the Reformation confession by the Pauline plea: The just shall live by faith without deeds of the law. But precisely this antithetical position of the Reformation confessions against Roman Catholicism can explain why the forensic, and not the eschatological character of the gospel has left is mark on the Reformation soteriology. It may be said that this position was the only possible and admissible one to adopt. But it cannot be said that the exegetical and homiletical approaches to Paul's epistles must forever be thus determined.[14]

We reexamine such approaches for a forensically lopsided soteriology held sway for centuries following the Reformation, and still does to an extent.. Writes Candlish:

> The Reformers had enough to do to vindicate 'the article of a standing or falling church'—justification by faith alone; to recover it out of the chaos of Popish error and superstition; and to reassert it in its right connection with the Doctrine of the Absolute Divine Sovereignty which Augustine had so well established. Their hands were full.

Similarly, Hugh Martin remarks: "On Justification by faith we have abundant and most precious authorship; for around that doctrine and

---

From 1500 to the Present Day, reprint ed. (Cambridge: Cambridge University Press, 1991), 69–86.

[14] Herman N. Ridderbos, *When the Time had Fully Come: Studies in New Testament Theology* (Jordan Station, Ontario: Paideia Press, 1982), 58.

privilege the great battle of controversy has raged. But the conquerors seem to have paused, exhausted or contented with the victory."[15]

Packer's cavalier claim that "Luther's grasp of adoption was as strong and clear as his grasp of justification," is challenged, then, by Lidgett's more accurate assessment, that, even when commenting on Galatians 4:7 (what we may call the *locus classicus* of adoption), Luther dealt more with redemption from the law than with the Fatherhood of God:

> Salvation is not conceived by Luther prevailingly under the form of realised and completed sonship, but as redemption, forgiveness, acceptance, confidence, and freedom, especially this last. . . . Luther speaks much here of the gift of the Spirit, of faith, of redemption, of freedom from the law of sin and death, of being heirs of God. All these blessings cluster for him around the gift of the Spirit of adoption. He speaks of the filial cry of believers, but he gives no exposition of the meaning of sonship, as the form, above all others, which the Christian life assumes. The freedom, confidence, and sense of heirship, which are so vital to Luther's experience and so closely consequent on sonship, engage his attention, rather than the nature of the relationship, which is their source.

Likewise, William Cunningham notes that "Luther applied very fully the true scriptural doctrine of justification to all the corruptions of the papal system which were *directly* connected with it, but he did not do much in the way of connecting the doctrine of justification with the other great doctrines of the Christian system." Nor, generally, has the Lutheran tradition. Explains George Hendry:

> There has sometimes been a tendency in Protestant theology, especially in the Lutheran Church, to lean too heavily on the doctrine of justification. This is understandable in view of the decisive importance of the doctrine at the Reformation. But the fullness of the gospel is too rich to be compressed into the framework of this doctrine alone. For when God extends his grace to us in Jesus Christ, he not only releases us from our guilt, he also receives us into his family; and the one thing cannot be separated

---

[15] Candlish, *The Fatherhood of God*, 192; Hugh Martin, *Christ's Presence in the Gospel History*, second ed. (Edinburgh: Maclaren, 1865), 80fn.

from the other without the risk of serious misunderstanding. The doctrine of adoption is sufficiently important to merit treatment alongside the doctrine of justification.[16]

The Reformed, by contrast, viewed justification as but one (privileged) doctrine in the scheme of salvation, rather than as *the* doctrine of soteriology. Yet, more variegated view of Reformed soteriology did not guarantee the inclusion of adoption.

Between 1530 and 1570 Protestants were compelled to defend tenaciously the freshly understood *sola fide* character of justification. Protestant defensiveness was occasioned by the Council of Trent (1545–63) and the anathematizing of those upholding the free grace of justification. According to James Payton, Rome's counteroffensive coincided with the division of Protestantism into Lutheran and Reformed camps and the loss of some of Protestantism's best church leaders and apologists. Yet, the real significance of the decrees of Trent lay, argues Alister McGrath, in the amount of attention the Roman church accorded the positive exposition of justification. The Council declared, *contra* the Protestants, that justification refers to Christian existence in its totality, and therefore includes both regeneration and adoption—the sinner's inner renewal as well as his or her pardon and acceptance.[17]

---

[16] James I. Packer, *Knowing God,* 1975 ed. (London: Hodder and Stoughton, 1988), 255; J. Scott Lidgett, *The Fatherhood of God in Christian Truth and Life* (Edinburgh, 1902), 251–52; William Cunningham, *The Reformers and Theology of the Reformation*, first published 1862 (Edinburgh: The Banner of Truth Trust, 1989), 337; cf., Sinclair B. Ferguson, "The Reformed Doctrine of Sonship," in Nigel M. De S. Cameron and Sinclair B. Ferguson, eds., *Pulpit and People: Essays in Honour of William Still* (Edinburgh: Rutherford House, 1986), 81; George S. Hendry, *The Westminster Confession for Today: A Contemporary Interpretation.* (Richmond, VA: SCM Press, 1960), 141.

[17] James R. Payton Jr., *Getting the Reformation Wrong: Correcting Some Misunderstandings* (Downers Grove, IL: IVP Academic, 2010), 190; McGrath, *Iustitia Dei,* 69–86.

The comparative neglect of adoption during the Reformation era became visible as early as the post-Reformation era. One only has to contrast WCF 11 and 12 to see this:

OF JUSTIFICATION

I. Those whom God effectually calleth he also freely justifieth; not by infusing righteousness into them, but by pardoning their sins, and by accounting and accepting their persons as righteous: not for any thing wrought in them, or done by them, but for Christ's alone: not by imputing faith itself, the act of believing, or any other evangelical obedience, to them as their righteousness; but by imputing the obedience and satisfaction of Christ unto them, they receiving and resting on him and his righteousness by faith: which faith they have not of themselves; it is the gift of God.

II. Faith, thus receiving and resting on Christ and his righteousness, is the alone instrument of justification; yet is it not alone in the person justified, but is ever accompanied with all other saving graces, and is no dead faith, but worketh by love.

III. Christ, by his obedience and death, did fully discharge the debt of all those that are thus justified, and did make a proper, real, and full satisfaction to his Father's justice in their behalf. Yet, inasmuch as he was given by the Father for them, and his obedience andsatisfaction accepted in their stead; and both, freely, not for anything in them; their justification is only of free grace; that both the exact justice and rich grace of God might be glorified in the justification of sinners.

OF ADOPTION

All those that are justified, God vouchsafeth, in and for his only Son Jesus Christ, to make partakers of the grace of adoption: by which they are taken into the number, and enjoy the liberties and privileges of the children of God; have his name put upon them, receive the Spirit of adoption; have access to the throne of grace with boldness; are enabled to cry, Abba, Father; are pitied, protected, provided for, and chastened by him as by a father; yet never cast off, but seal ed to the day of redemption, and inherit the promises, as heirs of everlasting salvation.

IV. God did, from all eternity, decree to justify all the elect; and Christ did, in the fullness of time, die for their sins, and rise again for their justification: nevertheless they are not justified, until the Holy Spirit doth in due time actually apply Christ unto them.

V. God doth continue to forgive the sins of those that are justified: and although they can never fall from the state of justificaiton, yet they may by their sins fall under God's fatherly displeasure, and not have the light of his countenance restored unto them, until they humble themselves, confess their sins, beg pardon, and renew their faith and repentance.

VI. The justification of believers under the Old Testament was, in all these respects, one and the same with the justification of believers under the New Testament.

The WCF's chapter on justification shows clear evidence of mature reflection, indicating in its positive and negative affirmations the pressures of the previous century, illustrating Schaff's comment that creeds and confessions include not only that which is "fundamental and sufficient," but "such points . . . as have been disputed."[15] By contrast, the chapter on adoption vindicates Candlish's lament that:

> The creeds and confessions of the Protestant and Reformed Churches, as well as the theological systems of their colleges, are for the most part extremely meagre and defective in what they say on the subject [of adoption]. In some it is not even noticed; in others it is made a part of justification, or a mere appendix to it; in none, I

---

[15] Philip Schaff, *The Creeds of Christendom: With a History and Critical Notes*, volume 1, ed. P. Schaff, rev. D. S. Schaff. Sixth ed. (reprinted from the 1931 ed.; Grand Rapids: Baker, 1990), 4.

believe, does it receive sufficiently full and distinct treatment. Hence [reflecting on Victorian liberalism] perhaps it is that the doctrine of the fatherhood has been so little understood and so much abused in recent days.[16]

There are several explanations for these dichotomized treatments of justification and adoption.

In the first place, debates over justification did not relent. Whereas the Reformation era was characterized by contention with Rome, in the post-Reformation era debates over justification developed within Protestantism. Despite the clarity of the Westminster Standards, these continued thereafter and took various forms, such as Arminianism and Neonomianism.[17] Arminianism espoused a universal view of the atonement. But how could Christ's death be efficacious, many Puritans asked, if all it accomplishes is the possibility of immunity from sin's penalty? Additionally, how can justification be free if faith, on the Arminian understanding, is not wholly God's gift but the exercise of free will? Without an able exponent other than John Goodwin, the Arminians struggled to answer such questions and to make inroads into Puritanism.

Neonomianism had greater success, for it was less radical in some senses than Arminianism and had the influential backing of Richard Baxter. Baxterianism, as Neonomianism was otherwise known, sought to defend God's free grace in justification against both Antinomian abuses and Roman Catholic charges that Protestants cheapened divine grace. Accordingly, Neonomians taught that in the gospel God requires a double righteousness—Christ's (which they called the new law) and the believer's (a believing and penitent obedience to the new law).

---

[16] Candlish, *The Fatherhood of God*, 193.

[17] In the following, I am indebted to J. I. Packer who, besides aberrant theology lists pride, spiritual frivolity, satanic hostility, and natural religion as the influences most influencing the defensive posture of the Puritans (*Among God's Giants: The Puritan Vision of the Christian Life* (Eastbourne: Kingsway, 1991), 196–99.

Critics of Neonomianism were quick to point out that when we supplement Christ's righteousness, we wrest justification from its sole foundation in the imputed righteousness of Christ. In this scheme, explains Packer, it is faith—constituting a real obedience to the gospel (God's new law)—and not Christ's righteousness that is imputed for righteousness.[18]

The debate over Neonomianism came to a head during the protracted Crispian controversy of 1690–99. It began with Baxter's vehement opposition to the republication of the said Antinomian sermons of Tobias Crisp (1600–1643), and kept Presbyterians and Congregationalists preoccupied with the respective merits and demerits of Neonomianism and Antinomianism, involving an array of doctrines: regeneration and conversion, the nature of Christ's death, the imputation of his righteousness to the elect, the nature of the covenant of grace, the free offer of the gospel, and the sins of the elect.

Philosopher John Locke spoke for many when he recalled how the controversy led him "into a stricter and more thorough inquiry into the question about justification." Yet the tensions resolved little and did nothing for the profile of adoption. They produced, it seems, more heat than light. Peter Toon writes of the debate: "Harsh controversy always seems to have the unfortunate effect of forcing most contestants logically to develop their thought to conclusions which they really never intended to reach. If this is so, heated theological controversy (as against "dialogue") is very dangerous. . . . Therefore, Christian charity should teach theologians to live peaceably with their brethren who hold different views."[19]

Second, in contrast with the WCF's distinguishing of justification and adoption, there developed the idea of subsuming adoption

---

[18] Packer, *Among God's Giants*, 207.

[19] Peter Toon, *Puritans and Calvinism* (Swengel, PA, 1973), 87–89 and 93–96, 100. John Locke as cited by Victor Nuovo in John Locke, *The Reasonableness of Christianity as Delivered in the Scriptures*, Reprint from 1794 ed. (Bristol: Thoemmes Press, 1997), x.

under justification. This we may trace back to Heinrich Bullinger: "Paul putteth faith for an assured confidence in the merits of Christ, and he useth justification for absolution and remission of sins, for adoption into the number of the sons of God, and lastly for the imputing of Christ his righteousness unto us."[20] J. V. Fesko lists William Perkins, John Davenant, Johann Heidegger, and Franz (Franciscus) Burman as also positing similar formulations.[21] Conversely, Fesko numbers John Owen amid those who treat adoption in its own right, and yet, as Edward Morris has pointed out, adoption was "not so much a separate or added benefit as an integral part or feature of justification itself—a presentation in the language of Owen, of the blessings of justification in new phases and relations".[22]

Although defenders of Protestant scholasticism advocate the avoidance of the blame game, the test case of adoption attributes the obscuring of the distinctiveness of adoption mostly to Francis Turretin's *Institutio Elencticae Theologiae*. Therein, Turretin discusses

---

[20] Quoted from Bullinger's *Decades* in J. V. Fesko, *The Theology of the Westminster Standards: Historical Context and Theological Insights* (Wheaton, Illinois: Crossway, 2014), 234.

[21] Fesko errs in including William Ames in his list. Ames treats adoption as distinct but inseparable from justification. Adoption is not subsumed under justification but is founded upon it (Cf., Fesko *The Theology of the Westminster Standards*, 235, and William Ames, *The Marrow of Theology*, transl. From the third Latin ed. (1629) by John Dykstra Eusden (Durham, North Carolina: The Labyrinth Press, 1968), 1.28.5–8 (165).

[22] Edward D. Morris, *Theology of the Westminster Symbols: A Commentary Historical, Doctrinal, Practical on the Confession of Faith and Catechisms and the Related Formularies of the Presbyterian Churches* (Columbus, OH: Champlin Press, 1900), 450. Morris, though, is not precise in lumping Owen and Thomas Watson together. Watson deals with adoption distinctly from justification as is clear from his *A Body of Divinity*, first published in 1692; reprinted as a revised edition in limp format (Edinburgh and Carlisle, PA: The Banner of Truth Trust, 1983), 231–40. To say, as Morris and Fesko do, that adoption is "a concomitant of justification" does not mean to say, as they seem to imply, that adoption is subsumed under justification. The one doctrine is a concomitant of justification simply because, literally, it follows on from justification in the explication of soteriology.

the nature of the adoption given *in* justification. Adoption, he opines, is but "the other part of justification . . . or the bestowal of a right to life, flowing from Christ's righteousness, which acquired for us not only deliverance from death, but also a right to life by the adoption with which he endows us."[23]

Turretin's view would not have mattered so much were it not for his protracted influence. We saw in the first chapter how his nephew, Pictet, in popularizing Turretin's thought helped extend it, but that was only the start. Commenting on Turretin's minimalist view of adoption, Douglas Kelly writes:

> The majority of Reformed teachers followed their great textbook master in this sad omission, thus removing much of the central Biblical picture of family relationship from the theological curriculum. None can doubt that this narrowing down of the crucial relationship of redeemed humans to the Holy God into only forensic terms (crucial as the forensic element is to the Gospel) impacted the preaching of their students into a more legal, and less familial direction.[24]

Notable among these Reformed teachers was the premier Princeton systematician, Charles Hodge (1797–1878). Drawing from Turretin's *Institutio* Hodge unsurprisingly makes next to nothing of adoption in his *Systematic Theology*.

Although Charles' son A. A. Hodge (1823–86) went the other way, suggesting that adoption is a capstone sitting astride justification and regeneration (the view more recently taken up by Lloyd-Jones and

---

[23] Francis Turretin, *The Institutes of Elenctic Theology*, vol. 2, transl. G. M. Giger and ed. J. T. Dennison Jr. (Phillipsburg, NJ: P&R, 1994), 666 (cf., Ferguson, "The Reformed Doctrine of Sonship," 83, and Candlish, *The Fatherhood of God*, 158).

[24] Douglas F. Kelly, "Adoption: An Underdeveloped Heritage of the Westminster Standards" (*Reformed Theological Review* 52:3 [Sept.–Dec. 1993]), 112; cf., Ferguson, "The Reformed Doctrine of Sonship", 83; Errol Hulse, "Recovering the Doctrine of Adoption," (*Reformation Today* 105 (1988), 10. Whaling is simply mistaken to say that "Turretin recognizes the central place of adoption in the application of redemption" ("Adoption," 234). Robert Webb is closer to the truth: Turretin "sinks [adoption] well-nigh out of sight" (*The Reformed Doctrine of Adoption*, 17).

now David Garner), the subsuming of adoption under justification was oft-repeated, even beyond Princeton.

Consider the thought of Robert L. Dabney (1820–98), of Union Theological Seminary, Virginia. In his 903-page *Syllabus and Notes of the Course of Systematic and Polemic Theology*, he allots adoption but twenty-two lines. While this was more than many others, his comment that Turretin devotes "only a brief separate discussion to it, and introduces it in the thesis in which he proves that justification is both pardon and acceptance" is complacent at best. Dabney opines: "The chief doctrinal importance of this idea . . . is, that we have here, the strongest proof of the correctness of our definition of justification, and of the imputed righteousness upon which it is based, in the fact that it is both a pardon and an adoption." [25]

The soteric battles of the Reformation era and the inevitable tensions and discussions of the post-Reformation era ensured the prolonging of the preoccupation with justification into the eighteen and nineteenth centuries. While the need to defend the free grace of justification was certainly real, a defensive mindset was forged accordingly which focused on the retrospective and forensic aspects of the gospel at the expense of those more prospective and relational (especially familial).

This prolonging was aided by the broader threats to theological orthodoxy of the age of reason. Therein, science, philosophy, and rationalism cast doubt on the supernatural content of Christianity; Deism, a reemergent Arianism, and Socinianism, were spawned; and Christianity began to be viewed relativistically amid the growing consciousness of the world religions. Inevitably, then, the need for a consolidating orthodoxy obscured the counterbalancing necessity of

---

[25] Robert L. Dabney, *Systematic Theology* (*Syllabus and Notes of the Course of Systematic and Polemic Theology Taught in Union Theological Seminary, Virginia*), first published 1871; facsimile reprint ed. [Edinburgh and Carlisle PA: The Banner of Truth Trust, 1985], 627).

one more creative. Thus, the defense of established truths took precedence over the enhancing of the Reformation heritage.[26]

Despite, then, the inclusion of adoption in the Westminster Standards, discussions of the doctrine became ever more isolated in Presbyterianism thereafter. From the mid-seventeenth century, the look and feel of everyday Presbyterian theology began to diverge from the Standards. Both retained a rather ratiocinated approach to the systemic layout of doctrine, but the former became increasingly retrospective and forensic.

We are heirs of this lopsidedness. Jonathan Edwards, for instance, is better known for his sermons on justification by faith (1734) than for his interest in adoption. Likewise, George Whitefield's appeals to the masses to be right with God (and to be born again) overshadow the little we know of his attention to adoption (chiefly the Spirit of adoption). Thus, the age of reason's isolated discussions of adoption highlights the doctrine's overall neglect in the everyday theology of Reformed orthodoxy. Such discussions, however, were insufficient to counteract it.

Typically, critics of the Reformed orthodoxy of the period failed to distinguish its general ossification among the Reformed orthodox from the theology of the Westminster Standards. In effect, the Westminster Standards suffer on account of their friends. Thus, the first step to a better defense of Reformed orthodoxy lies in recognizing the reactionary psyche our Protestant (specifically our Reformed) forebears developed in consequence of the recurring need to defend the free grace of justification.

Such recognition is two centuries late but is better late than never. Think back on McLeod Campbell's reaction to the ossified orthodoxy he encountered in early-nineteenth-century Scotland. His

---

[26] Tim J. R. Trumper, "An Historical Study of the Doctrine of Adoption in the Calvinistic Tradition" (University of Edinburgh: Ph.D. Diss., 2001), ch. 6; Tim J. R. Trumper, *When History Teaches Us Nothing: The Recent Reformed Sonship Debate in Context* (Eugene, OR: Wipf and Stock, 2008), 1–32.

protest for the paternal grace of God sought to balance the retrospective (what we are saved *from*) and prospective (what we are saved *to*) aspects of the atonement. This important kernel of truth was lost, however, on the Reformed orthodox of Campbell's day. Only in the 1860s did Candlish note in writing the shortcomings of our Reformation heritage. If, he wrote, the penal satisfaction of Christ

> is the only mode of God's dealing with Christ, and with those whom Christ answers for in the judgment . . . there may undoubtedly be some risk of its degenerating into barren and dogmatic orthodoxy. It would be a curious and interesting speculation to inquire whether we may not thus, to some extent at least, account for the lapse of the theology of the Reformation in the schools and colleges of the Continent, as well as among ourselves, first into rigid and frigid scholastic systematizing, and then into rationalism.[27]

Nevertheless, Jack Miller's latter twentieth-century replaying of McLeod Campbell's protest reveals our slowness to discern the need to balance the retrospective and prospective, as also the legal and the relational (familial) aspects of the gospel.

3. NEGLECT THROUGH EXCISION

It is one thing for the church to overlook adoption, especially when preoccupied by the defense of other biblical truths, but quite another for her members to suppress and/or to willfully excise adoption from the theology of the church. While such a claim sounds conspiratorial, the idea is supported by evidence that, previously, has been largely missed on account of the church's preoccupation with other doctrines.

The following examples of excision are standing tributes to the neglect of adoption, for what other soteric elements could suffer willful suppression with so few noticing? Imagine how a systematician's work would be received if he or she were to omit regeneration, justification, or sanctification from his or her soteriology, or to allow one of these elements to be so absorbed by a neighboring doctrine that it virtually

---

[27] Candlish, *The Fatherhood of God*, 166–67.

disappears. There would be a great demand for an explanation. Not so, to date, with excisions of adoption.

The case of John Wesley.

In Pauline theology, there is an inextricable link between adoption and predestination. In interpreting the apostle, Calvin understood Ephesians 1:4-5 to function as the *locus classicus* of predestination, taking precedence over Romans 9 by dint of its clearer pastoral, doxological, and practical implications. The connection between predestination and adoption is also clear in the WCF. The third chapter, "Of God's Eternal Decree," states, "Neither are any other redeemed, by Christ, effectually called, justified, adopted, sanctified, and saved, but the elect only" (3:6). The connection is replicated in the WSC.

Yet, when John Wesley revised the WSC he expunged every reference to adoption. Given Wesley's emphasis on the Spirit of adoption and assurance we ponder why he did so.[28] He may have felt that there are no words that adequately express the assurance the Holy Spirit works in the children of God. Yet, this does not explain why he would banish from his revised catechism a biblical term so expressive of the confidence of God's sons.

According to James MacDonald, Wesley was seeking to set in contrast justification and sanctification. Recall from the Westminster Standards how adoption sits between justification and sanctification, hindering, in a straight-through reading, an immediate comparison of justification and sanctification (WSC 33–35; WLC 70–75; and WCF 11–13). Certainly, by omitting adoption from the sequence, Wesley could

---

[28] John Wesley's "Revision of the Shorter Catechism," *The Banner of Truth Magazine* 47 (March–April 1967), 24, reprinted from James A. MacDonald's *Wesley's Revision of the Shorter Catechism* (Edinburgh: Geo. A. Morton, 1906), and taken in turn from Wesley's Christian Library, specifically An Extract from the Assembly's Shorter Catechism: with the proofs thereof out of the Scriptures (babel.hathitrust.org/ cgi/pt?id=hvd.ah4dqq; view=2up;seq=4, accessed October 19, 2017).

juxtapose justification and sanctification and demonstrate thereby that they are two distinct but inseparable blessings. Yet, MacDonald's description of the distinction as objective and subjective aspects of the gospel is too simplistic. Bear in mind that sanctification in its definitive aspect (Acts 26:18; 1 Cor. 1:2) is also objective. Also simplistic is the belief that Wesley omitted adoption from the WSC for reasons of brevity and symmetry.

MacDonald discerns, however, the most likely reason for Wesley's excisions, namely, his attempt to sidestep the close connection in the WSC and in Scripture between adoption and the decree of God. While I cannot go along with MacDonald's belief that predestination is a product of Scholasticism, how better to explain Wesley's deletion or alteration of all the questions and answers relating to the decree of God? Numbers 7, 8, 20, 31, 34 are deleted, and numbers 14, 21, 30, 32, 35, 36, and 37 are altered. Although Wesley approved of the WSC and its statements on adoption, he sought, in MacDonald's words, to shear it of all scholastic traces. Yet, predestination, the stubborn fact remains, is a biblical doctrine.

MacDonald is of the view, influenced by Wesley's works, that if Wesley had been of a mind to add to the WSC he would have replaced WSC 31 and 34 on effectual calling and adoption with material on the new birth. After all, the new birth is key to Wesley's theology and was the mainspring of the Methodist Revival. MacDonald's assessment, though, is questionable on two grounds.

First, from a Calvinistic perspective, the insertion of the new birth would do nothing to sidestep Westminster's affirmation of the absolute decree of God. After all, the new birth is, in Westminister's understanding, a monergistic work of the Spirit in the hearts of the elect (Jn. 1:13, 3:3-8). Wesley would have known this.

Second, had Wesley substituted Questions and Answers on the new birth for those on adoption, in MacDonald's words because the new birth "is everywhere in evangelical circles today recognized to be the grand truth brought fully into light in the New Testament, the doctrine around which the whole body of New Testament experiential theology circles,"[29] he would have demonstrated most clearly the neglect of adoption. As it is, MacDonald's positing of this possibility denotes that very reality.

Certainly, we revel in the biblical teaching of regeneration (the new birth) and affirm the importance of its inclusion in the discussion of the Christian faith, but we see no reason why the doctrine of adoption should be excised from our theology to make room for it, and certainly not on account of its close connection to predestination. Rather, we receive the Scriptures on their own terms.

The case of Thomas Erskine.

Transitioning from Wesley to Thomas Erskine of Linlathen, we advance from eighteenth-century England to nineteenth-century Scotland. Erskine's influence on the Victorian protest for paternal grace reminds us that a valid protest does not guarantee a valid solution. Indeed, his gradual substitution of the juridically lopsided Calvinism of his day for an eisegetical universalism of his own making caused more problems than it solved.

Ironically, the young Erskine had been one of the few Calvinists around to include adoption in his thinking. His earliest mention of the doctrine is found in his introduction to Richard Baxter's *The Saints' Everlasting Rest* (1824). There, he describes God's family as the adopted in Christ. They are the sons of God who first suffer with Christ and then are glorified together with him. Expressing the eschatological character of Pauline theology, Erskine notes that while God's sons have the charter of their adoption already (which authorizes them to speak to their heavenly Father), they wait in earnest anticipation of the full manifestation of their privileges—most obviously the redemption of their bodies. "There is," he says, "but one joy and one adoption; but they contain the principle of infinite expansion and enlargement."[30]

---

[29] *Wesley's Revision of the Shorter Catechism*, iii, viii–x, 9.

[30] Richard Baxter, *The Saints' Everlasting Rest*, with an introductory essay by Thomas Erskine *Esq.*, 1824, xxxii–xxxiii (no other details are given).

The following year Erskine wrote an introductory essay for the Collins edition of the *Letters of Samuel Rutherford*. Again, he expresses a familial understanding of the gospel within the full range of its juridical elements. This time he mentions adoption explicitly, but once:

> A restoration to spiritual health is the *ultimate object* of God in His dealings with the children of men. Whatever else God hath done with regard to men, has been subsidiary, and with a view to this; even the unspeakable work of Christ, and pardon freely offered through His cross, have been but means to a further end; and that end is, that the adopted children of the family of God might be conformed to the likeness of their elder brother,—that they might resemble Him in character, and thus enter into His joy.

Nevertheless, Erskine retains brief reference to the implications of adoption, writing, for instance, of "the rights and immunities of God's family [which] consist in possessing the favour of God, in approaching to him at all times as our Father, in enjoying what he enjoys, in rejoicing to see his will accomplished through the wide range of his dominions, and in being ourselves made instruments in accomplishing it."[31]

Later, in a letter dated November 11, 1832, Erskine mentions but in passing the Spirit of adoption. Evidently, then, a process was underway in his thought: the more he relinquished the need of adoption the more general his familial or filial references became. By the publication of his volume *The Doctrine of Election* (1837), his universalistic trajectory had become quite apparent: "I may observe here, that it was not merely to prove his love, and his readiness to make a sacrifice, that God gave his Son to the world; but because he desired to make the world *sons of God*. The gift of the Son was the gift of *sonship*; the only-begotten Son is the Fountain of adoption." In other words, in the gift of the Son the world has its adoption. Only, though, in his final book, *The Spiritual Order* (1871), which was published posthumously,

---

[31] *Letters of the Rev. Samuel Rutherford, with an introductory essay by Thomas Erskine, Esq.*, third ed. Glasgow: William Collins, 1830, x–xiii, xv (cf., xvi); John B. Logan, "Thomas Erskine of Linlathen: Lay Theologian of the 'Inner Light'," *SJT* 37 (1984), 24.

did Erskine reveal beyond doubt that he had become a Universalist. All references to adoption are gone.[32]

Erskine's defection from Calvinism to Universalism is regrettable for two reasons: First, because he could have influenced the Reformed orthodox to recover the familial side of the gospel, specifically the doctrine of adoption, and thereby to balance the legal and familial aspects of the gospel. Second, because his final Universalism ensured no place for adoption other than in some vague notion of the universal adoption in the gift of the Son. In actuality, Universalism renders irrelevant the receipt of adoption through faith in Christ. Reasons James Matthew,

> If all men are already, as men, God's children, and have always been so, it needs no adoption to make them so; if universal Fatherhood is a fact, and not a fiction, and by consequence if there be universal Sonship naturally belonging to all men, there is and there can be, so far as we can understand it, no such thing as Adoption. Adoption is, *per se*, a denial of such universality.[33]

Erskine arrived at his Universalism by pressing the theme of sonship to the exclusion of the particular language of adoption. The move weakened the link between predestination and adoption, broke Paul's inextricable connection between redemption and adoption (Rom. 9:4; Gal. 4:4-5; and Rom. 8:22-23), and eradicated the need of a legal transaction to secure sonship. In Erskine's use of *sonship*, all is exclusively relational or familial. The lopsided juridical gospel of the accepted orthodoxy of his day became an absolutist familial Unversalism.

Consider Erskine's treatment of Romans 1–9 in *The Spiritual Order*. By forgoing a sound hermeneutical and exegetical approach to

---

[32] *Letters of Thomas Erskine of Linlathen*, vol. 1 (1800–1840), ed. William Hanna (Edinburgh: David Douglas, 1877), 276; *The Doctrine of Election and its Connection with the General Tenor of Christianity*, second ed. (Edinburgh: David Douglas, 1878), 232. See also his comments on Rom. 8:12-25 (*ibid.*, 238–42).

[33] James Matthew, "The Doctrine of Sonship and the Sonship of Believers," *The Theological Review and Free Church College Quarterly* 2 (1886), 25.

the biblical text, he could make assertions concerning it without actually quoting it on more than a few occasions. When the need arose to cite an adoption text such as Romans 8:14-15, he translated υἱοθεσία as "sonship," thus swapping out the Authorized Version's (aka the King James Version's) translation of Romans 8:15 he had used in *The Doctrine of Election*. His reference to Christ as the "Fountain of adoption" is an exception, but this he changes to the "Fountain of sonship" in *The Spiritual Order*.[34]

While his slowly percolating Universalism was ingeniously concocted, Erskine's evasion of the hard graft of Spirit-led exegesis resulted from an inadvisable semi-pelagian confidence in humanity's "inner light." In effect, he exchanged trust in Scripture as the basis of his doctrinal formulation for confidence in his internal spiritual conscious-ness. Forgoing reliance on the illumination of the Spirit—which likely explains why he is so silent about the Spirit's ministry in the passage of *The Spiritual Order* under review[35]— he felt no need to justify his Universalism from the Spirit-inspired Scripture. Scripture serves, on Erskine's understanding, simply to confirm what humanity already recognizes, namely, that God is our Father. Yet Erskine underestimates the potent impact of the fall. While humanity retains the knowledge of God (Rom. 1:21), the entrance of sin into the created order has taken away our ability, outside of the gospel, to know God as Father. Only by the Spirit can men and women come by this knowledge. Our human experience can only validate the truth of the gospel in so far as it verifies, or comports with, biblical teaching.

We thus conclude, on the basis of Scripture and in line with its teaching, that Erskine's Universalism significantly distorted Scripture and denied the experience of those redeemed and adopted through

---

[34] Cf., *The Doctrine of Election*, 232 and *The Spiritual Order and other Papers Selected from the Manuscripts of the late Thomas Erskine* (Edinburgh: Edmonston and Douglas, 1871), 232.

[35] Erskine, *The Spiritual Order*, 84.

faith in Jesus Christ. His case teaches us that any theological "ism" requiring for its credibility the elimination of a biblical doctrine, can neither be of God nor merit the church's serious attention. It is important to say this, for Erskine was not the last to jettison adoption in the cause of liberal theology. We shall come in a moment to George MacDonald. Later, however, Adolf von Harnack also deemed adoption too closely related to predestination to warrant attention. In Paul's teaching, by contrast, predestination and adoption cast a luster on each other. The believer's adoption into God's household is divinely predestined, yet our predestination to adoption before the foundation of the world inspires our worship, comfort, and service as the sons and daughters of God.[36]

The case of George MacDonald.

Any doubt as to Erskine's intentional excision of adoption is removed by a remarkable sermon by Scottish man of letters, George MacDonald (1824–1905). It could not reveal more clearly the spirit of Victorian liberalism.[37]

Thirty-six years the junior of Erskine, MacDonald was born in Huntley, Aberdeenshire. Sadly, and of possible significance, his mother died in 1832. David L. Neuhouseer notes that MacDonald's father was "an earthly example of the loving heavenly Father" and proved to be "the early beginnings of his later beliefs."[38]

In 1840, MacDonald entered King's College, Aberdeen, gaining a Christian humanist education buttressed, writes Rolland Hein, by Reformed theology. Sabbath afternoons were spent studying the

---

[36] Adolf von Harnack, *What is Christianity?* Transl. Thomas Bailey Saunders (New York and Evanston: Harper and Row, Publishers, 1957), 172.

[37] The following is largely drawn from Rolland Hein, *George MacDonald: Victorian Mythmaker* (Nashville, TN: Star Song, 1993).

[38] David L. Neuhouseer, "George MacDonald and Universalism" in *George MacDonald: Literary Heritage and Heirs*, edited by Roderick McGillis (Wayne, PA: Zosima Press, 2008), 84.

Heidelberg Catechism. Later, in 1848, MacDonald entered training for pastoral ministry at dissenting academy Highbury College, London. The college shared the Calvinistic theology and evangelical spirit of his family. His relatives had been active in the Great Disruption of 1843 on the side of the Church of Scotland Free.

Even prior to entering Highbury College MacDonald began to distance himself from the evangelical world of his early years. The drift began with what MacDonald saw as an evangelical preoccupation with personal financial reward for righteous living and the outward or legalistic morality of the nation, preferring the British pound to biblical precepts, careless of the squalid poverty of the slums of London. The drift continued amid MacDonald's desire to understand his Christian experience. Reading John Bunyan's *Pilgrim's Progress,* MacDonald came to reject the doctrine of the imputed righteousness of Christ. As with others of the era, his interest in orthodox doctrine gave way to a predominant focus on the humanity of Christ and his teachings. In fairness, MacDonald was drawn to Christ's other-worldly outlook on life, contrasting it with the self-centeredness and worldliness surrounding him. Nevertheless, he substituted an important aspect of biblical revelation for the entire scope of it.

"All my teaching in youth seems useless to me—I must get it all from the Bible again," remarked MacDonald, yet, consistent with Victorian liberalism, his inner reality became the touchstone of what the Bible teaches. This emphasis on the inner reality he got not from the Bible but from German Romantics and British writers such as Samuel Taylor Coleridge (1772–1834) and William Wordsworth (1770–1850). Under their influence, he bristled at Highbury College against the propositional teaching and the "meticulous rationalist handling of theological ideas." In his view, theological reasoning needs imagination in order to be adequate.[39]

---

[39] Hein, *George MacDonald,* 37, 39, 46.

In 1850, MacDonald became minister of Trinity Congregational Church, Arundel, West Sussex, England. Yet, writes C. S. Lewis in his preface to *George MacDonald: An Anthology*, "by 1852 he was in trouble with the 'deacons' for heresy, the charges being that he had expressed belief in a future state of probation for heathens and that he was tainted with German theology." After successive pay reductions, MacDonald's position became untenable. Thus, in 1853 he left the pastoral ministry to become a freelance preacher and lecturer in literature, coming in 1856 under the patronage of Lady Byron. By that time, he had begun to write fantasy literature, developing thereafter his legacy as a novelist of Scottish life, a poet, and allegorist of man's pilgrimage back to God.

Of most interest to us is MacDonald's journey into Universalism and how his fantasist views gave rise to the most vocal attack on the doctrine of adoption known of in the history of the church. Several of the many influences on him are noteworthy.

First, there was the significant influence of Alexander John Scott (1805–66). Scott had had his license to preach revoked in 1831 by the Church of Scotland's Presbytery of Paisley for preaching Universalism and went on to fill the Chair of English Language and Literature at University College, London. Scott was like a second father to MacDonald.

Second, from the 1850s MacDonald came under the influence of the prominent Anglican theologian Frederick Denison Maurice (1805–72). Maurice emphasized the Fatherhood of God, rejected the idea of eternal punishment, and promoted the romantic idea that man has an "inner light" apart from Scripture for understanding truth. Although sounding like a Universalist, Maurice denied that he was one. And yet, as Hein writes, MacDonald "came out strongly on the side of F. D. Maurice (as well as the Unitarians) in the contemporary controversy concerning the duration of punishment of the wicked in the next life. He hoped for the eventual salvation of all people. (But in a manner quite different from the easy salvation the term *universalism* generally implies.)"[40]

Third, there is the influence of Thomas Erskine. Having retired early when his brother's estate came into his possession at Linlathen near Dundee, Erskine used his gift of hospitality to promote his views. We know that he hosted MacDonald at least once and that MacDonald shared with the older Erskine a firm assurance of God's Fatherhood. Following Erskine's death a series of "Broadlands Conferences" was held, 1874–1888, where his works were read. They were hosted by Lord and Lady Mount Temple, two of MacDonald's close friends, and organized by another friend, Russell Gurney. MacDonald was a major speaker at those conferences.[41]

Thus, we come to MacDonald's sermon "Abba, Father!" (Rom. 8:15)—a tirade against the doctrine of adoption. He begins with colorful descriptions of the doctrine. The "so-called doctrine of Adoption" is, he writes, "such a cold wind blowing at the very gate of heaven—thank God, *outside* the gate!" A "cold wind" because the doctrine is "evil," "hideous[ ]," and a "phantom." Yet, with an increasing number of Christians now awakening to the riches revealed in God's adoptive grace, we are bound to ask why MacDonald so resolutely opposed biblical teaching.[42]

MacDonald's hostility may be explained, as we have come to expect, by his Romantic notion of the inner light. He says that we may respect what good men have taught or believed, but their teaching and belief must not come between our souls and the spirit of the Father.

----

[40] Neuhouseer, "George MacDonald and Universalism," 86–87; Hein, *George MacDonald*, 188.

[41] Neuhouseer, "George MacDonald and Universalism," 85.

[42] I am indebted to Barton Priebe's *Adopted by God: Discover the Life-Transforming Joy of a Neglected Truth* (Independently published, 2021, 76), for awareness of this sermon. For support of what follows, see George MacDonald, *Unspoken Sermons: Series I, II, and III* (Radford, VA: Wilder Publications, 2008), 152.

This "feeling in human heart" creates the groaning under the weight of "the supposed authority" of the doctrine of adoption.[43]

Second, this prioritization of feeling led him to presuppose the teaching of Scripture. Gone is the Calvinist exposition of Scripture that man is by nature under the condemnation of God as Judge. Rather, all along the race has consisted of children of the Father who exist under his tutelage. Thus, "when a heart hears—and believes, or half believes—that it is not the child of God by origin, from the first of its being, but may possibly be adopted into his family, its love sinks at once in a cold faint: where is its own father, and who is this that would adopt it?" On MacDonald's reckoning, then, adoption is very unsatisfactory, for it implies we belonged to another before we belonged to the one in whose image we were made.[44]

Third, MacDonald proclaimed "Away with your Adoption!" because the teaching, based on the English translation of υἱοθεσία, misleads us in regard to what the apostle Paul taught. MacDonald thus impugns the motives of those translating υἱοθεσία as *adoption*. In contradictory fashion he writes:

> It is not for me to judge the learned and good men who have revised the translation of the New Testament—with so much gain to every one whose love of truth is greater than his loving prejudice for accustomed form—I can only say, I wonder what may have been their reasons for retaining the word *adoption*.

MacDonald supposes that the translation is a concession to popular theology. For support of his denial of the etymology of υἱοθεσία (the placement of a son [*child* says MacDonald]), he points to Luther's

---

[43] MacDonald, *Unspoken Sermons*, 152. C. S. Lewis notes that of all the stories of emancipation in the nineteenth century from Calvinistic upbringings which resulted in hatred for early influences, "I find no trace in MacDonald. It is not we who have to find extenuating circumstances for his point of view. On the contrary, it is he himself, in the very midst of his intellectual revolt, who forces us, whether we will or no, to see elements of real and perhaps irreplaceable worth in the thing from which he is revolting" (Preface, *George MacDonald: An Antology*, xxv).

[44] MacDonald, *Unspoken Sermons*, 152–53.

translation, *Kindschaft* (literally, childhood), and posits two arguments in favor of retranslating Paul's term. First, that Paul did not intend *adoption*. This MacDonald seeks to prove from Galatians 4:1-7, Romans 9:4, Ephesians 1:5, and Romans 8:23. Second, that the idea of adoption comes between God and our hearts.[45]

This outspoken rejection of the church's normative understanding of adoption requires a response. MacDonald was well aware of this, and thus supplies proactively his *coup de grâce*: "If to any reader my interpretation be unsatisfactory, I pray him not to spend his strength in disputing my faith, but in making sure his own progress on the way to freedom and sonship. Only to the child of God is true judgment possible." Stated alternatively, "If you don't agree with me, just forgo disagreeing!" Progress in freedom and sonship requires, however, an exegetical rather than an eisegetical understanding of Scripture and of Paul in particular.[46]

Debunking the belief in the universal Fatherhood of God and brotherhood of man requires a monograph. We can, however, offer a few remarks here.

First, MacDonald's supreme confidence in the human heart is rooted in emotionalism, one of the main historic challenges to the supremacy of Scripture. Scripture is challenged by traditionalism (notably but not exclusively in Roman Catholicism), and rationalism (what seems reasonable to the human mind, as in Enlightenment and post-Enlightenment thought). Emotionalism suppresses Scripture by subjecting its truth to what feels acceptable—a trend found in post-Enlightenment Romanticism and now also in Postmodernism. MacDonald's emotionalism caused him not to give up the Christian faith but to reshape it according to his feelings.

---

[45] MacDonald, *Unspoken Sermons*, 154–61. Despite the use of Romans 8:15 at the head of the sermon, MacDonald omits it from consideration without explanation, perhaps because it is a variant reading.

[46] MacDonald, *Unspoken Sermons*, 161.

He upheld, for instance, the justice of God, not as the condemnation from which God's justifying and adopting grace liberates us, but as God's paternal mercy in destroying the sins of his children. There is in MacDonald's schema, then, no place for God's just punishment of our sins. As is so often the case, error is discerned not by what it teaches but by what it omits. It *is* God's will, ultimately, to destroy the sins of his people, but first they are punished at the cross. We do need more of the spirit (better, Spirit) in the discussion of Christian doctrine, but whereas the human spirit, left to itself, leads us into error, the Holy Spirit, illuminating the Word he inspired, leads us into all truth (Jn. 16:13).[47]

Second, MacDonald's emotionalism meant, ironically, that he forewent, as a man of literature, a reliable reading of Holy Scripture. Making much of the humanity of Christ, we assume he would make much of the humanness of Scripture, its authorial diversity, multiple perspectives, and figures of speech. While they seem to bespeak contradictions in Scripture—between, for example, God's love and goodness in his general or creative Fatherhood over all creation and his justice in expelling his image-bearers from the Garden of Eden; and between our condemnation by nature and our adoption by God's paternal grace—such perspectives remind us that God and his ways are beyond us. To accommodate his revelation to our finite capacities, God has given us multiple individual glimpses of his character and saving grace which, seemingly contradictory, help us with our limited capacities to grasp important aspects of his being and his ways.

Instead of humbly accepting these tensions within the Bible's system of theology, MacDonald attempted to iron them out by his own ingenuity. By denying that Paul was "contribut[ing] towards a system of theology,"[48] he obtained for himself the freedom to pare down the juridical elements of the apostle's theology, reshaping the remaining

---

[47] See MacDonald's sermon, "Justice," in *Unspoken Sermons*, 268–89.

[48] MacDonald's sermon, "Abba, Father," *Unspoken Sermons*, 159.

familial elements into a theological system of his own making. MacDonald thus replaced the highly logicized systems of Reformed-orthodox theology with his emotionally driven equivalent.

Third, MacDonald's attempt to deny that υἱοθεσία has any connotation of adoption into sonship is now debunked by etymological, metaphorical, and exegetical studies. To transform Paul's uses of υἱοθεσία into more general references to the life of sonship is a nice try, but wholly flawed. This we shall demonstrate in the next chapter. Suffice it to say here, that MacDonald's attempt to promote a universalism in which the Father merely teaches his race of children to be what they were created to be, lacks both biblical and experiential credibility. It was, as his American readers understood, "a new gospel."[49]

4. NEGLECT THROUGH ABSORPTION

This fourth cause of the plight of adoption could have been included under the second (specifically, the preoccupation with the

---

[49] Hein, *George MacDonald*, 237. MacDonald's rejection of the Reformed and Evangelical faith of his youth for his "new gospel" renders complex C. S. Lewis' evangelical credentials. Lewis affirmed MacDonald as "my master," but note, not as a man of letters (deeming him a second rank writer at best), but as a "Christian teacher" (Preface, *George MacDonald: An Antology*). True, MacDonald's *Phantasies* brought Lewis out of atheism, but it is perplexing that Lewis' narration of his journey to Christianity in *Surprised by Joy* ends, as in Victorian liberalism, at the incarnation rather than at the cross. We thus rely on Lewis the disciple to make more of the atonement than on Lewis the convert. Alternatively, we are faced with the possibility that Lewis' conversion to Christianity was more intellectual than spiritual. The Lord knows. Either way, and without decrying his usefulness in Apologetics, his ownership of MacDonald as his Christian teacher raises concern about the appropriateness of the moniker "the patron saint of American Evangelicalism," and its propagation within the camp (Philip Ryken, "Lewis as the Patron Saint of American Evangelicalism" in *C. S. Lewis and the Church: Essays in Honour of Walter Hooper*, edited by Judith Wolfe and Brendan N. Wolfe [London and New York: T&T Clark International, 2011], 174–85; Alister McGrath, *C. S. Lewis: A Life* (Carol Stream, IL: Tyndale House Publisher, Inc., 2013), 371–76.

doctrine of justification), for here we take up the so-called NPP.[50] It could also have been included under the third (the excision of adoption), depending on how we interpret N. T. Wright's redefining of justification. Since, however, Wright has gone so far as to absorb adoption in justification, it seems fitting to see in his version of the NPP another reason for the neglect of adoption.

We focus on N. T. Wright not because he seminally influenced the NPP (think rather of Krister Stendahl, E. P. Sanders, and James Dunn), but because he developed as a theologian in conservative Reformed and evangelical circles, and because, in redefining the classic Protestant doctrine of justification, he became, in the popular mind, the voice of the NPP.[51]

Wright's understanding of justification was laid out originally and succinctly in his chapter, "Justification: The Biblical Basis and its Relevance for Contemporary Evangelicalism" (1980). There he expounds the doctrine in an appealing fashion, first from the Old Testament, and then from the various perspectives of the New Testament: The Gospels and Acts, Paul (Gal., Phil., and Rom.) and other authors. The methodology is sound, the details less so. Two features stand out: his communal or familial definition of justification and his silence about adoption. On these features hang the case for Wright's absorption of adoption in his redefined view of justification.

---

[50] The NPP label is not really about Paul. It is about first century Judaism. Moreover, it is not really new. See Peter Stuhlmacher, *Revisiting Paul's Doctrine of Justification: A Challenge to the New Perspective,* with an essay by Donald A. Hagner (Downers Grove, IL: IVP Academic, 2001), 33–52. "With its radical reinterpretation of Paul's gospel, especially his doctrine of justification," opines Seyoon Kim, "the New Perspective School is in many respects overturning the Reformation interpretation of Paul's gospel. The potential significance of the school for the whole Christian faith can hardly be exaggerated." (*Paul and the New Perspective: Second Thoughts on the Origin of Paul"s Gospel* [Grand Rapids: Eerdmans, 2002], xiv).

[51] See Wright's early coauthorship of *The Grace of God in the Gospel* with three other Oxford undergraduates, John Cheeseman, Philip Gardner, and Michael Sadgrove (Edinburgh: The Banner of Truth Trust, 1971).

"Justification," he says, "is God's declaration that certain people are within the covenant." In other words, "those who believe the Gospel are in the right, [and] are members of the covenant family."[52]

Wright clearly rejects Luther's individualistic definition of justification. While it comports with the biblical question, "how can a man be in the right before God?" (Job 9:2), it is detached from the larger picture of God's covenantal purposes for his people. "For Paul, as for Jesus," Wright argues, "the salvation of the individual is set in the context of God's redefinition of Israel, his call of a worldwide family whose sins are forgiven in the blood of the new covenant."[53] He errs, though, in the manner of his proceeding. The very notion of the covenant family begs talk of adoption, for there is in Paul an inextricable connection between the ideas of covenant and adoption. Adoption has its own term, context, and climactic use in three of Paul's major epistles. Adoption is the *telos* of predestination (Eph. 1:4-5), a way of understanding God's covenant dealings with his people in Old Testament history (Rom. 9:4), central to the gospel (Gal. 4:4-5) and the Christian life (Rom. 8:15-16); and is the climax of the entire history of salvation (Rom. 8:22-23).

It is bewildering that Wright should ignore adoption in his formative expositions of Galatians and Romans. Reminiscent of Erskine and MacDonald, Wright translates υἱοθεσία as *sonship* when citing Romans 8:14-17 and Galatians 4:1-7. Nowhere is his silence about adoption more deafening than when he states that, "Romans 8 points to

---

[52] Tom (N. T.) Wright, "Justification: The Biblical Basis and its Relevance for Contemporary Evangelicalism" in *The Great Acquittal: Justification by Faith and Current Christian Thought*, coauthored by Tony Baker, George Carey, John Tiller, and Tom Wright (London: Collins, 1980), 15. This definition has not changed over the years: "'Justification' is the doctrine which insists that all those who have this faith belong as full members of this family on this basis and no other." (*What Saint Paul Really Said: Was Paul of Tarsus the Real Founder of Christianity?* [Grand Rapids: Eerdmans, 1997], 133).

[53] Wright, "Justification," 21.

the crowning glory of Paul's doctrine of justification." Clearly, justification is of vital importance to Paul—"Who shall bring any charge against God's elect? It is God who justifies" (8:33)—but it is in Romans 8 that Paul introduces adoption as the climactic motif of all that has gone before, of our personal salvation, and the overall history of salvation. It is, writes Paul, for "the adoption" that the whole creation yearns (8:17-23).

Whereas Turretin, Dabney, Vos, and others said very openly that they understood adoption to be but the positive side of justification, in Wright's redefining of justification adoption is entirely absorbed, and without explanation. We are thus left to ponder whether:[54]

- Wright is influenced by the historic neglect of adoption and has forgotten the place of adoption in Pauline soteriology. This is possible but would question his authority to speak of historical theology when justifying his redefining of justification.
- Wright has forgone an investigation of the specific meaning of υἱοθεσία, and thus assumes his redefinition, utilizing *sonship*, accords with it. This, too, is possible but throws into doubt the quality of his investigation of the biblical text.
- Wright knows very well that υἱοθεσία means *adoption as son*, but has chosen the translation *sonship* to accommodate his new definition of justification. This also is possible but would constitute a willful distortion of the New Testament doctrine of justification and supply another example of the excision of adoption.
- Wright has been theologically unclear, and that all along he meant to do justice to adoption as well as to justification. This is possible, but he needs now to jetison publicly his redefining of justification.

---

[54] Wright, "Justification," 26, 27, 29, 36, and 116. See *What Saint Paul Really Said*, 95–133, for the same omission of adoption.

The several decades it has taken for the Christian community to appreciate the strategic significance of adoption for the refuting of Wright's redefining of justification demonstrates how deeply ingrained is its neglect. Too often refutations have constituted but loud repetitions of the classic Protestant understanding of justification, oblivious to the strategic role adoption plays in answering Wright's main concerns. As with responses to Victorian liberalism and, more recently, to Jack Miller, refutations of Wright have so fixated on what is awry with his redefining of justification as to overlook the kernel of truth in his protest against its historic Protestant expositions. Adherents of the classic doctrine have consistently missed the seismic opportunity adoption offers us to both defend the reformers' understanding of justification and to answer Wright's concern to balance the historical and the logical, the individualistic and the communal, and the juridical and the familial elements of biblical soteriology.

This in-house Protestant standoff over justification has been crystallized in counterstatements of John Piper and N. T. Wright. There follows the closest that Piper gets in *The Future of Justification* (2007) to scratching where Wright is itching:

> Our relationship with God is with One who has become for us an omnipotent Father committed to working all things together for our everlasting enjoyment of him. This relationship was established at the point of our justification when God removed his judicial wrath from us, and imputed the obedience of his Son to us, and counted us as righteous in Christ, and forgave all our sins because he had punished them in the death of Jesus.[55]

Piper's statement cries out, however, for the injection of the doctrine of adoption. In classic Protestant soteriology at its best, the communal and familial emphases of adoption complemented the juridical and personal implications of justification. Thus, attempts to refute a redefined justification entailing historical, corporate, and familial elements by

---

[55] John Piper, *The Future of Justification: A Response to N. T. Wright* (Wheaton, IL: Crossway Books, 2007), 185.

means of a classic definition of justification shorn of the distinct but inseparable and complementary historical, communal, and familial elements of adoption have inevitably failed. The retrieval of adoption thus challenges traditional Protestants to discern the kernel of truth in Wright's protest, while acknowledging their own historically lopsided, juridical, logical, and individualistic appropriation of the gospel. Correspondingly, the retrieval challenges Wright to jettison the historical novelty and exegetical fallacy of his redefined justification.

In pursuit of this retrieval, I concur with Wright that there is no pure return to the Reformation and that our priority must be to return to the New Testament. But before conceding a disjuncture between the New Testament and the reformers, we must consider the balance of Calvin, for it has been lost on advocates of both sides of the debate. Describing justification as the "main hinge on which religion turns," Calvin, as we saw in chapter one, nevertheless claims that the "grace of adoption . . . bestows salvation entire."[56] By according attention to both justification and adoption, Calvin held together the historical/logical, juridical/ relational (familial), and the personal/communal. We would do well to emulate his approach today.

Admittedly, the imputation of Christ's righteousness to the believer remains a contentious matter. Nevertheless, movement toward *rapprochement* remains possible since friends and foes of the NPP agree, that, to one degree or another, the New Testament *does* teach imputation. Listen carefully to what Wright says of 1 Corinthians 1:30:

> It is the only passage I know where something called "the imputed righteousness of Christ," a phrase more often found in post-

---

[56] *Inst.* 3:11:1 (*CO* 2 [30]:533). In his sermon on Lk. 1:5-10, Calvin preaches that justification is "the principle of the whole doctrine of salvation and of the foundation of all religion" (cited François Wendel, *Calvin* [London: Collins, 1963], 256). His assessment of adoption is found in *Calvin's Tracts and Treatises*, vol. 3, transl. Henry Beveridge, historical notes and introduction to the current edition by T. F. Torrance (Edinburgh: Oliver and Boyd, 1958), 275 [*CO* 7 {35}: 619]). Cf. N. T. Wright, *Justification: God's Plan and Paul's Vision* (Downers Grove, IL: IVP Academic, 2009), 72.

Reformation theology and piety than in the New Testament, finds any basis in the text. But if we are to claim it as such, we must also be prepared to talk of the imputed wisdom of Christ; the imputed sanctification of Christ; and the imputed redemption of Christ; and that, though no doubt they are all true in some general sense, will certainly make nonsense of the very specialized and technical senses so frequently given to the phrase "the righteousness of Christ" in the history of theology.[57]

Thus, even on this issue, there is some common ground. If we give due weight to the imputed redemption of Christ as is essential to the context of adoption (Eph. 1:3-7), then perhaps Wright can relax some when we affirm the reformers' teaching of the imputed righteousness of Christ as essential to justification. Unless, of course, Wright's druthers about imputation are more of a foil to lend credibility to his redefining of justification. In which case, traditional Protestants must ignore Wright on soteriology and concentrate on their own responsibility to retrieve adoption. It is, I posit, the complementing of justification and adoption which enhances orthodox or classic Protestantism and effectively answers Wright's protest.

Since first airing this response to the NPP in 2001, opportunities have arisen to pose in-person questions to Wright and to Piper. At the annual meeting of the Evangelical Theological Society in 2010, an opportunity arose to ask Wright why he consistently translates υἱοθεσία as *sonship* rather than as *adoption*. At the Evangelical Leadership Forum in Wisla, Poland, in 2016, there was likewise an opening to probe with Piper why he did not make more of adoption in responding to Wright. Since both men had just given public addresses, it was too hopeful to expect satisfactory off-the-cuff answers and would be an unkindness to quote them here.

Kevin Vanhoozer has, however, elicited from Wright some published comments on the place of adoption in his discussion of justification. Seeking "peace talks between New Perspectives and old Protestants," and affirming Wright's emphasis on the covenantal

---

[57] Wright, *What Saint Paul Really Said*, 123.

context and corporate dimension of soteriology, Vanhoozer sees fertile ground on which the "terrific half truth" of Wright's narrative approach (a quotation from Michael Horton) and the Pauline and Calvinian emphasis on union with Christ can meet. Vanhoozer has thus sought to bring together the forensic and participationist elements of the gospel: "To declare someone righteous is to declare that person as *incorporated into Christ's righteousness.*" This view, he fairly claims, resonates with the double grace of justification and sanctification which Calvin understood to issue from union with Christ.

In this biblically and historically attested schema, adoption, says Vanhoozer, is "the perfect mediating category." It brings together our legal standing before God (affording the rights of inheritance) and membership of the covenant (i.e., the family). Whereas, then, Calvin speaks of a *duplex gratia Dei*, Vanhoozer commends a *triplex gratia Dei*. In adoption, "Christians become members of God's covenant family by receiving the Son's status: *righteous sonship.*" Vanhoozer continues, "the *state of the union* and the *status of imputation* come together in the *sonship of adoption.*"[58]

We shall return in chapter six to the contemporary significance of union with Christ. Here, our focus remains on adoption. Wright has responded to Vanhoozer with the curious claim that adoption is vital to his thought: "I am surprised he hasn't seen this as central to my work. Perhaps I need to find ways of highlighting it further. Certainly, I have long seen it as vital." Yet, despite stating that "adoption-plus-incorporated-righteousness strikes [him] as a major step in the right (Wright?) direction," adoption still found no place in his index of select topics in *Paul and the Faithfulness of God* (2013) and is omitted from his delineation of the Reformed perspective of topics at the heart of Paul's thought.

---

[58] Kevin J. Vanhoozer, "Wrighting the Wrongs of the Reformation? The State of the Union with Christ in St. Paul and Protestant Soteriology" in *Jesus, Paul and the People of God: A Theological Dialogue with N. T. Wright*, ed. Nicholas Perrin and Richard B. Hays (Downers Grove, IL: IVP Academic, 2011), 235–59.

Only rarely does Wright use the term, arguing, ironically, and over against Hans Küng, that justification has a very particular meaning which cannot be expanded to cover neighboring aspects of Paul's soteriology. All the while, Wright's stretching of justification over the territory covered by adoption remains unrevised. To quote Wright, "'adoption' in Romans 8 or Galatians 4 is simply a way of exploring the meaning of 'justification', rather than a separate category."[59]

5. NEGLECT THROUGH PRESUMPTION

Further research may yet reveal other examples of overlooking, excising, absorption, or, minimally, the downplaying of adoption. It is not difficult to imagine, for example, how the doctrine contravenes feminist theology. Adoption's emphasis on the Fatherhood of God (the appropriation of the language of Αββα) and the sonship of his people (specifically Paul's play on the union of the Son [υἰὸς] and the sons [υἰοί]) cuts across the feminist demand to call God "Mother" and to jettison androgenic language irrespective of its theological underpinnings.

That said, others, far from purging adoption from the theology of the church, wrongly assume its ubiquitous presence in theological discourse. We have substantiated its neglect and here explain why it has been for so long obscured.

Possession of the Spirit of adoption.

Consider, first, the believer's possession of "the Spirit of adoption" (Gal. 4:4-7; Rom. 8:15-16). Each of us is indwelt by the Spirit of the now glorified Son, no matter whether we are conscious of or instructed about God's adoptive grace. Periodically we grieve the Spirit and need restoration, yet the presence and empowerment of the Spirit of adoption remains a permanent feature of the lives of God's adopted

---

[59] N. T. Wright, "Response to Kevin Vanhoozer," in *Jesus, Paul and the People of God*, 259–61; N. T. Wright, *Paul and the Faithfulness of God* (Minneapolis: Fortress, 2013), 39, 914, 925–26, 950 (cf., 528, 876–79, 941, 956, 976, 1,022).

sons and daughters. The Spirit sometimes hides from us but only so that we might follow harder after him. His work *in us* no more fails us, then, than either the Son's work *for us* or the Father's grace *toward us*.

Possessing, then, the Spirit of adoption, we pray to the Father through the merits of the Son and by the enabling of the Spirit—a pattern inverting the way our blessings come to us (from the Father, in Christ, and by the Spirit [Eph. 1:3]). Moreover, we sing to the Father. Our hymns portray the Son, who, by the ordination of the Father and through the propitiation and expiation of the cross, turned the Father's throne of judgment into one of paternal grace. Furthermore, we possess in life in general a filial consciousness before God. All told, then, our prayers, sung praise, and filial consciousness combine, at their most attuned, to obscure the neglect of adoption. Indwelt by the Spirit of adoption, we presume the church possesses a commensurate understanding of the theology of adoption.

How often, though, are our prayers more christomonist than trinitarian. The Son, and the Spirit are certainly coequal with the Father and rightly figure in prayer, but the Father is also coequal with the Son and the Spirit and is the one to whom prayer is normatively directed. Likewise, for all the hymns mentioning the Father, there are few which extol him in detail. Hymns specifically on adoption are rare and exegetically weak. If we only had the hymns of the church to go by, we would likely think that we are redeemed slaves or justified sinners and not also adopted sons.

In short, the church has known enough of the Spirit of adoption to think that the discussion of adoption is prevalent, but not so much of him as to insist that adoption receives the attention accorded other soteric doctrines. Either the Spirit has been grieved by the neglect, withholding from the church greater effusions of the consciousness of our filial privileges; has sovereignly chosen when and how to mature the church's understanding and appropriation of adoption; or both. This is a mystery known only to God. Whatever the truth of the situation, our confession of the historic neglect of adoption honors God, as does our dependence on the Spirit for the illumination and drive needed for its retrieval.

Polarized approaches to adoption.

Throughout the history of adoption, two ways of referencing the doctrine have predominated. By far the most prevalent is the piecemeal referencing of adoption. I refer to brief, passing comments and citations of adoption texts. Then there is the localized approach of gathered summaries (*loci*) of adoption. Ironically, both approaches, taken in isolation, have, in their own ways, helped obscure adoption.

The *prevalent approach* is found in Paul, and among the church fathers and reformers. The apostle wrote letters rather than treatises in systematic theology, and the fathers predated the development of the discipline of systematic theology. Yet, the tidbits on adoption have often been lost to view, appearing in isolation to say very little. Additionally, Michael Peppard observes that by the fourth century, adoption was no longer a crucial or visible element of Imperial theology (the cult of the emperor).[60] It, thus, lost some of its metaphorical appeal, leaving Paul's isolated references to adoption unassembled theologically and largely undiscovered in succeeding centuries.

While Calvin's interest in adoption stands out on account of the multiplicity of his references to the doctrine—at least, now that we know to look for them—his decision not to allot adoption a distinct chapter or section in his *Institutes* proved significant. His approach was likely influenced by various factors.

First, by the relevance of his adoption references to the broad scope of salvation history and to a plethora of issues germane to the application of salvation. In particular, Calvin viewed adoption as a powerful expression of union with Christ—a broad theme possessing incarnational, mystical, and spiritual dimensions. Thus, the panoramic scope of adoption proved inconducive to its confinement to a specific

---

[60] Michael Peppard, *The Son of God in the Roman World: Divine Sonship in its Social and Political Context* (Oxford: Oxford University Press, 2011), 5.

chapter or section. Not so the two stated benefits of union with Christ: justification and regeneration (sanctification).

Second, it has been said that metaphors play no functional part in Calvin's systematic theology. Could it be that he denied adoption a specific chapter or section because of its metaphorical status? This is unlikely since Calvin does not, so far as I have seen to date, refer to adoption as a metaphor, even though terms such as *metaphorae*, *figurae*, *similitudines*, and *comparatines* occur in his writings.

Whatever Calvin's reasoning, his approach had the effect of clouding the importance he placed on Paul's motif as also the clarity of his overall view of adoption. Had he combined his pervasive approach with a more intense localized discussion of adoption, he would likely have guaranteed the inclusion of adoption in subsequent explications of his theology. He could also have contributed to an arrangement of soteriology based on distinctive soteric images (although, in fairness, that would have placed him well ahead of his time [see part three]). All the same, recall the influence of Christian Humanism on Calvin with its emphasis on the constituent parts of Scripture, notably on the *corpus Paulinum*. This Humanist emphasis comports with the overt acknowledgment of Paul's unique use of υἱοθεσία.

There are uncertainties here, but clearly, Calvin's approach, while perceiving the richness of the apostle's doctrine, combined with the neglect of adoption from the mid-seventeenth century onward, to create the impression that, to quote Robert Webb's *faux pas*, Calvin wrote nothing "whatever" on adoption.

The alternative *localized approach*, dating back to Aquinas, is synonymous with the theological methodology of Medieval and Protestant Scholasticism. The approach has become normative in the Presbyterian (English-speaking) sector of the Reformed tradition, largely due to the WCF's distinct chapter on adoption. Writes Sinclair Ferguson, "There is a special emphasis in the Confession on the Fatherhood of God in a separate chapter devoted to the Christian's adoption into God's family." In this light, it seems churlish to question the Westminster commissioners' seminal inclusion of a chapter on adoption in the Westminster Standards.[61]

Had the *loci* been more substantive, Pauline, and redemptive historical, and its correlative themes and ramifications more visibly woven throughout the Westminster Standards, the Standards might have avoided the accusations of legalism and coldness to which they have been subjected. The localized approach unwittingly curtails most of the familial feel of Westminster Calvinism to its respective statements in the Westminster Standards, giving the impression that the Westminster commissioners were more at home with the legal than the relational content of the gospel. [62]

I posit, then, a center-right perspective on the Westminster Standards. Neighboring to the right is the orthodox-Reformed perspective (affirming Westminster's theology *and* methodology). Further away to the left is the revisionist–Reformed perspective (seriously questioning and rejecting Westminster's theology and methodology). In adjusting the orthodox-Reformed perspective, the constructive-Reformed question the highly ratiocinated method of the Standards while avidly affirming their theology. For more see chapter six and the Appendix.[63]

Typifying the spirit of this *via media* is Scottish Presbyterian

---

[61] Sinclair B. Ferguson, "The Teaching of the Confession" in *The Westminster Confession in the Church Today: Papers Prepared for the Church of Scotland Panel of Doctrine*, ed. Alasdair I. C. Heron (Edinburgh: The Saint Andrew Press, 1982), 28–39; Dewey D. Wallace Jr., *Puritans and Predestination: Grace in English Protestant Theology 1525–1695* (Chapel Hill: The University of North Carolina Press, 1982), 56–57.

[62] For an exposition of the strengths and weaknesses of the Westminster treatment of adoption, see Trumper, "An Historical Study," 217–46.

[63] Hitherto, these categories were named revisionist, orthodox, and constructive Calvinism since they originated amid the process of tracing adoption along the lines of both Calvinistic-Baptist and classically-Reformed thought. Here we update the labeling of these categories in line with the defense of Protestant Scholasticism, to and the concern to understand consider Calvin amid the breadth of the Reformed tradition.

Horatius Bonar (1808-89). States Kelly, he preferred "the more Biblical-story form of earlier Scottish Reformation Catechism to 'the skillful metaphysics and lawyer-like precision' of the more abstract and systematic Shorter Catechism." Similarly, Philip Schaff writes of the WSC, "It lacks [the] genial warmth, freshness, and childlike simplicity [of Luther's Catechism and the Heidelberg Catechism, and] it substitutes a logical scheme for the historical order of the Apostles' Creed. It deals in dogmas rather than facts." More recently, Peter Toon has commented that the WCF's emphasis on system "loses the dynamism of the Bible's portrayal of our sin and redemption in Christ," while T. F. Torrance, following Bonar but in a more revisionist Reformed vein, opines that "the Confession of Faith does not manifest the spiritual freshness and freedom, or the evangelical joy, of the Scots Confession of 1560, and was not so much a 'Confession' as a rational [better, ratiocinated] explanation of a constitutional establishment." [64]

As commentaries on the tone of the Westminster Standards, these claims are hard to deny. Yet there is a certain irony here. The Heidelberg Catechism (Lord's Day 13, Q and A 33), containing very little on the Fatherhood of God and adoption, is commended for its warmth, while the Westminster Standards, occupying a prominent place in the history of adoption, are deemed deficient on account of their juridical theology and clinical feel. The commissioners' approach to the exposition of adoption likely has contributed to this.

Passing references to adoption.

Third, the neglect of adoption (υἱοθεσία) has been obscured by its inclusion in the church's cross-denominational library of multilingual biblical dictionaries and lexical aids. Consider, for instance, *Dictionnaire de Spiritualité* (1872), "Grace (II. Le Mystère de la Filiation

---

[64] Kelly, "Adoption," 110; *Catechisms of the Scottish Reformation*, ed. Horatius Bonar (London: James Nisbet and Co., 1866, vii); Schaff, *The Creeds of Christendom*, 1:787 (see also 790–91); Peter Toon, *Puritans and Calvinism*, 60; T. F. Torrance, *Scottish Theology: From John Knox to John McLeod Campbell* (Edinburgh: T&T Clark, 1996), 127.

Adoptive)"; *Dictionary of Doctrinal and Historical Theology* (1872), "Adoption (υἱοθεσία); *Dictionnaire Latin-Français des Auteurs Chrétiens* (1954), "adoptarius" *et al.*; *A Greek-English Lexicon of the New Testament and other Early Christian Literature* (1957), "υἱοθεσία, ας, ἡ"; *A Patristic Greek Lexicon* (1961), "υἱοθεσία, ἡ"; *The Interpreter's Dictionary of the Bible: An Illustrated Encyclopedia* (1962), "Adoption"; *A Catholic Dictionary of Theology* (1962), "Adoption as sons"; *Theological Dictionary of the New Testament* (1972), "υἱοθεσία"; *Evangelical Dictionary of Theology* (1984), "Adoption"; *Dictionary of Paul in His Letters* (1993), "Adoption, Sonship." We could go on.

Whether such entrances predate the slowly growing awareness of the need to retrieve adoption or are testimonies to the reawakening of interest in adoption, it is hard to tell. When my research began in the early 1990s it was the presence of adoption in such reference works which led to some push-back against the claim that adoption is, so far as its treatment is concerned, the Cinderella of soteriological doctrines. Yet, there is a marked contrast between the coverage of adoption in the lexical tools and dictionaries of the church and her corpus. Since it is easier to look up a dictionary than to comprehend the fortunes of adoption in history, it is unsurprising that some have presumed the neglect of adoption to be mythic or exaggerated. In actuality, adoption has slidden from view somewhere between the lexical investigation of the Bible's terminology and the church's prayers and sung praise. Adoption is found in dictionaries and in the spirit of God's children, but is much harder to find in the annals of the church's theology.

6. NEGLECT THROUGH FEAR

We might be forgiven for thinking that the documentation of the history of adoption and the identifying of the causes of its neglect would guarantee the retrieval of adoption. We cannot underestimate, however, the impact of fear on traditions of theology. The fear that opts for the *status quo* and the defense of the received orthodoxy finds all sorts of suspicions about change.

This is difficult to substantiate, for we do not tend to own our fear and oftentimes do not recognize fear in ourselves. Nevertheless, the objectivity of hindsight can help us here, for fear-driven hyper defensiveness has led to unanticipated consequences. Recall how:

- The nervous defense of the free grace of justification after the Reformation led to the gradual ignoring of adoption, from the mid-seventeenth century on especially.
- The lopsided juridical feel of Reformed orthodoxy stirred, in turn, the nineteenth-century promotion in Victorian liberalism of the universal Fatherhood of God and brotherhood of man.
- To this day, there lingers a fear that to retrieve adoption will influence a slide into an errant liberalism or a superficial senti-mentality.

Our suspicions are not easily documented but can be felt. Many left to themselves prefer an historic lopsidedness to the fear that the relational or familial might eradicate the juridical or cause a slide into Universalism.

While fretting over the proverbial "thin end of the wedge" is sometimes warranted, less recognized is the way such fretting can backfire. Feeding ourselves on worst-case scenarios—which is what fretting does—has, in history, led us to forgo moderate, warranted reforms that could have enhanced Reformed orthodoxy. Instead, unyielding refusals to reform, contrary to our claim to reform according to God's Word, create a buildup of pressure which, as history demonstrates, can produce theological combustion, the fallout from which can be more damaging than what we fretted occurring in the first place. The process is somewhat akin to a water radiator exploding because it either lacked a pressure valve to release some air, or because the pressure valve went unreleased.

The Victorian protest for paternal grace illustrates this phenomenon very well, which all goes to say that in contemplating the reforms needed to retrieve adoption, fear can also be a danger. It can blind us to those current deficiencies the Spirit would have us address. Oftentimes, fear tempts us to set up buffers against heterodoxy that are neither required by Scripture nor are helpful. Manmade, they do more to spawn counterreactions against orthodoxy than they do to safeguard it, and tend to occasion division among God's people rather than unity.

In authentic Protestantism where the principle of *sola Scriptura* holds sway, the key to overcoming fear is a fresh engagement with Scripture. God's Word rather than the aberrations of theology form the touchstone of our faith. While *sola Scriptura* does not equate to *nuda Scriptura* (Scripture denuded of the historical and ecclesiastical context of its exegesis and interpretation), God's Word is nevertheless the fount to which the reformers encourage us to return (*ad fontes*). In so doing, we seek a positive construction of adoption which not only retrieves the doctrine, but which enhances our reflection of the balances of Christian theology. Our aim is not the safe regurgitation of a deficient history, but the reform of our understanding of the doctrine, simply following the biblical data where it leads us.

Long before the Protestant reformers rocked the professing church, Vincent of Lérins (died 450) in *A Commonitory* challenged her to overcome her fear:

> Shall there . . . be no progress in Christ's Church? Certainly; all possible progress. For what being is there, so envious of men, so full of hatred to God, who would seek to forbid it? Yet on condition that it be real progress, not alteration of the faith. For progress requires that the subject be enlarged in itself, alteration, that it be transformed into something else. The intelligence, then, the knowledge, the wisdom, as well of individuals as of all, as well of one man as of the whole Church, ought, in the course of ages and centuries, to increase and make much and vigorous progress; but yet only in its own kind; that is to say, in the same doctrine, in the same sense, and in the same meaning.

This "real progress" is what our understanding and expression of biblical soteriology needs. It is a progress, says R. B. Kuiper, illuminated by the Spirit through the study of God's Word. In this light, he continues, "It is no less necessary that the church be progressive than it be conservative. . . . The church's conservatism must be unto progressivism." Not to tear down what has been founded biblically, after the manner of liberalism, but that which builds on a true, demonstrable, biblical foundation. To so build is, says Kuiper, "at once healthy conservatism and true progressivism." Both we now pursue in parts two and three.[65]

~~~~

---

[65] *N and P-N F* (second series), 11:148 (cf., 129); R. B. Kuiper, "Progressivism," *The Glorious Body of Christ: A Scriptural Appreciation of the One Holy Catholic Church*, first published by Eerdmans, 1966; reprinted. (Edinburgh and Carlisle, PA: The Banner of Truth Trust, 2006), 83–84.

PART TWO

THE METAPHORICAL IMPORT OF ADOPTION

Some men, by feigned words, as dark as mine,
Make truth to spangle and its rays to shine.
"But they want solidness." Speak, man, thy mind.
"They drown the weak; metaphors make us blind."

Solidity, indeed, becomes the pen
Of him that writeth things divine to men;
But must I needs want solidness, because
By metaphors I speak? Were not God's laws,
His gospel laws, in olden times held forth
By types, shadows, and metaphors? Yet loath
Will any sober man be to find fault
With them, lest he be found for to assault
The highest wisdom. No, he rather stoops,
And seeks to find out what by pins and loops,
By calves and sheep, by heifers and by rams,
By birds and herbs, and by the blood of lambs,
God speaketh to him; and happy is he
That finds the light and grace in them be.

Be not too forward, therefore, to conclude
That I want solidness, that I am rude;
All things solid in show not solid be;
All things in parables despise not we,
Lest things most hurtful lightly we receive,
And things that good are, or our souls bereave.
My dark and cloudy words, they do but hold
The truth, as cabinets enclose the gold.

The prophets used much by metaphors
To set forth the truth; yea, who so considers
Christ, his apostles too, shall plainly see,
That truths to this day in such mantles be.

John Bunyan, The Author's Apology,
Pilgrim's Progress.

3

ADOPTION IN SCRIPTURE
Metaphorical Terminology

> We view language as providing data that can lead to general principles of understanding. . . . We have found that such principles are often metaphoric in nature and involve understanding one kind of experience in terms of another kind of experience.
>
> George Lakoff and Mark Johnson,
> *Metaphors We Live By.*

> Metaphor is . . . a pressing topic for theology and it is one often mentioned in doctrinal, philosophical, and exegetic studies—rarely, however, is it discussed in any detail.
>
> Janet Martin Soskice,
> *Metaphor and Religious Language.*

Having navigated the "Michigan Left," we now put "peddle to the metal." While it is helpful to know what is behind us, we turn here to the fresh terrain ahead. First, we pass through the deep forest of Linguistics, then through the field of Exposition. Most travelers bypass the forest, but they miss some of the very woods from which the timbers of Adoption have been taken. While they get to the town more quickly, they struggle to distinguish it from the neighboring municipalities of Regeneration and Justification. Look out in the forest, then, for three distinctive architectural features of Adoption.

~~~~

An examination of what the Bible says of adoption enables us to explain and to vindicate the prior evaluations of historic treatments of the doctrine. This examination is divisible into three sections.

1. THE TRANSLATION OF *ΥΙΟΘΕΣΙΑ*

Two facts of Scripture are fundamental and must be safeguarded for a correct understanding and consistent exposition of adoption.

First, that only Paul uses the term υἱοθεσία (Rom. 8:15, 23; 9:4; Gal. 4:5; and Eph. 1:5). There is no corresponding usage in the LXX, any other Jewish sources, or in the New Testament. Yet, before considering the translation of υἱοθεσία we must explain our inclusion of Ephesians 1:5 and Romans 8:23. The former is considered by critical scholars pseudepigraphical, the latter is a variant reading.

Among relevant scholars, Matthew Vellanickal, Brendan Byrne, James Scott, and Erin Heim omit consideration of Ephesians 1:5. Vellanickal references the text but does not expound it. Byrne is silent. Scott includes the text among those "crucial passages in Paul" warranting attention, but then ignores it. Heim offers convenient but uncompelling reasons for side-stepping it. Why, we may ask her, would the use of υἱοθεσία in Galatians 4:5 point to the original Pauline composition of the text, but not so in Ephesians 1:5? Heim claims that in Ephesians 1:5 υἱοθεσία occurs in the context of a prayer (1:3-14) rather than in the main argument of the letter. Would we on that basis also rule out what Paul has to say in the doxology of predestination, redemption, and the sealing of the Spirit?

This is an important matter, for the use of υἱοθεσία in Ephesians 1:5 is essential to the entire salvation-historical scope of God's adoptive dealings with his people, as also to the full extent of their theological implications. Simply put, Paul's use of υἱοθεσία in Ephesians 1:5 fully comports with his other four uses. Observes Garner, "rejecting the authenticity of Ephesians compromises the rich protological-to-eschatological contours of adoption implicit elsewhere in Paul but made explicit in the opening section of this letter."[1] The burden of proof for the omission of Ephesians 1:5 lies, then, with those cropping from consideration our predestination to adoption.

Neither Scott nor Heim excludes Romans 8:23. The textual variant υἱοθεσίαν has strong support and has likely come into question on theological grounds, namely, amid the confusion as to how those already adopted (v. 15) could undergo "the adoption" at the end of the age. Erasmus' principle, *lectio difficilior potior* is relevant here. By it he taught that the more difficult theological reading is probably the correct one since copyists would more likely turn a difficult reading into an easier one than *vice versa*. On this understanding, Romans 8:23 became a variant reading by dint of a copyist's failure to appreciate the wonderful truth that those adopted in this life, experience the consummation of their adoption in the life to come.

Second, υἱοθεσία is the only term in Scripture that specifically means adoption. Its uniqueness highlights its significance to the understanding of our salvation. If we lose sight of υἱοθεσία, or generalize its distinctive translation, we have no other biblical term to substitute for it. Ὑιοθεσία speaks incomparably of the Father's acceptance of us in Christ and the life of freedom to which he has called us.

---

[1] Matthew Vellanickal, *The Divine Sonship of Christians in the Johannine Writings* (Rome: Biblical Institute Press, 1977), 69, 73; Brendan Byrne, *"Sons of God"—"Seed of Abraham": A Study of the Idea of the Sonship of God of All Christians in Paul against the Jewish Background* (Rome: Biblical Institute Press, 1979); James M. Scott, *Adoption as Sons of God: An Exegetical Investigation into the Background of ΥΙΟΘΕΣΙΑ in the Pauline Corpus*, Wissentschaftliche Untersuchungen zum Neuen Testament ·2. Reihe (J. C. B. Mohr [Paul Siebeck]: Tübingen, 1992), xiii; Erin Heim, "Light through a Prism: New Avenues of Inquiry for the Pauline Ὑιοθεσία Metaphors," (Ph.D. Diss.: University of Otago, 2014), 1fn2, 145. Cf., David B. Garner, *Sons in the Son: The Riches and Reach of Adoption in Christ* (Phillipsburg, NJ: P&R, 2016), 58–60.

The general translation of *sonship* overlooks the unique usage and distinctive meaning of υἱοθεσία. This may seem a small matter until we remember from the theological history of adoption that the doctrine can ill afford to become obscured in translation. Not only does the unique idea of adoption need exposure, we have seen how the muting of its specificities has been used to eradicate the doctrine and its implications from consideration.

Not all, however, have an agenda in preferring the translation *sonship*. Others argue for this translation on contextual grounds. Byrne, for example, has taught that Paul meant *sonship* since the term (υἱότης), found among later Christian authors, was not available to Paul, and given that *sonship* more easily corresponds to the Old Testament sonship tradition. Trevor Burke notes, though, that Byrne changed his mind in the process of reviewing Scott's *Adoption as Sons of God*, and now prefers the compound form "adoptive-sonship." This accords with the recognition that υἱοθεσία does double duty, expressing both the adoptive act (the process of entrance into sonship) and the adoptive state (the ensuing life of sonship).

James Hester accepts the translation of υἱοθεσία as *adoption* in but two of its five occurrences: Galatians 4:5 and Romans 8:15. Conversely, the NIV translates the term as "adoption" on three occasions (Rom. 8:23; 9:4; Eph. 1:4-5), preferring *sonship* and *the full right of sons* in Romans 8:15 and Galatians 4:5, respectively. Evidently, dynamic-equivalent (thought-for-thought) translations render υἱοθεσία *adoption* when the adoptive act is in view and as *sonship* or *the full right of sons* when the adoptive state is implied. In formal-equivalent (word-for-word) translations, υἱοθεσία is uniformly translated *adoption* or *adoption as son*.[2]

---

[2] J. D. Hester, *Paul's Concept of the Inheritance: A Contribution to the Understanding of Heilsgeschichte*, SJT Occasional Papers, 14 (Edinburgh and London: Oliver and Boyd,

The matter is further confused in German-speaking theology, where options for translations of υἱοθεσία vary between the equivalents of *adoption* (*Kindschaft*), *sonship* (*Sohnschaft*), or *childhood* (*Kindheit*). Following Luther, the newer translation *Die Bibel nach der Übersetzung Martin Luthers* translates υἱοθεσία consistently by some form of the stem *Kind* (child): *Kindschaft* in Galatians 4:5, Romans 8:23, and 9:4; *kindlichen Geist* (Spirit of childhood) in Romans 8:15; and *Kinder* (children) in Ephesians 1:5.[3] Even supposing Luther originally intended us to understand the stem or noun to refer to adoption, *Kind*, as George MacDonald quickly pointed out, does not capture the adoptive act (manner of entrance into sonship). It captures only the life of sonship.

I have long pondered why Luther did not use the more literal German translation *die Adoption* or *die Annahme* rather than *Kindschaft* or even *Sohnschaft*. Historians of the German language can determine whether these alternatives were available to Luther. I suspect, however, that Luther's dynamic equivalence and his negligible interest in adoption were determinative. That said, there has since been some interest in this matter. In the nineteenth-century debate in Catholicism between Scheeben and Granderath, the former preferred *Gotteskindschaft* and *Kind*, the latter *Gottessohnschaft* and *Sohn*.[4]

More recently, the Swiss German translation, *Der heiligen Schrift das Alten und des Neuen Testaments* (Zürich, 1993) translated υἱοθεσία consistently by some form of the noun *die Annahme* and its

---

1968), 61. Brendan Byrne, *"Sons of God"—"Seed of Abraham,"* 80–81 (cf., Trevor J. Burke, "The Characteristics of Paul's Adoptive-Sonship (Huiothesia) Motif," *Irish Biblical Studies* 17, January 1995, 63fn.

[3] Jacob Grimm and Wilhelm Grimm, *Deutsches Wörterbuch*, V (Leipzig: S. Hirzel, 1873), 771.

[4] Edwin Hartshorn Palmer, *Scheeben's Doctrine of Divine Adoption* (Kampen: J. H. Kok N.V., 1953), 89–90.

verbal form *annehmen* (*an Kindes statt annehmen*). But even this form of translation does not explain why German translators have overlooked what appears to be the most obvious translation: *die Adoption*. This was the translation I used to describe my research upon arrival in Tübingen in 1994. Consistently, those hearing me assumed I was there to study christology (Adoptionism [in German, *Adoptionismus*]). Only after encountering Luther's translation of υἱοθεσία did I understand why my peers were mystified when hearing the research described in terms of *Adoption* or *Sohnschaft*. After some moments perplexed, they would exclaim: "Ah, du meinst nicht Christologie sondern Soteriologie. Du meinst 'Kindschaft'!" Nein! Of all the alternative translations to adoption or *Adoption*, only *Die Annahme* retains the distinctiveness of Paul's meaning. Even so, the latter noun captures but the core conceptual notion of adoption (acceptance). It does not possess the colorful metaphorical garb of *Adoption*.

Adoption or *adoption as son* names, then, the doctrine, implies its distinctiveness and allows for its breadth of meaning. The translation challenges the obscuring or dilution of the doctrine and renders its neglect more inexcusable. After all, it is not for the translator to determine whether Paul in any given use of υἱοθεσία refers to the adoption *in se* or to the subsequent state of sonship. That responsibility belongs to the preacher.

The practical pluses of the *adoption* translation aside, consider the etymological issues. No one has researched these from the Hellenistic period more than James Scott. He argues that the lingering influence of Graeco-Roman forms of adoption developed, by the New Testament era, a semantic range of apposite terms: εἰσποιεῖν; ἐκποιεῖν; τίθεσθαι; ποιεῖσθαι; υἱοποιεῖσθαι; and υἱοθετεῖν. His examination of them leads him to five conclusions.

- First, that υἱοθεσία is one of the most common terms for adoption in Hellenistic Greek. While rare in non-Christian literary sources, it was frequently used in Greek inscriptions.

- Second, that although Paul's religious application of υἱοθεσία is unparalleled, there is evidence of the theological use of some of the other terms. For example, Plutarch uses ποιεῖσθαι to refer to "adopted truth" or to a truth derived second hand; ἐκποιεῖν, to a moral transformation effected by divine punishment; υἱοποιεῖσθαι, to divine adoption; εἰσποιεῖν, to fraudulent adoption of which Alexander the Great and Solon were accused for claiming to be the adopted sons of Ammon-Zeus and of Fortune.

- Third, most of the word groups (excepting υἱοποιεῖσθαι) were used of Roman adoptions in addition to other forms, but not of Roman adoptions *alone*.

- Fourth, the relevance of most of these Greek terms to Roman *adoptio* suggests they refer etymologically to adoption.

- Fifth, the synonymy between the various terms, demonstrates that "adoption as son" rather than "fosterage" or some other translation renders υἱοθεσία most faithfully.

Assuming Scott is right, the faithful translation of υἱοθεσία as "adoption" or "adoption as son" establishes υἱοθεσία as a unique biblical category. There is no other adoption category in the Synoptic Gospels, Hebrews, or John (and Peter). Matthew speaks in very practical terms of the life of sonship under the phrase *sons of the kingdom*. John and Peter write of our new natures as those born as *children of God* into the kingdom, and Hebrews of the end of our fears and the beginnings of our chastenings as *sons of the Father*. [5]

---

[5] Scott, *Adoption as Sons of God*, 13–57. To track such authorial diversities, see Willi Twisselmann's work *Die Gotteskindschaft der Christen nach dem Neuen Testament*, Beiträge zur Förderung christlicher Theologie 41 (Gütersloh: Verlag C. Bertelsmann, 1939) and Witold Marchel's *Abba, Vater! Die Vaterbotschaft Des Neuen Testaments*, Die Welt der Bibel (Düsseldorf: Patmos-Verlag, 1963).

2. THE DISENTANGLING OF ΥἱΟΘΕΣΊΑ

The *sonship* translation of υἱοθεσία not only blurs the respective filial/familial themes of the New Testament, it facilitates the ignoring or downplaying of their distinctive structures. Most notable in this regard is the church's abiding habit of conflating Paul's teaching of adoption and John's (and Peter's) teaching of the new birth. So engrained is the conflation that the obtaining of a clear view of adoption requires that we first disentangle it from the new birth.

The reasons for disentanglement.

First, the disentanglement is necessary on account of the practice of referencing adoption in an isolated fashion. Recall that for large swathes of church history, dating back to the church fathers, such references were all the attention adoption received, with some amounting to little more than quotations of Paul. While better than nothing, these passing allusions could not encapsulate the apostle's full picture of adoption. Without a perception of the beautiful coherence of his scattered references, it was easy to comingle them with similar-sounding filial and familial terms from non-Pauline sources. Yet, we only have warrant for such admixtures where Scripture legitimizes them. To conflate what Scripture distinguishes obscures the clarity of divine revelation.

Second, the disentanglement is necessary on account of developments in the systematizing of Scripture. Against the flow of the defense of Protestant scholasticism, the case of adoption reveals more dogmatic construal of Scripture than defenders typically acknowledge. This became increasingly pronounced the more the systematization of Scripture developed. The problem lay not with the systematizing of biblical truth *in se,* for systematics gives rightful expression to the divineness and miraculous coherence of God's Word, revealing one God and one gospel. Yet, an orthodox doctrine of Scripture also teaches the humanness of the Bible, as discerned in its multiple authors, genres, books, and perspectives. In her systematizing, then, the church must do justice to both the divineness/oneness and humanness/diversity of Scripture.[6]

The devising of the *loci* (or topics) has been very helpful in incorporating both elements of Scripture in the systematizing of biblical doctrine. Popularized by Philipp Melanchthon's *Loci Communes* (1521; final edition 1560), the *loci* figured in both humanist and scholastic theologies. *Loci*, says Luco van den Brom, are clusters of concepts developed around a central theme or topic for clarity in the explanation of Scripture. These, dogmaticians identified and elicited from the text of Scripture, drawing from patristic materials, and arranging them in a salvation-historical sequence (*historica series ordo*): God, creation, human nature, the all, sin, covenant, Christ, the order of salvation, the church, and the last things.

Rather curiously, defenders of Protestant scholasticism deny that the *loci* were part of an all-embracing structure or system. More likely they mean that they did not coerce the *loci* to fit the propagation of a central dogma since each *locus* retained its own thematic focus and structure.[7] The weakness of the scholastic use of the *loci* lay (and lies), I shall argue, not in their *ad extra* connection to the overall system of theology but in their *ad intra* arrangement.

First, we read little in discussions of systematic method of how each *locus* should integrate doctrinal content drawn from the multiple

---

[6] In terms of models of biblical theology, dogmatic construal is closest to "biblical theology within categories of dogmatic theology" (Brevard S. Childs, *Biblical Theology of the Old and New Testaments: Theological Reflection on the Christian Bible* (Minneapolis: Fortress, 1993), 11–12.

[7] Luco J. van den Brom, "Scholasticism and Contemporary Systematic Theology," in Willem J. van Asselt and Eef Dekker, eds., *Reformation and Scholasticism: An Ecumencal Enterprise* (Grand Rapids: Baker Academic, 2001), 288. Richard Muller, "The Problem of Protestant Scholasticism—A Review and Definition," *Reformation and Scholasticism*, 58–59.

authors, genres, books, and perspectives of Holy Scripture. The dogmaticians' synthesizing of biblical doctrines has majored instead on ratiocination: the relationship of first causes, means, and goals. Thus, the arrangement of each *locus* has done little to factor in the underlying humanness of Scripture.

Second, and consistent with the foregoing, the internal arrangement of the *loci* has suffered from proof-texting. The claim by Richard Muller that this was not an issue in the Medieval, Reformation, and post-Reformation eras flies in the face of many historic expositions of adoption. Muller errs, it seems to me, in assuming that the scholastics' use of exegetical tradition guaranteed their evasion of proof-texting. The neglect of the history of adoption and the exclusion of biblical scholars from the assessment of scholastic exegesis indicate why the exoneration of the scholastics from the charge of proof-texting does not stand up to scrutiny. Treatments of adoption relied on exegetical tradition that did proof-text. Whereas the church fathers' proof-texting led to the conflation of different filial and familial motifs amid the absence of a systematizing of biblical truth, in the Middle Ages, the Reformation, and the post-Reformation eras, conflations arose from ratiocinated *ad intra* arrangements of the *loci*. The mantra proclaiming, for instance, that regeneration grants us the filial nature and adoption the filial standing is true, but it was arrived at in a way that overrode the exegetical and hermeneutical specificities of Scripture. Thus, the soteric *locus* joins the other *loci* in its want of sensitivity to the humanness and, thereby, the feel of Scripture.

Even Calvin's thought, for all its awareness of the history and genre of Scripture, of Paul's salvation-historical take on adoption, and, says Jane Dempsey Douglass, of the Bible's use of metaphors, was not without some traces of dogmatic construal.[8] Although influenced by the

---

[8] Jane Dempsey Douglass, "Calvin's Use of Metaphorical Language for God: God as

humanists to expound the Scriptures on their own terms, in aiming to prove Protestant distinctives Calvin at times perpetuated the confusion of regeneration and adoption inherited from the fathers. His sermon on Galatians 3:26-29 and his commentary on John 1:12-13 are illustrative.

At one level, the opening comments of his Galatians sermon are exactly right:

> Last time, we saw that the gospel has elevated us to a position of great dignity. Not only are we called to share the privileges that our holy forefathers enjoyed, who were so greatly blessed by God; but an even greater dignity and honour has been conferred upon us, because, unlike them, we have been delivered from bondage to the law. To reinforce this point, Paul states that we become children of God only through belief in the Lord Jesus Christ. *The same doctrine is taught in the first chapter of the Gospel of John* [italics inserted] (*John* 1:12).[9]

Faith is indeed the same instrument in the receiving of adoption (Gal. 4:5) as in the receiving of the right to be called God's child (Jn. 1:12), yet Calvin's cross-reference invites his readers to import more from Galatians 3 (and 4) into John 1:12 than the idea of saving faith.

Calvin's corresponding comments on John 1:13 confirm this, for there he reads adoption into John's perspective on the gospel: "The enlightening of our minds by the Holy Spirit belongs to our renewal. So faith flows from its source, regeneration. But since by this same faith we receive Christ, who sanctifies us by His Spirit, it is called the beginning of our adoption." In other words, the Spirit who regenerates,

---

Enemy and God as Mother" in Richard C. Gamble, ed., *Articles on Calvin and Calvinism*, Vol. 6. *Calvin and Hermeneutics* (New York: Garland Publishing Inc., 1992), 100.

[9] John Calvin, *Sermons on Galatians*, first published in 1563 (French) and 1574 (English), transl. by Kathy Childress (Edinburgh and Carlisle, PA: The Banner of Truth Trust, 1997), 341 (*CO* 28 [50]: 557). Care is needed here. In the translation and editing of Calvin, scriptural references from outside of the *corpus Paulinum* are sometimes inserted into the text. The reference to John 1:12 above is a case in point. Cf., the original and translation of Calvin's *Sermons, Eph*, 40 and *CO* 29 (51): 275.

inspires the faith through which we receive our adoption. This is true, but it does not follow that John writes of adoption in John 1:12-13, no matter how ingrained the belief that the apostle's use of ἐξουσία in verse twelve bespeaks adoption.

Calvin offers but the briefest explanation as to why he thinks it does. Ἐξουσία is, he says, a "circumlocution . . . better calculated to commend the excellence of grace than if he [John] had said in a word that all who believe in Christ are made sons of God by Him." "Sons of God," though, is Paul's terminology not John's (with one exception, Rev. 21:7). At this juncture, Calvin's dogmatizing takes priority over his exegesis:

> When the Lord breaths faith into us He regenerates us in a hidden and secret way that is unknown to us. But when faith has been given, we grasp with a lively awareness not only the grace of adoption but also newness of life and the other gifts of the Holy Spirit. For since, as we have said, faith receives Christ, it leads us in a sense to the possession of all His blessings. Thus, so far as our attitude is concerned, we begin to be the sons of God only after we believe. For since the inheritance of eternal life is the result of adoption, we see that the Evangelist ascribes the whole of our salvation to the grace of Christ alone.[10]

Neither the inheritance nor adoption, though, is entailed in John 1:12-13. John's imagery is that of birth into the kingdom, and while the idea of standing is present, it is our new nature and family likeness that is to the fore. A matter, let us recall, can be a truth of Scripture but not necessarily of the Scripture under review. It is, then, incumbent on proponents of a high view of Scripture to press on to a higher use of it. If, dare we say it, this applies to Calvin, one of the church's great expositors, how much more does it apply to us?

---

[10] *The Gospel According to St. John 1–10*, Calvin's Commentaries, transl., T. H. L. Parker, ed. D. W. Torrance and T. F. Torrance, 1959 ed.; reprint ed. (Grand Rapids: Oliver and Boyd, 1979), 17, 19.

The same conflation is found in Calvin's *Institutes*. In 3:3:10, Calvin states that, "the children of God (are) freed through regeneration from the bondage of sin." Yet, the idea of bondage adheres more to the context of adoption than the new birth (cf., Gal. 3:23–4:7 and Rom 8:15-16). Brian Gerrish confirms the conflation, "The theme [singular] of adoption, the new birth, the transition from 'children of wrath' to 'children of grace', takes us to the heart of the Reformer's protest against the prevailing gospel of the day." Although Garret Wilterdink appears to differ, remarking on Calvin's soteriology, that "Related to our adoption, yet distinct from it, is our rebirth or regeneration as children of God," he notes Calvin's commentary on 1 John 4, "where the emphasis falls on abiding in God." This emphasis, he adds, "Calvin interprets consistently in terms of adoption."[11]

Calvin's commitment to Paul's theology, and his sensitivity to the apostle's salvation-historical reading of adoption limits but does not entirely eliminate from his corpus the admixture of the New Testament images of the new birth and adoption. Yet, in the later Reformed orthodox, where the two essentials of a right perception of adoption are overlooked, the admixture is typically given free vent. Check for yourself. The admixture is pervasive.

While retaining the theological *loci* and maintaining generally the *historica series ordo*, the post-Reformation treatments of adoption consistently sacrifice its salvation-historical scope in order to demonstrate the ratiocinated connections germane to the application of salvation. In the process, they run together the filial language of the new birth and adoption. This does not mean to say that the Reformed orthodox taught serious error in their treatments of adoption, but it does mean to say that the exegetical traditon upon which they relied is

---

[11] Brian A. Gerrish, *Grace and Gratitude: The Eucharistic Theology of John Calvin* (Edinburgh: T&T Clark, 1993), 89–90; Garret Wilterdink, *Tyrant or Father: A Study of Calvin's Doctrine of God*, vol. 1 (IN: Wyndham Hall Press, 1985), 37 and 39.

not to be confused with Scripture. As Protestants we must remember this. Some illustrations go far to explain this.

Consider William Ames' summary of adoption in *The Marrow of Theology*. Of the twenty-seven points he makes, eight have no supporting biblical reference, six are supported by references drawn exclusively from Paul's writings, while another five points include reference to the Pauline corpus. A total of nine refer to the Johannine writings, of which four draw biblical support exclusively from John. Of the fourteen points outstanding, three are supported exclusively by references to Hebrews. Thus, Ames draws support for over half his points about adoption from texts written by authors other than Paul. Less than a quarter of them are supported solely by Pauline texts.[12]

Consider also the WCF's ground-breaking confessional treatment of adoption. Of the twenty-one biblical references appended to the twelfth chapter "Of Adoption," only nine are derived from the *corpus Paulinum*. Four are drawn from the Old Testament, eight come from New Testament books penned by authors other than Paul. Included in this number is John 1:12, which in the history of adoption rivals infelicitously Galatians 4:4-5 as the *locus classicus* of adoption.

We could go on with further illustrations of proof-texting, with few signs of it abating. In monographs, relevant *loci* in the systematic theologies, and popular treatments of adoption, the same pattern is evident. Observable across the denominational and theological spectrum, the presence of the pattern in Reformed orthodoxy is especially noteworthy. First, because no other tradition of theology appears to have shown as much interest in adoption since the Reformation. And, second, because it is the Reformed orthodox who have gone to such lengths to defend Protestant scholasticism from the charge of proof-texting.

---

[12] William Ames, *The Marrow of Theology*, transl. from the third Latin ed. (1629); ed. J. D. Eusden, (Boston, Philadelphia, 1968), 164–67.

The tension between the biblical data and historic expositions of adoption, suggests that, even from a sympathy for Protestant scholasticism, the refuting of proof-texting is one defense too many. Indeed, a close reading of those in print defending Protestant scholasticism reveals that there is some agreement in this regard. Admits Bert Loonstra, contra Richard Muller, the scholastics were not free of "dogmatic biblicism for the sake of the system."[13] Of four scholastic attitudes to the biblical text—belief in the inspiration of the Hebrew vowel pointing, the questioning if not the rejection of textual criticism, the affirming of the Bible's affirmations about science, and the use of biblical texts as logically exploitable arguments in a systematic discourse—it is the last that concerns us here.[14]

Loonstra openly concedes that biblical texts were used as proof-texts (*dicta probantia*). From them, universal truths were drawn by logical deduction, the logical conclusions bearing for Reformed scholastics the same authority as the text itself. Loonstra notes that the major difficulty with this practice was not that the logical inferences supported a certain theological position, but the "logical-systematic setting" in which the texts were handled. "The setting is foreign to the texts," he says, adding that "the scholastics were not very sensitive to this shift [from text to setting]." Loonstra goes still further:

> The logical framework in which the Bible was interpreted by the scholastics is a cultural-historical presupposition which affects the understanding of the texts. With its emphasis on the validity of its logical method of interpretation[,] Reformed scholasticism does not meet with approval anymore.

---

[13] Van Asselt and Dekker, "Introduction," in *Reformation and Scholasticism*, 24; Muller, "The Problem of Protestant Scholasticism—A Review and Definition," 4l7 (cf., van Asselt and Dekker, "Introduction" and van Asselt "Cocceius Anti-Scholasticus?" in *Reformation and Scholasticism*, 34fn., 69 and 241).

[14] Bert Loonstra "Scholasticism and Hermeneutics" in *Reformation and Scholasticism*, 296–306 (304 and 305 for the following quotations).

It is imperative in the present that we retain our respect for, and confidence in the unity of the system of truth in Scripture, while yet expressing the diversity that God has revealed in his Word:

> Reformed scholasticism concluded from the ontological unity of the truth, that both the revelation and experience of this truth participate in its logical uniformity. Biblical texts were interpreted by the scholastics as unequivocal expressions of doctrine. They were insufficiently aware of the fact that generally the structure of written revelation is not analytical-logical, but emotive-rhetorical.

Confirming our case study of adoption, specifically the treatments of adoption in Reformed orthodoxy, Loonstra writes: "The historical context and the specific scope of the texts are left out of consideration too easily." Recognizing the humanness of Scripture, he notes how the Holy Spirit conforms his inspiration to the personal and cultural-historical potentialities and limitations of the biblical speakers and writers. While it would be preferable for Loonstra to say that the Spirit makes use of the human factors of personality and cultural-historical context, he acknowledges that both salvation history and the authorial diversity of the New Testament must figure in the reform of scholastic method.

This less guarded defense of Protestant scholasticism opens the door for the full retrieval of adoption (see chap. six). Loonstra gets the ball rolling by, it seems to me, swapping out the questioning of the value judgments of the critics of Protestant scholasticism with a humbler commitment to consider our own value judgments.

Third, the disentanglement of adoption is required because, without it, historic conflations go unchallenged. Building on the industrious work of the last decades in resurrecting the Puritans, there now needs to be, under the supremacy of Scripture, an embracing of a sympathetic-critical response to their theological method. Historical studies such as Joel Beeke's chapter "The Apostle John and the Puritans on the Father's Adopting, Transforming Love (1 John 3)" are fine when understood as such, but without the inclusion of the correctives of Scripture they serve to perpetuate exegetical fallacies. These are then repeated in pulpits and pews without a second thought, for in the tradition of classic Reformed orthodoxy neither theological students nor, in turn, their congregants are encouraged, in esteeming the tradition, to attest it by Scripture.[15]

The recovery of the Puritans, needs, accordingly, a parallel recovery of the reformers' principle of *ad fontes*. Such a principle is essential for reading the Puritans through Scripture rather than Scripture through the Puritans. Happily, the retrieval of adoption offers us a significant opportunity to look afresh at our systematizing of Scripture, remembering that due respect for prior exegetical tradition is not to usurp the supreme authority of Scripture for faith and conduct (WCF 1:4, 10). Yet, traditions of exegesis and system building die hard, especially when confused with the text of Scripture itself. Misled by that confusion, such traditions become to us indispensable safeguards against heterodoxy. This is particularly so when we have no clear alternative approach or system in view.

There is today, however, a scholarly movement toward the recognition of the exclusively Pauline, salvation-historical use of υἱοθεσία. Less advanced to date is the awareness of the need to inject metaphorical considerations into the treatment of adoption. Together, these three developments—the first fundamental to the disentan-glement of adoption, and the second and third the fruits of it—remind us that the retrieval of adoption requires not only that more be written on the doctrine, but that more be written that accords with Scripture. All this said, we must now justify our claim that adoption is

---

[15] Joel R. Beeke, ed., *The Beauty and Glory of the Father* (Grand Rapids: Reformation Heritage Books, 2013), 79–105. Therein, David Murray goes furthest. I wish there were a gentler way to say that his eisegetical treatment of 1 John 3:1 entirely ignores John's focus on the new birth (cf., 1 Jn. 2:29). In its place, he imposes Paul's language of adoption, supporting his exposition with a misappropriation of Jn. 1:12-13 ("What Kind of Love is This?" in Joel R. Beeke, ed., *Calvin for Today* [Grand Rapids: Reformation Heritage Books, 2009], 3–12).

distinctive.[16]

The case for disentanglement.

The required disentanglement is two-directional. The history of adoption teaches us that the doctrine needs to be untwined from both the new birth and justification. Here we consider the case for the untwining of adoption from the new birth, comparing the contrasting of John (and Peter) and Paul, leaving the disentangling of justification and adoption for later when examining the internal workings of Paul's theology.

Although John is not alone in writing of the new birth (cf., 1 Pet. 1:3, 23), we focus on his corpus. First, because his writings belong, like Paul's, to the major books of the New Testament. Additionally, no New Testament author utilizes as many filial and/or familial terms as John. "In the Johannine writings, both in the gospel and also in the epistles," writes Twisselmann, "the perception of the Christian's sonship [*Gotteskindschaft*] and the Fatherhood of God has become completely central." Third, because it is John's teaching of the new birth which, more than anyone else's, has been conflated with Paul's teaching on adoption. Fourth, there is a real need for a fresh consideration of the semantic and theological differences between John's teaching on the new birth and Paul's on adoption. Just as distinct colors must first be washed separately before they can be stored or worn together, so the distinctive motifs of the new birth and adoption need to be understood on their own terms (which is to say, in their own contexts), before they can be juxtaposed in systems of theology, without threat to their

---

[16] At Puritan Reformed Theological Seminary there is developing an embrace of the salvation-historical approach. See Michael P. V. Barrett's excellent exegetical summary of adoption in *Complete in Him: A Guide to Understanding and Enjoying the Gospel*, ch. 8, "Adoption: The Privileges of the Gospel" (Grand Rapids: Reformation Heritage Books, 2017, 165–91). Note also the new Center for Reformed Biblical Theology.

clarity.[17]

Since the Christian church has one God and one Bible, communicating one gospel, we deal first with the commonalities between the thought of John and Paul.

First, they speak of the same heavenly Father. In Scripture, God is revealed to be the Father of humanity in a general sense, for he created us in his image. In the Old Testament, he reveals himself as Father of Israel his corporate son. Moreover, he promised to Israel the Messiah, his natural Son so to speak. But God is also, by his grace, Father of his people, both through new birth (John) and adoption (Paul).

Second, John and Paul both use the term *children of God* (τέκνα θεοῦ). This language is particularly prominent in John's references to the new birth. He uses it in John 1:12 and 1 John 3:1, 2, and refers in consequence of the new birth to "the children of God" (τὰ τέκνα τοῦ θεοῦ) in John 11:52 and 1 John 3:10 and 5:2. Paul also uses τέκνα in Romans 8:16, 17, 21; 9:8; and Philippians 2:15. Four of his references to God's τέκνα occur amid three of his uses of υἱοθεσία (Rom 8:16-17, 21; 9:8).

Third, John and Paul intend their filial or familial terminology to be understood metaphorically. Vellanickal points out that John refers to τέκνα on fifteen occasions. On seven of these, the use is metaphorical and followed by a genitive of a noun such as θεοῦ (Jn. 1:12; 11:52; 1 Jn. 3:1, 2, 10), Ἀβραάμ (Jn. 8:39) and διαβόλου ("devil," "slanderer" [1 Jn. 3:10]).[18]

Fourth, there are overlapping emphases in John and Paul. While the idea of status is front and center in Paul's teaching on adoption and

---

[17] Peter Stuhlmacher, *Wie treibt man Biblische Theologie?* Biblisch–Theologische Studien 24 (Neukirchen–Vluyn, 1995), 40; Twisselmann, "Die Gotteskindschaft der Christen nach dem Neuen Testament," 77.

[18] It is unclear why Vellanickal omits 1 John 5:2 from the metaphorical uses of τέκνα (*The Divine Sonship of Christians in the Johannine Writings*, 91–92).

arises from the adoptive act, we are not to think it is wholly absent from John's understanding of the new birth. Although the primary purpose of the new birth is to convey the idea of likeness of nature, talk of the new nature is possible precisely because those born again are children of God. Filial status is, then, implied. As John exclaims: "Behold what manner of love the Father has bestowed on us that we should be called the children of God [τέκνα θεοῦ], and we are!" (1 Jn. 3:1).

These commonalities go a long way to explain the ingrained conflation of the respective teachings of John and Paul. Factor in, though, the structural divergence of the new birth and adoption motifs and it becomes clear that the conflation muddles the two biblical themes and constitutes a coercive approach to the systematizing of biblical truth.

First, and most obviously, Paul uses the term υἱοθεσία, John does not. Nor is there in the Johannine writings another term capturing the distinctive meaning of υἱοθεσία ("adoption as son") or its breadth (inclusive of both the adoptive act and state). John uses the noun υἱός (son), but this he consistently reserves for Christ, except in Revelation 21:7 where he alludes to the eternal state in which God's children will at last resemble God's Son (cf., 1 Jn. 3:2). "Unlike John," observes Vellanickal, "Paul uses both *huioi* and *tekna* to express the divine sonship of man, while John reserves the term *huios* for Jesus."[19]

What then of John's use of ἐξουσία in John 1:12-13: "But as many as received him, to them he gave the authority [ἐξουσίαν] to become children of God [τέκνα θεοῦ], even to those who believe in his name: who were born not of blood, nor of the will of the flesh, nor of the will of man, but of God."? Despite influencing the early development of a new biblical dogmatic, John Murray remains wedded to the prior exegesis of the text *à la* Calvin, claiming that John 1:12 is among the most important passages in the New Testament bearing on adoption,

---

[19] Vellanickal, *The Divine Sonship of Christians in the Johannine Writings*, 69.

and distinguishing verse twelve (teaching adoption) from verse thirteen (teaching regeneration). Now, certainly, there is a clear distinction between John 1:12 and 13—verse thirteen accenting God's sovereignty in the birth of his children, and verse twelve our Spirit-enabled receiving of Christ in faith and of the authority to become God's children—but it is an assumption to think that the right or authority implies adoption.[20]

Were a prince born to everyday parents, the question of authority to be called the child of the monarch would rarely arise. But it becomes a matter of abiding importance when a child is born to royalty. The authority implies not that the royal child has been adopted, but that he or she truly belongs to the king. The authority bespeaks, then, the legitimacy of the child's royal status.

This is exactly John's point. Those born to God are born not of our own will, but by the will of God. Thus, in our birth into the kingdom of God, we receive authority to be called God's children (Jn. 1:12; 3:3-6). John's filial language differs markedly, then, from Paul's discussion of adoption as sons into the household of God (cf., Eph. 2:19).

Hattie Buell's line, altered to, "I'm a child of the King" is, then, the language of John rather than Paul. In John, there is not so much as one-time analogy of adoption, and certainly, nothing to compare with Paul's explicit fivefold references to adoption. Both John and Paul speak of *receiving* (cf., Jn. 1:12 [ὅσοι δὲ ἔλαβον αὐτόν] and Gal. 4:5 [τὴν υἱοθεσίαν ἀπολάβωμεν]), but the references to this receiving are to be

---

[20] Murray, *CW*, 2:226, 228. Marinus De Jonge also sees a distinction in 1:12-13, which turns on John's use of ἔλαβον and ἐγεννήθησαν, and, despite the order of the verses, wants us to understand the order of the new birth and faith: "In 1:12, 13, 'begotten of God' is connected with 'receive him' (that is, in this context, the Word), and 'believe in his name,' in such a way that the human decision is mentioned first, and then God's initiative. Yet faith is a response to, and not a pre-condition of, that initiative" ("The Son of God and the Children of God in the Fourth Gospel," in *Saved by Hope: Essays in Honor of Richard C. Oudersluys*, ed., James I. Cook [Grand Rapids: Eerdmans, 1978], 53).

understood within the ambit of their respective theologies. In John's corpus, we receive the right to royalty as children of the King; in Paul's, we receive as slaves the grace of adoption as sons.

Second, the respective models operate with contrasting uses of τέκνα (children). From the root τίκτειν (to beget, engender, procreate or give birth to), the noun does not have the profile in Paul's writings that it does in John's, nor is his primary concern to distinguish Christ's sonship from the childhood of God's people. Paul affirms the uniqueness of Christ but is rather concerned to bring together Christ (υἱὸς) and his people (υἱοί, as in υἱοθεσία). By this clever play-on-words Paul expresses the tight-knit union of the Son and the sons so central to adoptive sonship. By stating in effect that only in the Son (υἱὸς) can we become sons (υἱοί), he highlights the inextricable nexus between the believer's union with Christ and his or her adoption. Christ alone is the "natural" or firstborn (πρωτότοκος) Son (Rom. 8:29; Col. 1:18), yet in him the believer receives adoptive sonship. Paul's emphasis on Christ's sonship is, then, a theological rather than a sociocultural prioritization of the male gender (cf., his use of "daughters" [θυγατέρας] in 2 Cor. 6:18 and of τέκνα).

By contrast, John's use of the noun τέκνα and the aorist infinitive passive γεννηθῆναι (specifically the forms γεγέννηται in 1 Jn. 2:29 and 4:7 and γεγεννημένος in 1 Jn. 3:9 and 5:4, 18) are essential to his teaching of the kingdom. Τέκνα emphasizes the idea of origin and refers, gender neutrally, to those who have been born of God. In the distinction of the regenerate τέκνα θεοῦ and the only begotten υἱὸς θεοῦ, the Son alone possesses "a natural and essential relationship with the Father." He is μονογενὴς θεός who has uniquely experienced life in the bosom of the Father (εἰς τὸν κόλπον τοῦ Πατρὸς). Only he partakes of the being and nature of God (Jn. 1:18). John distinguishes, therefore, the ways in which God is the Father to his μονογενὴς and to his τέκνα, respectively. He also puts on record Jesus' consciousness of this distinction. Following his resurrection, he told Mary Magdalene to "go to my brothers (τοὺς ἀδελφούς μου) and say to them, 'I am ascending to my Father [τὸν Πατέρα μου], and your Father [πατέρα ὑμῶν]; and to my God [θεόν μου] and your God [θεὸν ὑμῶν]'" (Jn. 20:17b). While Jesus accepted unreservedly his sharing of his Father with his disciples (hence his identification with those the Father had given him), he sets apart his Sonship from their childhood (hence his deliberate choice of pronouns [τὸν πατέρα μου and Πατέρα ὑμῶν]). Whereas his Sonship flowed naturally from his eternal oneness with the Father, theirs was the product of a supernatural birth from above (a regeneration).[21]

The infinitive γεννηθῆναι occurs ninety-nine times in the New Testament, twenty-eight times in the Johannine corpus. Γεννηθῆναι is a derivative of the verb γεννάω (to beget, generate, produce, give birth to), and differs from τίκτω (the derivative of τέκνα), in that its reference to the giving of birth includes the prior conception. Likewise, in the LXX, γεννάω refers more to a mother's giving birth than to a father's begetting (יָלַד translates γεννάω, occuring 228 times and just twenty-

---

[21] Vellanickal, *The Divine Sonship of Christians in the Johannine Writings*, 90, 92, 143; Murray, *CW*, 2:226; Thomas A. Smail, *The Forgotten Father*, first published 1980, reprint ed. (London: Hodder and Stoughton, 1990), 143 (see also 62–64). John 20:17 figured in the Candlish/Crawford debate. Whereas Candlish insisted that the text identifies Christ with his brothers, Crawford argued that the distinguished commentators of church history denied this. Augustine, for instance, understood Christ to say that while his Sonship is natural, ours is gracious. To Crawford the omission of "our Father" is decisive: "It then appears that our Lord in His address to Mary Magdalene is *so far from identifying* His own sonship with that of his disciples, that *He most significantly and emphatically discriminates them from one another.*" (Robert S. Candlish, *The Fatherhood of God being the first course of the Cunningham Lectures delivered before New College, Edinburgh, in March 1864*. fifth ed. [Edinburgh: Adam and Charles Black, 1869], 117–29; Thomas J. Crawford, *The Fatherhood of God considered in its general and special aspects and particularly in relation to the atonement with a review of recent speculations on the subject*, second edition revised and enlarged with a reply to the strictures of Dr. Candlish, [Edinburgh and London: William Blackwood and Sons, 1867], 281, 283). More recently, Smail has argued that in John 20:17 there is both Christ's identification with the sons and his distinguishing of himself from them (*The Forgotten Father*, 142).

two times in maternal and paternal contexts, respectively). Γεννάω may thus be said to refer either to the beginning of a pregnancy (i.e., to the conception, in which case the mood is active, the tense aorist, implying male involvement) or to its termination (i.e., to the birth, in which case the mood is passive, the tense perfect, referencing female involvement)—Matthew 1:20 and Luke 1:35, respectively. Thus, the use of the verb is flexible. "What really matters for John," Vellanickal explains, "is the idea of an origin from God through generation. He deliberately does not envisage the different moments of conception and birth."[22]

Third, the respective teachings of John and Paul suggest different implications. Paul's motif speaks fundamentally of the Christian's standing before God (formerly a slave, now an adopted son), and draws our attention to our union with the Son (sons in the Son) and our acceptance with God. John's new birth motif implies a change of status (our birth into God's Kingdom) but implies most of all the Christian's new life (1 Jn. 2:28ff.). The graphic picture he paints of this life parallels the New Testament's comparable terms: τῇ παλινγενεσίᾳ (the regeneration, used of personal and cosmic salvation in Matt. 19:28 and Tit. 3:5) and ἀναγεννάω (1 Pet. 1:3).

Through the new birth, God's children come into possession of the same human nature as God's Son. Now blessed with his desire and ability to be holy, the newly born begin their journey into conformity to him. Explains Vellanickal:

> Teknon is used with a noun in the genitive to show that somebody bears a perfect likeness or a similarity of nature to some other person, to whom for the same reason some relation of paternity is attributed. In this expression is implied the derivation of a person's nature, and following therefrom, his character and belongings, though sometimes the one and sometimes the other element is prominent.

---

[22] Vellanickal, *The Divine Sonship of Christians in the Johannine Writings*, 98, 100.

Likewise, τέκνα, as a derivative of the Hebrew equivalent בְּנֵי (*sons*, meaning *peoples* or *tribes*), typically joined in Hebrew usage to the name of the progenitor (e.g., as in בְּנֵי יִשְׂרָאֵל [Gen. 42:5, 45:21; 46:5; Ex. 1:1] and בְּנֵי יְהוּדָה [Gen. 46:12; 1 Chron. 2:3,10; 4:1, etc.]), denotes descendency or posterity. Furthermore, the idea of similarity of nature arises from John's contrasting of the believer's and unbeliever's relationship to God and to the devil, respectively. His parallel phrases εἶναι ἐκ τοῦ θεοῦ and εἶναι ἐκ τοῦ διαβόλου (Jn. 8:41-47 and 1 Jn. 3:1-10) distinguish those who are of the world and those who are of the devil, as do his phrases τέκνα τοῦ θεοῦ and τέκνα τοῦ διαβόλου (1 Jn. 3:8-10; cf., Jn. 8:44). Whereas a child of God does the works of Abraham (cf., Jn. 8:39) and practices justice, the child of the devil does not practice righteousness nor love his brother.[23]

The remaining issue of disentanglement.

Clearly, John (and Peter) and Paul draw on similar filial and familial terms to unpack different but complementary aspects of our salvation. Notwithstanding, these compelling grounds for disentangling Paul's teaching of adoption from John's teaching of the new birth, we must nevertheless address a relevant matter internal to Paul's corpus. I refer to his fourfold use of τέκνα located amid three of his references to υἱοθεσία (Rom. 8:16-17, 21; 9:8).

Assuming the sound hermeneutical principle that we work from the clear to the unclear, we ask whether Paul intends his references to τέκνα to convey within his theology the juxtaposition of adoption and new birth models. To pose the question alternatively, should we read into Paul's uses of τέκνα the full array of etymological implications found in John's use of τέκνα, or just the surface translation *children*? In other words, are Paul's uses of τέκνα supportive of his teaching of adoption or are they intended additionally to teach the new

---

[23] Vellanickal, *The Divine Sonship of Christians in the Johannine Writings*, 91, 97.

birth albeit a way distinct from John and Peter?

Since Paul does not combine τέκνα with the use of γεννηθῆναι (John), ἀναγεννάω (Peter), or even his own use of παλιγγενεσίας (Tit. 3:5), the connection to birth is weakened.[24] In the context of Romans and of Paul's understanding of adoption, it is feasible to argue that Paul uses τέκνα to bring under one umbrella the hiatus and variegations of the old and new covenants (Rom. 9–11). Just as the children of Israel entered into the rights of primogeniture (Ex. 4:22; Hos. 11:1) by becoming God's corporate son, so Paul, according to this proposal, uses τέκνα to speak additionally of God's sons and daughters in the new Israel. τέκνα thus functions as a convenient collective term.

A second proposal broadens the collective use of τέκνα to include not only different filial terms but the salvation-historical development of the filial theme. On this understanding, Paul's uses τέκνα in Romans 8 qualify his earlier teaching in Galatians 4 of the coming of age of the church in this new covenant era. Whereas Israel was an underaged son of God, those now trusting in Christ enter into a mature sonship (Gal. 3:23–4:7). For so long, though, as the Father remains alive, his sons remain children (τέκνα). At no point are we independent of him, nor does he become frail and dependent on us. There is no role reversal, nor does the Father experience death.[25]

What term could Paul have used to tell us this, other than τέκνα? Infant (νήπιός) would not have worked, for this was the term Paul had used to describe the minority sonship of Israel under the old covenant (Gal. 4:1), and would imply the very opposite of what he

---

[24] He uses γεννάω in 1 Cor. 4:15, but of his relationship to his Corinthian readers and without use of τέκνα (Vellanickal, *The Divine Sonship of Christians in the Johannine Writings*, 77).

[25] Conversely, "a man ceases to be a Father when he dies himself, or when all his children are dead" (*The Works of the Rev. John Gambold, A.M., with an Introductory Essay by Thomas Erskine, Esq., Advocate* [Glasgow: Chalmers and Collins, 1822], vii).

conveys in Romans 8; namely, that the adopted are no longer possessed by the spirit of slavery as under the old covenant. Rather, they have the Spirit of adoption (cf., Rom. 8:15-16 and Gal. 1:1-3). While we call adult sons and daughters the children of elderly parents, we do not call them infants.

A third proposal suggests that Paul's use of τέκνα arose from the need to exemplify in his teaching of adoption (the union of the Son and the sons) that there is no male nor female in Christ (cf., Gal. 3:28). Consistently Paul underlines the value of sisters in Christ and would not want to imply that male believers alone are sons in the Son. What other term than τέκνα could communicate the inclusion of both male and female believers in God's adoptive purposes? The term τέκνα comports with Paul's utilizing of the covenant formula in 2 Corinthians 6:18: "I will be a father to you, and you shall be sons and daughters [καὶ θυγατέρας] to me, says the Lord God Almighty." To quote Heim, as we have already in the Preface, Paul's teaching of υἱοθεσία intends no statement of ontological superiority of one gender over another.[26]

Fourth, it is feasible to suggest that Paul intended nothing distinct when sometimes referring to the adopted as the sons of God and sometimes as God's children. Writes J. B. Lightfoot: "In St. Paul the expressions, 'Son of God', 'children of God', mostly convey the idea of *liberty*, as in iv. 6, 7, Rom. viii, 14sq. (see however Phil. ii:15), in St. John of *guileness* and *love* e.g. 1 Joh. iii. 1, 2, 10 in accordance with this distinction St. Paul uses *huioi* as well as *tekna*, St. John *tekna* only."[27]

Although Paul's uses of τέκνα do not necessitate the presence in his theology of a new birth model (since they are unaccompanied by γεννηθῆναι [John] and ἀναγεννάω [Peter]), what are we to make of two other texts in Romans 8? In the first Paul writes that, "the whole

---

[26] Heim, "Light through a Prism," 80.

[27] J. B. Lightfoot, *St. Paul's Epistle to the Galatians: A Revised Text with Introduction, Notes, and Dissertations* (London: MacMillan, 1892), 149.

creation ... groans together in the pains of childbirth" (v. 22) awaiting "the freedom of the glory of the children of God" (v. 21). Are we to discern here a parallel between the birth of God's children and the birth of the new world, comparable to the parallel between the adoption of God's sons and the adoption at the end of the age (vv. 15 and 23)? If so, how do the figures of birth and adoption interconnect *in Pauline theology*, especially since the idea of the birth of God's children has not figured in Romans or generally in his theology? Perhaps, Paul is simply heaping up pictures of the final day of salvation to convey the wonder of the occasion. This is possible given that at the *eschaton* all things are brought together in Christ (cf., Eph. 1:10).

Then, in verse 29 of Romans 8, the Lord Jesus is described as "the firstborn [πρωτότοκος] of many brothers" (cf., Col. 1:15). Although πρωτότοκος originally meant giving birth for the first time, it later came to mean firstborn or first in rank. By the time of the New Testament, the idea of birth had faded into the background. Yet, πρωτότοκος serves well in Romans 8 to distinguish the Son of God from the adopted sons of God. Yet, Paul generally seeks to bring the Son and the sons together in the adoption motif. In the immediate context, where Paul writes of the conformation in glory of the elect to the image of the Son, likeness of nature appears to be in view.

Clearly, such texts referring to birth amid references to adoption warrant further investigation. Two observations are noteworthy.

First, that all of the Pauline letters referencing adoption were written in the main decades prior to the Johannine and Petrine corpora. Whereas Galatians, Romans, and Ephesians were written in 49, 55, and 60 A.D., respectively, 1 and 2 Peter were not written until 63(–64) A.D., and John and 1–3 John not until the late '80s and early '90s A.D. This rules out any influences of the Johannine and Petrine emphasis on the new birth on Paul's adoption model.

Second, neither Paul's use of τέκνα in Romans 8 nor the two texts in Romans 8 utilizing the imagery of birth undermine the fundamental clarity of Paul's teaching on adoption. At most, τέκνα and the texts introduce us to what Vern Poythress calls the "fuzzy boundaries" of theological models, "interfer[ing] with the ideal of infinite precision."[28] Neither justifiy, then, our creation of fuzzy content, either by reading Paul's model of adoption into John's model of the new birth or by assuming that when Paul utilizes τέκνα and its accompanying themes he does so in a manner metaphorically coherent with the Johannine (or Petrine) model of the new birth.

3. THE FUNDAMENTALS OF ΥἱΟΘΕΣἹΑ

Having established that both the etymology and use of υἱοθεσία refer to adoption, we close the chapter with a consideration of Paul's use of *adoption* as a linguistic tool. To date, I have typically labeled the term a teaching, more formally, a doctrine, or a motif (or theme). I have, however, been coy about identifying and defining adoption linguistically. Here is why.

In the lopsided emphasis on the divineness of Scripture in traditional systematics, the linguistic categorization of adoption is overwhelmingly ignored. Systematicians typically delve straight into the propositions of adoption. The growing sensitivity to the humanness of Scripture, while increasing the descriptors of adoption, has yet to lead in the field of theology to much explanation or distinguishing of their meaning.[29] In biblical studies, adoption is referred to as a

---

[28] Vern S. Poythress, *Symphonic Theology: The Validity of Multiple Perspectives in Theology* (Grand Rapids: Academie Books [Zondervan]), 1987, 64–67, 81–82.

[29] Garner variously describes adoption as a concept, metaconcept, a metaphor or a model, but without defining his terms or explaining his choice of them (*Sons in the Son*, 19, 35, 36, 40, 52, 138fn77, 207, 211, 235, 250).

metaphor, but the categorization is assumed rather than unpacked. Let us begin, then, with three essentials of adoption as a linguistic tool.

First, and in line with historic Christian orthodoxy, we support the view that Paul's use of υἱοθεσία is reality-depicting. Adoption conveys real, eternal, and substantive truth, divinely revealed for our instruction, salvation, and mission. I reject, then, the postmodernist idea that adoption is merely a social construct formulated in our tribal grouping to explain life as we Christians find it. The grace of adoption is not a humanly created or bottom-up projection onto God. After all, left to ourselves, we reject God's existence or attribute to him evil intent. Adoption is, rather, a top-down, archetypal, divine revelation. The term and its image have been given to us in history through the mediation of Christ, and by the mind-opening and heartwarming revelation of the Spirit. We glean this from Paul's remark about the Fatherhood of God in Ephesians 3:14: "I bow my knees before the Father, from whom [—that's top-down—] every family in heaven and on earth is named". In other words, says Calvin, human fathers borrow their title from the Father of glory. Likewise, the language of adoption comes from God and not man. On this understanding, societal adoption evinces the fact that humanity is created in God's image, for, in pale ways and with limited reach, we mirror ectypally what God predestined for his elect in Christ before the foundation of the world (Eph. 1:5). Accordingly, divine adoption is of a higher order and broader historical scope than societal adoption.[30]

The second essential has to do with *how* adoption is reality-depicting. The positivist account of reality is irrelevant here, since positivists believe that man can only know observable realities and rely on logical empiricism to discover them. Neither is the idealist account

---

[30] John Calvin, *Sermons on the Epistles to Timothy & Titus*. Facsimile ed. of 1579. Reprint ed. (Carlisle, PA: The Banner of Truth Trust, 1983), 9 (*CO* 53 [81]:13). Garner expresses well the top-down view in *Sons in the Son*, xxi–xxiv.

germane, since it responds to human need rather than to external reality. Adoption was in the mind and purpose of God and was for many in history an external reality before it became for them a felt spiritual need. This leaves us with realistic accounts to consider.[31]

The naïve-, direct-, or common sense-realist account likely explains why, in history, substantive discussions of the language of adoption are rare. The naïve realist believes things are described as they are. On this understanding, God has given us access in the language of adoption to how he *actually* accepts us. The simplicity of this top-down approach is appealing, not least because Scripture does not describe adoption as a figure of speech, and although Calvin notes biblical *metaphorae* and *similitudines*, he does not, as far as I have found to date, describe the Fatherhood of God or adoption as figures of speech.

More recently, critical realism has found favor with those who, fearing that naïve realism idolizes language and thus blurs the Creator-creature distinction, nevertheless wish to uphold the transcendental (top-down) realist view of revelation. Critical realists support, accordingly, the metaphysical claims of Scripture but believe they are accessed non-directly, irrespective of whether biblical language is understood to be a mixture of the literal and the figurative or irreducibly figurative.[32]

---

[31] I interact in the following with Janet Martin Soskice's *Metaphors and Religious Language* (Oxford: Clarendon Press, 1987), 97–161.

[32] John Frame represents those understanding biblical language to be a mixture. While regarding all biblical language as analogical—since God views his revelation (the referent) in his divine capacity and we in our human capacity—Frame distinguishes the literal in Scripture from the metaphorical (Frame, *DKG*, 35–40, 227–28). He challenges, accordingly, those treating the Scriptures literalistically (without regard for its humanness [e.g., genres and figures of speech]). Alternatively, Kevin Vanhoozer challenges pragmatic views of biblical language which, conversely, state that "there is no non-metaphorical word that can be said of God." They diminish thereby the language

Either way, critical realists believe that there is more to the language of Scripture than meets the eye. They are, then, very much at home with the Bible's specific figures of speech, recognizing in them, despite their status as vehicles of revelation, indications of our limitations in speaking of God and his ways. Whether or not, then, other language of Scripture is taken literally, critical realists understand adoption to depict figuratively God's saving of his people and the privileges and responsibilities he grants them in his grace.

Critical realism is sometimes labeled moderate realism. Although the notion may date back to Aquinas, it is now employed by Kevin Vanhoozer. As a realist, he seeks amid the challenge of postmodernism to weave between absolutist traditional interpretations which seek a God's eye point-of-view true for all times and places, and anti-authoritarian, anarchic, postmodernist interpretations which contain no facts. With facts interpreted away, we are left, says the postmodernist, with the fictions we create. Biblical interpretation thus becomes invention. Vanhoozer seeks, accordingly, an interpretation of Scripture that yields sufficient knowledge for our faith, without it becoming either wholly determinate (absolutist) or wholly indeterminate (anarchist).

Going by this moderate realism, we can know what is meant by the grace of adoption, but inexhaustively so. Accordingly, we may add to our knowledge of adoption or even revise historical interpretations of it, yet without inventing new meaning. In this way, moderate realism upholds the infallibility of the Scriptures while rejecting the infallibility of the interpreter. Vanhoozer promotes, then, a regulative realism. In seeking the truth, he argues, we may arrive at a provisional consensus, even if not at the whole truth of reality. On this understanding, the truth

---

of Scripture, viewing it as but an exemplar of how to create theological models—ones which "work" for the present (Vanhoozer, *Is There Meaning in This Text? The Bible, the reader and the morality of literary knowledge* (Leicester, England: Apollos, 1998), 134.

of adoption outruns our best interpretations of the model, and yet gains among the community of interpreters a regulative (accurate but non-exhaustive) understanding of it.[33]

With modest confidence then, we come to the third essential: the category of the figure of speech or trope into which Paul's use of υἱοθεσία falls. Of all the possibilities—distant relations such as symbol, allegory, or satire, or nearer relations such as hyperbole, exaggeration, oxymoron, and litotes—most akin are synecdoche, metonymy, simile, and analogy:

- Synecdoche is too oblique a figure of speech to describe adoption. In a synecdoche, a comprehensive idea is implied by a narrower term. Here, the comprehensive idea is *the Fatherhood of God*, but that idea, servicing both adoption and the new birth, cannot of itself do justice to the specificities of adoption. Conversely, the narrower term of adoption cannot of itself do justice to the Fatherhood of God since the divine paternity also has relevance to the distinctively structured model of the new birth (as also to the filial and familial language or implications of the synoptic Gospels and of the author of Hebrews).

- Metonymy, meaning an adjunct standing for the whole, is also too oblique to describe adoption. The metonymy in this context is *sonship* (typically *Kindschaft* in German). It accounts in part for the historic neglect of adoption, for while, as an adjunct for adoption, *sonship* includes the adoptive state, it omits the prior adoptive act (the Father's placement of erstwhile slaves as sons into his family).

- Simile is too weak or indirect to describe adoption since its use of "like" or "as" injects qualifiers not found in Paul's teaching of adoption.

---

[33] Vanhoozer, *Is There Meaning in This Text?* 126–40, 300–303.

- Analogy, referring here not to the nature of biblical language, but to the specific figure of speech, teaches old words new tricks, and stretches language to fit new applications. It requires, then, no imaginative strain to understand the connection. When, for instance, we adopt a cat, we speak analogically, for while we stretch the language to fit the new application, it requires little imagination. When, however, we say that God adopts sons and daughters from among humanity, we not only stretch the language to fit a new application, but strain our imagination to understand how this can be. Divine adoption may, then, be understood analogically, yet analogy, as a figure of speech, does not do justice to the grace of adoption. In Scripture, adoption affords us a new picture of God and his grace toward sinners that we would not naturally perceive. For this reason, it is more appropriate to describe adoption as a metaphor.

Colin Gunton, noting Ingolf Dalferth's *Religöse Rede von Gott* (1981), estimates there are as many as 125 definitions of metaphor. He defines metaphor, though, as "a term belonging somewhere else . . . used in an unusual context." While this simple definition is likely insufficient to distinguish analogy and metaphor, it points us in the direction of the distinction, for a metaphor understands and experiences one kind of thing (acceptance with God) in terms of another (adoption).[34] Yet, dealing with the supernatural, metaphor reminds us that while God is knowable, his nature and ways are, remarks George Chrysides, not

---

[34] Colin E. Gunton, *The Actuality of the Atonement: A Study of Metaphor, Rationality and the Christian Tradition* (Edinburgh: T&T Clark, 1988), 27–28; George Lakoff and Mark Johnson, *Metaphors We Live By* (Chicago: University of Chicago Press, 2003), 5, 36, 117 (cf., Soskice, *Metaphors and Religious Language*, 15); Sallie McFague, *Models of God: Theology for an Ecological, Nuclear Age* (London: SCM Press, 1987), 29–31, 33.

statable, at least at a literal level.[35]

Metaphors, we may say, are one-time figures of speech fleeting in their use and minimalist in the information they convey. Writes Henri Blocher: "Some metaphors . . . are of little cognitive import and of little help in elaborating doctrine. They draw attention to superficial or accidental similarities." While we regularly formulate metaphors in passing, whether in preaching, prayer, or conversation, the ones we create do not carry the weight of biblical metaphors, nor are they binding. Adoption, however, is a particular kind of metaphor. It is a model.[36]

A model is what we may describe variously as a robust, weightier, dominant, master, large-scale, conceptual, extended, or theory-constitutive metaphor. To quote Sallie McFague, a model is "a metaphor that has gained sufficient stability and scope so as to present a pattern for relatively comprehensive and coherent explanation." In brief, a model is "a metaphor with staying power." Given Paul's five strategic uses of υἱοθεσία, the wealth of their theological content, and the climactic role adoption plays in his theology, we deduce that Paul's term refers to a model.[37]

Admittedly, the terms metaphor and model are, of themselves, no more likely to stir us doxologically than the alternatives. In particular, *model* conjures from days of youth something flimsy or

---

[35] George Lakoff and Mark Johnson, *Metaphors We Live By*, first published 1980 (Chicago: University of Chicago Press, 2003), 37, 59, 265; Soskice, *Metaphors and Religious Language*, 54–66; George Chrysides, "Meaning, Metaphor and Meta-Theology," *SJT* 38 (1985), 145.

[36] Henri Blocher, "Biblical Metaphors and the Doctrine of Atonement," *JETS* 47:4 (December 2004), 638.

[37] Sallie McFague, *Metaphorical Theology: Models of God in Religious Language* (Philadelphia: Fortress, 1982), 71, 117, and *Models of God*, 34; Frame, *DKG*, 227; Soskice, *Metaphor and Religious Language*, 102; Vanhoozer, *Is There Meaning in This Text?* 129.

artificial. As children, we received Airfix Models: cars, planes, ships, and the like. Moreover, we must distinguish a conservative use of the term from one that is liberal. Nevertheless, despite the nomenclature's drawbacks, thinking especially of Donald Macleod's opposition to its more liberal use, I believe, for want of a better substitute, that it is legitimate to continue to call adoption a model.[38]

First, it was from Professor Macleod that I learned, courtesy of Augustine, that in theology we sometimes use terms not because they are ideal but so as not to remain silent. Second, because there is an enriching conservative understanding of models which casts light on how the language of biblical revelation functions. This light has been greatly needed. Third, models, from a conservative standpoint, do not attempt to create revelation. We understand them to be God-inspired conduits through which his infallible revelation comes to us.[39]

I concur, then, with Macleod's rejection of a liberal view of model, but were we to reject the idea of models altogether, we would perpetuate lost opportunities to go deeper into the biblical use of language, and, as we shall discover in the next chapter, would miss out on how Paul's model of adoption functions and what the apostle sought to accomplish by his uses of υἱοθεσία.

However, in maintaining the category of model, two points must be made.

First, given the nature of Scripture, we understand biblical models, contra Sallie McFague, to be dicta for theology rather than

---

[38] Donald Macleod, *Christ Crucified: Understanding the Atonement* (Downers Grove, Illinois: IVP Academic, 2014), 104–6.

[39] Donald Macleod's use of Augustine in defense of the term *person* is taken from the father's *On the Trinity* (5:9): "When the question is asked, 'What three?' human language labours altogether under great poverty of speech. The answer, however, is given, Three 'persons', not that it might be (completely) spoken, but that it might not be left (wholly) unspoken". Calvin's defenses are gleaned from his *Institutes* 1:13:3 (*Shared Life: The Trinity and the Fellowship of God's People* (London: Scripture Union, 1987), 15–16, 27.

exemplars of how we may formulate our own. Let me say again, we have no liberty to create models which clash with revealed truth, nor to substitute them for the biblical models already revealed to us. Scripture is sufficient in the models given us to perceive the gospel, and while they are to be applied in the contemporary context, we have no self-appointed right to invent our own supposedly authoritative, Scripture-equaling, doctrine-shaping metaphors or models. Were we to take this right to ourselves we would "stampede away from the familiar images of the Fatherhood of God in an attempt to provide . . . new language" for our theology and, therefore, our faith.[40]

Second, we must note the variant way that Janet Soskice and Erin Heim understand the relationship between metaphors and models from the understanding I am working with here. They view models as logically prior to metaphors and therefore regard metaphors as based on models. Thus, models contain attributes that may or may not surface in their corresponding metaphors. I beg to differ, siding ironically with McFague in her view that models are aggrandized metaphors. Accordingly, models have greater structural capacity than metaphors. They are those "around which," says Frame, "a theological doctrine is organized."[41]

This variant use of *metaphors* and *models* is significant. Whereas Heim views the four uses of υἱοθεσία (recall, she omits Eph. 1:5) as multiple adoption metaphors—like bands of color appearing as a white light passes through a prism—I view the five uses, notwithstanding their revelation of different aspects of adoption, as constituting one coherent adoption model. Heim we would expect to disagree, and yet she seems to scupper her perspective by the

---

[40] Francis Lyall, *Slaves, Citizens, Sons: Legal Metaphors in the Epistles* (Grand Rapids: Academie Books [Zondervan], 1984), 188.

[41] Heim, "Light through a Prism," 16–17, 35, 36; Soskice, *Metaphor and Religious Language*, 50–51; Frame, *DKG*, 27.

inexplicable claim that each adoption metaphor (use of υἱοθεσία) is a discrete element or separate utterance *of the composite whole*. Rather than tell us what is the composite whole if not the adoption model, she states that the "synthetic endeavor, unfortunately, falls outside the purview of [her] study." Noting that the matter "is certainly a viable avenue for further research" we have taken it up here, revising her paradigm in the process.

As a coherent model, adoption possesses the theological robustness Blocher has in mind when speaking of those metaphors having a "fruitfulness for doctrine." The model meets all three criteria Blocher uses to identify which metaphors should be "granted privilege":

1. Frequency of occurrence, regularity, development, with a constellation of subordinate metaphors and other recurring arrangements, ensuring predictability, and raising the probability of doctrinal significance intended by the writer.
2. Consistent evidence that the author considered his metaphorical statements to be a springboard for understanding a matter, and a formation of a matrix of meaningful connections closely allied to a conceptual scheme. In effect, the author supplies a *metalinguistic* proposition accounting for the way things, which, while metaphorical, are logically related to reality.
3. The significance of the literary (or rhetorical) genre of the unit containing the metaphor. The more didactic the genre, the nearer the conceptual implications.[42]

On this understanding, we may delineate what the New Testament reveals of the metaphorical structure of the familial in general and of adoption in particular. The Fatherhood of God forms what we may call the supramodel, for it overarches the distinctively

---

[42] Henri Blocher, "Biblical Metaphors and the Doctrine of Atonement," *JETS* 47/4 (December 2004), 639.

structured filial models of the synoptic Gospels, John (and Peter). Paul, and Hebrews. The new birth and adoption models receive greater attention, though, given the authors using them, and since they are more substantive, clearly defined, amenable to doctrinal formulation, and address how we enter the filial state as also the subsequent experience of it (see Figure 3.2 overleaf).[43]

Considered on its own, adoption stands at the heart of a pyramidical structure. The Fatherhood of God, as supramodel, constitutes the capstone, the model of adoption the core, and the correlative themes (subordinate metaphors) the base:

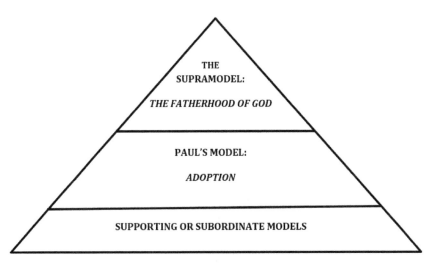

Figure 3.1
The pyramidical structure of supramodel, model,
and subordinate metaphors

---

[43] Poythress, *Symphonic Theology*,16; Soskice, *Metaphor and Religious Language*, 55, 112; Lyall, *Slaves, Citizens, Sons,* 79.

THE SUPRAMODEL OF THE FATHERHOOD OF GOD			
THE SONSHIP MODEL	**THE NEW BIRTH MODEL**	**THE ADOPTION MODEL**	**THE BROTHERHOOD MODEL**
LOCATION: SYNOPTIC GOSPELS	**LOCATION:** JOHANNINE AND PETRINE CORPORA	**LOCATION:** PAULINE EPISTLES	**LOCATION:** EPISTLE TO THE HEBREWS
KEY PHRASES: *Sons of God; sons of your Father; your (heavenly) Father; their Father; my Father; son of God; little children; Father.*	**KEY PHRASES:** *Children of God; born; born again; seeing and entering the kingdom of God; born of [God]; newborn infants; (many or my) sons.*	**KEY PHRASES:** *Sons of God; heir(s) (of or through God); (Spirit of) adoption as sons; sons; "Abba! Father!"; slaves; children of God; household; redemption.*	**KEY PHRASES:** *My Son; many sons; (my, his, or holy) brothers; children; slavery; God's house.*
MATTHEW: 5:9, 16, 45; 6:9, 14, 26, 32; 7:7-11; 13:43; 16:17; 18:19; 25:34; 26:29. **MARK:** 3:31-35. **LUKE:** 3:38; 8:19-21; 10:21-22; 11:2, 13; 15:11-32; 20:36.	**JOHN:** John 1:12-13; 3:1-8. **1 JOHN:** 1 John 2:28–3:3. **REVELATION:** 21:7. **1 PETER:** 1:3; 2:2.	**ROMANS:** 8:12-25, 9:1-5. **GALATIANS:** 3:23–4:7. **EPHESIANS:** 1:3-6.	**HEBREWS** 1:5-6; 2:10-18; 3:1-5.

Figure 3.2
The supramodel of the Fatherhood of God and its subordinate filial models

We mention these subordinate metaphors because the model of adoption is drawn not simply from the term υἱοθεσία (although we use it as shorthand), but from the term located in its sentences and pericopes. From its theological and syntactical context the adoption model calls forth an emotional, moral, and spiritual response.[44]

Note in closing, that, in contrast to ratiocinated treatments of adoption, we depart from the practice of mixing distinctively structured models unless or until we find Scripture to clearly mix them. Such models constitute particular or individual perspectives on the gospel, offering a different or, at least, a supplementary way, of parsing the doctrine of salvation than that offered by traditional *ordo salutis* arrangements.

Recall, that although unique, the gospel possesses such wealth of content and meaning that God, for our sakes, has couched its revelation in multiple perspectives. While distinct, they combine to help our finite minds to appreciate the profundity of the gospel. We shall come in chapter six to consider how they may be harmonized systemically, for as van Asselt and Dekker note, "systematic reflection is unavoidable for every form of theology."[45] Yet, we seek a harmonization which comports with the fullness of an orthodox doctrine of Scripture, its humanness as well as its divineness.

~~~~

---

[44] Besides υἱοθεσία, Vellanickal lists four relevant filial or familial terms used by Paul: (i) υἱοὶ θεοῦ (and equivalents in Rom. 8:14, 19; 9:26; 2 Cor. 6:18; Gal. 3:26; 4:6-7); (ii) τέκνα τοῦ θεοῦ (Rom. 8:16-17, 21; 9:8; Phil. 2:15); (iii) τέκνα ἐπαγγελίας (Rom. 9:8; Gal. 4:28); (iv) θυγατέρας (2 Cor. 6:18). We may also think of the correlative themes of Fatherhood, household (Eph. 2:19), and heirship.

[45] van Asselt and Dekker, "Introduction," in *Reformation and Scholasticism*, 32.

4.

ADOPTION IN THEOLOGY
Metaphorical Usage

> If biblical scholars are to appreciate the complex-
> ities of biblical metaphors, then their exegesis
> must also be founded upon a theory of metaphor
> that is both philosophically sound and exegetic-
> ally useful.
>
> Erin Heim, "Light through a Prism."

The road we are on runs farther into the forest of linguistics, bringing us to the thick foliage surrounding Metaphor, a town en route to Adoption. It is via Metaphor that we get to the heart of Adoption and gain the best view of the region of Retrieval. To bypass the forest is to miss out on the best view of both towns and to deny ourselves the opportunity to speak of them with optimum authority.

~~~~

1. THE PURPOSE OF THE ADOPTION MODEL

In contemplating Paul's adoption model, the question arises as to whether he was led by the Spirit to decorate a bare concept or concepts of the gospel, or to articulate fresh discoveries derived from the Spirit's illumination. To answer the question is to introduce competing theories of knowledge.[1]

---

[1] In what follows, I dialogue chiefly with Eberhard Jüngel, *Theological Essays*, transl. with an introduction by J. B. Webster (Edinburgh: T&T Clark, 1989), 16–17; *Gott als Geheimnis der Welt* (Tübingen: J. C. B. Mohr [Paul Siebeck], 1978), 357–408; Janet Martin Soskice, *Metaphor and Religious Language* (Oxford: Clarendon Press, 1985), 1–14, 24–53; and Erin Heim, "Light through a Prism: New Avenues of Inquiry for the Pauline Ὑιοθεσία Metaphors," (Ph.D. Diss.: University of Otago, 2014), 24–48, 80–88.

The Substitution or Comparison Theory.

Associated initially with Aristotle's *The Art of Rhetoric* and *Poetics* and his famous definition of metaphor as "a short form of comparison" or "the application of an alien name by transference,"[2] the substitution theory claims metaphors (and models we may add) are ornamental. They decorate bare concepts. Two characteristics of metaphor are essential to this decoration: the name (τό ὄνομα), in this case adoption; and the conceptual word(s) of substance (λόγος της οὐσίας), namely, relationship, standing, and acceptance.

The significance of the name underlines the importance of translating υἱοθεσία accurately, for the term *adoption* is very decorative of the bare conceptual ideas of relationship, standing, and acceptance with God. That day in the Free Church College when the word *adoption* jumped out at me, it was precisely the ornamental attractiveness of the term which warmed me to my assignment. The *Tertius Usus Legis* (the third use of the law)—a use I affirm—would not have had the same effect on me as did the metaphorical lingo, *adoption*.

Yet, the substitution or comparison raises some questions. First, whether the comparison is found in the transference from the conceptual words to the metaphor, or only in the product of the transference (what remains of the original conceptual words following the transference or *epiphora* [carrying over]).

Second, if, going by this theory, we simply say that our relationship to God, our standing with him, and our acceptance by him, is like an adoption, then are we not diluting the metaphor/model into a weakened simile, turning it from a direct into an indirect figure of speech?

Third, if the metaphor/model is but the substitution of the conceptual words, then has it not become expendable? We may still

---

[2] Cited by Colin Gunton, *The Actuality of the Atonement: A Study of Metaphor, Rationality and the Christian Tradition* (Edinburgh: T&T Clark, 1988), 28.

speak of our relationship, standing, and acceptance, albeit by means of bare, unadorned, tired, or repetitive conceptual words. Obviously, though, without the frills provided by the metaphorical dressing, we possess little understanding or facility of expression, and struggle to muster excitement. Our worship is reduced to repetition *ad nauseum* of nondescript conceptual words. Theologizing becomes impossible. In the absence of the ornamentation of adoption, it ends where it begins: "I have a relationship with God, a standing with God, and am accepted by God."

Thus, despite the long-standing popularity of the substitution or comparison theory, there is more to a metaphor or model than its decorative qualities. Writes Soskice, "Even where metaphor does function as an ornament, it does so by virtue of making some addition to significance, be that ever so slight."[3] In other words, in the ornamentation there is a substantive addition to the bare conceptual words. Their ornamentation takes us into the why, the what, and the how of our relationship, standing, and acceptance with God.

Emotive theories.

Emotive theories also operate with deviant word usage: a typical term used atypically. They, too, deny the addition of special cognitive content. Yet, this is where the common ground between the substitution and emotive theories ends. In emotive theories of metaphor, the emphasis is not on content (or meaning) at all, but on the emotional impact (or use) of the metaphor/model. What metaphors lack in cognitive content they make up for by stirring emotion.

Certainly, Paul's use of υἱοθεσία impacts emotions, but by formulating a model from υἱοθεσία, Paul seeks to do more than to rouse the emotions of his readers. The arousal happens precisely because of the wonderful truths the adoption model discloses. They are powerful

---

[3] Soskice, *Metaphor and Religious Language*, 25.

and beautiful, combining:

- Rich cognitive content, impressively germane to both the *historia* and *ordo* (better *applicatio*) *salutis*.

    and

- Affective influences, arising from its depiction of our personal salvation, the life of sonship, and hope of the new world to come.

Incremental theories.

Incremental theories differ from both the substitution theory (namely, that an idea can be expressed equally, whether conceptually or metaphorically) and emotive theories (namely, that metaphors offer an affective impact not a substantive increase of meaning). They claim, rather, that metaphor is a must. What is said by the metaphor/model can be said in no other way.

Several specific types of incremental theory are identifiable.

In the *intuitionist theory*, the metaphor/model forms, by an intuitive act, a complete transformation in which the literal meaning is eradicated. The act brings forth new, fully cognitive meaning, but is inexplicable. That suffices to sink the theory in its nonbiblical application, yet the intuitive act could be explained in biblical metaphors/models by divine inspiration. In the biblical scenario, God's exhaling of his Spirit on Paul granted him both the intuition to discern divine truths and the impulse to bring them together in a new, unique, and affective model of adoption.

In the *controversion theory* of Monroe Beardsley (*Aesthetics*), sometimes labeled a verbal-opposition or metaphorical twist, a meta-phor is recognizable by its logically incompatible modification of its subject. Going by this theory, metaphorical connotations must, strictly speaking, be false or logically absurd.

While Beardsley's theory is criticized for the vagueness of the connotations required to make it a metaphor, some logical absurdities are discernible in the adoption model. Recall how George MacDonald pounced on them. Would God as Father to Adam and Eve really condemn his children eternally? Since the race remains related to Father God, is it not logically absurd to speak of our being adopted back into his family? MacDonald proves, however, that post-Enlightenment Romanticism defeated Enlightenment Rationalism only by succumbing to it, for in seeking to iron out the logical absurdities of the adoption model, he lorded it over Scripture.

Leaving MacDonald aside, we can point to some of the other absurdities of the model. Since, for instance, Israel was adopted at Mount Sinai (Rom. 9:4) how come believing Jews are adopted upon trusting in Christ (Gal. 4:4-5)? If Jews and Gentiles are adopted when believing in Christ, how come the adoption is yet to come (Rom. 8:23)?

What appears absurd however, namely, the idea of adoption from slavery to sonship, makes sense once we realize the history of Israel and the common ground between Israel's redemption from Egypt and the Roman practice of adopting former slaves. The model's controversions or twists can thus be explained historically and theologically.

In the *interactive theory*, Max Black (*Models and Metaphor*) endeavors to build on the earlier contribution of I. A. Richards (*The Philosophy of Rhetoric*). Richards taught that in the principle of metaphor two active thoughts of different things are present in a single word or phrase. Its meaning becomes apparent by their interaction. The one thought, the tenor, covers the underlying subject (in this case, our relationship with God, standing, and acceptance, etc.). The other—the vehicle (or model of adoption)—expresses the tenor. Black maintained Richards' basic idea, but inadvisably, argues Soskice, changed the idea of two thoughts into two subjects, the principle and the subsidiary. In the interaction, the two commonplaces are acknowledged, but filters or screens are used to highlight some aspects and to suppress others. While these succeed in producing new, informative, and irreplaceable meaning, they inadvertently reduce the metaphor to a simile and diminish the notion of interaction.

Criticism of Black's interaction theory has led to an *interanimation theory*. It reverts to Richards' idea of the two active thoughts in a single word or phrase. Richards focused not only on the meaning of individual words or phrases but on their complete utterances and surrounding contexts. Metaphors/models he understood to be the product of the interanimation of the tenor and vehicle, and the vehicle and the tenor, in their complete utterances or whole units. Such utterances may also include subsidiary vehicles or metaphors. Take Galatians 4:4-7, for instance:

> But when the fullness of time had come, God sent forth his Son, born of woman, born under the law, to redeem those who were under the law, so that we might receive adoption as sons. And because you are sons, God has sent the Spirit of his Son into our hearts, crying, "Abba! Father!" So you are no longer a slave, but a son, and if a son, then an heir through God.

The interanimation of the adoption model involves the tenor (relationship, standing, and acceptance with God), the vehicle (adoption), and the subsidiary vehicles (slavery, sonship, and heirship). We may state this in terms of the pyramid in the previous chapter. The Fatherhood of God forms the supramodel or capstone, the vehicle or model of adoption forms the core and is expressed by the tenor, and the subsidiary vehicles or metaphors the base. The latter I regard not as isolated metaphors but as constitutive elements of the one adoption model. Slavery, sonship, and heirship are all found in the sources of Paul's adoption model: Old Testament history and contemporaneous sociocultural practices. This associative network of metaphors helps flesh out the adoption model:

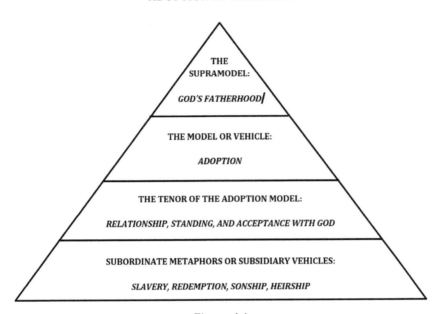

Figure 4.1
The pyramidical structure of the adoption model considered in terms of its interanimation

---

These competing theories and variations in terminological usage are fascinating, in that, in contrast with the way the doctrine has been perceived, they underline its profundity. Adoption is:

- *Both ornamental (à la* the substitution or comparison theory) *and heuristic (à la* the incremental theories). Paul spoke, says Jüngel, "more than the actuality of the world is able to say," yet, by communicating as he did, he was able to convey what is profoundly true and real. He went "beyond actuality [—which "represents being only in time"—] without talking around it." Yet, by "going beyond actuality, [he actually got] to grips with it."[4] While God has not adopted us in a literal sense as we humans

---

[4] Jüngel, *Theological Essays,* 16, 25.

understand adoption, the adoption model communicates the archetypal, celestial reality of our entrance into our relationship, standing, and acceptance with God. Were our talk of the relationship not metaphorical it would be a lie, for adoption deviates from the truth in order to remain within its bounds and to communicate its reality.

- *Both cognitive (à la* the substitution or comparison theory and incremental theories) *and affective (à la* the emotive theories). Adoption not only communicates discoveries of God's dealings with his people, it evokes praise within and among us for the blessings received from the Father, in Christ, and by the Spirit (Eph. 1:3). The model supplies, then, a sighting of God's grace far surpassing the communicative and inspirational abilities of the bare conceptual words or tenors of *relationship, standing,* and *acceptance.*

- *Intuitionist, controversionist, interactive, as well as interanimated.* Adoption is, first, intuitionist, not because Paul possessed inherent heuristic abilities, but because God breathed out on him. Thus, we relabel this version of the incremental theory, the theopneustic theory (from θεόπνευστος ["breathed out by God," 2 Tim. 3:16]). The adoption model is also controversionist in the sense that it contains apparent logical absurdities. Expounded in context, these features of the model are not absurd at all. They only appear absurd when read from a bottom-up, rationalist, or romantic perspective governed more by contemporary practices of adoption than by the exegesis of Scripture. Then again, the adoption model is interactive. Its new cognitive meaning arises from an exchange between the tenor (what it means to belong to God) and the vehicle (how adoption discovers for us that belonging). The tenor without the vehicle would have left Paul either silent about certain aspects of our relationship with God or severely limited or dull in expressing them. The vehicle without

214

the tenor would have rendered Paul's language of adoption a fiction. Finally, the adoption model is interanimated in that it includes not only the word υἱοθεσία, but completed utterances, sentences, and units containing references to the supramodel (God's Fatherhood), the tenor and vehicle, and the subsidiary metaphors of slavery, sonship, and heirship.

2. THE SOURCE OF THE ADOPTION MODEL

How rich is Paul's language of adoption! Clearly, God is its ultimate source, hence our top-down approach. Nevertheless, God's inspiring of Paul was organic not mechanical. He sovereignly ordained the earthly influences which Paul enlisted in constructing the model. I thus concur with G. B. Caird that there is a two-way movement in the forming of biblical models, but, contra Caird, believe the movement began in heaven rather than on earth:

> Metaphors derived from human relationships have a special interest and importance, because they lend themselves to a two–way traffic in ideas. When the Bible calls God judge, king, father or husband it is, in the first instance, using the known to throw light on the divine unknown, and particularly on God's attitude to his worshippers. But no sooner has the metaphor traveled from earth to heaven than it begins the return journey to earth, bearing with it an ideal standard by which the conduct of human judges, kings, fathers and husbands is to be assessed.[5]

---

[5] G. B. Caird, *The Language and Imagery of the Bible*, reprint ed. (Grand Rapids: Eerdmans, 1997), 19. Curiously, Herman Bavinck argues that the theory of knowledge ought to start with our ordinary everyday experience, since God reproduces in his human image-bearers the ectypal knowledge reflective of the archetypal knowledge in his own divine mind. While he posits this view over against the speculations of the philosophers, there seems to be something of a tension here in Bavinck's reflections *vis-à-vis* the obligation divine revelation places on us to begin with what God has revealed (*Reformed Dogmatics*, Volume 1: Prolegomena, gen. ed. John Bolt, transl. John Vriend [Grand Rapids: Baker Academic, 2003], 223 and 233; cf. 212).

The right priority established, we now turn to the perennial discussion of the earthly source(s) of Paul's use of υἱοθεσία. We know the term is Hellenist—one of the most common for adoption in the Graeco-Roman world, literally meaning "the placing of a son" (a compound of the noun υἱος and the verb τιθημι ["to place"]). Yet, cautions Scott, "the Hellenistic *meaning* of the term must be distinguished from a Hellenistic *background*." In other words, just because the term is Hellenist it does not follow that Paul derived his use of it from Hellenist practices. Was he then influenced by Roman practices? After all, Paul uses υἱοθεσία in letters written either from or to Rome, and always to communities under Roman rule: Ephesus, the leading city of the empire after Rome; Galatia, assuming the south Galatian theory; and Rome itself. Yet, Paul clearly fills the term with his reading of Old Testament history.[6] Given that he was a Jew ("a Hebrew of the Hebrews," Phil. 3:5), fluent in Greek and Aramaic (Acts 21:40, 22:2), and professing to be a Roman citizen (Acts 22:27), scholars inevitably probe which background influenced most his formation of the adoption vehicle or model.[7]

---

[6] James M. Scott, *Adoption as Sons of God: An Exegetical Investigation into the Background of υἱοθεσία in the Pauline Corpus*, Wissenschaftliche Untersuchungen zum Neuen Testament 2. Reihe 48 (Tübingen, J. C. B. Mohr [Paul Siebeck], 1992), 267; cf., 61 and his article "Adoption, Sonship," *Dictionary of Paul in His Letters*, Gerald F. Hawthorne, Ralph P. Martin, and Daniel G. Reid, eds. (Downers Grove, IL: IVP Academic, 1993); Herman Ridderbos, *Paul: An Outline of His Theology*, transl. J. R. de Witt (London: SPCK, 1977), 197–98; likewise, James I. Cook, "The Concept of Adoption in the Theology of Paul" in *Saved by Hope: Essays in Honor of Richard C. Oudersluys*, ed. James I. Cook (Grand Rapids: Eerdmans, 1978), 137. For a narration of how views shifted in favor of an Old Testament background, see Cook, "The Concept of Adoption in the Theology of Paul," 134–39.

[7] Daniel J. Theron writes, "there hardly seems to be any doubt that Paul's metaphor of adoption roots in the Jewish rather than in Graeco–Roman, or other traditions" ("'Adoption' in the Pauline Corpus," *Evangelical Quarterly* vol. 28 [1956], 14). Contrast David J. Williams' opinion in *Paul's Metaphors: Their Context and Character* (Peabody,

We shall not pause for long discussing the semitic background. Υἱοθεσία does not appear in the Masoretic Text of the Old Testament nor in the LXX. Much of what could be said theologically is germane to the exposition (chap. five).[8] Nevertheless, a word is apposite about the question of semitic practices of adoption. While there were no Old Testament laws regulating semitic adoptions, discussion continues as to whether the idea was present in Israel, such as in the case of Eliezer of Damascus (Gen. 15:3), Ephraim and Manasseh (Gen. 48:5), Moses (Ex. 2:10), Mephibosheth (2 Sam. 9:1-13) and Esther (2:7).

Supposing Abraham was influenced by Mesopotamian practices in adopting Eliezer, his adoption, argues Trevor Burke, would count for nothing once Isaac, the natural heir, was born. Regardless, the primacy of the natural-born son contradicts the co-heirship the adopted now share with Christ. As it happens, the adoption of Eliezer did not take root in Israel. When Jacob took his grandsons Ephraim and Manasseh on his knee, he was not adopting them but allocating succession within the family. No third party was involved. If Moses was adopted by Pharoah's daughter, there is no mention of it in the text. On the contrary, he refused to be considered an Egyptian (Heb. 11:23-26). The case of Mephibosheth is used by preachers to unpack adoption, but such sermons, predicated on the confusion of the filial models of the New Testament, read too much into the Old Testament narrative and draw too little from Paul. In the process, they create idiosyncratized

---

MA: Hendrickson, 1999), 83–84n.138. For other sample opinions see Allen Mawhinney, "υἱοθεσία in the Pauline Epistles: Its background, Use and Implications" (Ph.D.: Baylor University, Waco, TX, 1983); Francis Lyall, "Metaphors, Legal and Theological," SBET 10 (1992), 94–112 (especially 105-6) (Roman); Scott, Adoption as the Sons of God; cf., Russell Radoicich, "Adoption in the Pauline Epistles" (Crestwood, NY: St. Vladimir's Orthodox Theological Seminary, Crestwood, 1999) (OT/Jewish); Matthew Vellanickal, The Divine Sonship of Christians in the Johannine Writings (Rome: Biblical Institute Press, 1977), cf., 69 (OT/Jewish) with 71 [Roman]).

[8] Vellanickal, The Divine Sonship of Christians in the Johannine Writings, 69.

models of adoption which bear little resemblance to the specifics of the apostle's model. Finally, it is unlikely Esther was adopted. Even if she had been under Persian law, Hebrew law was still binding on Jews, yet it had no law governing adoption (Esther 3:8). In Israel, other practices were common for childless couples: the levirate marriage (hence the absence of adoption laws) and the unauthorized but divinely accommodated practice of bigamy.[9]

Although a Roman colony, Greek laws were operative in Paul's native Tarsus, as also in many cities to which he traveled. Much of our knowledge of Greek adoption comes from the fourth century B.C. Due to the city-states there was no overall body of Greek law. We know, however, of three processes to perpetuate the family line (*cultus*) or to secure the geriatric care of a childless father. From the civic code of Gortyn, we learn of *inter vivos* adoption wherein an adopter could adopt during his lifetime. Yet, the adopted son would not have rights as great as those of a natural son. Then there was testamentary adoption in which an adopted son was designated in the will or testament, which took effect following the death of the testator. The adoptee had to claim his inheritance by marrying the daughter of the testator, otherwise the adoption became null and void, with the inheritance going to the next of kin willing to claim the daughter and the estate. In posthumous adoption, where a man had died without a legitimate heir or adopted son, either the next of kin received the estate or a son succeeded to it by adoption. Yet, the antiquity of this data, the multiplicity of city-states,

---

[9] Trevor J. Burke, *Adopted into God's Family: Exploring a Pauline Metaphor*, New Studies in Biblical Theology (Nottingham, England: Apollos, 2006), 47, 198–201. For an infelicitous use of Mephibosheth, see Philip G. Ryken, *The Message of Salvation: By God's Grace, for God's Glory*, Bible Speaks Today (Downers Grove, IL: InterVarsity Press, 2002), 206–19.

and the rise of Roman law bring into question whether Greek law exclusively influenced Paul's adoption model.[10]

Most favor the influence of Roman adoption. By the time of Paul, the Roman Empire had replaced the Greek empire. The data we have about the Roman family is, thus, generally contemporaneous with Paul's letters. Υἱοθεσία occurs most often in the epistle written to the Christians at Rome (Rom. 8:15, 23; 9:4). Roman law was more unified than Greek adoption and would have been familiar to Paul, a citizen of Rome. He saw it applied throughout the empire, for it was common for emperors in the Julio-Claudian line to undergo adoption to succeed in the principate, such as in the cases of Octavian (Augustus), Tiberius, Gaius (Caligula), Claudius, and Nero. Evidently, adopted sons had equal rights with natural-born sons.

Although the picture of Roman adoption is somewhat sketchy, based on literary sources of the late Republic and the law code of the classical period, and evolved over the years, we know that the Roman family was hierarchical, ruled over by the father of the family (*paterfamilias*), with absolute and lifelong authority (*potestas*) over biological and adopted children, slaves, and their offspring. Adopted sons were cherished. They safeguarded the family from demise by ensuring the continued role of the *paterfamilias*, and thus gained social opportunities.[11]

While there were modes of Roman adoption analogous to *inter vivos* and testamentary adoptions, there was no equivalent to posthumous adoption. We encounter, however, a new mode. Requiring

---

[10] Burke, *Adopted into God's Family*, 58–60.

[11] The 1959 film *Ben Hur* offers a winsome visual of Roman adoption, wherein Roman Admiral Quintus Arrius adopts his slave Judah Ben-Hur to stand in the place of his lost son. "The formalites of adoption have now been completed," Arrius publicly declares. "Young Arrius is now the legal bearer of my name and the heir to my property. This ring of my ancestors would have gone to my son. So now it is yours."

public approval, *adrogatio* pertained to cases of a man (and only men) not under the legal *potestas* of his father. If he had children, they also came under the *postestas* of the new *paterfamilias*, thus ending the adoptee's original family and *sacra* (cult or family worship). Since, however, the practice of *adrogatio* was restricted to Rome until the third-century rule of Diocletian, Paul more likely had in mind the more private procedure of *adoptio*. This also entailed the adoption of a male, not *sui iuris* as under *adrogatio*, but *alieni iuris*, meaning one under the legal *potestas* of another. The fact that *adoptio* did not involve the eradication of the original family meant that it was more accepted than *adrogatio*, although it meant transferring submission from the original *potestas* to the new *paterfamilias*. The original *paterfamilias* sold his son into slavery, from whence the new *paterfamilias* could purchase him. The adoptive act was binding, legally witnessed, and generally changed the legal succession. It supplied the adoptee with the same rights as the biological son. In turn, the adoptee swapped his original family for the new family, gaining fresh privileges and responsibilities.[12]

Such features of *adoptio* led Francis Lyall to comment: "Only Roman adoption has a content that fully combines the profundities of both the elements of entrance into the status of 'son' and the incidents of that status, in other words, of becoming a son and being, or behaving as, a son." Burke warns us, though, against thinking that lessons drawn from *adoptio* exhaust our understanding of υἱοθεσία: "We must not automatically assume a simplistic one-to-one correspondence between the ancient social practice of adoption and Paul's metaphorical use of the term—no overlap is complete and there will always be discontinuities where the analogy breaks down."[13]

Note, first, that nowhere does Paul explicitly state the back-

---

[12] Burke, *Adopted into God's Family*, 60–70.

[13] Francis Lyall, *Slaves, Citizens, Sons: Legal Metaphors in the Epistles* (Grand Rapids: Academie Books [Zondervan], 1984), 68; Burke, *Adopted into God's Family*, 69–70.

ground(s) from which he draws. Second, in a top-down approach, it is the exegesis of Scripture that drives our understanding. While we do not isolate the exegetical from sociocultural considerations, the latter must not dictate to the former. Third, parallels are not the same as influences. Fourth, contemporary theories of knowledge teach us that Paul's use of υἱοθεσία need not mirror any one societal practice of adoption. There are issues of emotion and intimacy as well as cognition to take account of in weighing the influences on Paul.

It seems that Paul's inspired adoption model, consistent with his passion for the unity of Jewish and Gentile believers, takes account of two sectors of the Christian church: Jewish Christians, for whose sake he fills υἱοθεσία with a theological reading of the history of salvation; and Gentile Christians, for whose sake he includes parallels between the households of Rome and of God. In effect, Paul's colorful adoption model not only contributes to our understanding of the gospel, it illustrates his proclamatory and ecclesiological endeavors to bring together believing Jews and Gentiles (Eph. 2:11-22). We do not limit, then, the influence on adoption to one background or another. Rather, we exegete Paul's five uses of υἱοθεσία, reading the sociocultural parallels through the inspired texts, rather than *vice versa*. By means of this process, we better discern how Paul's adoption model creates, novelly, common ground on which Jewish and Gentile believers can stand, now that they are one in Christ. Paul draws both reading communities to himself, that he may impress on them their unity in the Lord Jesus.[14]

It is the fact, then, not the extent of the common ground which is important. Erode it and one reading community becomes alienated and the other privileged. In the common ground, each community experiences a mix of familiarity and unfamiliarity. Whereas the familiarity draws in the Jewish and Gentile reader, respectively, the

---

[14] Heim, "Light through a Prism," 89.

unfamiliarity raises their sights to the grace they share in divine or heavenly adoption. Paul rejoices and God is glorified in their coming together around their shared privilege in Christ. Note, additionally, that whereas Jewish believers needed Gentile believers in their stand against the Judaizers, Gentile believers needed Jewish believers in their withstanding of the social pressures of the imperial cult. Paul tells them in effect that it is they, rather than the Emperor, who are adopted into divine sonship.

The model thus displays not only the profundity of God but also his wisdom. Whereas its points of contact with the respective Jewish and Gentile backgrounds of Paul's readers render the model effective, the backgrounds are not so identified by the apostle that his uses of υἱοθεσία become inaccessible or inapplicable to later readers from diverse cultures and eras. What matters most, then, are not the background influences on Paul's model, but how he structures the model so as to communicate the riches of God's free grace and, on the level ground of that grace, to urge the unity within the household of God of believing Jews and Gentiles. That "how" is understood not, first and foremost, by sociocultural analysis but by the exegeting of Paul's letters.

3. THE TRANSMISSION OF ADOPTION

Evidently, before Paul could convey the idea of adoption, he had to come by it. "It is the communicator," writes John McIntyre, "who has received the insight into reality in terms of the metaphor in the first place, or, alternatively, to whom reality so revealed itself, and who then imparted it in these terms to the person listening or reading." This accords with Paul's claim that he received the gospel by revelation (Gal. 1:11-17). Gunton sheds light on this: "It is not that metaphor *precedes* discovery, helping to make it possible, but rather that new language and discovery happen together, with metaphor serving as the *vehicle* of discovery."[15]

Next came the transmission. A metaphor, writes Jüngel, "gets itself adopted, either by being accepted by its hearers or by being repeated in speech." The acceptance of adoption implies that Paul spoke of it as well as wrote of it. As meager as are the references to adoption, the fact that they can be traced back to the church fathers suggests that there was some repetition in the church of what was first heard from the apostle Paul.

Although adoption is not mentioned explicitly in any of Paul's sermons (Luke records in Acts but summaries of them), we know he preached in Judea, Antioch in Syria, through Asia Minor, and westward across the empire, and that adoption is mentioned in three of his letters recognized as Holy Scripture (2 Pet. 3:16). It is feasible but not necessary to the transmission that many, listening to the epistles read in their congregations, recognized Paul's references to adoption from the times he preached locally.

Paul's first canonical letter, Galatians, containing his first mention of υἱοθεσία (Gal. 4:5), was written in 49 A.D. (according to the "South Galatian Theory"), just after his first missionary journey. If we suppose, for the moment, the validity of the "North Galatian Theory," the epistle still appeared as early as 51/52 A.D., but certainly by the mid-'50s (c.55–57), which is to say within local memory of his first missionary journey. It is no flight of fancy to suggest, then, that the treatment of adoption in Galatians confirmed what Paul had preached from place to place.

---

[15] John McIntyre, *Theology After The Storm: Reflections on the Upheavals in Modern Theology and Culture*, ed. with a critical introduction by Gary D. Badcock (Grand Rapids: Eerdmans, 1996), 274; Gunton, *The Actuality of the Atonement*, 31.

Ephesians, Paul's eleventh canonical letter, was written likely around 60 A.D. from imprisonment in Rome, five years after the completion of his third missionary journey. During that missionary enterprise, Paul spent two years in Ephesus, "so that all the residents of Asia heard the word of the Lord, both Jews and Greeks" (Acts 19:10). Given the apostle's fondness for the adoption motif, it is difficult to imagine him ministering all that time without utilizing it to drive home to his hearers this free grace of God in Christ. The epistle mentions adoption amid an array of subsidiary metaphors: the believer's prehorizoning (προορίσας, 1:5), redemption (1:7; cf., 4:30), assurance and inheritance (1:13-14, 18), and membership of the household (2:19). Although these are subjects in their own right, they serve in relation to adoption as subsidiary metaphors to flesh out the model, either pointing to adoption (e.g., predestination to adoption) or elaborating on its ramifications.

The claim that Ephesians was written pseudonymously around 90 A.D. does nothing to negate the transmission of the adoption model. Instead of driving home what Paul had preached in Ephesus during his third missionary journey, a pseudonymous view of authorship would have to concede that what Paul had taught over forty years before had taken root in the mind of the church, for the pseudonymous author was so acquainted with Paul's thought as to make use of υἱοθεσία in a way entirely consonant with the apostle's other four uses of υἱοθεσία. Indeed, so surefooted is the pseudonymous author that he supplies the missing link in the history of God's adoptive grace, that which connects God's protological predestination to adoption to the outworking of his adoptive grace in space, time, and history.

Given the position taken that Paul did write Ephesians, it follows that in Romans alone were the references to adoption likely new to most of Paul's readers. While some passing through Rome may have heard Paul earlier on adoption, and others may have read copies of his letter to the Galatians, the fact remains that by 55 A.D. Paul was yet to visit the Lord's people in the capital of the empire (Rom. 1:10, 13; 15:22).

Could this be why three of the references to adoption are included in Romans (8:15, 23; 9:4), transmitting to them what had yet to be conveyed in person? Possibly, but not necessarily so, for the references in Romans are predicated on the fuller context of adoption found in Galatians. Writes Scott: "The use of υἱοθεσία in Rom. 8:15, 23 clearly builds on that in Gal. 4:5, for once again those who receive adoption as the sons of God participate in the sonship of the messianic Son based on the 2 Sam. 7:14 tradition (cf., 2 Cor. 6:18)."[16]

It is more likely that Paul includes the triple reference to adoption for the sake of the coherent statement of the gospel he lays out within the epistle. This gospel he had preached around the east of the Roman empire and would soon preach in Spain to the west (15:22-29). With persecution on the rise in Rome, there was also cause for Paul to point to the glorious future of the adopted sons of God. Continues Scott: "Rom. 8 also emphasizes a *future* aspect of υἱοθεσία, a point which, although adumbrated in Gal. 4:1-7 by the equation υἱὸς θεοῦ = κληρονόμος = κύριος πάντων, is more fully and explicitly developed in Romans." Regardless of the reason(s) for the triple use of υἱοθεσία, Paul uses the references to connect with his Jewish and Gentile readers in Rome by means of adoption's associated network of ideas (the sonship tradition in the Hebrew Scriptures and Roman *adoptio* and the adoption of the Emperor).[17]

The brevity of Paul's references to adoption in Romans 8 is, as Heim notes, a case of metalepsis or transumption. She quotes Richard Hays: "When a literary echo links the text in which it occurs to an earlier

---

[16] Scott, *Adoption as Sons*, 221.

[17] Scott, *Adoption as Sons*, 221; Jüngel, *Theological Essays*, 36; Michael Peppard, *The Son of God in the Roman World: Divine Sonship in its Social and Political Context* (Oxford: Oxford University Press, 2012), 5.

text [Galatians], the figurative effect of the echo can lie in the unstated or suppressed (transumed) points of resonance between the two texts" (*Echoes of Scripture*).[18] This, though, would assume their knowledge of Galatians, written six years earlier.

Whatever, then, the uncertainties of "how" adoption was transmitted, we know *that* adoption entered the church's theological vocabulary through the Spirit's guarantee of what Aristotle called the transference of an alien name.

Paul's hearers, unable to find reference to adoption in the Hebrew Scriptures, would have been intrigued by his reading of the old covenant history, and likely presuming that anything Roman was antithetical to the Christian faith, they would have been struck by his couching of the gospel in terms of adoption.

The very success of a metaphor or model relies, says Jüngel, on "the strangeness of a strange word." This strangeness is "intrinsic to metaphor." Typically, the strangeness lies not in the name *in se*, but in the name's unexpected usage. Far, then, from hindering the acceptance of the model, the strangeness and novelty of Paul's use of υἱοθεσία was crucial to its success. Under the guidance of the Spirit, Paul created the surprise element necessary to the success of metaphors and models.

In the surprise of Paul's adoption model lay not only the warmth and appeal of the gospel, but, to quote McIntyre, "the possibility of 'epistemic access' to the outside world [in this case the heavenly realm], the events that happen in it and the persons who live in it. These subjects are characterized in ways that would be impossible in flat, literal descriptions."[19]

The power of Paul's model lies, then, not simply in its surprising and endearing qualities, but in its use. Paul used υἱοθεσία sufficiently to ensure that it took hold in the minds and hearts of his hearers, but

---

[18] Heim, "Light Through a Prism," 258.

[19] Jüngel, *Theological Essays*, 36; McIntyre, *Theology After The Storm*, 271.

not so profusely that it lost the strangeness or surprise so crucial to its effectiveness. By restricting the use of υἱοθεσία to the five instances, Paul sustained the ability of the model to surprise and therefore to impact his readers. Moreover, by brilliantly and strategically establishing the five references to υἱοθεσία as periodic markers along the entire scope of salvation history (from the first things [Eph. 1:5] to the last things [Rom. 8:23]), Paul demonstrated just how significant the model is in biblical revelation. Each use functions not only as a milestone but as a doctrinal epicenter, whether of predestination (Eph. 1:5), covenant theology (Rom. 9:4), soteriology (Gal. 4:5), pneumatology (Rom. 8:15), or eschatology (Rom. 8:23).

Inevitably, the inscripturation of υἱοθεσία and the passage of two millennia have diminished the model's surprise element. The model died, as metaphors do, especially once the Roman Empire fell and the exaltation of adoption through the connection with Roman society (notably the adoption of the Caesar as son of God) became lost to history. Yet, what adoption lost in terms of its surprise element, it gained through the realization of the profound truths it teaches. Certainly, the historic neglect of adoption limited this realization, yet it remains the case, as George Lakoff and Mark Johnson observe, that "Our ordinary conceptual [or doctrinal] system, in terms of which we both think or act, is fundamentally metaphorical in nature."[20]

There is in the lifespan of conceptual words-become-metaphors an obtaining of transcendent insight connecting the divine revelation and the earthly experience. Yet, the metaphor returns, says McFague, to ordinary life in an appropriate form suitable for living a committed existence under God. That suitable form is doctrinal, but the doctrine

---

[20] George Lakoff and Mark Johnson, *Metaphors We Live By* (Chicago and London: The University of Chicago Press, 1980), 3. My use of Lakoff and Johnson does not imply agreement with their rejection of absolute objective truth, nor naivete in equating objective truth with absolute objective interpretation (*Metaphors We Live By*, 159–271, *passim*).

remains a model (robust conceptual metaphor) allowing for the study of its internal structure. The model is, then, neither "literal truth" nor a "mere metaphor." In the model certain aspects square with the earthly experience, others do not, for an extension of the literal truth has occurred. As we shall see, in divine adoption:

- The adopted receive the Spirit of the adopter and not only a standing in relation to him.
- The adopted have the assurance that the adopter never dies, and that an eternal relationship and inheritance is in view.[21]
- The adoption never fails. There is never a reversal or termination of the relationship.
- The adopted conform to the image of the firstborn.
  Around these extensions, Jewish and Gentile believers could and can unite.[22]

4. THE STRUCTURE OF ADOPTION

The model includes five separate but complete utterances or pericopes. These are to be understood in their individual contexts, "structuring and restructuring the perception of their intended audience" to quote Heim. Sometimes υἱοθεσία refers primarily to the history of salvation (Eph. 1:5, predestination to adoption; Rom. 9:4, the adoption of Israel; and 8:23, the consummation of adoption), other times more to its application (Gal. 4:5, the reception of adoption; Rom.

---

[21] This is not only a truth of Paul's adoption model but also shed's light on Jesus' parable of the prodigal son, in which the inheritance is granted while the Father is still alive (Lk. 15:11-32).

[22] Henri Blocher, "Biblical Metaphors and the Doctrine of the Atonement," *JETS* 47/4 (December 2004), 638; Sallie McFague, *Metaphorical Theology: Models of God in Religious Language* (Philadelphia: Fortress, 1982), 123–24; Peppard, *The Son of God in the Roman World*, 3–5. I am grateful to Pastor Bob Van Manen's exposition of Galatians (Little Farms Chapel, Coopersville, Michigan, Fall 2017) for suggestions in identifying the extensions in divine adoption.

8:15, the Spirit of adoption). Some uses more clearly distinguish the adoptive act from the adoptive state, leading to more interpretative translations of υἱοθεσία. Both the act and state are typically implied, although sometimes one is in view more than the other.

Such differences in usage are not absolute but gradient, allowing for the assembling of the shades of meaning of υἱοθεσία in the one single, coherent model of adoption. The cohesion is both theological (trinitarian) and historical (*heilsgeschichtliche*), belying Heim's emphasis on the disparate character of the adoption references or, in her words, metaphors.[23]

The theological structure.

Cognisant of Jüngel's Lutheran theology of the cross, we nevertheless affirm that, "Every theological metaphor must be compatible with the cross of Jesus Christ." The cross is, after all, the central discovery of Christianity, and possesses wide-ranging and far-reaching implications for the church and the world. It goes without saying that inscripturated metaphors and models possess the necessary compatibility. Indeed, the work of Christ inspires them. Writes Gunton, "All the main ways of spelling out the saving significance of the life, death and resurrection of Jesus contain a considerable metaphorical and imaginative content, drawing, as is often remarked, from a number of human institutions: notably the legal system, the altar of sacrifice, the battlefield and the slavemarket." Such models, depicting Easter, "enable the Christian community to declare how God, through Christ, remakes broken relationships." That said, we distinguish Christ-centeredness from Christomonism. The one is trinitarian the other is not.[24]

---

[23] Heim, "Light Through a Prism," 66, 73.

[24] Jüngel, *Theological Essays*, 65; Gunton, *The Actuality of the Atonement*, 17–18; cf., 46.

The adoption model's trinitarian credentials are plain for all to see. In Galatians 3:26–4:7 the Father sends the Son, and through union with the Son the Father adopts his people.[25] Yet, completing the triangular involvement, Paul teaches that it is in possession of the Spirit of the Son (πνεῦμα υἱοθεσίας) that the adopted cry out, "Abba, Father!" (Αββα ὁ πατήρ). Christ, however, is central:

- First, by dint of the grounding of the blessings of the adopted in their redemption by Christ: "when the fullness of the time was come, God sent his son, made of a woman made under the law, in order that he may redeem the ones under the law, that [ἵνα] we may receive the adoption of sons. And because you are sons God has sent the Spirit of his Son into your hearts crying, 'Abba, Father'" (4:4-6).

- Second, through the reception in adoption of Christ's Spirit. The Spirit puts on our lips the cry of liberation, enabling us to pray to the Father in the same way as did the Son (cf., Mk. 14:36). He teaches us to repeat the very vocative Christ uttered when in the garden of Gethsemane. The words so natural to Christ, become ours by the grace of the Father given us in the Son.

In Romans 8:15 the Trinitarianism is also clear, although the christocentric is not so overt. When urging the adopted to realize, through the Spirit of adoption, their freedom from the fearful spirit of bondage, Paul mentions the Father and the Spirit, but not Christ the Son. We should not read too much into this. As Vellanickal explains, Paul's doctrine has not changed, only his emphasis. Whereas in Galatians Paul's connecting of redemption and adoption is direct and explicit, in Romans 8 the connection is assumed from what Paul has written earlier in the epistle (see especially 3:21-26; 4:23–5:2, 6-21; 8:3-4, 11). Byrne explains that Romans 8 does not spell out the mechanics of redemption effected by Christ. "Only in the phrase . . . 'in the likeness of sinful flesh,'

---

[25] Vellanickal, *The Divine Sonship of Christians in the Johannine Writings*, 74–77.

does Paul hint at what might be termed the inner workings of redemption." In short, the epistles of Galatians and Romans both embrace the centrality of Christ's work, although in Romans 8 the embrace is presupposed.[26]

In Ephesians 1:5 the Trinitarianism is again explicit, as is the christocentricity. Paul's opening doxology flows from his trinitarian statement in 1:3: "Blessed be the God and Father of our Lord Jesus Christ, who has blessed us with every spiritual blessing in the heavenly places in Christ." The apostle indicates that God the Father is the source of all the blessings the adopted possess in Christ. Whereas the Father predestines or prehorizons (προορίσας) us to adoption through Jesus Christ (vv. 4-6), the son redeems us (vv. 7-12), and the Spirit seals us (vv. 13-14). He is the guarantee or down payment of our inheritance.

With certainty, then, the adoption model points us to the cross of Christ, but never at the expense of the persons and the works of the Father and the Spirit. States A. A. Hodge: "Adoption proceeds according to the eternal purpose of the Father, upon the merits of the Son, and by the efficient agency of the Holy Ghost."[27] Only *via* participation in Christ's sonship can we know God as our Father, and only by the Spirit of Christ uniting us to the Son can we call on Αββα as our God (Gal. 3:26-28; 4:6).

---

[26] Vellanickal, *The Divine Sonship of Christians in the Johannine Writings*, 83; Brendan Byrne, *"Sons of God"—"Seed of Abraham": A Study of the Idea of the Sonship of God of All Christians in Paul against the Jewish Background* (Rome: Biblical Institute Press, 1979), 94.

[27] A. A. Hodge, *Outlines of Theology* (New York: Robert Carter and Brothers, 1866), 400–401. For similar examples of christocentricity within a trinitarian framework see Thomas A. Smail, *The Forgotten Father*, reprint ed. (London et al.: Hodder and Stoughton, 1990), 145–46.

The historical structure.

Having disentangled the New Testament's new birth and adoption models, addressing how the adoption model functions, we are now well placed to display without obstruction the salvation-historical scope and contours of the adoption model. Indeed, it encapsulates the entire history of salvation, each use of υἱοθεσία (Rom. 8:15-16 excepted) serving as an epochal marker along the way. The model thus illustrates Geerhardus Vos' principle of periodicity/historical progression and the warrant for Richard Gaffin's remark that "in both overall structure and internal development, dogmatics needs to make clearer that soteriology is eschatology."[28] Moreover, "the Grounds of Adoption make up a great section of Biblical Theology."[29]

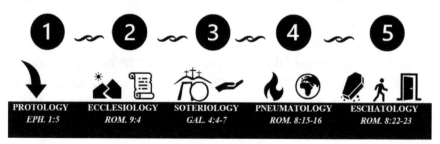

Figure 4.2
The salvation-historical contours of Paul's adoption model[30]

<hr />

[28] Richard B. Gaffin Jr., "The Vitality of Reformed Dogmatics" in *The Vitality of Reformed Theology: Proceedings of the International Theological Congress June 20–24th 1994, Noordwijkerhout, The Netherlands* (ed. J. M. Batteau, J. W. Maris, and K. Veling [Kampen: Kok, 1994], 31; cf., *Resurrection and Redemption: A Study in Paul's Soteriology*, 2nd ed. [Phillipsburg, NJ: P&R, 1987], 138; Theron, "Adoption," 13).

[29] Thornton Whaling, "Adoption," *The Princeton Theological Review* 21 (1923), 226.

[30] Geerhardus Vos, *Biblical Theology: Old and New Testaments* reprint ed. (Carlisle, PA: The Banner of Truth Trust, 1985), 16.

The seeds of this perception of the scope and contours of Paul's adoption model are found in Irenaeus, the father of biblical theology; in Clement of Alexandria; and Tertullian, but notably in Calvin. Whereas they left their references to adoption strewn throughout their works, there follows a comprehensive but nonexhaustive sketch of the historical and theological coherence of Paul's model and the reason why Ridderbos labels adoption "important." Whether the Southern Presbyterian minister Benjamin Morgan Palmer was thinking along similar structural lines or not, his claim is very *à propos*: "Probably no word in our science of theology more completely covers all parts of the system of grace than does this word, adoption." It is, says Robert Peterson, "an overarching way of viewing the Christian faith."[31] The following exposition of adoption helps explain such estimates.

~~~~

---

[31] Ridderbos, *Paul*, 197; Benjamin Morgan Palmer, *The Threefold Fellowship and the Threefold Assurance: An Essay in Two Parts*, reprint ed. (Harrisonburg, VA: Sprinkle Publications, 1980), 39; Robert A. Peterson, "Towards a Systematic Theology of Adoption," *Presbyterion* 27/2 (Fall 2001), 121.

PART THREE

THE BIBLICAL EXPOSITION OF ADOPTION

THE HISTORY OF OUR ADOPTION

Eph. 1:4-5; Rom. 4:13, 9:4; Gal. 3:23–4:7; Rom. 8:15-16, 22-23

1. Our blessèd God, One and yet Three,
Your purpose love, sov'reign and free!
Before the world, you chose us to be
sons in the Son, your glory to see.

2. Space, hist'ry, time, your sphere of grace!
From Eden's loss to Patriarch's place,
Your plan revealed, one seamless trace,
To your elect out of the race.[1]

3. To Abram was a vision giv'n,
A fam'ly like the stars of heav'n.
First enslaved and by masters driv'n,
Then redeemed, a–dopted for heaven.

4. Israel was young, much yet to learn,
With gov'nor, steward, taught to yearn.
Reared by You for full age to turn,
Then Faith came, our freedom to earn.

5. Of woman, born subject to law,
The Son a slave, slaves to adore!
He set us free, bondage no more,
Jew, Gentile, trust Christ, be secure!

6. A household one, we're sons, heirs, too!
One with Christ, we're in Father's view,
From *Abba* we've the Spirit, too!
We're fam'ly, siblings not a few!

7. Bound for new earth, destined in love,
God to worship, come down from above!
Adoption known, yet pangs we have,
God to enjoy, in bodies alive!

Words: Tim J. R. Trumper, 2017
Tune: Maryton, Henry Percy Smith, 1874[2]

---

[1] Verse 2 may be omitted without disturbing the flow of the hymn.

[2] The hymn was first sung at Little Farms Chapel (OPC), Coopersville, Michigan, during evening worship on June 11, 2017.

5.

ADOPTION IN OUTLINE
A Fresh Exposition

> When we consider . . . the passages where Paul
> expressly speaks of the sonship of believers and of
> their adoption as sons, it becomes clear at once that
> he is again thinking in redemptive-historical,
> eschatological categories.
>
> Herman N. Ridderbos,
> *Paul: An Outline of His Theology.*

Welcome to Adoption!
Coming out of the plains of history and the forest of linguistics, we finally arrive in the city of Adoption. We are here to take in the sights, to document what we find, and to send out pictures of its expanse and beauty. We seek an accurate tourist map, an increase of visitors, ways to settle into Adoption, and the road to the wider county of Retrieval.

~~~~

As a model or metaphorical concept, adoption lends itself to exposition and to the discussion of its contribution to the overall edifice of the church's theology. Within this edifice, to paint a picture applicable just to this chapter, adoption possesses its own elongated room. In it, the references to υἱοθεσία standing as pillars, supplying the room with strength and beauty. Upon entering the room, we swirl around each pillar in turn until we reach the far end. The pillars (aka the adoption texts) guide our movement through the entire scope of salvation history, from protology to eschatology.

MOVEMENT ONE: PREDESTINATION TO ADOPTION

Blessed be the God and Father of our Lord Jesus Christ, who has blessed us in Christ with every spiritual blessing in the heavenly places, even as he chose us in him before the foundation of the

237

world, that we should be holy and blameless before him. In love he
predestined us for adoption as sons through Jesus Christ, according
to the purpose of his will, to the praise of his glorious grace, with
which he has blessed us in the Beloved. (Eph. 1:3–6)

This first reference provides a mile-high snapshot of the totality
of our adoption. Although the protological details are to the fore,
already we sense that God's adoptive interest stretches to the far
distant horizon of the last things. While the text does not give us the
intervening details, it does provide the theological foundation upon
which the adoption of God's people rests. Thus, "Sonship," Ridderbos
rightly counsels, "is not to be approached from the subjective
experience of the new condition of salvation, but rather from the divine
economy of salvation, as God foreordained it in his eternal love (Eph.
1:5), and realized it in principle in the election as his people."[1]
Accordingly, we begin with this text because our predestination to
adoption, belonging to protology, is logically prior to all that follows.

In Ephesians, Paul sets our predestination to adoption in the
context of our soteric blessings. These are triunely bestowed (v. 3).
They come *from* the Father (vv. 3-6), *in* the Son (vv. 7-12), and *by* the
Spirit (vv. 13-14). The apostle refers to the Trinity not ontologically but
economically. The theologians' use of the Greek term οἰκονομία refers,
fittingly, to God's "household management" (see, for example, Eph.
1:10). By the economic Trinity we indicate the way in which God,
through the respective roles of each person of the Godhead, manages
the household that he, in grace, has brought into being.

Paul begins with the role of the Father (vv. 3-6). It is in relation
to him that he introduces the term υἱοθεσία. In the Father, adoption's
associated network of ideas unite. Gentile readers of Ephesians would
immediately recall from the theological use of υἱοθεσία the
fundamental importance of the *paterfamilias* in Roman *adoptio*. This

---

[1] Herman N. Ridderbos, *Paul: An Outline of His Theology*, transl. J. R. de Witt (London:
SPCK, 1977), 198.

surprising allusion would have thrilled them, for it would indicate to them that they are included in the divine grace of adoption. Jewish readers, for their part, would have shared the surprise. Although their Hebrew Scriptures include general references to God's overall Father-hood of the cosmos (albeit as a simile [e.g., Deut. 1:31, 8:5; Ps. 103:13; Mal. 3:17]), to his specific Fatherhood of Israel (Is. 63:16, 64:8; Jer. 3:4, 19, 20, 31:9, 20; Hos. 11:1-4; Mal. 1:6) and of the king (2 Sam. 7:14; 1 Chron. 17:13, 22:10, 28:6; Ps. 89:26), Ephesians strengthens and universalizes the divine name. From the letter, Jewish readers learned that the election of Israel, while still in effect (for God is faithful, cf., Rom. 9–11), anticipated the inclusion or ingrafting of Gentiles.

Thus, under the role of the Father, and by means of the adoption model, Paul began to integrate believing Jews and Gentiles within the one church or household of God. Despite their disparate backgrounds, they had come to share in the one Father and his predestinating grace.

Note, consistent with the juxtaposition of humanist and scholastic influences at the time of the Reformation, we, too, may unpack Paul's depiction of the Father's role in terms of Aristotelian categories of causality. We follow Calvin, then, in making use of them when they flow naturally from the exegesis of Scripture.[2]

The efficient cause of adoption.

The *efficient* cause of adoption refers to the grace of the Father in adopting a people as his own for no other reason than "the good pleasure of his will." In other words, there was nothing outside of God that compelled the Father to adopt us. His adopting of his family has always been and ever shall be *sola gratia*! If we may speak at all of his

---

[2] See Calvin's *Institutes*, 3:22 for instance, and his commentary on Ephesians (*CC* XXI, 196–201); cf., Richard A. Muller, *After Calvin: Studies in the Development of a Theological Tradition*, Oxford Studies in Historical Theology (Oxford: Oxford University Press, 2003), 55, 35.

compulsion to adopt us, we do so in terms of his internal will to love us and of the love of his will to do so.

Within, the Godhead had known eternally the internal flow of perfect, full, selfless, reciprocated, and satisfying love. The Father had, accordingly, no need to love outside of himself in order to be love. Contrary to ancient forms of adoption, he was not motivated by the need to perpetuate his name after his days. Moreover, as an everlasting Father he had an eternally begotten Son, and therefore had no need to adopt to make up for what he could not have naturally. Rather, within the triune counsel of the Godhead, the Father eternally, sovereignly, graciously, lovingly, communally, and freely extended the divine love beyond the community of the three persons. This would have made sense to Gentile readers, for in Roman adoption the adopter had to be both older than the adoptee and free to adopt. The Father utilized this freedom magnanimously, electing an innumerable number to adopt. Thus, we may say, without demeaning the beneficence of ectypal or human forms of adoption (whether ancient or contemporary), that "Gods [sic] ways are not man's ways. It is free grace only, and not need, that puts the heavenly Father to adopt any of his creatures."[3]

After all, there was nothing spiritual, moral, or ethical that God foresaw in us to compel the Father to adopt us. The Father predestined his elect not because he foreknew we would be holy, but "that," in a reversal of the fall in which our first parents broke loose from him, "we should be holy and blameless" (v. 4). Nothing he foresaw in the race or in us personally could quench his love for us. Finding us in space, time, and history in the household of the living dead—physically alive but living as the "sons of disobedience" and the "children of wrath," dead in trespasses and sins, under the sway of the prince of the power of the air (cf., Eph. 2:1-5)—he not only adopted us but ensured, through Christ

---

[3] *The Complete Works of the Late Rev. Thomas Boston* vol. 1, Rev. Samuel McMillan, ed., reprint ed. (Wheaton, IL: Richard Owen Roberts, Publishers, 1980), 652.

and by the Spirit, that we should ever after be holy and alive within his household (cf., Eph. 2:19). No wonder Paul exclaims, "Blessed be the God and Father" (v. 3)![4]

The material cause of adoption.

The efficient and material causes of our adoption are tied together. Due to God's gracious will to adopt us, the Father *predestined*, literally prehorizoned (προορίσας), his people to adoption. Although predestination is cosmic, entailing the foreordaining of all things which come to pass, epicentral to it is the Father's election of the adopted in Christ.

While the election is not of all without exception, it is of all without distinction. Those chosen to adoption are from every race, tongue, tribe, and people. The election takes in the expanse of history and the extent of the globe, but it stops short of Universalism. How could God faithfully reveal himself or be known in a full representation of his glory if his justice lay latent in his being with no evidence thereof? Hence, in part at least, God's ordaining (establishing the fact thereof) of the fall.

Paul, a Jew, writing in Ephesians predominantly to Gentiles, illustrates both the generosity and the particularity of predestinating grace. Note his use of "our," "us," and "we" in verses 3-6. The Father named his elect as his own (cf., 3:14). They are his exclusively through (διὰ) Christ his Son (v. 5; cf., v. 7). Those predestined to adoption have been eternally bound together with Christ in the mind and heart of the Father. He has forever loved the Son for himself, but through the predestination of the elect unto adoption he has ever loved him as the firstborn of many brothers (cf., Rom. 8:29). Seeing Christ, the Father

---

[4] The phrase "broken loose" is Calvin's, from his commentary on Paul's address to the Athenians (*The Acts of the Apostles 14–28*, transl. John W. Fraser, ed. David W. Torrance, and Thomas F. Torrance [Edinburgh and London: Oliver and Boyd, 1966]), 117).

thinks of us, and seeing us he sees Christ. He loves us as he does all his creatures for what is his in us by creation, but he loves us particularly and supremely in his saving grace as sons in his Son.

There is no greater evidence of the Father's love than that he should give up his Son unto death for us. It is by Christ's shed blood that we are redeemed from slavery and adopted by the Father (cf., v. 7). This would make sense to Paul's readers. Gentile believers would recall how, in Roman *adoptio*, the new *paterfamilias* would buy the adopted son from enslavement, while Jewish readers would recollect how Israel's redemption from Egyptian enslavement was followed at the Exodus by the inauguration of Israel as God's son. Thus, in the model's associated network of ideas, our divine, spiritual, and beneficent Father replaces the earthly, carnal, and dictatorial paternity of Pharaoh and Caesar, respectively. They embodied the prince of the power of the air, but he is the heavenly *paterfamilias* with whom no human father can compare.

The instrumental cause.

We do not come by the blessings of redemption and adoption automatically. The *faith* in Christ to which we are called is the *instrumental* cause of both our redemption and adoption. In the one movement of resting on Christ, we are liberated from the household of the living dead and adopted into the household of the living lively. Through faith, Christ becomes both our Redeemer and our elder brother. This faith operates both retrospectively and prospectively. In believing, we confess that we are utterly unable to liberate ourselves and are unworthy of being liberated, yet we hope in the blessings the liberation portends. These come to us, Paul repeatedly states, "in Christ" (vv. 3, 9, 12), or "in him" (4, 7, 10, 11, 13 twice). Whereas then, the Father elects us to adoption, the Son redeems us for adoption, and the Spirit inspires the requisite faith needed to receive it.

The final cause.

What began with God's grace has his *glory* for its *final* cause. We taste it in this life through the realization of how blessed we are in the Beloved (v. 6). Yet, God lavishes his grace on us in all wisdom and insight so that we grasp the mystery of his will, namely, his purpose to unite all things in heaven and on earth. Thus, "in the fullness of time" (v. 10) we shall see the Father's display of his own glory, as seen in his grace (v. 6). Deduces Whaling, adoption is "the supreme illustration of grace, and the highest reach of glory for the redeemed."[5] Our adoptive state of sonship is, then, characterized by a yearning for the grand family gathering planned for the end of the age. There praise of our triune God for his grace of adoption will echo unto the ages of eternity to come and across the expanse of his household, no matter the location in space and time we have occupied. What a sight and a sound that will be!

MOVEMENT TWO: THE PRIVILEGE OF ADOPTION

> I am speaking the truth in Christ—I am not lying; my conscience bears me witness in the Holy Spirit—that I have great sorrow and unceasing anguish in my heart. For I could wish that I myself were accursed and cut off from Christ for the sake of my brothers, my kinsmen according to the flesh. They are Israelites, and to them belong the adoption, the glory, the covenants, the giving of the law, the worship, and the promises. To them belong the patriarchs, and from their race, according to the flesh, is the Christ who is God over all, blessed forever. Amen. (Rom. 9:1-5).

In this second movement, we swirl from the pretemporal to the temporal, filling in the details of God's adoptive dealings with his people as they were revealed to Paul.

---

[5] Whaling, "Adoption," 223.

Preliminary matters.

The first preliminary matter pertains to the metanarrative we call salvation history. During the second half of the twentieth century, *Heilsgeschichte* came under serious criticism, suffering from the Barthian differentiation of *Geschichte* (popular and interpreted history) and *Historie* (real, scientific, and factual history); the rightful recognition that not all Old Testament material is historical; and the distinction between history and subsequent tradition.[6] Clearly, though, Paul trusted the Hebrew Scriptures, as did Jesus. Their confidence in them, confirmed by Calvin, has encouraged a growing support of the salvation-historical model of biblical theology.

This begs the question, second, as to where we begin depicting God's adoptive dealings. In Eden, with God's creation of Adam and Eve and his relationship to them, at the fall and its immediate aftermath, or thereafter?

Certainly, the historical Adam is significant in Paul's overall theology, notably in connection with the Adam-Christ parallel so essential to the apostle's presentation of the gospel in his letters to the Romans (5:12-21) and to the Corinthians (1 Cor. 15:42-49). Drawing on the father of the human race was especially relevant for Christians living and serving the Lord Jesus in Rome, the capital of the known world, and in iniquitous Corinth. But several factors have combined to make more of Adam than is required by the adoption model.

First, traditional Reformed systematics tend toward giving the impression that the Adam-Christ parallel is one that is flat rather than ascending. This has the unfortunate effect of playing down the progression of revelation from the first to the second or last Adam. Scripture furnishes us with considerably more data concerning Christ's

---

[6] Robert Gnuse, *Heilsgeschichte as a Model for Biblical Theology: The Debate Concerning the Uniqueness and Significance of Israel"s Worldview.* College Theology Society Studies in Religion 4 (Lanham *et al.*: University Press of America, 1989), 1–2.

person and work than Adam's. Stellar Reformed pastor-theologian Hugh Martin helps us to redress the balance of Scripture, and thereby to understand why the injecting of Adam into the adoption model is neither exegetically warranted nor theologically necessary. It, in fact, blurs the clarity of what Paul wishes to say of the Abraham- and Moses-Christ parallels:

> it will uniformly be found that the theology which is meagre in reference to the Covenant of Grace, is still more so as to the covenant of works. The first Adam was but "the type of him that was to come," the shadow of the "last Adam." And where the "last Adam" is little recognised as a covenant head, there can be little reason or inducement to recognise the "first" in that light either. It is in Christ pre-eminently that the doctrine of covenant takes fullest shape; and apart even from express verbal affirmations of it, we find that it is continually subsumed in Holy Scripture's descriptions of His work in the days of His flesh, and of His reward in His risen glory.[7]

Second, as Martin indicates, the intrusion is not only of Adam but of the covenant of works. Since the seventeenth century, the covenantal framework of Scripture (old covenant/new covenant) has been overshadowed in confessional Presbyterianism by a logicized covenantal structure, which, seeking to encapsulate the whole scope of the system, extends the covenantal framework back to Eden. There is very little biblical evidence proffered for this in the detail found in the WCF. Recall, that WCF chapter 7, "Of God's Covenant with Man," was the first confessional chapter on covenant so far as we know, although the Irish Articles of 1615 refer to covenant. It is unlikely the Westminster commissioners considered it a definitive arrangement or the last confessional word on the subject.

Before venturing further, understand that I am not in the slightest questioning the historicity of Adam and Eve, the garden of Eden, the trees of life and of the knowledge of good and evil, the probation, and the fall. My only question concerns the pedagogical

---

[7] Hugh Martin, *The Atonement in its Relation to the Covenant, the Priesthood, the Intercession of our Lord* (Edinburgh: Knox Press, 1976), 35.

construct of a covenant of works.[8] Exegetically, the biblical evidence claimed is slight (e.g., Hos. 6:7 [margin], Ex. 19:5, Deut. 4:13, Rom. 3:27, and Gal. 4:24).[9] Historically, Calvin's version of federal theology, and John Murray's for that matter,[10] demonstrate that a covenant of works is not the *sine qua non* of covenant theology. Richard Muller acknowledges that "the language of the doctrine is certainly different from the language of the Reformers and even from that of earlier successors to the original Reformers."[11] Muller has implied that the formulation of a covenant of works began as a pragmatic attempt to undergird the Reformation principle of salvation by grace alone.[12] Yet manmade buttresses against heterodoxy often produce more heat than light, and more division than unity in the truth.

Third, the prominence of Adam in expositions of Paul's adoption model has arisen from the nineteenth-century quest to refute

---

[8] Michael S. Horton, "Law, Gospel, and Covenant" and mine, "Constructive Calvinism and Covenant Theology," *Westminster Theological Journal* 64 (Fall 2002), 285–86, and 387–404, respectively.

[9] Re the list of texts, Herman Witsius' use of Rom. 3:27 on the contrasting of the law of works and the law of faith seems, in the context, a stretch to assume the distinction between the covenant of works and the covenant of grace (*The Economy of the Covenants Between God and Man: Comprehending a Complete Body of Divinity*, vol. 1, reprint ed. [Kingsburg, CA: den Dulk Christian Foundation, 1990], 48–49). Richard Muller offers a lengthier list: "the doctrine [of a covenant of works] was a conclusion drawn from a large number of complex texts, among them, Gen. 1:26-27; Lev. 18:4-5; Matt. 19:16-17; 22:37-39; Rom. 1:17; 2:14-15; 5:12-21; 7:10; 8:3-4; 10:5; Gal. 3:11-12; 4:4-5, with Hos. 6:7 and Job 31:33 offered only as collateral arguments. It was, moreover, a conclusion largely in accord with the exegetical tradition" (*After Calvin*, 183). Again, reliance on an exegetical tradition, while useful, does not guarantee the exegetical warrant for the supplanting of the Bible's explicit old/new covenant framework.

[10] *CW*, 2:47–59.

[11] Horton, "Law, Gospel, and Covenant", 287; Muller, *After Calvin*, 189.

[12] Muller, *After Calvin*, 184.

the universal Fatherhood of God and brotherhood of man. Prior to the Victorian era, it was assumed that Adam was God's son, his subject, or both. The question, though, does not seem to have come under scrutiny until Candlish's Cunningham Lectures in 1864 and their subsequent fallout. The apostle Paul, however, does not share the preoccupation with Adam's pre-Fall standing when discussing adoption.

Even when Paul describes man as God's offspring in Acts 17:28, he is quoting the ancient poet Aratus (*Phainomena*), seeking at Mars Hill to draw a point of contact with the Athenian intelligentsia. When he alludes in Romans 8 to Adam's creation in the *imago Dei*, which is an argument for Adam's creation as a son of God, Paul's thought is not oriented retrospectively toward Eden but prospectively toward the *eschaton*.[13]

We avoid, then, imposing on the adoption model systemic questions not directly germane to the adoption model and to what Paul is seeking to accomplish by utilizing it. The model, covering the grand metanarrative from the *proton* to the *eschaton*, focuses within the history of salvation not on the epoch from Adam to Israel, but on that stretching from Israel (notably the Abrahamic and Mosaic eras) to Christ. The knowledge we now have of Calvin's well-rounded understanding of Paul's theology of adoption helps us here. Calvin teaches us that what interested the apostle was not the "then but no moreness" of what we were in Adam, but the "now but not yetness" of what believing Jews and Gentiles are in Christ.

Doubtless, the question of Adam's original relationship to God is important for the overall understanding of what salvation accomplishes, as is the context of the fall. The construct of a covenant of works

---

[13] Trevor J. Burke, *Adopted into God's Family: Exploring a Pauline Metaphor*, New Studies in Biblical Theology (Downers Grove, IL: InterVarsity Press, 2006), 192. For a summary of the nineteenth-century discussions of adoption see Tim J. R. Trumper, "An Historical Study of the Doctrine of Adoption in the Calvinistic Tradition" (Ph.D. Diss.: University of Edinburgh, 2001), chaps. 8–9.

will survive in logicized systematics, but it is more doubtful whether the covenant of works/covenant of grace paradigm will survive a biblical-theological revamping of systematic theology.[14] Two questions which loom large, but are scarcely if ever asked, at least not in public, are worth at least posing here: Why do we insist in Presbyterian circles that the covenant of works/covenant of grace is a nonnegotiable of covenant theology, given that the Bible has its own paradigm (old covenant/new or better covenant)? And why do we insist on imposing the former on the latter?

This we see no need to do, nor does the exegesis of Paul's adoption model require us to. We thus bypass Adam in this outline of adoption, the question of his standing before God and the probation he faced. These are issues germane to biblical revelation but are not essential to the immediacy of Paul's model of adoption.

In this regard, David Garner's welcome salvation-historical reading of adoption assumes Adam was God's son, and thereby goes some way to reorientate Presbyterians toward Christ, yet his omission of the workings of the structural distinctives of biblical models, and his admixture of two models of biblical theology—the salvation-historical and Brevard Childs' identification of "Biblical Theology within dogmatic categories"—leads him to the compulsion to fill in or to "complete" the front end of revealed history not covered by Paul's adoption model. By injecting Adam and the covenant of works into its story-of-Israel framework, Garner overextends the temporal scope of the model.[15]

---

[14] This domination was not always the case. See John L. Girardeau, *The Federal Theology: Its Import and its Regulative Influence* (J. Ligon Duncan III, ed., with an introduction by W. Duncan Rankin. Greenville, SC, 1994) and his *Discussions of Theological Questions*, first published 1905 (Harrisonburg, VA, 1986), 68–69; cf., Martin, *The Atonement*, 29–30.

[15] David B. Garner, *Sons in the Son: The Riches and Reach of Adoption in Christ* (Phillipsburg, NJ: P&R, 2016), 6, 79, 263, 284. Brevard S. Childs, *Biblical Theology of the Old and New Testaments: Theological Reflection on the Christian Bible* (Minneapolis: Fortress, 1992), 11–13.

Garner defends his inclusion of Adam and the covenant of works by repeatedly warning of "the word-concept fallacy" (the idea that concepts must be named in order to be present). While I affirm that such a fallacy exists, also Garner's belief that Paul's soteriology must be understood covenantaly, finding his formula, "the created sons became the alienated sons who become the adopted sons of God," like the mantra "the new birth gives us the natures of sons, adoption the standing of sons," to be true, the traces of dogmatic construal in his treatment of adoption (supported by non–Pauline authors) coerces the model to do more than it was intended to do. Whereas the latter very much includes Adam, the former does not in an explicit or vital manner. "It is true," writes Edwin Palmer in summarizing Matthias Scheeben's thought, "that from Adam on, man's supernatural end was adoption but this was not clearly expressed at the first." In short, Garner has adopted the salvation-historical reading of adoption without breaking free of the methodological demands of traditional systematics.[16]

In adhering closely to a biblical-theological reading of Paul's model, there is one more preliminary issue to address, namely, Paul's reading of the Old Testament. Israel's relationship to Yahweh is described in profuse ways. Israel is a daughter (Jer. 31:21b-22a), a wife (Hos. 2:2-3), a whore (Hos. 2:4-5), sheep (Ezek. 34:11-16), clay (Rom. 9:20-22), dough (Rom. 11:16), and branches of an olive tree (Rom. 11:17-24). Prominent in the Old Testament, however, is the sonship tradition (e.g., Ex. 4:22; Deut. 8:5, 14:1, 32:5-6, 18; Is. 43:6-7; Jer. 31:9; Is. 63:8; Hos. 1:10, 2:1, 11:1; and, depending on the interpretation, Mal. 2:10). The tradition also figures in the Intertestamental literature (e.g., the book of Wisdom 12:19-22 and 18:1-4; Joseph and Aseneth 19:8; 3 Maccabees 6:27-28, 7:6-7; Sirach 36:16-17; Judith 9:12-14; and Psalms

---

[16] For my review of Garner's *Sons in the Son*, go to *JETS*, vol. 62, no. 1 (March 2019), 204–9.

of Solomon 17:26-29, 18:4-5).[17] Significantly, the adoption of Israel is not mentioned in the Old Testament, although some believe Hosea 11:1 speaks of it: "When Israel was a child, I loved him, and out of Egypt I called my son."

How then are we to understand Paul's use of the sonship tradition given that adoption does not figure in the Old Testament? Through the revelation of God and the inspiration of the Spirit, Paul reread the sonship of Israel as an adoption. Clearly, there is overlap between the two readings. Both regard sonship as a privilege of ethnic Israel and portray the relationship covenantaly. Thus, Paul's rereading would not have sounded strange to ancient Near Eastern ears. It was quite usual for father-son imagery to be employed in the drafting of covenants. Quoting D. J. McCarthy, Richard Patterson writes, "the father-son relationship . . . is essentially that of the covenant. And there is no doubt that covenants, even treaties, were thought of as establishing a kind of quasi–familial unity."

The adoption model, however, offers a surplus of information on the theme of Israel's sonship, and introduces elements of variation, even tension, between the sonship tradition and Paul's adoption model. To draw from Heim, Paul's adoption model sings in harmony but not in unison with the sonship tradition. Through his conversion to Christ (and, I add, his reception of the revelation and inspiration of the Spirit), Paul has, to quote Richard Hays' *Echoes of Scripture in the Letters of Paul* (1989), "grappled his way through to a vigorous and theologically generative reappropriation of Israel's scriptures." He became thereby a major interpreter of the tradition and the creator of the adoption model. The theme of sonship continues but has been transposed by the

---

[17] Heim, "Light Through a Prism," 263–82.

apostle into the metaphorical concept or model of adoption through the typological idea of Yahweh's adoption of Israel retroactively applied.[18]

The preparatory adoption of Israel.

Paul, we argue then, continues the theme of adoption in space, time, and history not with Adam but with Israel; not with the creation but with God's covenantal dealings with his chosen people.

Note the two steps he takes.

First, Paul tells us that a promise of inheritance was given to Abraham, namely, that through the righteousness of faith he would be "heir of the world" (Rom. 4:13). This corresponds with the use of adoption in Galatians 3:23–4:7, where all who are Christ's are Abraham's offspring and heirs according to the promise (Gal. 3:29). Calvin is mistaken, however, especially in his *Genesis* commentary, to introduce the language of adoption in connection with the Abrahamic era. Paul does not start reading the Old Testament sonship tradition in terms of adoption until the Mosaic era (cf., Gal. 3:16-18). Prior to that, Abraham was given the promise of an inheritance that his posterity would one day come by the grace of adoption. Significant in the intervening period was the numerical development of that posterity such that upon redeeming Israel from Egypt Yahweh inaugurated Israel as a nation. The children of Abraham had long since ceased to constitute a nuclear family.

Second, Paul focuses in on the inauguration of the nation of Israel as Israel's adoption as a son of God. Yahweh thus granted Israel not only a negative liberty *from* the enslavement in Egypt but a positive liberty *to* sonship as his heir. This sets the pattern for what is to come through Paul's reading of the gospel at the outset of the new covenant

---

[18] Heim, "Light Through a Prism," 245, 285–91, 292, 310; Burke, *Adopted into God's Family*, 49; Richard D. Patterson, "Parental Love as a Metaphor for Divine-Human Love," *JETS* 46:2 (June 2003), 212.

era. Writes Vellanickal, "in all these [adoption] texts, the idea of liberation from the bondage of slavery is predominant."[19] Slavery not orphanhood is the essential backdrop of adoption.

For the evidence of this, we turn to Romans 9:4. The text, as we noted in chapter four, is metalyptic. It constitutes, says Heim, "a predication without explanation."[20] Whereas a fuller explanation of Israel's sonship will come in Galatians, we must understand here why Paul refers specifically to the adoption of Israel in the coherence of his *Romans* presentation of the gospel. We begin answering this by remembering that this coherence was contingent on his need to defend the message of grace that he preached and his need to enlist the support of the Roman church for his forthcoming mission to Spain.[21]

The defense begins in 3:1-8. There Paul anticipates four criticisms of his message of free grace in Christ. These he answers chiastically, responding immediately to questions three and four in terms of the doctrines of justification and sanctification (chaps. 3–8):

- "But if our unrighteousness serves to show the righteousness of God, what shall we say? (v. 5).

---

[19] Edwin Hartshorn Palmer, *Scheeben's Doctrine of Divine Adoption* (Kampen: J. H. Kok N.V., 1953), 12; Trumper, "An Historical Study" chap. 2.3.i (cf., John L. White, *The Apostle of God: Paul and the Promise of Abraham* [Peabody, MA: Hendrickson, 1999], xxv); Matthew Vellanickal, *The Divine Sonship of Christians in the Johannine Writings* (Rome: Biblical Institute Press, 1977), 70.

[20] Heim, "Light Through a Prism," 242.

[21] Scholars differ about the contingency and coherence of Paul's letter. For more, see J. Christiaan Beker, *The Apostle Paul* (Edinburgh: T&T Clark, 1980), especially 23–37, and N. T. Wright's reflection on Beker's case in *The Climax of the Covenant, Christ and the Law in Pauline Theology*, reprint ed. (Edinburgh: T&T Clark, 1993), 259f.; James M. Scott, *Adoption as Sons of God: An Exegetical Investigation into the Background of YIOΘΕΣΙΑ in the Pauline Corpus*, Wissenschaftliche Untersuchungen zum Neuen Testament 2. Reihe 48 (Tübingen: J. C. B. Mohr [Paul Siebeck], 1992), 221.

- "But if through my lie God's truth abounds to his glory, why am I still being condemned as a sinner? And why not do evil that good may come?" (vv. 7-8).

Yet, the first two anticipated charges he takes up in Romans 9–11:

- "What advantage has the Jew? Or what is the value of circumcision?" (v. 1).
- "What if some were unfaithful? Does their faithlessness nullify the faithfulness of God?" (v. 3).

It is in the context of answering the charge that he has undermined the privilege of Israel that he speaks of the nation's adoption.

The ninth chapter opens with Paul's "great sorrow and unceasing anguish" that for all Israel's privileges under the old covenant, his kinsmen had proven unfaithful to God and had rejected the covenant with him. Paul mentions six weighty privileges:

- The adoption (ἡ υἱοθεσία).
- The glory (ἡ δόξα).
- The covenants (αἱ διαθῆκαι).
- The giving of the law (ἡ νομοθεσία).
- The temple service (ἡ λατρεία).
- The promises (αἱ ἐπαγγελίαι).

The corresponding endings of the Greek terms, Scott very helpfully observes, reveal two groups of three. The first of the first group (ἡ υἱοθεσία) corresponds to the first of the second group (ἡ νομοθεσία), the second of the first group (ἡ δόξα) to the second of the second group (ἡ λατρεία), and the third of the first group (αἱ διαθῆκαι) to the third of the second (αἱ ἐπαγγελίαι). Thus, Scott deduces (contra Calvin and Heim), that the adoption (ἡ υἱοθεσία) took place at the giving of the law (ἡ νομοθεσία).[22]

---

[22] Scott, *Adoption as Sons of God*, 148–49. With the possible exception of δόξα, Heim notes, υἱοθεσία is the only privilege that is metaphorical ("Light Through a Prism," 244, 247, 248, 249–50).

The law was given at the time of the Exodus. In those days, Near Eastern religions customarily regarded their gods as having consorts who bore them sons. Yet, being without equal, Yahweh had no consort, and, therefore, no son either. Yet, we read, "Thus says the LORD, Israel is my firstborn son, and I say to you, 'Let my son go that he may serve me.' If you refuse to let him go, behold I will kill your firstborn son" (Ex. 4:22; cf., Deut. 14:1-2 and 32:6; Is. 1:2-3 and 63:7-8; Jer. 31:9; Mal. 1:6 and 2:10). In effect, Yahweh sought to assure Israel, in entering his sonship to God, that he possessed all the rights of primogeniture. He communicated to Israel in so many words that he was as special to him as a firstborn son. Israel was not, then, to compare his sonship unfavorably to the "natural" sonship that surrounding peoples claimed they had in relation to their gods.

Paul thus picked up on an inherited collection of ideas to recast the sonship tradition as an adoption: Yahweh's sovereign and gracious choice of an otherwise insignificant Israel (cf., Deut. 7:1, 7), Israel's redemption from Egypt, Yahweh's play on the idea of birth to the gods, and Israel's possession by grace of the rights of primogeniture. The language differs in Exodus 4:22 (Israel as firstborn son) and Romans 9:4 (the adoption of Israel), but not the underlying constitutive elements of God's grace toward his people.[23]

Paul's adoption model is, contra Heim, sufficiently robust to envelop both the adoption of Israel (the adoptive act) and his subsequent sonship (the adoptive state). As God's son, Israel would spend his liberation undergoing fifteen hundred years of education as a spiritual maturing supervised by Yahweh. Writes Calvin, this "was the actual youth of the church [*ecclesiae adolescentia*]" preceding "the age

---

[23] James I. Cook, "The Concept of Adoption in the Theology of Paul" in *Saved by Hope: Essays in Honor of Richard C. Oudersluys*, ed. James I. Cook (Grand Rapids: Eerdmans, 1978), 138; contrast C. J. H. Wright, *God's People in God's Land: Family, Land and Property in the Old Testament* (Exeter: The Paternoster Press, 1990), 15–23.

of manhood [*virilis aetas*] down to Christ's last coming, when all things shall be fully accomplished."[24]

Despite the role of Romans 9:4 as a "predication without explanation," Paul's rereading of the sonship tradition in Romans 9:4 accomplishes numerous purposes. First, it underscores the vital nexus between predestination (election) and adoption. Second, it distinguishes the origins of Israel's sonship from that of Christ, the firstborn (πρωτότοκον [cf., Rom. 8:29; Col. 1:15]). Whereas Christ's Sonship is said, metaphorically speaking, to be natural or biological, the believer's is adoptive. Third, it paves the way for Paul's argument in the wider context of his letter that since the privileges of the gospel are by grace there is nothing to prevent God from also bringing Gentiles to himself. Surmises C. J. H. Wright, Israel was called in Exodus 4:22 the firstborn son precisely because there were other sons to come.

Paul's use of υἱοθεσία in Romans 9:4 points prospectively, then, to the unity of God's dealings with his people across the hiatus of the old and new covenants. It also bespeaks the internal coherence of the adoption model. Besides its role in interpreting the Old Testament sonship tradition, the model, in teaching God's grace in Christ, serves as a place of intimacy. It enables Jewish readers to look back on Israel's history with much gratitude to Yahweh for his grace of adoption and his commitment to Israel, his son. That is why Paul lists Israel's privileges in the present tense. God's calling to Israel and gifts are irrevocable (Rom. 11:29). Believing Jews belong to the new Israel. But Gentile believers, too, have reason to rejoice. God has graciously included them in God's adoptive purposes. Such connections between the old and new covenants and the Jews and Gentiles help us segue from Romans 9:4 to Galatians 3:23–4:7.

---

[24] John Calvin, *Commentary on the Prophecy of Isaiah*, vol. 4, transl. William Pringle (Edinburgh: The Calvin Translation Society, 1853), 136 (*CO* 15 [37]: 270).

MOVEMENT THREE: THE RECEPTION OF ADOPTION

> But when the fullness of the time had come, God sent forth his Son, born of woman, born under the law, to redeem those who were under the law, so that we might receive adoption as sons. And because you are sons, God has sent forth the Spirit of his Son into your hearts, crying, "Abba, Father!" So you are no longer a slave, but a son, and if a son, then an heir through God. (Gal 4:4-7).

No adoption passage is more relevant, straightforward textually, complex historically, and rich theologically than Galatians 3:23–4:11. It provides simultaneously the apex of Paul's teaching in Galatians and the *locus classicus* of adoption (4:4-7).[25] Predating Romans 9:4 in its publication, the passage conveys the bulk of what Paul says of Israel's preparatory adoption and the full adoption of believing Jews and Gentiles. The one adoption is analogous to the other.

Preliminary matters.

First, understand Paul's letter. In Galatians, he aims to offset his readers' temptation to buy into the Judaizers' hybrid "gospel"—faith plus works (circumcision and obedience to the Mosaic law). He, therefore, emphasizes throughout the letter the gospel he had received by revelation (1:11-12). It is received, to summarize the implications of his argument, by grace alone through faith alone in Christ alone. This he demonstrates in terms of two main models: justification and adoption.

Since Luther, Galatians ("his Katie") has been known mainly for its teaching of justification. Less recognized is its teaching of adoption, despite the familiarity of 4:4-7. Thus, I posit here the view that juxtaposed in the heart of Galatians are the models of justification (2:15–3:14) and adoption (3:25–4:11). Since Paul is writing a letter, and at haste (1:6-10, 6:11), it is no surprise that there are some fuzzy

---

[25] Heim, "Light Through a Prism," 152, 252. The language of preparatory and full adoption Heim attributes to John Murray, C. B. Cranfield, and Douglas Moo.

boundaries between them (3:15-24). Nevertheless, the recognition of their distinctives is both possible and helpful. Whereas the model of justification possesses a legal framework and speaks of sinners, law, Christ, righteousness, curse, the tree, and faith, the model of adoption, possessing legal undercurrents, is more relational and speaks of guardians, managers, slaves, sons of God, Christ, faith, "Abba! Father," and heirs. The fuzzy boundary is observable by the overlapping use of law and sin (justification) and covenant and inheritance (adoption):

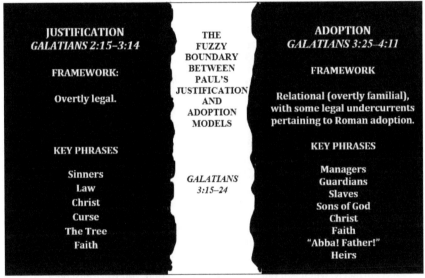

Figure 5.1
The juxtaposition of justification and adoption in Galatians

Second, understand Paul's oscillation. Throughout 3:23–4:11 he goes back and forth between the first and second persons: The first-person plural ("we") and the plural possessive ("our") in 3:23, 24, 25; and 4:3, 5, and 6 on the one hand, and the second person ("you") on the other in 3:26, 27, 29; and 4:6, 7, 8, 9, 10, 11:

"We" and "Our"

23Now before faith came, we were held captive [ἐφρουρούμεθα] under the law, imprisoned until the coming faith would be revealed. 24So then, the law was our [ἡμῶν] guardian until Christ came, in order that we might be justified by faith [δικαιω- θῶμεν]. 25But now that faith has come, we are [ἐσμεν] no longer under a guardian.

"You"

26For in Christ Jesus you are [ἐστε] all sons of God, through faith. 27For as many of you as were baptized [ἐβαπτίσθητε] into Christ have put on [ἐνεδύσασθε] Christ. 28There is neither Jew nor Greek, there is neither slave nor free, there is no male and female, for you are [ἐστε] all one in Christ Jesus. 29And if you are [ὑμεῖς] Christ's, then you are [ἐστε] Abraham's offspring, heirs according to promise.

"We"

4:1I mean that the heir, as long as he is a child, is no different from a slave, though he is the owner of everything, 2but he is under guardians and managers until the date set by his father. 3In the same way we [ἡμεῖς] also, when we [ἦμεν] were children, were enslaved to the elementary principles of the world. 4But when the fullness of time had come, God sent forth his Son, born of woman, born under the law, 5to redeem those who were under the law, so that we might receive [ἀπολάβωμεν] adoption as sons.

"You" and "Our"

6And because you are [ἐστε] sons, God has sent the Spirit of his Son into our [ἡμῶν] hearts, crying, "Abba! Father!" 7So you are [singular, εἶ] no longer a slave, but a son, and if a son, then an heir through God. 8Formerly, when you did not know [εἰδότες] God, you were enslaved [ἐδουλεύσατε] to those that by nature are not gods. 9But now that you have come to know [γνόντες] God, or rather to be known [γνωσθέντες] by God, how can you turn back [ἐπιστρέφετε] again to the weak and worthless elementary principles of the world, whose slaves you want [θέλετε] to be once more? 10You observe [παρατηρεῖσθε] days and months and seasons and years! 11I am afraid I may have labored over you [ὑμᾶς] in vain.

While it is tempting to understand Paul in his use of "we" and "our" to refer to his fellow Jews (3:23-25; 4:1-5), and in his use of "you" to the now included Gentiles (3:26-29), this straightforward distinction, although appealing, only works in 3:23–4:4, and then only if we understand the "you" to refer to both believing Jews and Gentiles. Yet, the understanding breaks down entirely in the heart of the passage, 4:4-7. If, when Paul says that Christ's redemption procures adoption, he has in mind but the Jews ("that we might receive the adoption"), how could he then include the Gentiles in his declaration of sonship in verses 6-7 ("and because you are sons")? Given that Paul includes the Gentiles exclusively in the use of "you" in the next verse, v. 8 ("when you did not know God"), the "we" (Jews)/"you" (believing Jews and Gentiles) seems implausible.

Perhaps, alternatively, we are to understand Paul to write randomly in the first and second person. Certainly, such inconsistency fits with his writing in haste with a burdened heart. But I doubt he is entirely random. Could it be that when he refers to the age prior to Christ's coming, he underscores the distinctiveness of Jews and Gentiles by the respective uses of "we"/"our" and "you" (cf. 3:23-25 and 4:1-4 with 4:8)? And when he refers to the current age, now that Christ has come, he uses the "you" inclusively, to show how Christ has brought believing Jews and Gentiles together? This fits with his use of the second person in 3:26-29 and 4:6-7, 9-11. On this understanding, the residual "we" in 4:5 serves as a hinge. It completes Paul's references to Old Testament history and readies the reader for the inclusion of the Gentiles once more from v. 6.

This interpretation mediates between the simplistic and untenable claim that the "we"/"our" refer to the Jews and the "you" to believing Jews and Gentiles, and the alternative claim (especially as regards 4:1-3, 8) that Paul is entirely indiscriminate in his manner of expression.[26] Yes, he wrote his letter in haste but not unthinkingly. This

---

[26] Richard Longenecker, *Galatians* Word Biblical Commentary 41 [Dallas, TX: Thomas Nelson, 1990, 164; contrast Heim's consideration of 4:1-9 in "Light Through a Prism," 145–49.

interpretation better indicates how Paul employed his pronouns to show how God's free grace in Christ brings together believing Jews and believing Gentiles.

Third, we return to Paul's appropriation of the sonship tradition. While heir to a great estate (cf., "the world," Rom. 4:13), Israel was a child under age (νήπιός [4:1]).[27] Thus, his earthly circumstances were more akin to servitude. The law with its multiple ceremonies kept custody of him, hemming him in with the minutia of rules and regulations appropriate to a child, especially to one of great significance in the purposes of God. The law—specifically the ceremonial law by this stage of the letter—functioned as Israel's tutor (literally, "child-leader" [παιδαγωγὸς]), guardian, or governor (ἐπιτρόπους), 3:23; and his steward, administrator, or manager (οἰκονόμους [4:2]). It was divinely designed to point Israel to Christ and to prepare him for the inheritance. Its burden of rules, while suffocating, matured Israel, educating him in holiness and creating within him a yearning for the day he would come of age and enter into the blessings of the great estate. He had, says Paul, to learn "the elements [or basic principles, τὰ στοιχεῖα τοῦ κόσμου] of the world" (Gal. 4:3). During this course of education, which lasted from the inauguration of the nation throughout the duration of the Old Testament era, there was little awareness in Israel of a personal Father-son relationship with Yahweh. That was yet to come in the new covenant era with the freedom of full adoption. For now, Yahweh's redeemed son must give heed to his responsibility to obey his tutor, guardian, and administrator.

Obviously, Gentiles were not included in Yahweh's adoption of Israel, nor in the subsequent education he underwent under the ceremonial law as heir to the great estate. Nevertheless, they, too, were

---

[27] I differ here from James Scott who reads 3:23–4:3 as the enslavement of God's people in Egypt rather than as Israel's post-Exodus imprisonment to the Torah (specifically the ceremonial law). Cf., Burke, *Adopted into God's Family*, 85fn.33.

enslaved, to "the elements [or basic principles, τὰ στοιχεῖα τοῦ κόσμου] of the world." The diverse meanings of the phrase allow Paul to use it not only for the ceremonial law as in the case of the Jews, but in reference to pagan idols (those enslavers which "by nature are not gods" [cf., 4:3 and 8]).[28]

These respective enslavements were asymmetrical. The Gentiles had no loving Father promising them a great estate, but the prince of the power of air ensuring them of nothing but the chains of sin and death (cf., Eph. 2:1-3). They underwent no education in the knowledge of God, of themselves, or of the Christ to come, but only one in sin. All the same, they were brought by their embroilment to the point of yearning for a redeemer, and in their darkness found no hope until Christ came. All those now believing in Christ, whether Jew or Gentile, are redeemed by Christ, adopted by the Father, and possess the Spirit of Christ the Son. These three vital elements of unity in the gospel bring us to the heart of adoption (4:4-7). We consider them in turn.

Redeemed by Christ (vv. 4:1-5a).

The first advent of Christ signaled a major hiatus in salvation history. For Jews, it meant the epochal transition from the old to the new covenant, coinciding with the coming of age of God's people. Writes Paul, "after faith has come we are no longer under a tutor" (3:25). Rather, those receiving Christ entered "the full right of sons" (the NIV's correct interpretation/dynamic–equivalent translation of υἱοθεσία [4:5]). To quote Herman Witsius:

> God . . . has displayed his manifold, and even his unchangeable wisdom . . . in suiting himself to every age of the church: . . . a stricter and pedagogical discipline was better suited to her more advanced

---

[28] For the different ancient meanings of τὰ στοιχεῖα, see the work of Gerhard Delling, cited by Longenecker, *Galatians*, 165–66; Palmer, *Scheeben's Doctrine of Divine Adoption*, 174–75; G. B. Caird, *The Language and Imagery of the Bible*, first published 1980 (Grand Rapids: Eerdmans, 1997), 239–40.

childhood, but yet childhood very unruly and headstrong. And adult and manly age required an ingenuous and decent liberty. Our heavenly Father therefore does nothing inconsistent with his wisdom, when he removes the pedagogue, whom yet he had wisely given his son during his nonage; and treats him, when he is now grown up, in a more free and generous manner.[29]

For Gentiles, Christ's advent signaled the entrance of those trusting in Christ as redeemer into the majority or mature adoptive sonship of the new covenant era.

Paul mentions Christ's birth twice. He who was sent out (ἐξαπέστειλεν) of heaven by the Father next appears in authentic humanity. He is "born [γενόμενον] of a woman, born [γενόμενον] under the law, to redeem those who were under the law." Paul is thinking not so much of the virginal conception, the payment of the ransom, or even redemption from the curse of the broken moral law (a truth more *apropos* to Paul's earlier model of justification). Rather, he is thinking in the categories and meaning of adoption. The model teaches, contrary to nineteenth-century Universalism, that although the incarnation renders humanity redeemable, we cannot be redeemed without Christ's accomplishment of redemption.

Scott comments that Paul uses ἐξαγοράζω only in Galatians 3:13 and 4:5. He notes that a consensus of scholars believe his use of it in Galatians 4:5 should be translated as "to redeem" (or "to deliver") rather than the usual and simple infinitive "to buy." [30] The distinction is interesting, for whereas the prior use is found in the context of justification and is pertinent to Christ's taking on our curse, the latter is used as a precursor to Paul's reference to adoption. The more general idea of deliverance in 4:5 is likely due to his endeavor to draw from both the sonship tradition (for Jewish readers) and Roman *adoptio* (for Gentile readers). While the price would have been familiar to Gentile

---

[29] Witsius, *The Economy of the Covenants*, 2:380.

[30] Scott, *Adoption as Sons of God*, 172.

readers on account of the process of Roman *adoptio* (in which the adopter purchased the adoptee from a slave owner—cf. the use of ἀπολύτωσιν and its cost of blood in Eph. 1:7), the relevance of the ransom price is not so obvious from Paul's reading of the adoption of Israel at Sinai. Whom, we may ask, did God pay in order to redeem Israel from Egypt?

This said, the specificities of the adoption model comport with the Protestant reformers' description of the gospel as a "wonderful exchange." God's Son was "imprisoned" under the law so that "we" (believing Jews and Gentiles) may be liberated from our respective enslavements. Clothed in our flesh (albeit an unfallen experience of it [cf., Rom. 8:3; 2 Cor. 5:21]), Christ stretches out to humanity a brotherly hand, conferring on believers a right of fraternal alliance beyond that procured through his *assumptio carnis*.[31] Clearly, both the sonship tradition and Roman *adoptio* teach us that redemption is prerequisite to God's adoption of sons.

Adopted by the Father (v. 5b).

Writes Ridderbos, "The adoption of sons is . . . the object of the great eschatological redemptive event and . . . the direct result of redemption." He continues, "Sonship is . . . a gift of the great time of redemption that has dawned with Christ. It is the fulfilment of promise that was given of old to the true people of God (Rom. 9:26; 2 Cor. 6:18)."[32] Nowhere is this more clearly proven than in Galatians 4:5.

There, redemption and adoption are juxtaposed, being distinguished by a ἵνα clause: Christ redeemed those under the law "so that [ἵνα] we might receive adoption as sons." The clause indicates that redemption is logically prior to adoption. This does not mean to say that adoption is what Max Black calls a "subordinate metaphor" (read model

---

[31] These expressions are Calvin's (Trumper, "An Historical Study," 120–21).

[32] Ridderbos, *Paul*, 197, 198-199; Theron, "Adoption," 10–11.

for metaphor). Rather, redemption and adoption are coequal models with complementary functions within the gospel.

Obviously, redemption is a model in its own right, but it is, says John McIntyre, "an incomplete symbol." It does not tell us explicitly what was given or received at Calvary and, of itself, leaves us asking for what end God's people are delivered or liberated. Writes Scott, "The goal is rather redemption *to* a relationship with the Father established by 'adoption'." Adds John Murray, "Redemption contemplates and secures adoption as the apex of privilege." Conversely, adoption presupposes redemption and functions as its *telos*. Without redemption, adoption would make no sense to Paul's Jewish and Gentile readers. [33]

The models are, then, mutually supportive. Together, they highlight God's lavish grace in granting the believer the *titulo redemptionis* and *adoptionis*. The ἵνα clause ensures they remain distinguishable as models with their individual integrities safeguarded (see Figure 5.2 opposite).

The complementary relationship between redemption and adoption is substantiated theologically in two ways. Whereas redemption conveys what McLeod Campbell labeled in *The Nature of the Atonement*, the retrospective aspect of the atonement (what we are saved *from*), adoption bespeaks its prospective aspect (what we are saved *to*). Redemption answers our past enslavement, but adoption opens up our life of sonship. Moreover, whereas redemption, predicated on the gift of Christ, accents God's sovereignty, adoption, in

---

[33] Vellanickal, *The Divine Sonship of Christians in the Johannine Writings*, 72; M. Black, *Models and Metaphors: Studies in Language and Philosophy* (Ithaca, NY, 1962), 42–43; John McIntyre, *The Shape of Soteriology: Studies in the Doctrine of the Death of Christ* (Edinburgh: T&T Clark, 1992), 33. Scott, *Adoption as Sons of God*, 174; Samuel King, "The Grace of Adoption," *The Union Seminary Magazine* 22 (Oct., Nov. 1910), 31; and John Murray, *CW*, 2:228. The fact that adoption appears in Ephesians 1 prior to redemption in contrast to Galatians 4 suggests the coequality of the models.

this passage, emphasizes the responsibility of men and women to trust in Christ. God redeems, but man receives. Redemption and adoption, in their complementarity, thus possess, through the instrument of faith, a shared resonance and a mutual dependence. [34]

Figure 5.2
The juxtaposition of models in Galatians elaborated

Evident in Paul's depiction of the logical progression from redemption to adoption is the unity of the Godhead. Those the Son redeems the Father adopts. Three blessings accrue from the Father's adoptive act.

First, adoptees gain a *new standing*. They cease to be slaves and are now sons. The context points to this, as does the term υἱοθεσία ("the placing of a son"). Verse seven is emphatic: "You are no longer a slave,

---

[34] John McLeod Campbell, *The Nature of the Atonement and its relation to Remission of Sins and Eternal Life*; fourth ed. (London: James Clark and Co., 1959), particularly chaps. 1 and 7; Heim, "Light Through a Prism," 214–15.

but a son." On reflection, the Father would have been most generous had he but redeemed us from slavery and left it at that. Certainly, the Israelites would have settled for redemption when crying to God from their bondage in Egypt. But no, in grace the Father as *paterfamilias* grants his sons a place in his household. His sovereign love and commitment toward us in our full sonship follow the pattern of his love and commitment to Israel in his minority.

States Edwin Palmer, the two versions of sonship—the old covenant sonship of Israel and the new covenant sonship of the new Israel of believing Jews and believing Gentiles—are in "fundamental agreement . . . [for] the two are essentially one and the same." Nevertheless, like Calvin, Palmer perceives their continuity and discontinuity. Concluding his comments on the reformer's exposition of Paul, Palmer writes:

> This is in general accord with the Reformed principle of the unity of the covenant under the two dispensations. Although there are two different administrations, the covenant, the promises, and the law are one. The old one was an earlier and less perfect phase, but it had the same gospel based on Jesus Christ. The new dispensation does not destroy the old one, but fulfills it. And so it is also with adoption: The New Testament adoption is a richer fulfillment of the Old Testament one.[35]

Turning specifically to our new covenant era, of importance re the new standing of the adopted is its legality. In building an associated network of ideas for his Jewish and Gentile readers, Paul cannot afford to be too explicit. The idea of law helps Paul connect with Gentile readers familiar with Roman adoption, but with the Jews less so. Although the inauguration of Israel as Yahweh's son coincided with the giving of the law, there was no legal practice of adoption to satisfy. That said, Jewish readers, dispersed in regions occupied by Rome, would

---

[35] *Scheeben's Doctrine of Divine Adoption*, 176.

likely have been familiar with Roman *adoptio* and could join with Gentile readers in resonating with Paul's network of ideas.

Thus, both sets of readers would know that in Roman society, *adoptio* entailed, first, a transfer from another household (cf., Eph. 2:1-3); second, the destruction of the prior *potestas* of the previous father; third, the retrieval of the adopted son from the slavery into which he had been sold by the original *paterfamilias*; fourth, the entry into the new family as adopted son, eligible for all the rights of sonship and inheritance; fifth, the belonging of the adopted son and all he possesses to the new *paterfamilias*; sixth, the beginning indicated by the adoption of a new life as the legally recognized son of the new *paterfamilias*; and seventh, a ceremony to mark the adoption corresponding in spiritual adoption to baptism.

Yet, for all these commonalities between Roman and spiritual adoption, we need care in weighing the legal content of the adoption model. It is the model of justification that carries the main juridical freight of the gospel. It is no more fitting to expand adoption to cover the ground of justification, than it has been to expand justification to cover the ground of adoption. In justification God is the Judge who, in righteousness, demands satisfaction of his justice. In adoption, God is the Father who graciously adopts. While God must meet his own adoptive criteria, it is difficult to see from the text that in the adoptive act the satisfaction of legal adoptive requirements is Paul's overt concern. Paul emphasizes rather the Father's placing of his sons in the Son (hence υἱοθεσία). His concern, then, is with the union of the sons and the Son.

This is confirmed by Paul's mention of baptism. Although the sacrament publicly recognizes the entrance of the sons of God into the family of God, the significance of baptism in the context as the *symbolum adoptionis* emphasizes not the completion of a legal process but the oneness between the Son and the sons: "For as many of you as were baptized into Christ have put on Christ" (Gal. 3:27). James Cook reminds us, then, that adoption is anchored to love and to grace rather than to a legal institution. This, I may add, helps to explain why Paul does not identify the source(s) of his model.[36] The union of the Son and the sons to which the Father's love and grace lead remind us that God's adoption of his people goes far beyond any bare legal transaction could express or realize.

The idea of the legality of our adoption is present (especially in resembling Roman *adoptio*), but, to repeat, it is not Paul's focus. The heavy emphasizing of the legality of adoption arises more from bottom-up perspectives which read the text through human practices, as influenced by the juridical lopsidedness of Protestant soteriology. WCF 12, in this light, is not wrong to say that the adopted have God's name "put upon them," but this is more an extrapolation from Scripture than it is demanded by Paul's model.

Note that the Westminster commissioners drew the idea not immediately from Paul but from Jeremiah 19:9, with support from 2 Corinthians 6:18 and Revelation 3:12. The idea comports with God's frequent practice of renaming (e.g., Abram/Abraham, Sarai/Sarah, Jacob/Israel, etc.) but is more a general truth of Scripture than it is of Paul's adoption model. Paul concentrates more on the relational—what Jewish and Gentile believers are (sons not slaves)—than on the legal mechanism of the adoptive act. There is a practical explanation for this. Had Paul gone into great detail about the dynamics of adoption he would have undermined the effective association of ideas intended to bring his Jewish and Gentiles readers together. He would have diminished in the process his emphasis on the union of the sons in the Son.[37]

Second, adoptees gain a *new relationship*. We discern this from Paul's ongoing adaptation of the Hebrew (Old Testament) sonship

---

[36] Cook, "The Concept of Adoption in the Theology of Paul," 139–40.

[37] Lyall, *Slaves, Citizens, Sons*, 86–88.

tradition. The adaptation is twofold.

On the one hand, his model depicts a development from the communal or collective sonship of Israel to the individual or personalized sonship of the new covenant believer. While there are traces of filial individuality in the Old Testament amid an otherwise collective view of Israel's sonship (2 Sam. 7:14; Prov. 3:12; Ps. 68:5; 103:13; Is. 43:6),[38] in the New Testament, the collective is assumed (note the reference to the church as the household) behind more overt references to the individual enjoyment of adoption.

On the other hand, the adoption model includes a development from the minority sonship of Israel to the majority sonship of the Jewish and Gentile believers. With the coming of Christ, God's people came of age. Thus, Jews now believing in Christ enter into the majority sonship of God's people. The entrance is personalized in the cry of liberation: "Abba, Father!" The Gentile believers, without participating in the maturing of Israel, now enter the same mature relationship to the Father as do believing Jews. Buffeted by their old *paterfamilias*, the prince of the power of the air, and doubtless vexed by their years as the sons of disobedience and children of wrath, they, too, cry out in freedom as they receive from the Father their adoption. Clearly, then, the popular treatments of adoption which depict the adoptive relationship as that of a little child to his or her father err. The relationship is rather of one come of age newly liberated. The entrance into the relationship is typified by the vocative. *Abba* Smail describes as "a new word for a new relationship."[39]

Third, the Father's adoption grants a *new experience*. Nothing in Israel's old covenant experience of sonship compares to the privilege of crying out so directly, personally, and fully, "Abba, Father!" *Die Bibel*

---

[38] Allen Mawhinney, "God as Father: Two Popular Theories Reconsidered," *JETS* 31.2 (1988), 184.

[39] Smail, *The Forgotten Father*, 40

nach der Übersetzung Martin Luthers captures somewhat dynamically the emotion of the cry: "Abba, Lieber Vater!" (cf., Rom. 8:15).[40] As sons of disobedience and children of wrath, the Gentiles danced to the tune of their "father," the devil. He had no affection for them. His rule over them was for their ruin in the bondage and death of sin. How contrary our experience, now that we are in relationship with a beneficent heavenly Father! He has loved us from eternity, chosen us for his family, placed us in the Son, and purposes that we should live in the freedom of holiness and in enjoyment of the inheritance.

What, though, are we to make of Paul's use of the Aramaic *Aββα*? Scholars understand it variously. Joachim Jeremias opines that Aββα was familiar children's talk in Jesus' day meaning *Daddy*. Yet, adult sons could also address their fathers that way. Since it would have seemed disrespectful to address God as Aββα, Jeremias deduces that Aββα was a novel way of addressing God. It was introduced by Jesus in the Garden of Gethsemane, as Mark records (Mk. 14:36). James Barr agrees that Aββα was familiar language in Jesus' day, distinct from more formal or ceremonious usage, but argues that Aββα was not an expression comparable to "Daddy."[41]

Wherever the truth lies, our understanding of Aββα is informed not only by the original usage of the vocative in Jewish culture, but by Jesus' use of it in Gethsemane—the only occurrence of "Aββα ὁ πατήρ" outside the Pauline corpus (cf., Mk. 14:36, Gal. 4:6, and Rom. 8:15). There, the vocative bespeaks a personal relationship to the Father. Listen to Jesus amid the lonesomeness of his Passion: "Abba, Father, all

---

[40] Luther's translation of Mk 14:36 reads "Abba, mein Vater . . . !"

[41] Joachim Jeremias, *Prayers of Jesus*, SBT II 6 (London: SCM, 1967), 11–65; James Barr, "'Abba' isn't 'Daddy,'" *Journal of Theological Studies* 39.1 (1988), 28–47. For a summary of the argument and the sources, see Mary Rose D'Angelo, "*Abba* and 'Father': Imperial Theology and the Jesus Traditions" *Journal of Biblical Literature* 111.4 (winter, 1992), 611–30.

things are possible for you. Remove this cup from me. Yet not what I will, but what you will." The trauma of Gethsemane powerfully reminds us, though, that the personal character of the relationship is not manipulated by sentiment. Even were Αββα to mean *Daddy*, we are not to read the vocative sentimentally as if the Father is a big softy capable of being played at will. Quite the contrary, Christ's use of Αββα reveals the seriousness of filial love, devotion, and obedience; for while the Father is most loving and gracious, he ever remains a holy Father. As such he has predestined us to be holy, too (cf. Rom. 8:29 and Eph. 1:5). He personalizes and blesses our providences to this end, determining to love us without ever spoiling us, and calling us to defer to him in all matters of faith and conduct. There is, then, nothing "cutsie" about Αββα. When Jews called on him they were recognizing his paternal authority. Writes Edward Schillebeeckx,

> the father is the one charged with authority, with *exousia*, complete authority, whom the children are in duty bound to obey and treat with piety. The father is also the one available to look after and protect his own, the family, to come to the rescue and to give advice and counsel. He is the focus of the entire family (paternal house), everything revolves around him and through his person forms a community. There is no contending with the father's authority in Judaism.[42]

Gentile believers join their Jewish brothers and sisters in recognizing God's paternal authority. Freed from the evil authority of the prince of the power of the air, they look not for a weak Father who permits their freedom in Christ to degenerate into the anarchy they once knew, but for a loving yet authoritative Father who, taking possession of all that we are, bestows on us his beneficence. This understanding of divine Fatherhood Paul's Gentile readers could relate to from their knowledge of the societal *potestas* of the *paterfamilias*.

---

[42] Edward Schillebeeckx, *Jesus: An Experiment in Christology*, transl. Hubert Hoskins, reprint ed. (New York: Vintage Books, 1981), 262.

Indwelt by the Spirit (vv. 6-7).

Whereas the Son redeems the elect, and the Father adopts them, the Spirit ensures their experience of adoptive sonship. He applies in us what the Son does for us and the Father does to us. In this application, the Spirit displays the profundity of his multivalent ministry. We shall have more to say of it in regard to the use of υἱοθεσία in Romans 8:15-16. Note, though, in connection with Galatians 3–4 six aspects of the Spirit's work.

First, the Spirit is *the inspirer of faith*. Although the adoption of God's sons is guaranteed by the Father's grace in predestining us and the Son's grace in redeeming us, we are not sons of God until we receive the adoption. Paul is not saying that Jewish and Gentile slaves can thwart the Father's adoptive purposes, but that adoption, no less than justification (2:15-16), is received through faith. Receiving the adoption (ἀπολάβωμεν, v. 5) is all we can "do" with it. It is a free gift of our triune God! Even the ability to receive adoption is attributable to his grace, for it is the Spirit who inspires the faith through which we take possession of it.

Paul's allusion to faith in Galatians 4 is not surprising. It follows on from his debunking throughout the letter of the Judaizers' claim that the gospel is received through an admixture of faith and the works of the law. Fearing that the Galatians have been bewitched into believing the Judaizers, Paul asks: "Did you receive the Spirit by the works of the law or by hearing with faith? . . . Having begun by the Spirit, are you now being perfected by the flesh? . . . Does he who supplies the Spirit to you and works miracles among you do so by works of law, or by hearing with faith?" (3:2-3). Obviously, Paul intends his readers to understand the "hearing with faith" to be the correct answer. Possession of the gift of the Spirit without the works of the law proves, then, that it is faith alone in Christ which is God's ordained means whereby we receive the benefits of salvation (cf., 3:14; 4:6). If faith could operate without the Spirit—that is to say, by our own initiative and energy—then neither justification nor adoption would be of God's free grace. In fact, adoption is as much *sola gratia* and *sola fide* as justification.[43] While it is "through the Spirit, by faith we ourselves eagerly wait for the hope of righteousness" (5:5), we await likewise our inheritance as God's sons.

Second, the Spirit is *the bond of the union* between the adopted sons of God and their older brother. The faith the Spirit inspires has no sense or meaning without the Son, for it is in him we trust. We not only look to Christ but are bound to him by the Spirit. In the language of the passage before us, the sons of God are "in Christ" (3:26; cf., v. 28), "baptized into Christ" (v. 27), "put on Christ" (v. 27). In short, we "are Christ's" (v. 29). These explicit references to union with the Son cast light on the subtler reference to the union in 4:5b. In adopting us, the Father places us as υἱοι in the υἱος (hence υἱοθεσία), yet it is through the Spirit that our sonship in the Son is forged. Paul is emphatic about this: "Because you are sons, God has sent the Spirit of his Son into our hearts" (v. 6a).

There is much more here than a legal transaction or a replication of societal forms of adoption. God gives us of his Spirit in a way that is impossible in human community. Not only are the adopted *in Christ*, but he is *in us*! Not physically, for he ascended bodily to heaven. Rather, our heavenly Father, in adopting us, sends the Spirit of his Son into our hearts. Thus, indwelt by the Spirit, experiencing within an ectypal echo of the perichoretic experience within the Trinity, we are enabled to address God as Father, as did the Son in the garden of Gethsame. The union with Christ, the firstborn, is that tight![44]

Third, the Spirit is *the source of the believer's assurance*. Paul specifically says that it is the Spirit of God's Son who cries out, "Abba! Father!" There are two extraordinary truths revealed here. First, that it

---

[43] Cf., Whaling, "Adoption," 227–28.

[44] Longenecker, *Galatians*, 154; cf., Trevor Burke, "Pauline Adoption: a Sociological Approach" *EQ* 73:2 (2001), 121fn. 9, 127.

is the Spirit of the Son who first uses this vocative in the hearts of the adopted. While we may assume that the Spirit of the Son prays for us, the initial use of the vocative is best understood as the Spirit teaching newly released slaves how to pray to God now that he is their Father and they are his adopted sons. Since this knowledge does not come to us naturally, the Spirit is given to show us what we should call God. He preps us in addressing God filially. Also, we learn that it is the energy of the Spirit that is operative within us. He so rushes through our hearts in the moment of adoption that we *cry out*, "Abba! Father!" The cry, coinciding with the transition from slavery to sonship, was for first-century Jews of faith a breaking of the dam of a pent-up yearning following long centuries under the burdensome ceremonial law. For Gentiles, the cry bespeaks the enlivening power of God. He causes us to realize that in the Son we have a new *paterfamilias* who has prehorizoned us to live as his sons (cf., Eph. 2:5).

Fourth, the Spirit *gives expression to the believer's liberty*. He cries out within us to pry open our hearts and mouths, thereby facilitating our liberty in prayer and inaugurating our experience of sonship. The Spirit's intent is that this newfound liberty should flow through our entire lives. Listen to Paul again: "You are no longer a slave, but a son" (v. 7). This liberty is obtained for us through the Son's redemptive work. It is confirmed by the Father's adoption of us, and is animated by the indwelling of the Holy Spirit. Besides elevating our spirits, the Spirit points us as God's sons to the perfect example of the Son, challenging us thereby to use our freedom to serve rather than to sin. Thus, authentic liberty is manifested in filial obedience to God.

Later in Galatians, Paul tells us how our liberty is preserved and grows. While God's sons have a responsibility to stand fast in it (5:1), the Spirit fights for us against the flesh, daily reminding us that we are not to use our liberty as occasion for the flesh (5:13, 17). Rather, we use it to become embodied summaries of the law, loving our neighbor as ourselves. This begins with our service to God's household (cf., 5:13-14 and 6:10), but it does not end there. While works make no contribution to our adoption, we have been adopted to live and to walk by the Spirit (cf., Eph. 2:10). Instead, then, of pursuing the works of the flesh (sexual immorality, impurity, sensuality, idolatry, sorcery, hatred, strife, jealousy, anger, rivalries, dissensions, divisions, envy, drunkenness, and orgies), we seek the Spirit's power to live loving, joyful, peaceable, patient, kind, good, faithful, gentle, and self-controlled lives (5:16-26).

Fifth, the Spirit *develops our fellowship within God's household.* Paul has already alluded to this in his piling up of descriptions of the believer's union with Christ (3:26-28). Our identity as sons in the Son supersedes, he insists, our ethnicities, social statuses, and genders. Joined supremely to Christ, our fellowship embraces those whom society shuns. This fellowship is not on our personal terms, but on the terms of free grace set by the gospel. Thus, Paul rebuffs the Judaizers' demand for Gentile believers to be circumcised and to uphold the ceremonial law for their acceptance in God's household. He will not have it that Gentile believers need to become Jews in order to take their place in the family of believers. Nor must we. Stresses Paul, "you are all one in Christ Jesus" (v. 28). Believing Jews have ceased to be Jews primarily, since their identity, like that of believing Gentiles, is in Christ. By grace, we share the same redemption, the same adoption, and the same indwelling. We pray to the same Father and belong to the same household.

The juxtaposition of the Aramaic Αββα and the Greek ὁ πατήρ in the cry of liberation makes the point beautifully. Since Galatians was written around the Council of Jerusalem (A.D. 48 or 49), somewhere between (A.D. 48–51), it was likely written prior to Mark's Gospel (A.D. 40–65). On this understanding, Paul drew the vocative "Abba! Father!" from the common knowledge of Jesus' prayer in the Garden of Gethsemane (hence his forgoing of an explanation of its use).[45] By

---

[45] Burke, *Adopted into God's Family*, 91.

A.D. 56 Paul repeated the double vocative in his letter to the Romans (8:15). Alternatively, Mark, assuming he had access to Paul's letter to the Galatians or the newly distributed letter to the Romans, made use of the internationalized double vocative in Galatians 4:6 to communicate the relevance of Jesus' vocative to his readers in Rome. Regardless of its origin, its combination of Aramaic and Greek typify the intent of the model to encourage intimacy between believing Jews and Gentiles. The double vocative expresses very well the unifying purposes in Paul's vision of the household of God. The household is not simply for Jews (Aramaic speakers) but for the nations (Greek speakers). God's household is run by the grace which provides an equal footing on which his multiethnic sons can fellowship with him and with each other.[46]

The unity of the household was not a light matter to Paul. In Ephesians (A.D. 60–62) he elaborates on the point. Writing to the Gentiles, formerly known as "the uncircumcision," recalling how they were "separated from Christ, alienated from the commonwealth of Israel and strangers to the covenant of promise, having no hope and without God in the world" (v. 12), the apostle, formerly a Hebrew of the Hebrews, rejoices that "in Christ" Gentile believers have been brought near to God and to believing Jews. Because of the blood he shed on the cross, Christ has become "our peace." Speaking from experience, Paul writes: "He has made us both one and has broken down in his flesh the dividing wall of hostility by abolishing the law of commandments expressed in ordinances, that he might create in himself one new man in place of the two, so making peace, and might reconcile us both to God in one body through the cross, thereby killing the hostility" (vv. 14-16).

---

[46] Heim, "Light Through a Prism," 307–308. For a discussion of the dating of Mark, see William Hendrickson, *The Gospel of Mark*, reprint ed. (Carlisle, PA: The Banner of Truth Trust, 1987), 14–16. On the dating of Galatians, I have gone by Herman N. Ridderbos' discussion in *The Epistle of Paul to the Churches in Galatia*, reprint ed., transl. Henry Zylstra (Grand Rapids: Eerdmans, 1981), 31–32.

Christ, then, is critical to the unity of the household. By his blood, as applied by the Spirit, Gentiles are built together with the Jews as a dwelling place for God (v. 22). This building amounts to more than a Jewish and Gentile tolerance of one another in a peaceful but unloving coexistence. Paul's proclamation in Galatians that there is no Jew nor Gentile in Christ becomes in Ephesians 2 a more positively stated proclamation that there is now one new man in Christ. The old Israel which Paul regarded as possessing the preparatory adoption, takes a back seat to the new "Israel of God." Only the latter experiences the full adoption (Gal. 6:16). I word this carefully for, as was stated earlier, God remains faithful to his ancient people (Rom. 11:29). When Jews receive the adoption either personally or in a national restoration (Rom. 9–11), they enter the new Israel, which is the household of God.

Sixth, the Spirit is *the guarantee of the inheritance.* Accompanying the gift of sonship is that of heirship (Gal. 4:7). This connection in Paul's model between adoptive sonship and heirship is ineradicable, and has not been lost on those in history who have written on the doctrine where the two themes appear repeatedly. The inheritance functions in regard to Paul's adoption model as a supportive subsidiary metaphor, and yet, more broadly speaking, the inheritance also functions as a theological model in its own right.

To summarize the long-standing context of Galatians 4:7, we may note that the promise of an inheritance was first given to Abraham but became Israel's upon the nation's adoption as God's son. To carry Gentile readers with him, the apostle weaves into this historical context ideas of inheritance found in Roman *adoptio.* Yet, divine adoption goes much further, for the indwelling of the Spirit of the Son, in proving the authenticity of our sonship, guarantees that the sons of God are also heirs of God and of the world (cf., Gal. 4:7b and Rom. 4:13). States Paul's cross-reference in Ephesians 1:11: "We have obtained an inheritance, having been predestined according to the purpose of him who works all things according to the counsel of his will." He teaches in effect that once we possess the Spirit of the Son we are *already* coheirs together with Christ the Son (cf., Rom. 8:17).

In the moment of faith, we come, in this life, into possession of our heavenly Father. Here and now, we are able to call him ours! Yet, the Father has promised us that what he is *and* all that is his become ours at the end of the age. The Spirit indwelling us assures us of this. He is, writes Paul, the divine seal notifying us that we belong to God. Thus, we can never be lost to the Father, for the Spirit seals us unto the day of redemption (cf., Eph. 1:13-14; 4:30). He is, to utilize Paul's additional imagery, the guarantee or down payment on the inheritance to be received on that day.

The church, though, has rarely given attention to the question of the identity of the inheritance and the occasion of our receipt of it. Recently, though, Miguel G. Echevaria Jr. has given himself to this subject and identified three schools of thought.[47]

First, there are those who, in positing that the adopted already possess their inheritance, claim that it is purely spiritual. Up for question is not the thought that the inheritance is as certain as their election and adoption by the Father, their redemption by the Son, and their sealing by the Spirit, but whether the spiritual nature of the inheritance exhausts what we are to understand of it.

This spiritualization has been emphasized by James Hester in his seminal treatment of the subject, *Paul's Concept of the Inheritance*, and has been advocated by scholars William D. Davies, Bruce Waltke,

---

[47] Miguel G. Echevarria Jr.'s *The Future Inheritance of Land in the Pauline Epistles* (Eugene, Oregon: Pickwick Publications, 2019) was written for two reasons: To supplement James Hester's *Paul's Concept of the Inheritance* (1968) and out of dissatisfaction with Hester's spiritualization of the theme. See Echevarria pages 5–18 for the following schools of thought. Along a similar line, see also Esau McCaulley's *Sharing in the Son's Inheritance: Davidic Messianism and Paul's Worldwide Interpretation of the Abrahamic Land Promise in Galatians* (London, *et al.*: T & T Clark, 2019).

and Sam Williams. They hold that the inheritance is fulfilled "in Christ" and by the indwelling of the Spirit, and thus has been fulfilled in a landless or deterritorialized way.

Echevarria is rightly dissatisfied with this understanding. The adopted are already heirs in view of a future enjoyment of a physical inheritance. This "already-not yet" view is held representatively by Edward Adams, G. K. Beale, Paul Hammer, and D. R. Denton. It considers the Old Testament promise of the inheritance to be already fulfilled spiritually in Christ, with a literal or earthly fulfillment to come at the end of the age. On this understanding, we are both possessors of the inheritance and co-heirs with Christ.

Echevarria supports, though, the "not yet" view held representatively by Mark Foreman, Yon-Gyong Kwon, and N. T. Wright, which posits that there is no present fulfillment of the promise of the inheritance. The fulfillment is all to come in the future world.

To the "not yet" we shall come. Here we have sought to do justice to the Spirit's present evincing of the inheritance. I see no exegetical warrant, then, for the "not yet" swallowing up the "already." As sons of God we are already heirs of God. We have, to cross-reference Ephesians 1, the downpayment of the inheritance and the promise of its fulfillment. In our souls, we already have what is incomparable in human adoption, namely, the Spirit of God. Yes, the Spirit of the adopter! This wonderful privilege explains our yearning for the consummation of the inheritance in a redeemed cosmos. Our possession of the down payment of the inheritance is, then, psychical, but our consummate possession of it shall also be bodily, tangible, and cosmic. More of that to come.

MOVEMENT FOUR: THE ASSURANCE OF ADOPTION

For all who are led by the Spirit of God are sons of God. For you did not receive the spirit of slavery to fall back into fear, but you have received the Spirit of adoption as sons, by whom we cry, "Abba! Father!" The Spirit himself bears witness with our spirit that we are children of God, and if children then heirs—heirs of God and fellow heirs with Christ, provided we suffer with him in order that we may also be glorified with him. (Rom 8:14-17)

Although we move from one text or pericope to the next, here we have the sole use of υἱοθεσία in which there is no progress along the trajectory of salvation history. Paul focuses rather on the experience of adoptive sonship. This, the Puritans, Methodists, and Brethren knew very well. To say, however, that this fourth movement is theological and experiential rather than chronological does not mean to say that it is not also soteriological. Thus, I differ from Heim's claim that only the use of υἱοθεσία in Galatians is soteriological. For sure Galatians 4:4-7 emphasizes the action of the Father in sending his Son, but to so limit the soteriological to the personal is to encourage the exclusion of the salvation-historical (Eph. 1:4-5, Rom. 9:4, and 8:22-23) and the salvation-experiential (Rom. 8:14-17). Such a move is more Western than biblical.[48]

That said, Paul's adoption model has an impressive array of personal applications. Some of these we have touched on already. Yet, in Romans 8, Paul, writing after his Galatian epistle, communicates further lessons pertaining to adoptive sonship. We don't exaggerate the extent of these, for Romans 8:14-17 offers us no more of "a predication without explanation" than Romans 9:4. What difference there is lies in the fact that the latter adoption text appears in the section in which Paul answers the first two questions in 3:1-8 (concerning God's faithfulness to his covenant), while the former appears in the section answering the

---

[48] Heim, "Light Through a Prism," 163, 190. In fairness, Heim notes the eschatological "now" but "not yet" tension running through the uses of the υἱοθεσία metaphors (to use her wording), but she undermines the eschatological force of the adoption model by omitting Eph 1:5 from consideration and by perforating the continuity in the structure of Paul's adoption model by treating his references to adoption as individual metaphors (ibid., 189, 222–23). Heim's criticisms that I do not, in making much of the eschatological, probe more the implications of adoption other than those which are soteriological, are due, it seems to me, to her overlooking of my *SBET* article on the exposition of adoption and its implications (ibid., 190fn6, 206–7).

third and fourth questions (relating to God's free grace in Christ). From it we draw three observations about the believer's experience of the adoptive state.

First, the verb κραζω reappears. It does so not in a vacuum but amid Paul's depiction of the Christian life. A Christian is one, who, freed in Christ from the law of sin and death, possesses the Spirit of life. He, therefore, walks according to the Spirit rather than according to the flesh. These two lifestyles are distinguishable by the use of the mind. Those walking according to the flesh set their mind on things of the flesh and those according to the Spirit on the things of the Spirit. The former is death because it is hostility against God, the latter life and peace (8:4-8). Paul is not distinguishing the mythical, so-called carnal Christian from the spiritual Christian, but the Christian from the non-Christian. His logic is straightforward: Either we are in Christ and his Spirit is in us, or we are not in Christ and his Spirit is not in us. Authentic sons of God owe the flesh nothing. Rather, those living by the Spirit put to death the deeds of the body, for the Spirit leads us to mortify sin. Our willingness to be so led affords clear evidence that we are sons of God (8:9-14).

Against the backdrop of this contrast of the true and the false, Paul warns his readers of the danger of falling back into a fearful enslavement. To do so is to lose the family resemblance. With sanctified dogmatism, he tells his readers that they did not receive the Spirit of slavery to fall back into fear, but the Spirit of adoption as sons, "by whom we cry [κράζομεν], 'Abba! Father!'" This title given the Spirit, πνεῦμα υἱοθεσίας, is unique to Paul in Scripture. But note here, in contrast to Galatians 4:6, that Paul says that it is the adopted rather than the Spirit of the Son who cry, "*Abba!*" or "Father!" depending on their ethnicity. In effect, Paul is saying that whereas the Spirit teaches us as former slaves newly adopted to converse with the Father, it becomes normative for us to cry to the Father thereafter. We ought not to think, though, that the Spirit having kick-started our prayers is absent from our lives thereafter. He intercedes for us (8:26), yet without negating the need of our own prayers. Common to both the Spirit's initiation of our prayer life and its continuation is our liberty and confidence as sons of God in crying out to our Father. Prayer, then, is an obvious way in which the adopted sons of God are distinguishable from those yet enslaved.

Although God is unchanged, our fears in prayer, whether "in the closet" or in the prayer meeting, are a denial of our adoption—a reversion to the sobering atmosphere in the household of the living dead. This is not the Father's will for us. Jewish believers are no longer to pray and to live as if trembling at the foot of Mount Sinai, or as if hemmed in by the ceremonial law's minutia. Nor are Gentile believers to live hopeless lives in the pagan or immoral addictions from which they are redeemed. The Spirit grants us freedom from servile fear. He is given us by the Father to demonstrate that we are in the Son and that the great estate is ours. How can anything less satisfy us?

Note, second, the additional feature. The Spirit witnesses supernaturally and personally with our spirits (συμμαρτυρεῖ) that we are authentic children of God (v. 16). Two matters are intriguing about this witness. First, the question arises as to whether the Spirit witnesses to our spirits or with them. Going for the prior rendering is the dative τῷ πνεύματι (to [our] spirits), and for the latter the compound verb συμμαρτυρεῖ (to bear witness with). In the former option, the Spirit witnesses independently in a direct revelation informing the believer that he or she is an adopted son of God. In the latter, the Spirit comes alongside our spirits to combine his witness with ours, that we are God's children. On this rendering, which is the preferable one theologically, the Spirit and our spirits come together to fulfill the biblical requirement of dual or multiple testimonies for the establishment of a truth (cf., 2 Cor. 13:1; Deut. 17:6, 19:15). Paul may also have had in mind practices of Roman adoption in which the adoptive act was performed publicly before witnesses.[49] They did not witness to the adopted of their adoption, for the adopted were conscious of what was happening, but they did witness with the adopted that the adoption was actual and, subsequent to it, that the adoption had happened.

Third, the Spirit witnesses with our spirits that we are children of God (τέκνα θεου). Recall from the third chapter our outline of four possible reasons why Paul, having made so much of adoption as *sons*, should state here that the Spirit witnesses that we are God's *children*. Is he, we asked, underlining to believers from the children of Israel that the adopted are now part of a new Israel, the children of God? Or, that as mature as is our sonship under the new covenant, we remain children for so long as the Father is alive? Or, that there is no male nor female in Christ? Perhaps, alternatively, he has nothing distinctive in mind. There is another possibility, however. It is said that a Roman adoption was, existentially, like a new birth, for the slave was no longer existing, but now lived in possession of all the rights of his new family: freedom from debt and a share in the inheritance.[50]

Regardless of Paul's reason or reasons for the use of τέκνα θεου in the context of his adoption model, the integrity and the clarity of its structure is undiminished. The term τέκνα θεου comports with the

---

[49] Trevor J. Burke, "Adoption and the Spirit in Romans 8," *EQ* 70:4 (1998), 322. Burke rightly sides with John Stott *vis-à-vis* Martyn Lloyd-Jones concerning the Spirit of adoption, seeing no evidence in Romans 8 that the possession of the Spirit of adoption arises from a specialized form of assurance experienced subsequent to conversion by those who seek it (*Adopted into God's Family*, 143fn45).

[50] To admit this idea is not to go back on the distinctive structure of the Pauline adoption model. First, because we are talking within the confines of the Pauline corpus and theology. Second, because we are still speaking of adoption (albeit as a birth) and not necessarily of a competing new birth model within his theology. Third, because it is the exegesis of Paul's adoption model and not the possibility of a Roman likening of adoption to a birth which carries the theological freight.

apostle's connection of freedom and the inheritance in verses 15-17a, as also of the possession of the Spirit and the inheritance (cf., Paul's use of subsidiary metaphors in Eph. 1:13-14: the Spirit as down payment, guarantee, or pledge [ἀρραβών]). Were Paul, then, to allude in his use of τέκνα θεου to the Roman comparison of an adoption to a birth (or new life), he would not be seeking to muddy his adoption model. The comparison has not to do in the context of Romans 8 with how we come into a filial relationship to God, but with the legitimacy of the believer's standing with God as one of his heirs. The Spirit's witness with our spirit that we are *children of God* underlines, accordingly, the reality of the inheritance. The inheritance belongs, after all, only to children. This sets us up nicely to consider the receiving and the essence of the inheritance.[51]

MOVEMENT FIVE: THE CONSUMMATION OF ADOPTION

> For we know that the whole creation has been groaning together in the pains of childbirth until now. And not only the creation, but we ourselves, who have the firstfruits of the Spirit, groan inwardly as we wait eagerly for adoption as sons, the redemption of our bodies. (Rom. 8:22-23).

This fifth and final use of υἱοθεσία supplies the fourth epochal marker along the trajectory of salvation history. Having advanced through Paul's elongated model from our predestination to adoption, to the preparatory or typological adoption of Israel, and on to the full adoption of believing Jews and Gentiles, we now complete our exposition of the model with a consideration of its consummation. This final usage, like the previous one, is found in Romans 8. Byrne claims this usage refers to the adoption *simpliciter.* Only here, he argues, is adoption defined. While his claim could lead to an undue narrowing of the tenor of the model to the redemption of the body (the prior uses of υἱοθεσία pertain to the redemption of Israel and of the soul), the

---

[51] Lyall, *Slaves, Citizens, Sons*, 110–11.

epexegetical descriptor of adoption as "the redemption of the body" constitutes a worthy climax to Paul's salvation-historical reading of God's adoptive dealings with his people.[52]

The climax is, of course, the coming Day of Jesus Christ. This likely explains Paul's bringing together in Romans 8 a number of themes (subsidiary metaphors and models). These converge like multiple train lines narrow down to a singular track upon nearing a train station. Some of the lines are connected to the entire epistle (creation, the image of God, suffering, and resurrection) and some more specifically to the adoption model (redemption, adoption, childhood, and the inheritance). They remind us of the eschatological tension in which we live. We entered in this new covenant era the full adoption rather than the preparatory adoption of Israel, and possess the Spirit of God's Son and all the benefits of adoption he applies, yet we experience the Spirit as "the gift of the interim." [53] The fullness of the full adoption is yet to come, for the faith in Christ which establishes our sonship once-and-for-all in time and eternity (as also our justification and [positional] sanctification), is to be consummated on the Day of Jesus Christ.

Romans 8:17-25 infers that the consummation of our adoption entails, first, an end to our sufferings. Adopted in Christ, our sonship follows the pattern of his Sonship: suffering first, glory later. While his sufferings were satisfactory and ours castigatory, says Puritan Thomas Watson, we nevertheless suffer as fellow heirs (συγκληρονόμοι) with him (v. 17).[54]

---

[52] Byrne, *"Sons of God"—"Seed of Abraham,"* 109–10.

[53] Ridderbos, *Paul*, 200.

[54] Thomas Watson, *All Things for God*, first published in 1663 as *A Dvine Cordial* (Edinburgh and Carlisle, PA: The Banner of Truth Trust, 1986), 29. Burke distinguishes well the sufferings of the Son and the sons: "I use the word 'similar' rather than 'same,' as Christ's suffering was unique" (*Adopted into God's Familiy*, 148fn58).

How important it was for the persecuted Christians of Rome to understand this. This truth would help them to endure, for "provided" (εἴπερ) they suffer with Christ (συμπάσχομεν) they would be glorified with him (σσυνδοξασθῶμεν). To aid this endurance, Paul reminds them (as also the sons of God in all ages), that the present sufferings, no matter their intensity or extensity, are not worth comparing to the glory to be revealed to us. Not only are they incomparable in their contrast (the glory far surpassing in brilliance the darkness of the sufferings), so they are in their duration. Whereas the sufferings are, literally, of the now time (τοῦ νῦν καιροῦ), the revealed glory lasts forever (v. 18).

Second, the consummation of adoption signals the end of waiting (vv. 19-25). In explaining this, Paul speaks of creation in personified terms as waiting for the revealing of the sons of God (υἱῶν τοῦ θεοῦ). In the model's unique but indirect allusion to our first parents, Paul reasons that whereas creation became unwillingly bound in futility through the fall of our first parents, so creation has waited with eager longing for the apocalypse or unveiling (ἀποκάλυψιν) of God's sons. For although God's subjecting of the creation at the fall was an act of justice, he nevertheless graciously subjected it in hope of a new world to come (v. 20).

Prominent in this hope is a twofold freedom: freedom *from* the bondage of corruption and *of* the glory of the children of God (τέκνων τοῦ θεοῦ). As creation suffered through the fall of man, so creation is liberated through his glorification. There is, then, an inextricable and divinely supervised link in the fortunes of man and the creation. In man's fall creation is subjected to futility, in the glorification of the sons of God creation is liberated. We are not surprised at this, for man is, in God's economy, the crown of creation. As fallen, he lives in an enslaved context and cannot know glorification unless his context is liberated. Unsurprisingly, then, the sons of God, elevated by grace yet remain a part of creation, share its eager longings (note the respective uses of ἀπεκδέχομαι in vv. 19 and 23). Although God's sons are already adopted, they know freedom only in their souls, and even there only partially right now. Sometimes, the eager longing is such that we cannot pray intelligibly. In such instances, the Spirit groans on our behalf, interceding for us according to God's will in a way too deep for words (cf., vv. 16 and 26-27).

Only with the final deliverance of creation from the bondage of corruption shall God's sons be fully, perfectly, eternally, and psycho-somatically free. All traces of their former enslavement shall have vanished and all hopes for the inheritance shall be realized. The world we shall inherit with Christ shall be filled with the consciousness of the Father and of his joy in witnessing the family gathering he planned from before the world began. With Christ, our elder brother, we shall forever treasure the inheritance. Even so, it belongs to him by nature and to us by grace. Yet, never shall that enjoyment dim. We shall utterly and always be filled with the Spirit, glorifying God for all he is and for all the love and mercy he has bestowed so lavishly on us. He in turn, ever alive, shall rejoice to see his children revel in their inheritance—the new earth first promised to Abraham.

Third, and following on, the consummation of adoption marks, for God's people, the end of death. The creation yearns or stretches forward to see the consummation of all things, not in the throes of death as if hanging on to this life, but in birth pangs heralding the new world Jesus promised (cf., Matt. 19:28). The terminus of New Testament hope is not, then, heaven in its intermediate state—the paradise believers enter upon death—but heaven in its final state: a redeemed creation filled with God's presence and purged of the corruption of the old order of this first world. We yearn for this consummated heaven with an eagerness that survives death. In the beautiful words of the WLC (Ans. 86):

> The communion in glory with Christ, which the members of the invisible church enjoy immediately after death, is, in that their souls are then made perfect in holiness, and received into the highest heavens, where they behold the face of God in light and glory,

waiting for the full redemption of their bodies, which even in death
continue united to Christ, and rest in their graves as in their beds, till
at the last day they be again united to their souls.

Critical in the realization of this deathless context is the
ministry of the Spirit. Whereas we have presently the first droplets of
the Spirit (Calvin), then we shall know the fullest flow. This effusion of
the Spirit's power and life Paul speaks of by means of a subsidiary
agricultural metaphor. By stating that the adopted have the firstfruits
of the Spirit he implies that at the consummation the adopted shall
experience the full harvest of the Spirit's ministry. The firstfruits are
grown by the Spirit in our souls, but the full harvest will be felt
additionally in the bodies of the adopted as also in the cosmos at large
(hell excepted). Neither God's people as individuals nor the creation,
then, can be said to be consummatively redeemed unless and until their
bodies are also delivered from all effects of the fall (cf. Gal. 4:4-5). The
consummation of adoption heralds, then, the psychosomatic wholeness
of the adopted (individually and communally as God's household), in a
creation redeemed from its futility and bondage to corruption.

Interestingly, Paul refers to the bodies of the adopted in the
singular (σώματος). He does not tell us why, but our bodies, party to
the union of our persons with Christ and to our communion with the
saints, are, for all their individuality, somehow united in their
redemption with the bodies of each of the adopted. All the adopted, in a
moment at the *eschaton*, experience simultaneously the redemption of
their bodies. Life returns to them in the same moment, and their graves
open in unison (1 Cor. 15:52). Thus, while our individual bodies are
unique to each of us, the unified and spontaneous nature of the
resurrection legitimizes Paul's use of the singular when speaking of the
adoption as a bodily redemption.

Fourth, the consummation of adoption will end the hiddenness
of God's dealings. In "the now time" we know our Father's acceptance
in our souls. We cry out, "Abba, Father!" Yet, despite living life out of our
adoptive sonship, and possessing in the indwelling of the Spirit of God's

Son an infallible but nonconsummate assurance, the certainty of our adoption cannot be perfectly or entirely discerned by the human eye. The day of consummation will throw up some surprises. Some we assume are God's sons shall be understood by their absence from the household-inheritance to have been the sons of disobedience. Some we fear presently are children of wrath may in fact turn out to be children of God. It goes without saying that the verdict is God's (2 Tim. 2:19), but the fact that Paul writes of the revelation of God's sons implies that only on the day of redemption will the exact complement of God's household be known. Our authenticity as God's sons will be revealed by the visible redemption of our bodies unto eternal life.[55] In contrast to those resurrected unto eternal death, we shall know the Father's public and eternal acceptance and the embrace of our persons, then psycho-somatically whole.

The full adoption, beginning personally and privately in the soul at the dawn of faith in Christ and professed in the church or household of God, shall be confirmed and publicized throughout the new cosmos. The consummation of our adoption shall be enshrouded in a display of the glory of God surpassing the clearest discernings of it in this life. For this full adoption we hope, awaiting it and all its accompaniments with patience (vv. 24-25).

---

[55] Heim makes the valuable observation that some make an exegetical leap from Paul's talk of redemption to the resurrection. Certainly, the redemption of our bodies occurs on the day of resurrection (cf., Eph. 4:30), nevertheless, Paul retains the language in Romans 8 of redemption due to the backdrop of slavery. This contrasts with 1 Cor. 15 where he uses the language of resurrection ("Light Through a Prism," 201 [cf., 209fn 93 for Moo's differentiation of redemption and resurrection]). Heim highlights, then, the importance of not treating the adoption model and the letter to the Romans as coextensive. I shy away, however, from her description of redemption and adoption as "twin metaphors." They are certainly not identical twins, nor are they a diptych (a work made up of two matching parts). It is better to think of them as distinct but coequal models.

Fifth, the consummation of adoption entails our reception of the full inheritance. In the gift of the Spirit the adopted already experience the inheritance (Eph. 1:11, 14; Rom. 8:17), yet at the consummation of our adoption, with all suffering done, the "not yet" becomes the "now and evermore."

Romans 8 teaches us that the Father will disperse the inheritance to both the Son as God-man and the sons, for we are co-heirs with him. The dispersal shall coincide with our glorification with the Son (v. 17). Our shared glorification shall be manifest in our sharing of the inheritance. The Son receives the inheritance for what he in our humanity merited; we receive it due to his merit expended for our sake, and thus as pure grace. What a delightful scene that will be! The Father, as alive as ever, granting to us what rightly belongs to him, the Son sharing it with us in sheer joy and without a hint of jealousy, and the Spirit filling us to overflowing with the assurance and perception that the inheritance is ours!

Since the inheritance, as we noted earlier, has been spiritualized or deterritorialized away, we must, as Echevarria rightly notes, make more of it:

> The theme of inheritance has suffered from severe neglect in biblical scholarship. Interpreters prefer to speak of heaven rather than eternal life in the land promised to Abraham, i.e., the inheritance. One may speculate that this is due to platonic or gnostic influences throughout the history of the church, which deny the goodness of creation in favor of a bodiless existence in a realm devoid of matter. Consequently, the goal of a new creation for mankind has largely been forsaken, replaced by spiritualized themes such as "heaven" or "life in Christ."[56]

We welcome, then, Echevarria's and McCaulley's making more of the physical "not yet" of the inheritance.

---

[56] Echevarria, *The Future Inheritance of Land in the Pauline Epistles*, 1.

The inheritance received by the adopted at the consummation is, in short, the fulfillment of the promise of land given initially to Abraham and to his descendants. Canaan, in which God's people came to dwell, thus became a type of the eternal inheritance in which all God's sons shall one day dwell. Canaan's role as but a type was accentuated by the inability of the Hebrews to drive out all the inhabitants of the land. Thus, the people looked for a fuller rest and an enhanced inheritance.

The enhancement includes, first, the extension of the land promise from Canaan to the whole earth. Indeed, from old covenant times God encouraged his son Israel to look beyond Canaan to a greater inheritance to come:

> Ask of me, and I will make the nations your heritage,
> and the ends of the earth your possession. (Ps. 2:8)
> . . . the court shall sit in judgment, and his [the beast's] dominion shall be taken away, to be consumed and destroyed to the end.
> And the kingdom and the dominion and the greatness of the kingdoms under the whole heaven shall be given to the people of the saints of the Most High; their kingdom shall be an everlasting kingdom, and all dominions shall serve and obey them (Dan. 7:26-27).

Obviously, the inheritance includes people, but it also includes land. The apostle Paul clarified this in the new covenant era, describing Abraham as "heir of the world" (Rom. 4:13). Already possessing the Spirit, we yearn as the new Israel for this aggrandized territorialized inheritance.

Second, the consummated inheritance is qualitatively as well as quantitatively superior. Within their experience of the new earth, the children of God will receive their vindication and reward for their faithfulness and witness on earth. Ours will be a righteous existence, free and far from oppression and terror. No longer afflicted and storm-tossed we shall be comforted in splendor, and shall be secure (Is. 54:11-17).

Speaking poetically through Isaiah, the Lord, in 65:17-25, brings together the quantitative and qualitative excellencies of the inheritance:

> "For behold, I create new heavens and a new earth, and the former things shall not be remembered or come into mind. But be glad and rejoice forever in that which I create; for behold, I create Jerusalem to be a joy , and her people to be a gladness; no more shall be heard in it the sound of weeping and the cry of distress. No more shall there be in it an infant who lives but a few days, or an old man who does not fill out his days, for the young man shall die a hundred years old, and the sinner a hundred years old shall be accursed. They shall build houses and inhabit them; they shall plant vineyards and eat their fruit. They shall not build and another inhabit; they shall not plant and another eat; for like the days of a tree shall the days of my people be, and my chosen shall long enjoy the work of their hands. They shall not labor in vain or bear children for calamity; for they shall be the offspring of the blessed of the LORD, and their descendants with them. Before they call I will answer; while they are yet speaking I will hear. The wolf and the lamb shall graze together; the lion shall eat straw like the ox, and dust shall be the serpent's food. They shall not hurt or detroy in all my holy mountain."

We could continue into Isaiah 66, and quote other passages beside. The point is this: The consummation of the inheritance to which Paul refers in Romans 8 is predicated on old covenant prophecies.

Thus, in looking to the end of the age, Paul is comparatively brief. The adopted, now made up of Gentile as well as Jewish believers, shall inherit a new world wherein all suffering, corruption, and every taint of the fall is gone. Therein, the sons of God are fully and perfectly revealed, and are entirely free—that is to say, redeemed—in body and soul. We shall know the ministry of the Spirit fully and unceasingly. What an eschatological inheritance we have to look forward to as the household of God. Contextualized by the ever-present and all glorious triune God, the inheritance assured us could not be more tangible or delightful.

There coincides in Romans 8, then, not only the glorious climax of adoption and of the inheritance, but also the climax of salvation history. Contradicting once more Heim's denial of adoption as a soteriological model, Paul writes, "in this hope [—the hope of adoption and the redemption of our bodies—] we were saved" (v. 24). His use of the aorist indicative passive (ἐσώθημεν) reminds us that what the Father predestined in grace he will, through the accomplished salvation (aorist) procured by Christ at the cross and confirmed in his exaltation, bring about in glory.

What an encouragement to Paul's beleaguered readers in Rome, and what intimacy he established with them! To underline the wonder of the *eschaton*, he brings together several images since on that day all shall "unite . . . in [God]" (Eph. 1:10):

- *The climax of the creation's birth pangs and the adoption of God's sons.* Just as the Romans saw in adoption an analogy to new life, so the creation yearns for fresh life from the graves at the coming adoption. Indeed, Heim opines that the jarring of the images of birth and adoption serves to emphasize the latter.[57]

- *The redemption of our bodies and, thus, the consummation of our psychosomatic adoption.*

- *Our adoptive standing and the fulfillment of the Father's will that we be conformed to the image of his Son, who is the firstborn among many brothers.* Paul thus balances the privilege of adoptive sonship and our responsibility as the Father's sons to be holy, just as the Son is holy. To holy sonship we, the adopted, have been eternally predestined. Only in holiness, reflecting the Son, may we be pleasing to our Father (cf., Eph. 1:5 and Rom. 8:29).

Holding together all these convergent ideas and images is our eschatological hope. This hope Paul had preached in the east of the empire and was shortly to preach in the west, in Spain (Rom. 15:24). To this day, hope is given to all who, through faith in Christ, receive the

---

[57] Heim, "Light Through a Prism," 214.

adoption.

CONCLUSION

General observations.

The profundity of Paul's model confirms, *theologically*, its overt Trinitarianism. All three persons of the Godhead figure prominently throughout. Respective texts may emphasize more the role of one divine person than another, but the model points admirably to the coequality of the three persons. Burke notes, however, that expositions have focused more on the roles of the Father and the Son. Not so of late. Garner's volume, rich in many ways, so focuses on christology and pneumatology as to underplay the model's patrology.[58] Given the essence of adoption, the Father's placement of his sons in his household, that is some accomplishment.

Methodologically, our exposition confirms (as does Garner's otherwise) that biblical-theological (specifically salvation-historical) concerns precede the doctrinal questions which occupy the systematicians. Our fundamental task in expounding adoption is, accordingly, not how regeneration, justification, and sanctification correlate, but how the references to adoption combine to determine the shape and feel of Paul's adoption model. Only thereafter ought we to probe how a salvation-historically fashioned doctrine may be included in current soteriologies shaped by the order of salvation, and what that means for the connectedness of its neighboring soteric elements.

Spiritually, Thomas Law was exactly right to promote adoption in the nineteenth century as "a topic full of comfort to the Christian heart, and one which opens up a grand field for religious thought and inquiry." Yet, all the thought and inquiry in the world cannot negate Lyall's remark that figures of speech "aim at comprehension, not at explication." As finite creatures we quickly arrive at the limits of what

---

[58] Burke, *Adopted into God's Family*, 126.

we can explain. But before we dismiss a term like adoption as a mere metaphor, it is worth bearing in mind that without it we would be severely handicapped in speaking substantively, soothingly, and doxologically of the way we are embraced by God. To draw on the lessons of chapter four, Paul's adoption model provides the decoration, the heurism, the emotion, and the intimacy whereby we can speak of our wonderfully privileged relationship, standing, and acceptance with God.[59]

Specific observations.

We would be amiss to close out the chapter without considering a claim that would have sidetracked our sketch of adoption, namely, that Christ's adoption precedes our own. The idea is drawn from Romans 1:3-4 where Paul writes that Christ, "who was descended from David according to the flesh [κατὰ σαρκα] . . . was declared [ὁρισθέντος] to be the Son of God in power according to the Spirit [κατὰ πνεῦμα] of holiness by his resurrection from the dead, Jesus Christ our Lord."

Those supportive of the claim argue that Paul depicts the fulfillment of the promise given to David a millennium earlier:

> When your days are fulfilled and you lie down with your fathers, I will raise up your offspring after you, who shall come from your body, and I will establish his kingdom. He shall build a house for my name, and I will establish the throne of his kingdom forever: I will be to him a father, and he shall be to me a son. (2 Sam. 7:12-14a)

In the context, David had received a tremendous consolation from the LORD *in lieu* of his desire to build the temple: a son to establish the Davidic throne forever. These many centuries later, all agree that the promise of an eternal kingship is fulfilled in Jesus Christ. That, however, is about where the interpretation of Romans 1:3-4 ends. Leaving aside

---

[59] Thomas Law, "The Grace of Adoption," *Southern Presbyterian Review* (April 1879), 277; Francis Lyall, "Metaphors, Legal and Theological," *SBET* 10 (Winter 1992), 97.

the question as to whether Paul was quoting a pre-Pauline creed, we consider whether Christ's resurrection, ensuring the eternal nature of his kingship as the God-man, entailed specifically his adoption as the Son of God.

Much hangs on the declaration of Christ's divine Sonship. Scott argues that ὁρισθέντος can be translated as the *setting* or *appointment* of the Son of God and is a circumlocution for the adoption formula in 2 Samuel 7:14a: "I will be to him a father, and he shall be to me a son."[60] The text speaks within the election of Israel to adoptive sonship of the specific election of the Davidide to divine Sonship. On this understanding, God's covenant faithfulness to Israel (note the covenant formula in 2 Sam. 7:14) includes the LORD's provision of a divine Son.

Now having earlier concluded that there is a sonship tradition in the Old Testament but no specific evidence of adoption, we conclude that Scott's case for the adoption of a divine Son reads too much into 2 Samuel 12. The promise of a divine Son to sit on the throne of David does not require his adoption. Yet, this bloated reading becomes the basis on which the setting or appointment of the Son in Romans 1:3-4 is thought to mean his adoption.[61]

As Burke rightly notes and as our summary of the model has shown, Paul employs the term υἱος for Christ but reserves υἱοθεσία for the standing of God's people with their heavenly Father. We are not obliged, then, to understand either 2 Samuel 7 or Romans 1:3-4 in terms

---

[60] The adoption formula is said to be clearer there than in Psalm 2:7 ("I will tell of the decree: The LORD said to me, 'You are my Son; today I have begotten you'") and in 89:26-29:

> He shall cry to me, "You are my Father, my God and the Rock of my salvation." And I will make him the firstborn, the highest of the kings of the earth. My steadfast love I will keep for him forever, and my covenant will stand firm for him. I will establish his offspring forever and his throne as the days of the heavens.

[61] Scott, *Adoption as Sons of God*, 97–117, 223–44 (especially 241, 242).

of adoption. Paul uses ὁρισθέντος christologically, but υἱοθεσία soteriologically. The one term signals the exaltation of the incarnate Son of God to cosmic Lordship as the Savior of humankind, the other the believer's receipt of adoptive sonship. Thus, we understand the Father's declaration (aka his setting or appointment) in Christ's resurrection to constitute not his adoption as Son of God but his divine Sonship *in power or authority* (ἐν δυνάμει). Indeed, this is surely the *prima facie* understanding of the text.

Since, however, Christ is the eternal Son of God, coequal with the Father and the Spirit in power and glory, we might ask why this declaration was necessary. In his *Resurrection and Redemption* Gaffin helpfully notes two Reformed interpretations of Romans 1:3-4. The older represented by John Calvin, Charles Hodge, and B. B. Warfield understands the verses to refer, ontologically, to the humanity (κατὰ σάρκα) and divinity (κατὰ πνεῦμα) of Christ. On this understanding, the declaration, occasioned by the resurrection, was an affirmation of his divinity. The newer interpretation, while not denying the underlying ontological realities of Christ's humanity and divinity, perceives the verses to speak predominantly of two successive stages in the ministry of God's Son: his humiliation and exaltation. Agreement with it, however, does not oblige us to concur with Gaffin's deduction that Paul's participle ὁρισθέντος refers to Christ's adoption.[62]

Even supposing we go along with Gaffin's view that ὁρισθέντος includes elements of both an appointment and a declaration, there are good reasons for rejecting the view that the appointment requires adoption.

First, there is what Gaffin calls the text's "unmistakable juridical tone." This he supports by appeal to the use of ὁρισμος in the LXX

---

[62] Richard B. Gaffin Jr., *Resurrection and Redemption: A Study in Paul's Soteriology*, second edition (Phillipsburg, NJ: P&R, 1987), 100–114. In what follows, see Gaffin, *Resurrection and Redemption*, 117ff.

version of Numbers 30:3-15 (a binding oath or obligation entered into by a vow). Even supposing, though, the Father was juridically bound or obligated by a vow to exalt his Son—"I'll appoint you to be the Son of God in power by raising you from the dead if you serve unto death as the seed of David"—it does not follow *ex necessitate* that the Father was divinely obligated to adopt his own Son. To exalt him, certainly; but to adopt him?

Second, Gaffin reads Adam into Romans 1:3-4: "The resurrection of Jesus is his *adoption* (as the second Adam)." Given that Adam has made no prior appearance in verses 1 and 2 of the letter and that the historical focus is on David, the introduction of Adam *ex extra* suggests a dogmatic construing of the text through the reading into it of a figure yet to appear in the letter.

Third, Gaffin also reads the use of υἱοθεσία in Romans 8:23 back into 1:3-4. While it is true in "the family map" of Romans 8 that the resurrection of Christ is the firstfruits of the resurrection of his siblings, it does not follow that because our resurrection constitutes our adoption that, retrospectively, Christ's must have done so as well.[63] We noted in the previous section Heim's observation that while in Romans 8 the resurrection of the adopted is in view, Paul opts to call it a redemption given the affinity between redemption and adoption. Since the adoption of Christ is not in view in Romans 1:3-4, Paul writes straightforwardly of Christ's *resurrection*.

In short, then, Gaffin is essentially correct in promoting Vos' newer interpretation of the text bespeaking the humiliation/exaltation of Christ, but overdogmatizes the meaning of ὁρισθέντος in an appealing but unpersuasive manner. Nevertheless, two of Gaffin's students have followed his line of thought: Lane Tipton who formerly taught at Westminster Theological Seminary and David Garner who, at the time of writing, still does. We focus on Garner, since he has written

---

[63] For the term "family map," see Heim, "Light Through a Prism," 197.

a monograph on adoption, allowing, in my view, his otherwise admirable exposition to become hijacked by the theory, sailing confidently but perilously close to Nestorianism.[64]

Specifically, Garner's interpretation of Romans 1:3-4 errs on account of its—

- *Exegetical dubiety.* His interpretation relies on non-Pauline passages for its substantiation.

- *Theological dubiety.* First, the interpretation underplays the role of the Father in adopting his people. In so focusing on the Father's adoption of the Redeemer, on Christ's qualification for his resurrection-adoption, and on the Spirit's uniting of the sons to the Son, Garner largely ignores the Father's adoption of the redeemed. Yet, in the economy of redemption, it is he who places us in the Son and, thereby, in his household.

Second, Garner's interpretation swaps out Galatians 4:4-7 for Romans 1:3-4 as the central text of Paul's adoption model. In the former text, which is the *locus classicus* of adoption, it is explicitly Christ's death-redemption which is the basis of our adoptive sonship, not a supposed resurrection-adoption. The redemption-adoption sequence at the heart of Galatians 4:4-7 comports with both Paul's reading of the Old Testament sonship tradition (Israel's redemption *from* Egypt unto sonship) and the process of Roman adoption. Thus, when the Father places us in the Son, he does so because his natural Son paid the price of our

---

[64] Visit www.facebook.com/reformedforum/videos/270556298144566 (accessed June 1, 2021) for Lane Tipton's articulate but briefly stated affirmation of the case for Christ's resurrection-adoption. Garner in *Sons in the Son* goes to great lengths to explain and defend the position. For my fuller sympathetic-critical review of Garner's study, look up *JETS* 62/1 (March 2019), 204–9. It is also linked to https:// fromhisfullness.com/adoption, accessed June 2, 2021.

redemption. In this light, the adoption of the natural Son makes little sense, either metaphorically or theologically.

The denial of Christ's adoption ought not, however, to be read as a denial of his resurrection. The Father's raising of his Son confirms that the Christ's payment of our redemption went through, and that those he places in the household share with the natural, living Son a filial relationship to him. Both call God "Father," the Son by nature (ontologically) and the sons by grace (legally and spiritually). The adoption of Christ is, thus, an unnecessary complication and side-tracking of Paul's model.

Third, Garner's perspective underplays the adoptive state. His fascination with Christ's resurrection-adoption over-shadows the believer's life of adoptive sonship, its privileges and responsibilities.

- *Apologetical dubiety.* Garner keenly distinguishes Christ's resurrection-adoption from Adoptionism. "Asserting that Christ became Son in a new way does not," he explains, "presume or demand that he became Son for the first time or that he became divine; instead, it secures his redemptive efficacy as the Son *confirmed* in covenant righteousness." Nevertheless, we question not only the degree to which this fine distinction is preachable and can be readily understood in the pews of the church, but also Garner's associating of Christ's Sonship with his natures rather than with his person. Although he is careful to speak of the static and progressive *dimensions* of Christ's Sonship (singular), it is worth asking at what point these contrasting dimensions of Christ's Sonship devolve into different sonships.

Significantly, Thomas Aquinas long ago denied that Christ could have two Sonships (the one natural the other adopted). Sonship, he taught, adheres to his person and not to his natures, and thereby safeguarded the church's christology from a resurrection of Nestorianism. I do not doubt that Garner would wish to do the same, yet his misstep in expounding Romans 1:3-4 and his claim that his interpretation of the text is a *sine qua non* of a faithful understanding of Paul's doctrine of adoption prepares fertile soil from which Nestorianism can reemerge. That danger is mitigated, I suspect, as much by the difficulties of preaching the resurrection-adoption of Christ as by his denials of the danger of the hypothesis.

In preaching Romans 1:3-4, Christian and particularly Reformed orthodoxy would do better, it seems to me, to focus on the power of the resurrected Son than on the claim that he was adopted at his resurrection.

First, because the resurrection-adoption of Christ is not the first theological theory, powerfully and beautifully advocated at points, to lack biblical warrant. "What makes theological errors compelling is not their flagrancy," Garner ironically observes, "but their proximity to biblical truth and their captivatingly fresh redefinitions."[65] Precisely!

Second, because, in Garner's case, he is overly bold in attributing denials of Christ's resurrection-adoption in Romans 1:3-4 to the "word-concept fallacy." Doubtless, we may err in overlooking the presence of a doctrine in a text simply because the relevant term is missing. Nevertheless, Garner is too hasty in brushing off those unpersuaded by the reading of Romans 1:3-4 as Christ's resurrection-adoption. Sometimes the relevant term is missing from a biblical text simply because the idea it represents is not there either.[66]

Significantly, for all Calvin's fondness for the adoption motif, he makes no claim in commenting on Romans 1:3-4 that Christ's resurrection constituted his adoption. He views the resurrection not as a statement of Christ's adoption but as a proof of his divinity: The apostle "says that he [Christ] was declared by power, because power,

---

[65] Garner, *Sons in the Son*, 190, 195, and 201.

[66] Garner, *Sons in the Son*, 183–95, 202–16, 281–82.

peculiar to God, shone forth in him, and uncontestably proved him to be God; and this was indeed made evident by the resurrection"[67] This power Christ knew eternally as the Son of God. Now he knows it theanthropically, as the exalted God-man.

Third, because as welcome as is Garner's attempt to reinject creativity into Reformed orthodoxy, his endeavor largely fails. His teaching and use of the two dimensions of Christ's Sonship remind us of Candlish's warning: "we [must] take care that our diggings shall do no damage to any of the far more important mines which they [the Reformers and their successors] did explore—and explored so thoroughly and so well." The diggings Reformed orthodoxy needs are methodological rather than theological. To them, we now turn. [68]

~~~~

---

[67] John Calvin, *Commentaries on the Epistle of Paul the Apostle to the Romans* (*CC*, vol. XIX, 46).

[68] Robert Candlish, *The Fatherhood of God Being the First Course of the Cunningham Lectures*, fifth edition (Edinburgh: Adam and Charles Black, 1869), 195.

6

ADOPTION IN RETRIEVAL
A Renewed Theology

> Of course, it had never been doubted or
> concealed by any worthy expositor of the ways of
> God in salvation, that we are children of God by
> faith in Jesus Christ. Adoption is a Christian
> benefit. But much depends on the place in the
> mind given to a thought like this, and, especially,
> much depends on the dogmatic form it assumes,
> and the virtue allowed to it in the system.
>
> Robert Rainy, "Dr. Candlish as a Theologian,"
> William Wilson's *Memorials of Robert Smith
> Candlish.*

There is plenty more to discover of Adoption, but we have seen enough to commend it heartily to those needing to add it to Regeneration, Justification, and Sanctification on their bucket list of places to visit and revisit.

At this juncture, we merge onto Methodology Highway. It's been under construction for some time. We have caught sight of it periodically, running parallel to the route we've been on. Yet, now we make our way down the slip road to drive out into the wider county of Retrieval. Our aim is to redraw the county boundary, reassigning Adoption to the neighboring county of Essential.

That these two roads merge in Adoption is surely evidence of a governing hand. The city needs Methodology Highway for the encouragement of visitors, but Methodology Highway needs to pass through Adoption to highlight its value.

~~~~

Our journey together has aimed at more than an in-depth consideration of adoption. It *is* that, but has also sought to retrieve the doctrine from obscurity. That pursuit has built on the earlier endeavors of others. Yet, to do justice to adoption in the worship, message, and ministry of the church, "much depends," writes Scottish churchman

Robert Rainy (1826–1906), "on the dogmatic form it assumes, and the virtue allowed to it in the system."[1]

Having, thus, considered in prior chapters the scope and profundity of adoption, we come, finally, to probe—

- Why the retrieval is slow in coming.
- What is needed for adoption to take its place uncompromised in the overall theology of the Christian church.
- Our present-day opportunity to implement the methodological reforms needed to attain the full retrieval of adoption.
- The foreseeable benefits of making the necessary reforms.

1. THE ROADBLOCKS TO RETRIEVAL

Systematicians are nowadays more inclined to include adoption in their theologies, yet endeavors to do so on its own terms remain hampered. Without addressing the obstacles to inclusion, the retrieval of adoption, which has now come so far, will, proverbially, spin its wheels.

This, then, is a good time to address systemic reforms. Coincidentally, around the time this research began, Gordon Spykman remarked, "Since the middle of this century [the twentieth century] . . . it has become increasingly apparent that this scholastic model of theologizing [specifically, Louis Berkhof's] is losing its appeal." Whether Spykman is exact to trace the break back to the "fresh winds of a more original Calvinist dogmatics" found in G. C. Berkouwer's *Studies in Dogmatics*, of greater relevance is Richard Muller's defense of Hodge and Berkhoff. Neither theological stalwart, we recall, shows more than the scantiest of interest in adoption, nor are their systems set up to include the scope of Paul's model of adoption. The reforms we shall come to, arise, then, not from a succumbing to neoorthodoxy as

---

[1] William Wilson's *Memorials of Robert Smith Candlish, D.D.* (Edinburgh: Adam and Charles Black, 1880), 615.

Muller consistently suspects, but from biblically grounded moves from within the halls of Reformed orthodoxy. Why, then, their delay?[2]

First, the delay may be explained by the stubborn persistence of exegetical fallacies, chiefly those born of the admixture of the Johannine (and Petrine) model of the new birth and the Pauline model of adoption. For so long as these are accorded credibility, the necessity of reforming systematics to accommodate Paul's exclusive elongated model of adoption is deemed neither necessary nor pressing.

Second, the delay is explained by fear. The ratiocination of classic systematics, being centuries old, is considered safe. This fear forgets, though, the distinction made by defenders of Protestant scholasticism between rationalism and ratiocination. In the reform of systematic theology, we envision not, in the accessing of biblical truth, the substitution of faith with reason, but the reshaping of the arrangement of objective truth divinely revealed in Scripture. The reforms countenance, then, no diminution in our commitment to the objective truth of God's Word. Quite the contrary! By maintaining a high view of Scripture and enhancing our use of it, I envision the reforms to improve our buttress against error in our day.

Third, even where the reform is deemed necessary and overdue, it has been delayed due to uncertainty as to the specific reforms required. Within this context, expositors of adoption have preferred to settle for imprecise exegesis of the relevant texts than to set about the daunting task of overhauling the discipline of systematic theology.

Fourth, the delay is fed by suspicion. Since history helps to shape our reactions we are not surprised that, after tracing the denigration of Protestant scholasticism back to the nineteenth century (characterized, among other things, by the dubious creation of the Calvin versus the Calvinists' hypothesis), defenders of Protestant

---

[2] Gordon J. Spykman, *Reformational Theology: A New Paradigm for Doing Dogmatics* (Grand Rapids: William B. Eerdmans, 1992), 7.

scholasticism are bullish in rejecting criticisms of classic systematics. Yet, the defense of Protestant scholasticism seems to have bred among some a hyper-defensiveness that is neither wholly convincing nor entirely attractive.

The defensiveness manifests itself in a suspicion that criticisms of Protestant scholasticism are built on theological prejudice.

> When . . . the antagonism to scholastic theology is framed in terms of contrasts between rationalistic or speculative thinking and nonspeculative, biblical, dynamic, personal, and relational thinking in theology, it offers evidence of its own theological roots in neoorthodoxy and the Biblical Theology movement of the mid-twentieth century. It draws on the view, characteristic of much of that theology, that a strict distinction could be drawn between Hebraic and Greek mentalities and that the Hebraic view of truth was fundamentally one of "personal encounter" and relationship, while the Greek view of truth was fundamentally propositional, impersonal, and nonrelational. It would take an entire essay, longer than this one, to discuss the historical and linguistic fallacies involved in this and similar dichotomies.[3]

Doubtless, neoorthodoxy has set the stage for the defense of Protestant scholasticism, but the study of adoption reveals that not all concerns about it are theologically driven. Indeed, the exegetical concerns with ratiocinated systematics that a back-to-Scripture approach to adoption has raised, support the softer core defense of Protestant scholasticism by the likes of Bert Loonstra than that which is offered by Richard Muller.

Instead of allowing for reform from within the ranks of the Reformed orthodox, Muller's endeavor to undercut sweeping pejorative claims against Protestant scholasticism comes across, after a while, as a shutting down of virtually all objective evaluation. History reveals, however, that few things have done more to encourage the

---

[3] Richard A. Muller, *After Calvin: Studies in the Development of a Theological Tradition*, Oxford Studies in Historical Theology (Oxford, *et al.*: Oxford University Press, 2003), 94.

wholesale rejection of Reformed orthodoxy than the want of healthy self-criticism in Reformed orthodox ranks.

What is more, the suspicion, it seems to me, has led to a contradiction within the defense of Protestant scholasticism. On the one hand, the defense draws support from the distinction between method (ratiocination) and theology (reason), and yet it seems open to neither the necessity nor possibility of reform that is overwhelmingly methodological. It is chiefly methodological reform I propose in what follows. Such reforms do not loosen the opposition to rationalism, but they can significantly challenge criticisms of Protestant scholasticism which confuse its ratiocination with rationalism.

Fifth, the reform of systematics is hindered by the want of interdisciplinary cooperation. Writes Spykman:

> In the past, high and almost insuperable walls of separation have been erected between [biblical and systematic studies]. This has led to serious breakdowns in communication between those engaged in these two branches of learning. Often they have gone their separate ways, each group defensively staking out its field of inquiry, each laying claim to its own distinctive methodology, each holding its own exclusive conferences, each calling the academic respectibility of the other into question. Often there has been a glaring lack of cooperation between dogmatic and biblical studies. Students often sense this tension most keenly.[4]

Note van Asselt's and Dekker's *Reformation and Scholasticism*, a volume I have drawn from with much profit. Among the thirteen contributors, seven ply their trade in church history, four in systematic theology, one in philosophical theology, and one in pastoral ministry. While we would not expect Old and New Testament scholars to be authorities on the Reformation or on scholasticism, given Muller's extolling of the exegetic excellencies of the scholastics would it really be problematic to have confessional biblical studies professors involved in evaluating the exegesis and hermeneutics of the scholastics?

---

[4] Spykman, *Reformational Theology*, 8.

The defense of Protestant scholasticism has made understandable claims about the philological expertise within the prior tradition, but has not, at least so far as adoption is concerned, proven that the exegetical tradition was correct. Indeed, we have found marked contrasts between historic treatments of adoption and the biblical data. These were not unique to the scholastics, but they were formalized by them, and today are defended by the heirs of the Reformed orthodox without demonstrative proof from Scripture.

I repeat that I am not saying that Protestant or specifically Reformed scholastics taught error, but I do believe, going by what we have learned from our study of the doctrine of adoption, that the biblical texts adduced as evidence of the doctrine were not always fitting. Thus, the test case of adoption, now factored into the evaluation of Protestant scholasticism, demonstrates the need for inter-disciplinary cooperation. It also points to the need of back-to-Scripture investigations of other doctrines as well.

Sixth, we may ponder whether, underlying the reasons for delay in reform, there is a want of humility. Humility does not require us to agree with the overall criticism of Protestant scholasticism, but it does open us up to the thought that God, in his sovereignty, can test his people's fidelity by such criticism on the one hand, and bring to light needed reforms of Reformed orthodoxy on the other. As the history of adoption has shown, a challenge to Reformed orthodoxy may be very awry in general and yet contain a kernel of truth to which we would do well to take heed.

Understandably, defenders of Protestant scholasticism are in reactive mode, and have likely felt themselves to be up against the academy. Nevertheless, there can be an edge to the defense, even a snobbery dare I say it, which I have not found among those neo-orthodox often singled out for criticism by the Reformed orthodox. I refer to professors Thomas F. Torrance (1913–2007) and James B. Torrance (1923–2003). My recollections of them are fleeting and idiosyncratic, yet they are relevant, for the very yearning to retrieve adoption arose amid a felt need to answer their criticisms of Reformed orthodoxy.

T. F. Torrance was present, seated front row center, for my 1997 paper at the Edinburgh Dogmatics Conference on adoption in the Westminster Standards. Although a novice at speaking in academic settings, I came prepared, seeking courage from God to offer a well-reasoned rebuttal of his critique of the Westminster Standards. My abiding memory is of the surprise I felt during the lecture that he was ready to take in my defense of the Westminster Standards, and of his initiative afterwards in reaching out to me with genuine warmth and friendliness. He offered no self-defense, asking only if I had looked at the work of James Candlish. While I wish he had proffered other feedback to consider, I recall with affection his endearing down-to-earth demeanor. It is worth emulating amid the animosities of our day.

Likewise, I recall from Edinburgh in the 1990s a public lecture given by James Torrance, claiming that the federal theology of the Reformed orthodox is a legalistic construct. When pointing out in the Q and A the contradictory evidence of the WCF's seminal inclusion of a chapter on adoption, he offered a very gracious concession that he had not considered the matter nor factored it into his argument. At the end of the proceedings, we spoke together. Again, I recall, with much appreciation, the warmth with which he spoke of the late Professor John Murray. He referred to him not in a spirit of hostility but as one who was akin to an old friend.

While I still beg to differ from such scholars, I am drawn to the memory of their generosity of spirit and of their greater passion for the gospel and for mission than for winning academic arguments. This is something from which we, who see ourselves as Reformed orthodox, can learn. Maybe a chastened defense of Protestant scholasticism will help us get there. Let us then glean the input of biblical scholars faithful to Scripture and factor in lessons from the history and doctrine of adoption. In regard to the latter, it is worth remembering that for all Richard Muller's scholarly clout he represents a continental Reformed tradition that has done little to include adoption in its theology.

I advocate, then, a chastened defense of Protestant scholasticism, envisioning a reduction of inter-disciplinary suspicions. Dogmaticians need not regard biblical theologians as but eclectic thinkers preoccupied with bits and pieces of biblical data. Conversely, as respect for biblical theology rises, we may anticipate a reduction among biblical theologians of the disdain for the systematizing of biblical truth. The more the systematizing does justice to the humanness as well as the divineness of Scripture, the greater the common ground. A back-to-Scripture approach to the retrieval of adoption demonstrates just how possible is this inter-disciplinary cooperation. It offers a wonderful opportunity for biblical and dogmatic theologians to come together as a new generation of mutually supportive system builders. After all, the bits and pieces of biblical studies, when assembled, constitute the building blocks from which systems of theology are built and renewed. The system I envision encapsulates both the teaching and feel of Scripture.

2. THE ROUTE TO RETRIEVAL

The renewal of systematics feeds off their tremendous classical strengths:

- Belief in the divineness of Scripture and its emphasis on the one God, one Bible, and one gospel.
- Commitment to objective, immutable, unified truth.
- Freedom from the traditionalism of church authority.
- And belief that truth can be accessed by faith.

These strengths we greatly treasure, seeking to preserve them. Nevertheless, there are other reforms that can and ought to be made.

One such reform is covered by John Frame's advocacy of the *communicatio salutis*. He argues in effect that systematicians should no longer be selective in including biblical genres in their systems of theology. God reveals his saving grace not only through history, doctrine, and application, but through song, prophecy, love, poetry, court drama, confession, genealogy, lament, riddle, wisdom, prophesy, parable, epistle, and the apocalyptic. The inclusion of these not-to-be-forgotten elements of biblical revelation comports with the principle that "all Scripture is . . . profitable" (2 Tim. 3:16). Thus, all ought to be included in systems of theology, at least in representative fashion. Accordingly, the sources from which we assemble our systems of theology are to match the scope of God's definitive and infallible revelation.[5]

In the following, we assume the essential correctness of the *communicatio salutis*, pondering its ramifications for the reform of classic systematics, but focus on those reforms arising specifically from the history and exposition of adoption. There are six of them.

First reform: The biblical contextualization of doctrine.

Since the connection between biblical theology and the doctrine of adoption stretches all the way back to the apostle Paul, and is replicated in Irenaeus, the father of biblical theology, in a number of other fathers, and in Protestant reformers such as Calvin, it follows that doctrinal treatments of adoption must reflect the salvation-historical scope of the model. The alterations to systematic method that would allow for this engage us in the perennial debate about the correlation of biblical and systematic theology.

This debate is not new nor resolved. A narration of several of its historical phases indicates that the issue of the salvation-historical contextualization of biblical doctrine is not going away.

The earliest phase we consider takes us back to the seventeenth century and to Reformed orthodox theologian Johannes Cocceius (1603–69), and his significant volume *The Doctrine of the Covenant and*

---

[5] *DG*, 7–8, 197.

Testament of God (*Summa doctrinae de foedere et testament dei*, 1648). Cocceius preferred the terms of Scripture to the terms of theology, insisting that the latter be attested by the former. He, thus, explained the scholastic terms he deemed adequate for biblical exposition, merely tolerating those he felt less than ideal but obliged to retain. Scholastic terminology, Cocceius feared, "created an artificial language over-growing and obscuring the language of Scripture." As his 1656 letter to his cousin, Martin Hundius states:

> You are right in writing that today the words of St. Paul are rather enigmatic to us, because we are so used to scholastic terminology and have such a delight in it that we turn up our nose at investigating the meaning of words used by the Holy Spirit in Scripture, that is the reason why we no longer understand so well those who use them.[6]

Cocceius' reform of scholasticism needed improvement. Packer mentions "some inadequacies and errors that poor exegesis in the Cocceian camp had fathered."[7] Nevertheless, it is significant, given the

---

[6] Willem J. van Asselt, "Cocceius Anti-Scholasticus?" in *Reformation and Scholasticism: An Ecumenical Enterprise*, Willem J. van Asselt and Eef Dekker, eds. (Grand Rapids: Baker Academic, 2001), 235–36. Cocceius' observation mirrors my confusion on first learning covenant theology. "Why," I thought in effect, "are we pursuing an external construct of covenant theology [covenant of redemption, of works, and of grace] when the Bible utilizes the language of old covenant/new covenant?" Three decades later I have not heard a satisfactory answer to this question, and marvel at how easily we live with this tension. I do not doubt Muller's claim that the external construct arose from exegetical considerations ("The Problem of Protestant Scholasticism—A Review and Definition," in *Reformation and Scholasticism*, 61, 63), but it does not follow that these justify the imposition of a separate structure on one already pre-existent in Scripture. We go awry, Cocceius rightly warns, where we prefer extra-biblical constructs over those which are biblical, and oppose attempts to reformulate covenant theology along the lines of the old covenant/new covenant framework found in Scripture.

[7] J. I. Packer, Introduction to Herman Witsius, *The Economy of the Covenants Between God and Man: Comprehending a Complete Body of Divinity*, vol. 1, reprint ed. (Kingsburg, CA: den Dulk Christian Foundation, 1990).

distinction in scholasticism between method and content, that Cocceius felt he could, at one and the same time, uphold Reformed orthodoxy and renew its method and feel. Given this, it is altogether too simplistic to assume that the questioning of the scholastic method and tone arises necessarily from later post–Kantian theological predilections, liberal theology, or neoorthodoxy. Cocceius' wrestlings demonstrate that the questioning long preceded such modern developments.

Cocceius was opposed by Gisbertus Voetius (1589–1676). He believed Cocceius to have overemphasized the historical in Scripture, fearing that the new approach—beginning not with the doctrines of the Reformed church but with the Bible—would undermine Reformed dogmatics and practical Christianity. Yet, van Asselt notes traces of scholasticism in Cocceius' writings, especially in his doctrine of God (in his main systematic work, *Summa theologiae ex Scripturis repetita* [1662]). It is "an easy matter to compose a fine anthology from Cocceius' works which reflects his use and mastery of the scholastic method and its tools, such as linguistic, philosophical, and logical analysis." The *quaestio* technique, van Asselt continues, is present in both his systematic (*Aphorismi per universam theologiam* and *Disputationes selectee*) and exegetical works. His critique of Scholasticism pertained notably to the Medieval schoolmen's formulating and solving of "stupid questions" and its heretical content. The stubborn fact remains, however, that Cocceius believed a new approach to the systematizing of biblical truth was needed and that we ought to be troubled when the Reformed orthodox look down on the wording of Scripture.[8]

Despite the efforts of Herman Witsius' (1636–1708) to mediate between the Voetians and Cocceians in his *The Economy of the Covenants between God and Man* (*De oeconomia foderum Dei cum hominibus*, 1677), the relationship between what is now known as

---

[8] van Asselt, "Cocceius Anti-Scholasticus?" in *Reformation and Scholasticism*, 233.

biblical and systematic theology arose again two centuries later.[9]

Dutch-American scholar Geerhardus Vos (1862–1949) would have known of Cocceius, Voetius, and Witsius, but was likely influenced in his immediate context by the endeavors of compatriots Abraham Kuyper and Herman Bavinck to insert greater exegetical considerations into the systematization of biblical truth.[10]

In 1893, Vos was installed in Princeton Theological Seminary's newly inaugurated chair of Biblical Theology, an appointment that afforded him the opportunity to further his salvation-historical exegesis. The Bible, he taught, is more of an historical book of dramatic interest than a dogmatic handbook. In it, the dynamically unfolding content of God's covenant is fundamental. Thus, Vos recognized "the substance of the 'critical' charge," that Reformed orthodoxy had accorded inadequate attention to the historical character of the Bible. He believed, accordingly, that "by giving greater, more adequate attention to the salvation-historical structure and content of biblical revelation, or, in other terms, by attending to the rootage of that revelation in the dynamically unfolding history of God's covenant" he could counter-balance the ratiocination of systematic theology.[11]

---

[9] Packer, Introduction to Herman Witsius, *The Economy of the Covenants Between God and Man*, Muller, "The Problem of Protestant Scholasticism—A Review and Definition," in *Reformation and Scholasticism*, 54. Curiously, Joel R. Beeke's and Randall J. Pederson's *Meet the Puritans: With a Guide to Modern Reprints* (Grand Rapids: Reformation Heritage Books, 2006) includes Voetius and Witsius but not Cocceius, leaving us to ponder whether the omission indicates an ambivalence toward Cocceius' attempt at biblical-theological reform.

[10] For an expansion of the historical trajectory which follows, see Tim J. R. Trumper, "John Frame's Methodology: A Case Study in Constructive Calvinism," in *Speaking the Truth in Love: The Theology of John M. Frame*, edited by John J. Hughes (Phillipsburg, NJ: P&R, 2009), 145–72.

[11] Richard B. Gaffin Jr., "The Vitality of Reformed Dogmatics" in *The Vitality of Reformed*

Vos' work receives greater attention today than during his lifetime. With hindsight, we see clearly that he set in motion a twentieth-century trajectory bent on attesting systematic method by the Word of God. Of particular interest is his influence on a young John Murray. Murray studied at Princeton in 1924–27 and became an instructor there in 1929–30. Writes Iain H. Murray:

> It was the Seminary, and perhaps the instruction of Geerhardus Vos in particular, which instilled in [Murray] the conviction that doctrine must be arrived at through a painstaking examination of the Scriptures in their original languages. While the Puritans themselves held that view, the greater exegetical precision of the more modern commentators was scarcely known to them. At Princeton, then, Murray's commitment to the Reformed Faith was not changed, but it became, in a new way, rooted in the Bible itself.[12]

Thus, Murray began to inject salvation-historical considerations into his teaching of systematic theology, especially after his transfer to the fledgling Westminister Seminary in 1930. "Vos and Murray" came, says Richard Gaffin, to "agreement in their conception of biblical theology and its relationship to systematic theology" such that "this aspect of their thinking constitutes a direction."[13]

Loyal to Reformed orthodoxy, Murray sought to conserve the prior tradition and the core values of predictability and regularity. His Calvinism was, to quote Darryl Hart, as "unoriginal" as Charles Hodge's.

Theology: Proceedings of the International Theological Congress, June 20–24th 1994, Noordwijkerhout, The Netherlands, Eds. J. M. Bateau, J. W. Maris, and K. Veling (Kampen: Uitgeverij Kok, 1994), 23; Geerhardus Vos, *Reformed Dogmatics*, five volumes, first published 1896 (handwritten) and originally printed in 1910, transl. and ed. by Richard B. Gaffin Jr. (et al.), (Bellingham, WA: Lexham Press, 2012–16).

[12] *CW*, 3:29. Cf., *CW*, 3:375 for firsthand evidence of Murray's appreciation of Vos.

[13] Richard B. Gaffin Jr., "Systematic Theology and Biblical Theology" in *The New Testament Student and Theology*, vol. 3 ed. John H. Skilton (Phillipsburg, NJ: P&R, 1976), 42–43.

Even Murray's druthers about the covenant of works and his attention to adoption had Reformed (specifically Calvinistic) precedence.[14]

Hodge, though, was, for Murray, "never the starting point upon any subject." His interest in adoption illustrates this. Rather, Murray developed a methodological hybrid. Utilizing scholasticism's distinction between method and substance, and fascinated, like Hodge, in biblical facts and their internal relations, he nevertheless made little of systematic theology as a science. Murray preferred to ground his systematics in exegesis and in the salvation-historical contextualization of doctrine. His aim was not to dismantle the discipline of systematic theology but to correct its imbalances. After all, classic systematics had been strong on the divineness of Scripture, but weak on its humanness; strong on the unity of the Bible's system of truth, but weak in reflecting its authorial diversity; solid in the Bible's propositional content, but inattentive to its salvation-historical context; reliable in its orthodoxy, but questionable in some of its methods; and compelling in its doctrine, but alien to Scripture in its tone and feel.

Although Murray's work preceded the recognition of all these imbalances, he nevertheless shifted over time from an uncritical to a more sympathetic-critical appreciation of Reformed orthodoxy.[15] He was influenced not only by Vos but by the renaissance in Calvin studies. This renaissance began flourishing in Murray's native Scotland from the

---

[14] D. G. Hart, "Systematic Theology at Old Princeton Seminary: Unoriginal Calvinism," in *The Pattern of Sound Doctrine: Systematic Theology at the Westminster Seminaries*, ed. David VanDrunen (Phillipsburg, NJ: P&R, 2004), 5.

[15] *CW* 3:93. Hart, "Systematic Theology at Old Princeton Seminary: Unoriginal Calvinism," 7–9, 22. Cf., Murray's discussion of the discipline in "Systematic Theology," *CW*, 4:1–21; and his review of Ridderbos' work *When the Time had Fully Come: Studies in New Testament Theology* (Jordan Station, ON, Canada: Paideia Press, 1982), (*CW*, 4:355–57). The phrase "sympathetic criticism" comes from Klaas Schilder (Gaffin, "The Vitality of Reformed Systematic Theology," *The Faith Once Delivered: Essays in Honor of Dr. Wayne R. Spear*, ed. Anthony T. Selvaggio (Phillipsburg: NJ: P&R, 2007), 29–32).

mid-twentieth century and was shaped by fresh translations of Calvin produced by the Torrance brothers, Ronald Wallace, and others. Observes Iain Murray:

> Every careful reader of Calvin, especially of his *Institutes*, detects what may be called his biblico-theological method in contra-distinction from the more scholastic method of his predecessors in the medieval tradition and of many of his successors in the Protestant tradition. This does not mean that Calvin is not systematic. He was a humanist before he was a reformer. And logic in argumentation and in the sequence and arrangement of his topics is manifest on every page.[16]

Murray thus developed a hybrid methodology that began to challenge the dominance of the scientific or ratiocinated systematics of earlier centuries, and encouraged a modest or careful creative orthodoxy among the Reformed orthodox of his day. This fresh approach was not unique to him. Consider Cornelius Van Til's ordination charge to Norman Shepherd:

> You must not be a slave to tradition. You must not merely carry on what you yourself have learned from teachers. You must by all means cultivate originality. You must be yourself as you teach biblical and systematic theology. Only if you cultivate your independence of judgment will you make a genuine contribution to theology. But such originality cannot be attained otherwise than by ever going back of all the theology you have learned to the Christ who ever speaks to you in his Word.[17]

Irrespective of whether Shepherd subsequently crossed over into a critical-sympathetic appropriation of the Reformed tradition—history

---

[16] *CW*, 1:308. For evidence of Murray's interest in Calvin see his *CW*, 1:305–11; 3:337–39; 4:158–204 (reproduced in *Calvin on Scripture and Divine Sovereignty*. First published 1960 (Welwyn, Hertfordshire: Evangelical Press), 1979), 302–4.

[17] My thanks to Rev. Norman Shepherd for sharing his copy of Van Til's charge. Incidentally, John Murray preached the sermon at the installation service. On Shepherd's loss to Westminster Theological Seminary, see Ian Hewitson's account, *Trust and Obey: Norman Shepherd and the Justification Controversy at Westminster Theological Seminary* (Minneapolis, MN: NextStep Resources, 2011).

and heaven, I anticipate, will be more generous and discerning judges—the advance toward a new method of systematization continued despite Shepherd's premature departure from Westminister.

Sinclair Ferguson replaced Shepherd, yet, despite his contribution to the retrieval of adoption, it is to Richard Gaffin that we turn, to learn how the discussion of method unfolded. Not only was Gaffin an erstwhile student of Murray, he reflects Murray's hybrid methodology in his transition at Westminster from the New Testament to the systematic theology department, and there continued the injection into systematics of salvation-historical considerations. Besides his teaching, he took to editing the writings of Vos and Herman Ridderbos, and, walking cautiously the fine line between traditionalism and iconoclasm, has also written *Resurrection and Redemption: A Study in Paul's Soteriology* (1987), which he dedicated to Vos and to Murray, and *By Faith, Not by Sight: Paul and the Order of Salvation* (2006). Specifically, Gaffin emphasized the centrality of Christ as pivotal to the connectedness of salvation accomplished and applied.[18]

Gaffin's salvation-historical revamping of systematics has left their *loci communes* (commonplaces) untouched: revelation, God, man, salvation, ethics, the church, the last things—

> A redemptive–historical approach [does not] necessitate[ ] abandoning the so-called loci method of traditional *dogmatics*. After

---

[18] Re Gaffin's editing, see, for example, Herman N. Ridderbos, *Redemptive History and the New Testament Scriptures* (formerly *The Authority of the New Testament Scriptures*), Biblical and Theological Studies, transl. H. De Jongste and revised by Richard B. Gaffin Jr.; first published 1963; second revised ed. (Phillipsburg, NJ: P&R), 1988; Gaffin's foreword to Vos' *The Pauline eschatology* (Grand Rapids: Baker), 1979; *Redemptive history and biblical interpretation: the shorter writings of Geerhardus Vos*, ed. Richard B. Gaffin, Jr. (Phillipsburg, NJ: P&R), 1980; and, more recently, Gaffin's translation and editing of Vos' *Reformed Dogmatics* (*op. cit.*). Re his writing, see also other pieces such as "Redemption and Resurrection: An Exercise in Biblical-Systematic Theology" in *A Confessing Theology for Postmodern Times*, ed. Michael S. Horton (Wheaton, IL: Crossway, 2000), 229–49.

all, strictly speaking, that method simply calls for a topical
presentation of doctrine, and it is difficult to see why the biblical
materials preclude such an approach.[19]

They don't! Essential to the progress of divinely inscripturated
revelation is an organic unity running through the Old and New
Testaments. Each *locus*, then, may be unpacked in a *heilsgeschichtliche*
manner, by tracing the progressive unfolding of each in turn.

This idea is not new. The salvation-historical contextualization
of each *locus* and its component parts is already seen in treatments of
the Trinity (its Old Testament hints and New Testament fulfillment),
and of the person and work of Christ (Old Testament prophecies and
prefigurements of him). Yet, more could be done to extend this
approach, say to the doctrine of salvation. This would go some way to
challenge the charge, to quote Ferguson, that the *ordo salutis* "distorts
the basic NT (Pauline) emphasis on *historia salutis*, substituting for it a
less than biblical emphasis on personal experience."[20]

We could go on. Suffice it to say, that the appeal for the injection
of greater salvation-historical concerns into the systematizing of
biblical truth is neither new nor wayward. It furthers a concern that has
appeared and reappeared in church history. The exposition of adoption
demonstrates why this has been the case, the retrieval of adoption now
calling systematicians to operate out of a systemizing of biblical truth
allowing for a full, uncompromised space for the doctrine.

Second reform: The recognition of authorial diversity.

When the WCF extols the Scriptures for the "consent of all [its]
parts" speaking in unison of the "full discovery . . . of the only way of

---

[19] Gaffin, "The Vitality of Reformed Dogmatics," in *The Vitality of Reformed Theology*,
28–29.

[20] Ridderbos, *Redemptive-history and the New Testament Scriptures*, 49; *NDT*. 1988. S.v.
"Ordo salutis," by Sinclair Ferguson. Cf., George S. Hendry, *The Westminster Confession
for Today: A Contemporary Interpretation*. (Richmond, VA: SCM Press, 1960), 16.

man's salvation" (1:5), we must be mindful that the consent runs not only through the Scriptures (along the trajectory of salvation history) but across them. Such a consent is miraculous, for the Bible was written across 1,600 years, by forty-plus authors, from different times and places. Evidently, most did not know each other and could not have colluded. The consent, however, is not a bland or gray uniformity. It is a unity *of the parts*: two Testaments, sixty-six books, tens of authors, varying genre, distinctive content, different figures of speech, unique writing styles, and intent. The Scriptures thus possess a diversity in unity.

Classic systematics, understandably stressing the divineness of Scripture, major on Scripture's unity, yet they underplay its humanness and resultant diversity. Hence Murray's caution:

> The various passages drawn from the whole compass of Scripture and woven into the texture of systematic theology are not [to be] cited as mere proof texts or wrested from the scriptural and historical context to which they belong, but [are to be] understood in a way appropriate to the place they occupy in this unfolding process, [and are to be] applied with that particular relevance to the topic under consideration.[21]

Gaffin agrees, noting "the tendency" of the Protestant dogmaticians "to treat Scripture as in the interests of the system, as a collection of more or less isolated proof texts (*dicta probantia*), without adequate attention to context," and "as a manual of 'timeless' first principles of static truths."[22] Thus, they not only minimized the salvation-historical

---

[21] Murray, *CW*, 4:21; Similarly, Wilfrid J. Harrington writes, "it is manifest that the New Testament writings must be taken according to their natural groupings, or be studied individually where it is necessary to do so" (*The Path of Biblical Theology* [Dublin: Gill and Macmillan, 1973]), 211; cf., Ridderbos, *Redemptive-history and the New Testament Scriptures*, 71.

[22] Gaffin, "The Vitality of Reformed Dogmatics," in *The Vitality of Reformed Theology*, 23. Regrettably, Gaffin omits this criticism from a later version of this article, but it is

context of doctrine, they ran together the variant voices across the New Testament. The problem lay not with their aim—the systematization of biblical truth—but with the route they took. It too often coerced the specificities of biblical exegesis and ignored complementary perspectives of the different authors of the New Testament.

A back-to-Scripture exposition of adoption highlights the need for clearer recognition of the authorial diversity of Scripture in systems of theology. The recognition is made easier on account of Paul's exclusive references to adoption. These should have been sufficient to distinguish adoption in the minds of systematicians from the soteric models of other New Testament authors. After all, states Gaffin, "Reformed theology has always thought itself to be distinctively Pauline, more sensitive than other traditions to the deeper motives and trends of the apostle's teaching and more consistent in its expression of them."[23] Yet, the history of adoption, with its conflation of Pauline and Johannine (and Petrine) thought, qualifies this assessment. It indicates that there has not been enough sensitivity and consistency in expounding either Paul's thought or that of the other apostles.

Systematicians can glean much, then, from the sensitivities of biblical scholars. Note the following samples which recognize the authorial diversity of the New Testament and, thereby, the organic coherence of Scripture.

The first is rather generic and is found in Adolf Schlatter's outline of the development of New Testament theology in *The Theology of the Apostles*. His second, third, and fourth chapters are most relevant:

---

one by which he ought to stand (cf., Richard B. Gaffin Jr., "The Vitality of Reformed Systematic Theology," in *The Faith Once Delivered*, 7.

[23] Richard B. Gaffin Jr., *Resurrection and Redemption: A Study in Paul's Soteriology*, first published 1978 (Phillipsburg, NJ: P&R, 1987), 11.

Chapter II. The Convictions Upheld by Jesus' Followers
A.   The Aim Set for the Church by Peter
B.   The Establishment of Recollections about Jesus by Matthew
C.   The Purification of Jewish Devotion by James
D.   The Refutation of Gnosticism by Jude
E.   Jesus' Message to the Greeks According to John

Chapter III. The Calling of the Nations through Paul
A.   Paul's Task
B.   Christ's Gift
C.   God's Presence in Christ
D.   The Church
E.   Conditions Affecting Pauline Teaching

Chapter IV. The Share of Apostolic Associates in Doctrinal Formation
A.   The Simplification of the Gospel by Mark
B.   The Enrichment of Recollections of Jesus through the Witnesses Consulted by Luke
C.   The Incorporation of Careful Regard for History into the Church's Body of Conviction through Luke
D.   Resistance to a Return to Judaism through the Epistle to the Hebrews
E.   The Renewed Determination of the Church's Goal in the Name of Peter[24]

More specifically, we have noted Willi Twisselmann's and Witold Marchel's identification of the New Testament's various authorial depictions of the Father, the filial, and the familial:

Die Gotteskindschaft der Christen nach dem Neuen Testament (Gütersloh: Verlag C. Bertelsmann, 1939) Willi Twisselmann	*Abba, Vater! Die Vaterbotschaft des Neuen Testaments* (Düsseldorf: Patmos-Verlag, 1963) Witold Marchel
I. Divine Sonship in the Non-Christian Religions	1. Part One: Faith in God the Father before Christ

---

[24] Adolf Schlatter, *The Theology of the Apostles: The Development of New Testament Theology*, originally published as *Die Theologie der Apostel* (Stuttgart: Calwer Vereinbuchhandlung, 1922, transl. Andreas J. Köstenberger (Grand Rapids: Baker Books, 1999), 51–359.

Twisselmann and Marchel understood the importance of viewing individual texts in their specific authorial, bibliographical, and pericopal contexts. This is crucial for safeguarding the distinctive structures of the New Testament models. Only having done so are we able to probe ways of systematizing the models without compromising them.

Nineteenth-century Scottish scholar, George Smeaton, understood this. We can only "attain a full view of the New Testament doctrine ... except in a biblical-historical way; and have abstained from the artificial construction to which systematic theology has recourse, as well as from merely subjective combinations."[26] Smeaton referred in the "biblical-historical way" not only to the salvation-historical contextualization of doctrine but to the recognition of the authorial diversity of the New Testament, applying such reforms to the atonement in particular. From his set of volumes on Christ's and the apostles' doctrine of the atonement, note the main contents of volume two:

Chapter I: The Apostles' Doctrine of the Atonement

Chapter II: The Testimony to the Atonement in the Pauline Epistles

Chapter III: The Testimony to the Atonement Contained in the Epistle to the Hebrew

Chapter IV: The Testimony of the Apostle Peter

Chapter V: The Testimony of the Apostle John

---

[26] See George Smeaton, *Christ's Doctrine of the Atonement*, but especifically *The Apostles' Doctrine of the Atonement* (both republished from the 1870 editions [Edinburgh and Carlisle, PA: The Banner of Truth Trust, 1991]), v.

Leon Morris has taken a similar approach in *The Cross in the New Testament*:

1. The Cross in Matthew and Mark
2. The Cross in the Lukan Writings: The Gospel
3. The Cross in the Lukan Writings: The Acts
4. The Cross in the Gospel According to St. John
5. The Cross in the Pauline Epistles: The Plight of Man
6. The Cross in the Pauline Epistles: The Salvation of God
7. The Cross in the Pauline Epistles: Man's Response
8. The Cross in the Epistle to the Hebrews
9. The Cross in the Catholic Epistles and Revelation[27]

Likewise, we find evidence of the same approach in George B. Stevens' early twentieth-century volume *The Christian Doctrine of Salvation.* Part I: The Biblical Basis of the Doctrine runs as follows:

Chapter I: The Sacrificial System

Chapter II: The Prophetic Doctrine of Salvation

Chapter III: The Teaching of Jesus According to the Synoptic Gospels

Chapter IV: The Pauline Doctrine

Chapter V: The Doctrine of the Epistle to the Hebrews

Chapter VI: The Johannine Doctrine

Chapter VII: Summary and Conclusions[28]

This allowance for the Scripture's diversity in unity needs to spread further across the gamut of biblical doctrines. In fairness, there is some of this in Louis Berkhof's *Systematic Theology.* We do not expect full-blown analyses of the neighboring perspectives of New Testament authors on each key doctrine, but the discipline could yet benefit from much more sensitivity to the authorial diversity of the New Testament. As things stand, the widespread and unguarded running together of differing authorial perspectives helps explain some of the prevalent

---

[27] Leon Morris, *The Cross in the New Testament*, Mount Radford Reprints, No. 19, originally published by Wm. B. Eerdmans, 1965 (Exeter: Paternoster Press, 1976).

[28] George Barker Stevens, *The Christian Doctrine of Salvation*, International Theological Library, first published 1905, reprint ed. (Edinburgh: T & T Clark, 1930), 1–135.

cynicism about systematic theology.

Third reform: The limitation of the use of the ordo salutis.

Having considered the internal reform of the *loci* of theology we now zoom in on the particular *locus* of salvation. Attempts to arrange soteriology go back at least as far as the Reformation. Only, however, in the early eighteenth century—that is to say, after the development of seventeenth-century Reformed orthodoxy—did the term *ordo salutis* come into usage, at which point, says Richard Muller, the doctrinal model became a standardized way of highlighting the causality of grace in our receipt of salvation. The idea was built on Paul's words in Romans 8:29-30. It became known as a "golden chain" of grades, gradation, or degrees of belonging to the work of salvation:

> For those whom he foreknew he also predestined to be conformed to the image of his Son, in order that he might be the firstborn among many brothers. And those whom he predestined he also called, and those whom he called he also justified, and those whom he justified he also glorified.

Writes Geerhardus Vos, *ordo salutis* is "The series of acts and steps in which the salvation obtained by Christ is subjectively appropriated by the elect." When talking of *ordo salutis* we have in view, then, not the accomplishment of salvation but its application (what we may refer to alternatively as the *applicatio salutis*).[29]

Nowadays, the *ordo salutis* has fallen somewhat out of favor. There are several reasons for this.

First, scholars like Berkouwer question whether Paul intended us to see in Romans 8:30 an (or the) *ordo salutis*. After all, the list of soteric elements is partial. For whatever reason, Paul omits regeneration, union with Christ, faith, repentance, adoption, sanctifi-

---

[29] On the history of the *ordo salutis*, see Richard A. Muller, *Calvin and the Reformed Tradition: On the Work of Christ and the Order of Salvation* (Grand Rapids: Baker Academic, 2012). Vos, *Reformed Dogmatics*, 4:1.

cation, assurance, and preservation (or perseverance). In particular, the omission of union with Christ (the reality of being "in Christ"), which was so dear to Paul, suggests the apostle intended something other than a full and orderly itemization of the elements of salvation.

Second, Vos notes that the *ordo salutis* is complicated by differing definitions of some of its elements. He mentions variously understood interpretations of the relationship of calling to regeneration and of regeneration to conversion, as also of the meaning of repentance (whether understood as immediate or as lifelong).[30]

Third, the elements of the *ordo salutis* differ in kind. There are those directed to the will of man. These have in view his moral suasion but fall short of transforming him inwardly, such as is the case with the general or external element of calling. However, it is effectual or inner calling which is more germane to the *ordo salutis*. Then there are divine acts that affect a change of status in our relationship to God (reconciliation, justification, and adoption). There are also the elements of regeneration and glorification which bring about a real and inherent change in God's people.[31]

Fourth, John Frame, a near peer of Gaffin's, and another notable student of John Murray, in following Murray's rejection of "stagnant traditionalism" and in "caution[ing] us not to remain content with even the best formulations of past theologians,"[32] points, like Vos did prior to Murray, to the construct's causal inconsistencies:

> The *Ordo Salutis* has always seemed to me to be a confused idea, because the various items are not related to one another in the same

---

[30] Vos, *Reformed Dogmatics*, 4:2–4.

[31] Vos, *Reformed Dogmatics*, 4:4–11.

[32] Frame states: "I turn to him [Murray] more than to any other writer" (John M. Frame, *Salvation Belongs to the Lord: An Introduction to Systematic Theology* [Phillipsburg, NJ: P&R, 2006], 352). John M. Frame, "Background to My Thoughts," in *Speaking the Truth in Love*, 18; "In Defense of Something Close to Biblicism," *Westminster Theological Journal* 59 (1997), 276.

sense of "order." Regeneration is the efficient cause of faith, but faith is not the efficient cause of justification. It is the "instrumental cause," as we say; but justification is neither the efficient nor the instrumental cause of adoption. So on we go . . . such inadequacies of the traditional scholastic approaches were another factor in leading me to seek another way of teaching systematics, which, for better or for worse, is the method of the Theology of Lordship.[33]

Frame, though, does not advocate abandoning the *ordo salutis*. While "confused" in some senses, he believes the construct can continue to teach us about different aspects of soteriology. After all, it gathers together a significant amount of biblical data, and communicates some important elements of sequential prioritization which we need to know. From Romans 8:30 we learn that predestination precedes calling, calling justification, and justification glorification. Elsewhere, the New Testament also teaches us that between calling and justification regeneration precedes faith and repentance.

We ought to retain, then, the *ordo salutis* construct. Nevertheless, the biblical data calls into question its exclusive use in arranging the application of salvation. The data suggests the warrant for supplementing the use of the *ordo salutis* with other constructs. This should not surprise us. After all, we seek to grasp with finite minds what the author of Hebrews was inspired to call "a great salvation" (2:3).

In ways we shall explain, this scaling back suits the retrieval of adoption, since classic uses of the *ordo salutis* have not always included adoption, and when they have, they typically crop the salvation-historical scope of Paul's model (by eliding the significance of Romans 9:4 and Galatians 3:23–4:7—the comparison of the minority sonship of Israel and the majority sonship of God's sons and daughters today) and blur its uniqueness.

---

33 Personal email, May 2, 2003, used with kind permission.

Fourth reform: The christocentrifying of soteriology.

Continuing the discussion of the *ordo salutis*, we have cause to consider in greater detail our union with Christ, specifically the two challenges it presents to the *ordo salutis*. While I do not argue that emphases on the *unio* and the *ordo* are mutually exclusive, as if we must choose between them, if our use of the *ordo salutis* is to continue we must consider how the *unio* and *ordo* may be better correlated in explicating soteriology.

The first challenge pertains to the location of union with Christ within the construct. The WCF gives the impression that the doctrine of salvation consists solely of a chain of events. In that chain, union with Christ is treated rather subliminally, for the theme is allotted no chapter from which we could identify its location. There is, however, an explicit reference to union with Christ, but it does not appear until 26:1 in the chapter, "Of the Communion of Saints": "All saints, that are so united to Jesus Christ their Head, by his Spirit, and by faith, have fellowship with him in his graces, sufferings, death, resurrection, and glory."

Two centuries ago the Welsh Calvinistic Methodist Confession (1823) sought to amend the WCF, positing a valuable article on union with Christ between those on effectual calling (Art. 22) and justification (Art. 24). Article 23, "Of Union with Christ" reads:

> Those who are effectually called are brought into a mystical union with Christ. Though they were elected in Christ from eternity, and represented by him in the eternal covenant, nevertheless they are by nature the children of wrath, even as others, enemies of God, and far from Christ, until the Holy Ghost is sent to convince them of sin, show them their state of misery, reveal Christ to them, draw them to him, and create them in him; then will they be members of his mystical body, and will be in him as the branches are in the vine; then Christ and his salvation become theirs; the Holy Ghost dwells in them; and they receive every grace from the fulness of Christ. This union is intimate and loving; quickening and fruitful; strong and eternal: because the Head lives, the members shall live also. They are no more in the first Adam, as their covenant-head, nor under that covenant or

328

> its curse; but they are in Christ, the head of the covenant of grace, and
> have a right to all the blessings of the covenant.

Evidently, the awareness of the need to heighten the profile of union with Christ in the WCF and to identify its true location in the order or application of salvation is not new.[34]

Within the last century, Murray began remedying theologically the WCF's treatment of union with Christ. "Nothing," he writes, "is more central and basic than union and communion with Christ." He then explains that the breadth of the theme proves problematic to the treatment of it within the application of salvation. Union with Christ, he says,

> is not simply a step in the application of redemption; when viewed, according to the teaching of Scripture, in its broader aspects it underlies every step of the application of redemption. Union with Christ is really the central truth of the whole doctrine of salvation not only in its application but also in its once-for-all accomplishment in the finished work of Christ. Indeed, the whole process of salvation has its origin in one phase of union with Christ and salvation has in view the realization of other phases of union with Christ.[35]

Appreciating the difficulty, there is nevertheless a disappointment with Murray's treatment of union with Christ.

First, by expounding the union penultimately in *Redemption: Accomplished and Applied* (just prior to glorification), Murray appears

---

[34] Notice, in comparing the soteriologies of the WCF and CMC, the greater emphasis in the latter on the Holy Spirit (Arts. 20 and 21), the distinguishing of effectual calling and regeneration (cf., WCF 10 with CMC 22 and 26), and the insertion of articles on union with Christ (Art. 23) and peace of conscience (Art. 32). Although, then, Philip Schaff correctly states that the CMC "accords substantially in spirit and arrangement with the Westminster Confession," his view that the CMC "is far inferior to [the WCF] in ability and accuracy" is open to question (*The Creeds of Christendom: With a History and Critical Notes*, Volume 1: *The History of Creeds*, Philip Schaff ed., revised by David S. Schaff, reprint ed. [Grand Rapids: Baker, 1990], 903).

[35] John Murray, *Redemption: Accomplished and Applied*, first published by Eerdmans, 1955; reprint ed. (Edinburgh and Carlisle, PA: Banner of Truth Trust, 1979), 161.

to belie the "basic" importance of union with Christ in the application of salvation. Second, he missed the opportunity to clarify the Westminster commissioners' belief, according to WLC 65 and 66, that union with Christ occurs at the front end of our receipt of salvation:

> *Q. 65. What special benefit do the members of the invisible church enjoy by Christ?*
>
> A. The members of the invisible church by Christ enjoy union and communion with him in grace and glory.
>
> *Q. 66. What is that union which the elect have with Christ?*
>
> A. The union which the elect have with Christ is the work of God's grace, whereby they are spiritually and mystically, yet really and inseparably, joined to Christ as their head and husband; *which is done in their effectual calling* [italics inserted].

By cross-referencing the WCF and WLC we learn that union with Christ follows on logically from effectual calling and regeneration. These are treated together at the opening of Westminster's statement of the application of salvation in chapter ten, "Of Effectual Calling." Third, Murray has lent plausibility to Thomas Torrance's later claim that, in the WCF's "*ordo salutis*," union with Christ is reached in medieval fashion through various stages of grace.[36]

By seeking to anchor union with Christ toward the front end of our understanding of the order of salvation, we emphasize two principles. On the one hand, that our salvation is of God and not of man. Whereas the Father calls us into union with Christ, the Son bestows on us the benefits of our union with him, and the Spirit inspires in us the faith through which the bond of union occurs. On the other hand, we ensure that our attention is fixed first and foremost on God and only then on the benefits we receive in Christ.

Second, union with Christ challenges the appearance within the *ordo salutis* of the isolation of our Savior from the saving benefits he bestows. Any hint of this isolation challenges the workability and

---

[36] T. F. Torrance, *Scottish Theology: From John Knox to John McLeod Campbell* (Edinburgh: T&T Clark, 1996), 128.

therefore the existence of the gospel. In Calvin's words, "our whole salvation and all its parts are comprehended in Christ" (*Inst.* II.16. 19). Such a glorious truth the *ordo salutis* struggles to express.

Even if we reform the construct, front-loading it with union with Christ, the *ordo salutis* still struggles to display the inseparable connection between Christ and his benefits. In a linear diagram, each successive element of our salvation appears to take us further away from Christ. Moreover, we tend to speak more of individual elements of salvation than of the one event of the believer's union with our Savior in his death and resurrection. Furthermore, it is questionable whether the *ordo salutis* does justice to the eschatological character of our salvation. Raised with Christ in spirit in the moment of faith we yet await our bodily resurrection when Christ returns in power and glory. Justified, adopted, and sanctified in that moment we now await the consummation of such blessings on the day of our Lord.

While no human diagram can do justice to the magnitude of our salvation, Gaffin challenges dogmaticians to review their traditional formulations in the light of Scripture.[37] He pleads in effect for a christo-centrification of the application of salvation. Such a reform suggests, in effect, that in addition to the linear scope of the minimized *ordo salutis* we ought to adopt a circular representation of the inextricable connection between Christ and his benefits (chiefly justification, sanctification, and adoption). Hence the figure which follows. It seeks to show how Christ is the essential benefit of our salvation, and that without him we cannot receive those individual benefits bestowed and received simultaneously in him:

Figure 6.1

The soteric circle of nonsequential benefits of union with Christ

The commissioners of the Westminster Assembly understood this. WCF 12 clearly locates adoption in Christ: "All those that are justified, God vouchsafeth, *in and for his only Son*, Jesus Christ, to make partakers of the grace of adoption." Yet, the absence of an earlier chapter on union with Christ, and the sequential arrangement in which adoption follows justification has led subsequent theologians to camp out on the relationship between justification and adoption rather than on the conjoined connectedness of justification, adoption, and sanctification to Christ.

This misreading of both Scripture and the WCF persists. In his exposition of the WCF on adoption (found ironically in his chapter on justification), J. V. Fesko notes that, subsequent to the Westminster Assembly, "Reformed theologians [came to] view adoption as the consequence of justification."[38] When we recall, however, that most were rarely speaking of adoption, and that, among those who were, there was the practice of subsumed it under justification, we must deduce that Fesko is reading his own view into his review of the theological tradition:

> Believers receive all of these benefits [of adoption] as a consequence of their justification. In other words, because of the imputed obedience and satisfaction of Christ, received through faith alone, believers are designated as heirs of eternal life and possess numerous benefits only befitting princes.

Fesko's view is neither what Scripture teaches nor what the WCF states. Neither justification, adoption, nor sanctification stand in consequence of one another. Rather, they stand alongside one another as benefits of Christ. The WCF simply says that those justified are adopted. Adoption thus occurs not in consequence of our justification, but in consequence of our being in Christ. We are made partakers of the grace of adoption, it bears repeating, "in and for his only Son, Jesus Christ." On this reading, it is Christ and not our justification that is centralized in the *ordo salutis*.

The christocentrification of our soteriology is, then, both a significant and a live issue. The *ordo salutis* calls for the christo-centrification, as does the frequent treatment of union with Christ. This reform challenges what David Garner helpfully observes is a "forensic fixation."[39] The fixation has been influenced by history but must be tempered by Scripture.

Fifth reform: The injection of perspectivalism.

The language of perspectivalism has arisen as a more recent extension of the break from Hodge's scientific or objectivist theological

---

[38] J. V. Fesko, *The Theology of the Westminster Standards: Historical Context and Theological Insights* (Wheaton, IL: Crossway, 2014), 236.

[39] David B. Garner, *Sons in the Son: The Riches and Reach of Adoption in Christ* (Philipsburg, New Jersey: P&R, 2016), 224–30, 301.

method. Instead of falling prey to Schleiermacher's subjectivism, John Frame has proposed "something close to Biblicism."[40]

Frame's *near Biblicism* warmly embraces biblical theology. "It is especially important for systematic theologians today," he writes, "to be aware of the developments in biblical theology, a discipline in which new discoveries are being made almost daily."[41] Yet, while lauding biblical theology as "an exciting discipline,"[42] Frame refuses to replace an uncritical traditionalism with an unqualified enthusiasm for biblical theology. Biblical theology, he opines, is more of a perspective on theology than a separate division or department.[43]

Frame differs from Gaffin at this juncture. Gaffin "thought, and still does evidently, that biblical theology should control systematics. I have always thought that no theological discipline is primary but that all should provide checks and balances for one another." Frame also fears the belief that biblical theology, with its closeness to the text and vocabulary of Scripture, is more biblical than systematic theology, and, furthermore, the fanatical assumption that biblical theology requires "applicationless" salvation-historical preaching. It is expository preaching well done, I add, that is the true heir of biblical theology.[44]

---

[40] The following summarizes and at times quotes from *DKG*, 77–81—a significant discussion overlooked by Hart's support of Princeton's science-influenced unoriginal Calvinism.

[41] *DKG*, 212.

[42] For Frame's thought on salvation history, see *DG*, 207–9; "Systematic Theology and Apologetics at the Westminster Seminaries," in *The Pattern of Sound Doctrine*, 96.

[43] See #22 in "Reflections of a Lifetime Theologian," interviewed by Andrew Sandlin in *Christian Culture* (April–May 2008); *DKG*, 206.

[44] Frame, "Thanks for Dick Gaffin's Ministry," *DG*, 7–8. Frame's concerns I have compressed from the eight he itemizes in *DKG*, 209–11. Cf., the objections listed by Richard Gamble in "Biblical Theology and Systematic Theology" in *Always Reforming: Explorations in Systematic Theology*, ed. A. T. B. McGowan [Downers Grove, IL: IVP Academic, 2006], 228–32).

Warning, then, of pride in imbalanced attachments to individual perspectives and of anti-abstractionism in embracing the biblical-theological perspective, Frame argues instead for multiple perspectives in what is his most novel, distinctive, and relevant contribution to the restructuring of systematic theology. Note, though, in engaging his "exegetically based epistemology," that (multi-)perspectivalism has a broader and narrower reference.[45]

Broadly speaking, perspectivalism reminds us that while God in his omniscience sees everything at once, we finite creatures see but one perspective at a time. While not all human perspectives are right, Frame explains that the kernel of truth in other perspectives balances our own and helps us to reflect better the infallible, harmonious, multi-perspectival content of Scripture.

Narrowly speaking, perspectivalism observes that in Scripture "there is a pervasive pattern of threefold distinctions which, though mysterious, provide us with considerable illumination."[46] The Trinity is the archetypal triad, others are ectypal: divine Lordship (control, absolute authority, presence), revelation (general, special, existential [illumination]), the offices of Christ (King [control], Prophet [authority], Priest [presence]), aspects of salvation (salvation accomplished, law of God, salvation applied), human knowledge of God (object [world as God's control], norm [God's authority], subject [the knower standing in God's presence]), ethics or the knowledge of right and wrong (norm [obedience to God's Word], situation [application of the Word],

---

[45] Frame, "Systematic Theology and Apologetics at the Westminster Seminaries," 92. For Frame's perspectivalism, go to "A Primer on Perspectivalism"; *DKG*, 1, 165–346 (especially); John M. Frame, *The Doctrine of the Christian Life* (Phillipsburg, NJ: P&R, 2008), 131–382; cf., Poythress' *Symphonic Theology: The Validity of Multiple Perspectives in Theology* (Grand Rapids: Academie Books [Zondervan], 1987). Frame now questions the appropriateness of *perspectivalism* since its spelling closely resembles Nietzsche's relativistic perspectivism (*DKG*, 1n7).

[46] "A Primer on Perspectivalism," *DKG*, 4.

existential [inner satisfaction]).[47] In these triads, Frame sees the normative (the use of Scripture); the situational (the application of Scripture to the world of our experience); and the existential (the use of our faculties and skills in knowing and applying Scripture).[48]

It is the broader understanding which is germane to the retrieval of adoption and the restructuring of systematic theology. Doubtless, the normative, situational, and existential categories are useful when exegetically justified, but Scripture does not always speak in triads. It includes twelve tribes, emphasizes the number seven, and has four Gospels, etc. While there is a general benefit in regarding justification, adoption, and sanctification as a triad (*triplex gratia Dei*; cf., WCF 11–13), the categorization of justification as the normative, adoption as the situational, and sanctification as the existential perspectives on salvation is too convenient. It is better to say that justification, adoption, and sanctification each contain normative, situational, and existential elements and applications.

We resist, accordingly, a perspectival construal of Scripture as much as a dogmatic construal. Frame agrees: "Sometimes in a moment of overweening pride, I think that my three perspectives are an incredibly deep insight into the fundamental structure of biblical truth. But most of the time I just think they are a good pedagogical device, a set of hooks on which to hang the doctrines of the faith."[49]

The broader use of perspectivalism suffices, then, to challenge the tendency in classic systematics to absorb the humanness of Scripture in its divineness. In perspectivalism's reassertion of the "double-authorship of Scripture," Frame seeks not the equal ultimacy of Scripture's divineness and humanness (for Scripture ever remains

---

[47] Frame's list of triads is endless. See "A Primer on Perspectivalism," *DKG*, 10, where he points readers to *Salvation Belongs to the Lord* and Appendix A of *DG*.

[48] *DKG*, 167–346.

[49] Frame, *Salvation Belongs to the Lord*, 330; cf. "A Primer on Perspectivalism," *DKG*, 10.

God's Word), but a greater reflection of its genres and language.[50] This is important, for as we recall, such is the richness of the gospel that it cannot be encapsulated by a single perspective. Janet Martin Soskice makes this same point utilizing the language of models: "Both science and religion, theologians have been quick to note, rely on a multiplicity of models, each have a partial adequacy in describing the subject, and all being held in tension as a control against taking any one model as descriptively privileged."[51]

Sixth reform: The factoring in of theological models.

Soskice's language of models helps us to segue into this final reform, for some of the richest perspectives of the New Testament are stated by means of theological models, whether by supramodels (e.g., the Fatherhood of God), models (e.g., adoption), or subordinate metaphors (e.g., slavery, redemption, sonship, heirship).

As forms of complementary perspectives, neighboring models serve a number of purposes. Fundamentally, they empower biblical perspectives, for their colorful imagery enables them to stick in our memories, affording us avenues through which we can describe realities otherwise eluding or exceeding ordinary speech. Recall from earlier, they decorate bare concepts, discover truth (the substitution and incremental theories), evoke emotions of worship and adoration (the emotive theories), and so forth.

Second, models validate multi-perspectivalism. God has given us multiple models in Scripture to convey accumulated perspectives that, together, cover what he has revealed. Take, for instance, the doctrine of God. While God is anonymous (exalted and incompre-

---

[50] *DKG*, 199.

[51] Janet Martin Soskice, *Metaphor and Religious Language* (Oxford: Clarendon Press, 1985), 103.

hensible), he has nevertheless revealed himself polyonymously.[52] His multiple names help us, in our finitude, to take in different aspects of his self-revelation, one at a time. So it is with the revelation of his saving grace. Since his salvation cannot be encapsulated by a single perspective or model, God has revealed his lavish grace to us via multiple perspectives or models.

Few theologians have sought to articulate this truth over the centuries. John Dick is a rare exception. In his volume *Lectures on Theology*, he follows up his chapter on justification with the thought:

> [Adoption] appears to me to be virtually the same with justification, and to differ with it merely in the new view which it gives of the relation of believers to God, and in the peculiar form in which it exhibits the blessings to which they are entitled. As it implies a change of state, it must be the same; for this change can take place but once; and whether we say that a sinner passes from a state of guilt and condemnation into a state of favour with God, or that he is translated from the family of Satan into the family of heaven, we express the same fact, and only diversify the terms. He who is justified is adopted, and he who is adopted is justified. But as the Scriptures make use of the term adoption, to denote the change of relation which takes place when we are effectually called, and believers are often exhibited in the character of the children of God, the subject is well worthy of our attention, and has a claim to a separate illustration.[53]

While Dick underplays somewhat the function of the "separate illustration[s]" of justification and adoption, he was ahead of his time in recognizing the New Testament's multiple perspectives or models.

---

[52] Herman Bavinck, *The Doctrine of God*, transl., edited, and outlined by William Hendrickson; first edition, Eerdmans, 1951, reprinted (Edinburgh and Carlisle, PA: The Banner of Truth Trust, 1991), 90.

[53] John Dick, *Lectures on Theology*, two volumes (Philadelphia: F. W. Greenough, 1838), 2:224 (available at https://babel.hathitrust.org/cgi/pt?id=njp.3210106370 2136& view=1up&seq=230, accessed April 28, 2021).

Nearer our time, Edwin H. Palmer (1922–80), who taught at Westminster Seminary (1960–64), states that,

> The elect sinner enjoys one, great, indivisible salvation from God. In order to portray that in all of its fullness and richness, the Bible uses different descriptions. One aspect concerns God's holiness, which has been offended and violated by sin.... But this describes salvation from only one point of view, even though a glorious one. Another aspect, which is not, and cannot, be included in the idea of justification is the fact that in salvation the sinner does not only come to stand in a correct and proper relation to God's holiness and justice, but that he becomes the object of a tender, fatherly love. This side of redemption is expressed by the illustration of adoption.[54]

More recently still, N. T. Wright has affirmed this. "Granted," he says, that "Paul uses many metaphors and multiple models, ... there is a clear single narrative within which the metaphors and models make their distinctive and appropriate contribution."[55]

Conversely and thirdly, theological models counter the temptation to reduce an overall view of the gospel to a single perspective. Writes Trevor Burke, "Paul's understanding of what God in Jesus Christ has done for sinful humanity is so rich, diverse and kaleidoscopic, that it *ought not to be* reduced to a single expression."[56] This is historically relevant, for it counters the Lutheran tendency to absorb soteriology in justification. Writes Luther,

> The article concerning justification is the Master and Prince, Lord, Leader and Judge of all kinds of doctrine. It preserves and steers every church doctrine and allows our conscience to stand before

---

[54] Edwin H. Palmer, *Scheeben's Doctrine of Divine Adoption* (Kampen: J. H. Kok N.V. 1953), 168.

[55] N. T. Wright, "Response to Kevin Vanhoozer," in Nicholas Perrin and Richard B. Hays, Eds., *Jesus, Paul, and the People of God: A Theological Dialogue with N. T. Wright*, 261.

[56] Trevor Burke, *Adopted into God's Family: Exploring a Pauline Metaphor* (Downers Grove, IL: InterVarsity Press, 2006), 37 (italics inserted).

> God. Without this article the world is nothing but death and darkness.[57]

Counters Lutheran theologian Wolfhart Pannenberg, the only center controlling everything in Pauline theology is Jesus Christ. It is in him that the doctrines of justification and adoption link up. In this enhancement of Lutheran theology, Pannenberg continues:

> There is no reason to *subordinate* [other NT accounts of believer's participation in salvation] to the idea of justification, particularly as Paul himself already presupposed faith fellowship with Christ in the verdict of justification and then developed this theme in terms of adoption into the filial relation to the Father.[58]

What is more, the stating of perspectives in terms of neighboring models challenges the specific Reformed absorption of adoption in justification, and, more generally, the conflation of models which, although distinctively structured, share the same feel. The model of adoption stands alongside other major perspectives, such as justification and sanctification. It offes a distinctive perspective on salvation in its own right.

Fourth, perspectival models confirm the need to supplement in soteriology the more selective use of the *ordo salutis*. Notes Palmer, the application of salvation

> is not a question of either temporal or logical priority, but of a definition or description of another facet of the same object. Justification and redemption do not precede adoption, but are, as it were, alongside, parallel to, it. They are simply terms or descriptions that Paul uses to clarify for us the significance and varied richness of our salvation; but in reality, with God, whose thinking and actions

---

[57] Quoted in Eberhard Jüngel, *Justification: The Heart of the Christian Faith*, transl. Jeffrey F. Cayzer and introduced by John Webster, third edition (Edinburgh and New York: T&T Clark, 2001), 18.

[58] Wolfhart Pannenberg, Systematic Theology, Volume 3, transl. Geoffrey W. Bromiley (Grand Rapids: Eerdmans, 1993), 213 and 235.

are not to be compared with ours, it is impossible to speak of a logical priority, let alone a temporal one.[59]

More recently, Brenda Colijn has spoken similarly. She notes that while the New Testament does not give us a systematic doctrine of salvation, it offers us a variety of images. These she explains in terms of the complexity of both the human problem and its solution.[60]

Fifth, the stating of perspectives in theological models encourages us to revisit the comparative importance of soteric models. Historically, the sequence of Westminster soteriology led Candlish to describe adoption as "the crown of Calvinism," and Murray, a century later, as "the apex of redemptive grace and privilege." Does, however, the substitution of a sequential approach to the arrangement of soteric doctrine alter these assessments? Recall, we have posited that adoption—

- is a neighboring model to justification, rather than, as some readings of the *ordo salutis* imply, a result of justification.

- occurs in the same moment as justification and sanctification, through union with Jesus Christ in his death and resurrection.

I do not believe it does. The fresh arrangement of soteriology changes not the conclusion, but the way in which we arrive at it.

Whereas justification is the fundamental benefit of union with Christ, a case can be made for claiming that adoption and sanctification are higher benefits. Whereas justification describes those united to Christ as justified sinners, sanctification describes them as sanctified

---

[59] Palmer, *Scheeben's Doctrine of Divine Adoption*, 182–83, 168 (cf., 172).

[60] Brenda B. Colijn, *Images of Salvation in the New Testament* (Downers Grove, IL: IVP Academic, 2010), 13, 14, 19. While the New Testament images Colijn delineates distinguish redemption, regeneration, justification (etc.) from adoption, her lumping together reconciliation, adoption, and peace under the idea of "No Longer Strangers" (ch. 8) brings into question an adequate view of models or what we might also call metaphorical concepts.

saints, and adoption as liberated sons. Thus, sanctification and adoption take us higher in Christ. Although none can be either saints or sons of God without first being justified sinners, our sanctification and adoption rest not on our justification but on our being united to Christ. Likewise, we are justified in union with Christ.

The foregoing we can attempt to depict diagrammatically:

Figure 6.2

Alternative depiction of the benefits of union with Christ, in side profile.

Given the limitations also of this figure, we might be forgiven for thinking that there is little to distinguish this arrangement of such models from the notion of A. A. Hodge, Lloyd-Jones, and Garner in which adoption is a capstone sitting astride regeneration and justification. In their reckoning, regeneration and justification are subsumed under adoption. That arrangement would seem, though, to bring into question the metaphorical integrity of the models of the new birth (regeneration) and justification. Here we seek to maintain that integrity while nevertheless showing that adoption and sanctification take us higher in our union with Christ than justification. Our justification in Christ is foundational, but our sanctification and adoption in Christ are transformational and elevational, respectively.

3. THE RATIONALE FOR RETRIEVAL

Having posited plausible hindrances to reform, and identified those viable enhancements of systematic theology calling for our attention, we now argue the case for pressing on with the work of reform. It rests on two realities.

The first reality: The old wineskins are bursting.

Among the prevalent schools of Reformed thought in our day (see the Appendix), the revisionist Reformed have, by definition, jettisoned a commitment to the Reformed orthodoxy of classic statements such as the Westminster Standards. While Barth and the Torrances have shown interest in the products of Reformed scholasticism, the neoorthodox they represent, in pushing back against theological liberalism, have not returned to a theological conformity to Reformed-orthodox summaries of Holy Scripture. For them, the old wineskins have perished methodologically *and* theologically, and have little practical use today.

Thus, we focus here on those remaining committed to the theology of the Westminster Standards, noting ongoing, in-house discussions about theological methodology between those identifiable as orthodox and constructive Reformed. Consider representative figures Robert Godfrey and Richard Gaffin. Whereas Godfrey is content to defend uncritically both the methodology and theology of Reformed scholasticism, and opposes endeavors to reform the former, Gaffin belongs to that sympathetic-critical trajectory of reform dating back most recently to Geerhardus Vos, the grandfather of the constructive Reformed, and to John Murray, their father. This reform has been encouraged immensely by the renaissance in Calvin studies.

It is important to note that Gaffin upholds confessional subscription, believing the subscription should be "flexible full," which is of a tighter sort than system subscription (a general subscription to what is Christian, Protestant, Reformed). Nevertheless, Godfrey believes that Gaffin's advocacy of a sympathetic-critical (in that order!) approach to historic Reformed standards undercuts our confidence in them. Gaffin, though, believes Godfrey has misread his use of Klaas Schilder's epithet *sympathetic-criticism* and fears that Godfrey's rebuttal undermines the ability of the Reformed to reform according to the Word of God. Gaffin thus defends his plea for a creative orthodoxy agreeable to confessional subscription *ex animo*. After all, confessions of faith are subordinate to God's Word. Where, in Protestantism, the Bible is the "norming norm" (*norma normans*) of our faith and conduct, the church's confessions are "normed norms" (*norma normata*) and are therefore answerable to Scripture.[61]

Now, I do not question the theological orthodoxy of Robert Godfrey or of the orthodox Reformed. They love the biblical faithfulness and courage of our forefathers, as do the constructive Reformed. Some have been very effective in our day in introducing significant numbers to the Reformed faith. Yet. as many as have been welcomed through the front door, there is a back door through which the disenchanted continue to exit. I believe the working imbalances of Reformed expression and praxis have something to do with that. We are forthright on calling others to reform according to God's Word, but tend to be somewhat reserved about discerning and implementing the reforms that we need to make.

By seeking to reverse the somewhat oblivious trend of reading Scripture through our confessions of faith (instead of *vice versa*), the constructive Reformed pursue the recovery of a creative orthodoxy which aims to dissuade the disenchanted from leaving the Reformed community. While pertaining chiefly to our theological method, the

---

[61] Cf., W. Robert Godfrey, "Westminster Seminary, the Doctrine of Justification, and the Reformed Confessions" in *The Pattern of Sound Doctrine: Systematic Theology at the Westminster Seminaries (Essays in Honor of Robert B. Strimple)*, (Phillipsburg, NJ: P&R, 2004), 135 and 142, and Gaffin, "The Vitality of Reformed Systematic Theology," *The Faith Once Delivered*, 29–32.

creative orthodoxy in view challenges the danger of a quasi-Roman Catholic traditionalism wherein our confessions and catechisms threaten to rival the authority of Scripture. Such a traditionalism atrophies our thinking processes, and settles for the regurgitation rather than the renewal of the Reformed faith. Thus, the constructive Reformed, while holding on to the family silver, seek to polish it. To change the metaphor, we are committed to the old paths, but believe we could do with newer shoes to walk them. To draw from Jesus' metaphor, the older wineskins of ratiocinated system building are bursting. For the sake of the good wine of Reformed orthodoxy we argue for newer wineskins. Yet, among the constructive Reformed, there are differing views on what such wineskins look like.

In weaving, in constructive-Reformed fashion, between "unprecedented radicalism and profligate experimentation" and the temptation "to be merely reactionary" (what Bavinck calls the "deadly embrace of a dead conservatism"), Gaffin proposes rather daringly that we abandon the nomenclature *systematic theology*. He reasons that *biblical theology* is sufficient.[62]

This proposal is tempting, but it raises several issues. First, as John Bolt remarks, "a strictly 'biblical theology' . . . is impossible. Even efforts to be purely 'biblical' reflect the ecclesiastical and social environment in which they rise."[63] Second, in the wrong hands, biblical theology could lose sight of the significance of doctrinal synthesis, becoming but a replica of the biblical studies on which biblical theology is built. Third, biblical theology does not typically allow for the inclusion of excursions into the history of doctrine.

Thus, Frame, another of the constructive Reformed, retains the nomenclature *systematic theology*. Instead of implying that biblical

---

[62] Gaffin, "The Vitality of Reformed Systematic Theology," *The Vitality of Reformed Theology*, 2–3.

[63] John Bolt, Editor's Introduction, Bavinck, *Reformed Dogmatics*, 1:20

theology can absorb systematic theology (although this is not Gaffin's meaning), Frame regards biblical and systematic theology as distinct but inseparable perspectives. This duality, however, does not preclude the biblical-theological reform of systematic theology, for, as Frame's *Systematic Theology* illustrates, there is included more salvation-historical contextualization of the *loci* as also his tri-perspectivalism.

Although differing on the way forward, Gaffin and Frame, thoroughly Reformed orthodox in their belief, demonstrate by their consideration of the reform of theological method that the old wineskins of Reformed-orthodox methodology are bursting. Under today's latent pressure to prove our Reformed-orthodox credentials, Gaffin has, it seems to me, pulled back somewhat from his earlier freedom in speaking of methodological improvements to Reformed orthodoxy. Not so Frame. There is needed, however, an open conversation about what the reform of theological methodology means for subscription to the Westminster Standards, especially if that subscription obliges methodological as well as theological conformity.

The second reality: New wineskins are in the making.

On the basis of the aforementioned reforms of systematic theology, and gladly acknowledging the methodological influence of Vos, Murray, Gaffin, and Frame, I seek to probe further how we may assemble new wineskins to carry forward the good wine of Reformed-orthodox belief. Specifically, I wish to recommend, alternative to Gaffin's abandonment of the nomenclature *systematic theology* and to Frame's retention of it, a new nomenclature that aims to incorporate both the influence of biblical theology and the doctrinal synthesizing so essential to systematic theology.

The renaming of systematic theology is not so revolutionary. The belief that Scripture possesses a thematic coherence is very old, yet the names given it have been subject to numerous alterations. Origen referred to the search for thematic coherence in terms of "principles" (Ἀρχων), Theognostus as "outlines," and Lactantius as "Institutes."

Augustine preferred the nomenclature "Little Handbook" (*Enchiridion*), John of Damascus "Treatise," Isidore of Seville "Sentences" (generally replaced in the thirteenth century by "Summa Theologiae"), and Melancthon "*Loci.*" During the Reformation, Calvin returned to the nomenclature "Institutes," and with the increase of theological disciplines, accompanying adjectives came to be used, such as "didactic," "systematic," "theoretical," or "positive."

Only in 1659, so far as we know, did the adjective "dogmatic" appear, as in L. Reinhart's *Synopsis theologiae dogmaticae.* Over time the adjective became a noun, *dogmatics*, to which other adjectives were attached. Herman Bavinck labeled his dogmatics *Reformed* so as to underline his commitment to Reformed orthodoxy and its high view of Scripture as divine revelation. Karl Barth described his as *kirchliche* (churchly), opening declaratively with, "Dogmatics is a theological discipline. But theology is a function of the church." The church not only confesses God, but also humanity and the responsibility of our actions. Accordingly, the church produces theology by subjecting herself to self-examination.[64]

It is the label *dogmatics* that I prefer for the revamping of systematics. On the one hand, it has greater biblical resonance than the word *systematics*. Dogmatics comes from the Greek δόγματα which, in turn, comes from δοκεῖν. Although δοκεῖν has the idea "to be of the opinion," its meaning is discerned not simply from its etymology but from its use. In the LXX and in the New Testament, δοκεῖν is stronger than we might imagine given the relativism of today. It is used of government decrees (Esther 3:9; Dan. 2:13, 6:8; Lk. 2:1; and Acts 17:7), the statutes of the old covenant (Eph. 2:15; Col. 2:14), and of the

---

[64] Herman Bavinck, *Reformed Dogmatics*, Volume 1: Prolegomena; Gen. Ed. John Bolt, transl. John Vriend (Grand Rapids: Baker Academic, 2003), 26–28. Karl Barth, *Church Dogmatics*, Volume I.1, *The Doctrine of the Word of God*, edited by G. W. Bromiley and T. F. Torrance, first published in English T & T Clark, 1936 (Peabody, Massachusetts: Hendrickson, 2010), 3.

decisions of the Council of Jerusalem (Acts 16:4). In our derived use of δοκεῖν, we understand dogmatics to speak of the whole inscripturated revelation. Writes Herman Bavinck, dogmatics constitute "the knowledge that God has revealed in his Word to his church concerning himself and all his creatures as they stand in relation to him."[65]

On the other hand, the relevance of *dogmatics* to the whole of biblical revelation reminds us that the discipline can incorporate both the *communicatio salutis* and the specific reforms suggested. *Dogmatics* emphasizes, accordingly, the unity, and thus the coherence, of scriptural content. The dogmatician, writes Bavinck,

> does not come to God's revelation with a ready-made system in order, as best he can, to force its content into it. On the contrary, even in his system a theologian's sole responsibility is to think God's thoughts after him and to reproduce the unity that is objectively present in the thoughts of God and has been recorded for the eye of faith in Scripture. That such a unity exists in the knowledge of God contained in revelation is not open to doubt; to refuse to acknowledge it would be to fall into skepticism, into denial of the unity of God.[66]

It is the scope and unity of inscripturated revelation which, through the study of adoption, leads me to prefer and to specify that the revamped systematics be described as *biblical* dogmatics. Although sharing Bavinck's adherence to the Reformed faith, as also some of his reaction to Pietism and the biblical theologians,[67] the qualifying adjective is intended to stress that a Reformed dogmatics must be reforming, grounded on a high view of Scripture but also pursuing a higher use of it. The label, then, although sounding tautologous, is not.

Although I have arrived at *biblical dogmatics* independently, it turns out that the nomenclature is not original to me. Andrew George

---

[65] Bavinck, *Reformed Dogmatics*, 1:25.

[66] Bavinck, *Reformed Dogmatics*, 1:44–45.

[67] Bavinck, *Reformed Dogmatics*, 1:54.

Voigt, professor of systematic theology and dean of the Theological Seminary, Columbia, South Carolina, published in 1917 an evangelical Lutheran systematic theology under the title *Biblical Dogmatics.* Incidentally, it omits a chapter or section on adoption. Some decades later Pierre Marcel wrote, "Dogmatics cannot be either New or Old Testament Dogmatics: it must be *biblical* dogmatics, that is to say, it must take into account the whole of revelation." Such prior uses at least demonstrate the viability of the label.[68]

Bavinck feared, however, that the adjective *biblical*, while not assuming "a sharp contrast between Scripture and church doctrine," communicates a greater readiness to accept a disjuncture between inscripturated truth and the truth summarized in creeds and confessions of the Christian church. The use of the *biblical dogmatics* I envision accepts unreservedly, though, the normative integrity of the church in seeking to codify (rather than to "develop") the truth of Scripture. Nevertheless, the term *biblical* is a reminder that creedal or confessional standards are ever to remain subordinate summaries of Scripture, and that they can err. Indeed, we need go no further than the doctrine of adoption to realize, to quote Bavinck, that a matter may "be properly set forth in Scripture" and yet not receive normative exposure in the teaching or confessions of the church.[69]

This is why, then, we read the creeds and confessions of the church through Scripture, and not Scripture through her creedal or confessional standards. The former practice corrects or updates the subordinate standards, the latter limits the Scriptures to what has been

---

[68] Andrew George Voigt, *Biblical Dogmatics* (Columbia, S.C.: Lutheran Board of Education, 1917). Pierre Ch. Marcel, *The Biblical Doctrine of Infant Baptism: Sacrament of the Covenant of Grace*, transl. by Philip Edgcumbe Hughes; first published 1953, reprinted (Cambridge, England: James Clarke, 1981), 15.

[69] Bavinck, *Reformed Dogmatics*, 1:19 (John Bolt's "Editor's Introduction"), 30, 54. Karl Barth, *CD*, I.1, 3 "Church Proclamation as the Material of Dogmatics."

formulated historically. Thus, the nomenclature *biblical dogmatics* gives expression to a systematizing of biblical truth which allows for, and in fact encourages, reform according to God's Word. *Biblical dogmatics* is also, then, genuinely Reformed (reforming), *à la* Bavinck, and also churchly, *à la* Barth.

Obviously, to realize the new biblical dogmatic, we need to turn from the semantics to the implementation of the reforms, This is no small matter. Richard Gamble rightly observes that while many in the Reformed community are pondering the restructuring of systematic theology, there is a heavy responsibility that comes with the work. For all the exegetical and hermeneutical care needed, the biblical dogmatic will remain viable, if, says Gamble, "the relationship between biblical and systematic theology . . . continue[s] to develop so that the strengths of biblical theology inform the development of a 'biblical' 'system' of theology."[70]

Certainly, this is my intent. To actualize it, there follows a checklist of tasks to aid biblical dogmatists. The aim of it is to overturn Emil Brunner's concern about scholastic theology. Commenting in regard to the doctrine of God, he observed, "Anyone who comes for the first time from the Bible into the world of Scholastic Theology feels himself in a foreign world." Closer to home, Donald Macleod has similarly remarked, "The traditional doctrine [of God] is too far removed from the thought-world of the Bible and too much influenced by philosophy."[71]

---

[70] Gamble, "The Relationship Between Biblical Theology and Systematic Theology," 224–39.

[71] Donald Macleod, *Behold Your God* (Fearn: Ross-shire: Christian Focus Publications, 1990), 7, 8.

LOCI COMMUNES / CHECKLIST	SALVATION-HISTORICAL CONTEXT (*historia salutis*)	LITERARY & AUTHORIAL SPECIFICS (*communicatio salutis*)	DISTINCT MODELS & CONCEPTUAL AFFINITIES (*metaphorae salutis*)	APPLICATION TO WORSHIP, LIFE, SERVICE (*applicatio salutis*)
REVELATION				
GOD				
MAN				
SAVIOR				
GOSPEL				
ETHICS				
THE CHURCH				
THE LAST THINGS				

Figure 6.3

A checklist for a new biblical dogmatic

Our concern, however, is with the particular arrangement of soteriology, specifically the inclusion of a biblically sensitive under-standing of adoption. Given the inability of the *ordo salutis* construct to adequately depict our salvation in Christ, it is significant that complementary moves are afoot to increase the constructs we utilize in the expounding of soteriology.

Colijn has influenced Michael Bird along these lines. True to his goal of providing a biblical and systematic introduction to *Evangelical Theology*, Bird breaks down "The Gospel of Salvation" into different sections:

- *Salvation history*. Five acts: creation and fall, the Patriarchs and Israel, Jesus, the church, and the consummation.
- *The order of salvation*: Affirming Romans 8:29-30 as "the basic outline of an *ordo salutis*" ("the golden chain of salvation"), Bird understands salvation's past-present-future sequence to run as follows: predestination—>calling—>regeneration—>faith and repentance—>justification—>transformation—> glorification.
- *The images of salvation*. Whereas the section on the *ordo salutis* deals with the logical outworking of the gospel, under the images of salvation Bird envisions the results of the gospel and includes redemption, rescue, reconciliation, justification, peace, adoption, eternal life, and *theosis*.
- The scope and security of salvation.

Bird's diversification of the arrangement of the Bible's soteriology is a very positive advance in our expression of the nuances and wealth of soteric meaning. It lacks, however, the significance of the distinct metaphorical structures of the New Testament. Moreover, Bird outlines regeneration in his section on the order rather than the images of salvation, even though the New Testament's main references to it are metaphorical (the new birth). He is obligated to include justification in the *ordo salutis* since it is included in Rom 8:29-30, but also includes it at greater length among the images of salvation. Rightly, he evades identifying the center of salvation, other than in the triune God.

To build on Bird and to bring a specifically Reformed perspective to the multilayered arrangement of biblical soteriology, I suggest the following elements:

- *Historia salutis* (recall figure 4.2). Again, five acts, going under the labels of protology (predestination to life, in view of creation and the fall), ecclesiology (the development of God's people, the church under age), soteriology (the death and resurrection of Christ), pneumatology (Spirit baptism of the penitent/entrance by faith into the church come of age), and eschatology (the return of Christ, the resurrection of the dead, the Judgment, and the inauguration of the new earth).
- *Ordo salutis.* Now freed from dependence on Romans 8:29-30, and scaled back to those soteric elements forming a sequential or causal relationship:

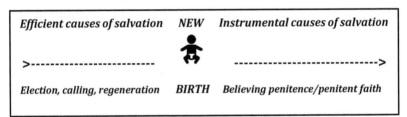

Figure 6.4
A scaled back *ordo salutis*

- *Metaphorae salutis.* Of all the images Bird lists—redemption, rescue, reconciliation, justification, peace, adoption, eternal life, and *theosis*—redemption, rescue, and reconciliation are not immediately relevant to the application of salvation since they are accomplishments Christ procured once-for-all at the cross. Christ does not undertake redemption every time a person comes to faith. Rather, through faith we receive the redemption that Christ accomplished once-for-all at Calvary. The same can be said of *rescue* and *reconciliation.* We thus focus in this layer of soteriology on the benefits of union with Christ, chiefly justification, sanctification, and adoption (see Figures 6.1 and 6.2).

- *Spes salutis.* Our hopes of salvation are realized in the reception of salvation. Such hopes point us to the consummation of salvation since they include peace, eternal life, *theosis,* assurance, perseverance (or preservation), and have to do with the existential experience of God's saving grace. Peace with God makes possible the peace of God. Eternal life commences on entrance into Christ and continues hereafter. Our participation in the divine nature now (2 Pet. 1:4) anticipates a moral likeness to God in the hereafter. Our assurance supports our blessed hope, and our perseverance is an evidence of it.

Having already depicted diagrammatically the *historia* and *ordo salutis,* there follows a figure combining the *metaphorae* and *spes salutis:*

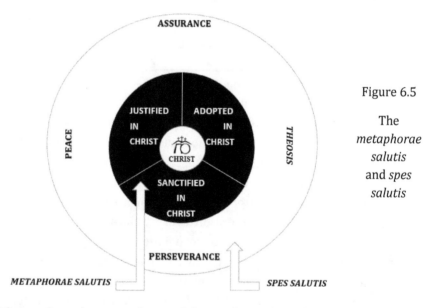

Figure 6.5

The *metaphorae salutis* and *spes salutis*

These four layers of soteriology—*historia salutis, ordo salutis, metaphorae salutis,* and *spes salutis*—can be boiled down pictorially to the *historia salutis* and the *applicatio salutis.* The *historia salutis* we depict again for the contrast with the *applicatio salutis.* The latter incorporates the *ordo, metaphorae,* and *spes salutis.*

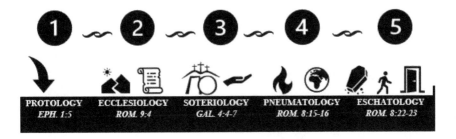

Figure 6.6
Historia Salutis (top) and *Applicatio Salutis* (bottom)

The bottom, combined figure depicting the *applicatio salutis* does several things. It—

- Retains what we can of the *ordo salutis.*
- Christocentrifies the believer's union with Christ in his death and resurrection.

355

- Maintains the distinctive structures of the major models of salvation while yet retaining the connectedness of their benefits to Christ.
- Includes the *spes salutis*, which arise from our mystical union with the risen Christ.

It bears repeating that no amount of diagramming can fully explicate the mysteries of our great salvation. Historically, Holy Spirit baptism has been omitted from arrangements of salvation. I have not sought to rectify that here. Additionally, I have limited the diagram reflecting the *applicatio salutis* to personal hopes arising from our oneness in Christ. Furthermore, in depicting the orderly route to our union with Christ, the diagram potentially misleads. To be clear, I have distinguished regeneration and the new birth, not because they differ but simply to show how the efficient causes of salvation, culminating in regeneration/the new birth enable the instrumental causes of salvation (believing repentance and penitent faith). Nor ought the diagram be read to infer a time lag between our new birth and our repentance and faith, and between our repentance and faith and our union with Christ. Moreover, we ought not to deduce that the union occurs through justification. Note that it states explicitly that we are justified in Christ.

For all their limitations, the figures convey that there *is* a way forward in creating fresh wineskins to hold securely the old wine. Specifically, they visualize for us how adoption may be included in biblical dogmatics without blurring or diminishing it.

4. THE REWARDS OF RETRIEVAL

This complex discussion begs the question as to the theological and spiritual fruits accruing from the full retrieval of adoption. Two words summarize them: biblical balance. "It would be quite misleading," Gaffin remarks, "as is often done by its more enthusiastic advocates, to create the impression that biblical theology brings something totally new into the life of the church. Rather it is largely a matter of correcting and balancing certain trends of the more recent post-Reformation past."[72] Here, then, are six correctives I envision from an untruncated and unmanipulated inclusion of adoption in a fresh biblical dogmatic.

1. The balancing of our view of the God of salvation.

The retrieval of adoption holds the promise of the juxtaposing on equal standing the Bible's theological supramodels (most relevantly, the Justice and Fatherhood of God) and its soteriological models (in the present context, justification, sanctification, and adoption). Permit me to explain.

While in Christ the throne of God's judgment is turned into a throne of paternal grace, we cannot reflect God adequately (contra Victorian liberalism and a lopsided orthodoxy) without according attention to both these supramodels. They are equal in essence, for neither, linguistically or theologically, is less than the other. God's role as Judge is not subordinate to his role as Father, as if one is a supramodel and the other something less, nor is the Fatherhood of God subsumed as some lesser category under the Justice of God.

Likewise, in Christ we receive simultaneously the escalated blessings of justification, sanctification, and adoption, becoming at once, in the moment of saving faith, justified sinners, sanctified saints, and adopted sons. And yet, despite the escalation of blessing, justification, sanctification, and adoption remain coequal models. We are not to think of justification as the model and sanctification and adoption as some lesser references to be absorbed by justification; nor are we, in reaction, to imply that because sanctification and adoption take us higher in Christ, that justification can be downplayed. No, the notions of coequal supramodels and coequal models ensure due exposure to the multiple facets of perspectives of divine revelation.

---

[72] Gaffin, "Systematic Theology and Biblical Theology," 43.

Confining ourselves here to the supramodels of God, it is only right that we are sensitive about how God is viewed. Guarding against a doctrine of the universal Fatherhood of God is appropriate, as also against populist or sentimental demands that we call God "Daddy," irrespective of his holiness. Historically, this guarding has accented God's sovereignty and his justice, which would have been fine, but for the simultaneous downplaying of his Fatherhood. After all, the defense of biblical orthodoxy requires us to be as aware of the dangers of excessive reaction as of the aberrations which produce the reactions in the first place.

When we consider the New Testament, the prominence of the language of divine Fatherhood is unmistakable. As a supramodel, God's Fatherhood has relevance across the New Testament in the multiplicity of its filial or familial models. How advantageous it would be for the fresh balancing of the juridical and the relational (specifically the familial) were all the New Testament's individual portraits of God's Fatherhood to be recovered, their distinctive structures acknowledged and utilized, and their commonalities celebrated. God, after all, is Father as well as Judge, eternally and constantly. Neither role eliminates the other, even though Christ has, for the believer, propitiated the Father's righteous anger, and, by the Father's foreordination, turned the throne of judgment into a throne of grace.

Yet, before conservatives in general and the Reformed orthodox in particular have gotten around to answering fully the Victorian protest for paternal grace, today's progeny of Victorian liberals has moved on, at least in their feminist strand, to advocate God's "Motherhood." Thus, the opportunity is before us today to answer jointly the respective nineteenth- and twentieth-century protests for paternal and maternal grace.

Since we have argued that the Justice and Fatherhood of God are coequal, are we to assume that the Fatherhood and "Motherhood" of God need counterbalancing, too? Not exactly, since we are not to address God as Mother. First, because nowhere does the New Testament call us to, and neither, historically, has the church. As one study report states, "The obvious reluctance of theologians of the past generally to admit feminine conceptuality acts as a warning today, some of us believe, against widespread expansion of our theological models into the realm of the feminine."[73] Second, by pressing ahead and ignoring the language of Scripture we contradict what it says of the maternal. For Paul, it is not God who is mother but the "Jerusalem above" (Gal. 4:26).

The crux of the issue is found, though, not in varying interpretations of Paul but in contrarian views of Scripture. For those for whom Scripture is normative, the matter is settled. God is Father not Mother. Yet, for others, Sallie McFague, for example, Scripture is not a dictum for theology but an exemplar of how we may create theology for ourselves. This relativistic view of revelation lays the basis for a different faith. Gresham Machen articulated this danger a century ago in *Christianity and Liberalism*. It has not gone away.

Leaving aside the problematic theological underpinnings of Feminism, consider the practicality of the matter. For every person who has suffered at the hands of a brutal father and who, therefore, shies away from the idea of God's paternity, there is another rendered a nervous wreck by a screeching mother. If talk of divine Fatherhood is inappropriate because of a minority of brutal fathers, then, to be consistent, a minority of psychologically destructive mothers precludes us from speaking of God as Mother. Thus, moving *in perpetuam* from one model of God to another, we eventually break our increasingly tenuous attachment to inscripturated revelation and exhaust the possibilities of speaking of God at all. Once, then, we make personal

---

[73] *The Motherhood of God: A Report by a Study Group appointed by the Woman's Guild and the Panel on Doctrine on the invitation of the General Assembly of the Church of Scotland*, ed. Alan E. Lewis (Edinburgh: St. Andrew Press, 1984), 44, 53.

experience the basis of our faith, we eventually jettison Christianity altogether.[74]

This said, there are opportunities for those of us affirming the normativity of Scripture to mature in our understanding. In our inadequate attention to the functioning of metaphors and models, there lingers in at least populist theological conservatism the danger of a naïvely sexist use of the language of Αββα. But God, we insist, is not male.

Moreover, we must realize, as John McIntyre reminds us, that metaphors have downsides. These become apparent where the name of the metaphor differs from the substance. We may, for instance, so load God's Fatherhood with male imagery as to make out that God's love is insufficient since it is exclusively paternal. Such downsides of metaphor are "offset by a nucleation of other relevant metaphors, which among them reduce the danger of what would otherwise be misinterpretation."[75]

In the case of God's Fatherhood, the downside is offset by the indications in Scripture that God's divine paternity incorporates archetypally all that is also best of a mother's love. Included in the supramodel is, then, an associated network of ideas that teach us that while we are not to call God *Mother*, God's paternity is also motherly in expression. Thus, the Bible underlines the sufficiency of God's love, each relevant text indicating in turn the degree to which the maternal

---

[74] Harvie M. Conn, "Normativity, Relevance, and Relativism" in *Inerrancy and Hermeneutic: A Tradition, A Challenge, A Debate*, ed. Harvie M. Conn (Grand Rapids: Baker Book House, 1988), 209.

[75] John McIntyre, *Theology After the Storm: Reflections on the Upheavals in Modern Theology and Culture*, ed. Gary D. Badcock (Grand Rapids: Eerdmans, 1997), 276.

is in view in portrayals of God.[76]

Jürgen Moltmann argues specifically that the new life, when thought of as *rebirth* or as being *born* again, alludes to the maternal role of the Holy Spirit. This idea was familiar in the early centuries of Christianity, especially in Syria, but was lost sight of in the patriarchy of Roman society. If, then, believers are "born" again from the Holy Spirit, the Spirit is in some sense "the mother" of God's children and can also be termed a "feminine" Spirit. As Paraclete, the Spirit comes alongside the born just as a mother does so when comforting her own (cf., Is. 66:13). Now, if Moltmann is right in all this, then Johannine (and Petrine) theology, differentiated from Pauline, portrays God as the Father who begot us (1 Pet. 1:3), the Spirit as the Mother who conceived us, Christ as our brother, and we as the newborn children of God.[77]

Obviously, exegetical and theological care is needed in understanding the Bible's allusions to the maternal love of God, for they do not trump the normative or predominant revelation of his Fatherhood. We must recall the top-down nature of divine revelation. This safeguards us from the dictates of any "ism," whether traditional or liberal, and the recreation of God in our image. The faith we profess must emanate from within the bounds of Scripture. No matter how much God's Fatherhood encompasses biblical expressions of motherly love, Packer remains correct to say, that, "If you want to judge how well a person understands Christianity, find out how much he makes of the thought of being God's child, and having God as his Father. . . . Our

---

[76] For the biblical evidence of the maternal expression of God's love, see *The Motherhood of God*, 29–43; cf., Smail, *The Forgotten Father*, 62–64. John W. Cooper addresses some of this in *Our Father in Heaven: Christian Faith and Inclusive Language for God* (Grand Rapids: Baker Books, 1998), 265–94.

[77] Jürgen Moltmann, *The Spirit of Life: A Universal Affirmation*, transl. Margaret Kohl (London: SCM Press, 1992), 157, 159–60.

understanding of Christianity cannot be better than our grasp of adoption."[78]

2. The balancing of our view of salvation accomplished.

Whereas a balanced view of God affects the overall feel of Christian theology, a balanced view of the accomplishment of salvation impacts our perception of the work of Christ. Critical to it are the events or acts of salvation history. I refer to the incarnation and the cross in the plural, for while their plurality has never been denied, part of the seismic revolt against theological orthodoxy in the nineteenth century was driven by the claim that the incarnation had become excessively overshadowed by the cross. Yet, such was the liberal reaction that the value of the cross came under threat from the incarnation.

I am not saying that Scottish Calvinists had no doctrine of the incarnation, nor that they focused on the atonement to insist that it is limited in its extent.[79] They do seem, however, to have lost something of Calvin's idea of Christ's union with our race in its humanity. Conversely, the positing of the gospel in the incarnation seems to have been driven by a rejection of a penal view of atonement and of the specific salvation of the elect. Indeed, it was the relocation of the epicenter of the gospel from the cross to the incarnation which paved the way for the promotion of a universal Fatherhood of God and

---

[78] *The Motherhood of God*, 62; J. I. Packer, *Knowing God*, first printed 1973 (London *et al.*: Hodder and Stoughton, 1975), 224.

[79] Limited atonement is better labeled *definitive atonement* or *particular redemption*. While the initial term indicates the extent of the atonement, namely, the death of Christ for the elect, the adjective *limited* describes Christ's work in the negative, and, appearing to undermine the sheer number for whom Christ died, has misled some to assess the value of the atonement in terms of what is assumed to be the small count for whom Christ died. It is assessed, rather, in terms of the invaluable Christ who did the dying. The alternatives, *particular redemption* and *definitive atonement*, are more positive, affirming Christ's atoning for the sins of an innumerable elect people.

brotherhood of man. On this understanding, Christ entered our humanity solely to educate us by his example. Such a schema allows no place for Paul's idea of receiving in faith Christ's redemption and the Father's adoption. To the Universalist, these blessings are irrelevant or superfluous. George MacDonald considered them "evil."

While the incarnate Christ certainly expresses generally the love of God for all humanity—a truth the Reformed ought to be less shy in affirming—any shortchanging of the atonement obviously raises a red flag. The gospel is found exclusively in neither the incarnation nor the atonement. Rather, it is found in the unbreakable continuum between them. Understood in terms of the earthly experience of Christ as sin-bearer, the continuum runs downward to the abyss of the cross. Understood in terms of the accomplishment of the heavenly mission it runs uphill to Christ's climactic declaration, "It is finished" (Jn. 19:28, 30). There is in the continuum, then, no atonement without the incarnation, nor could there be fulfillment and hope had not the incarnation lead to atonement.

The *locus classicus* of adoption, Galatians 4:4-6, clarifies this and more beside. There, the incarnation makes no sense without the redemptive work of Christ; the redemption has no victory without the resurrection, and the resurrection has no confirmation without Pentecost. Within this continuum the death-resurrection of Christ is central, but it requires the incarnation for its grounding and Pentecost for evidence of its accomplishment.

Stated alternatively, the atonement is neither a mere suffix of the incarnation, nor the incarnation a mere prefix to the atonement; nor is the resurrection merely a prefix to Pentecost, nor Pentecost merely a suffix of the resurrection. Within the death-resurrection of Christ, the resurrection adds neither value nor completion to the work of the cross; yet, without the resurrection we have no assurance that Christ's redemptive work has been accepted by the Father. There is, then, writes Herman Witsius, "some latitude to that fullness of time[ ] in which the

New succeeded the Old Testament." Says Paul: God sent forth Christ not ultimately to be human, to educate, or to be an example, but to redeem (Gal. 4:4-5).[80]

3. The balancing of our view of salvation applied.

Balancing our view of the accomplishment of salvation, helps us segue into a consideration of the believer's union with Christ. This theme, also needing retrieval, is enjoying something of a renaissance in both Pauline and Calvin studies. Having touched on its significance in strategizing a breaking of the impasse over the NPP, we now consider more generally its role in helping us regain some theological balance in our orthodoxy. [81]

Viewed broadly, union with Christ is two-sided. On the one side, there is Christ's incarnational union with us in our humanity (Heb. 2:14-18), and his representational union with our race as the second or last Adam (Rom. 5:12-21; 1 Cor. 15:45-49). On the other, there is the believer's pneumatological union with Christ. This is both mystical or definitive (1 Cor. 1:9, 6:7; Eph. 5:30), and spiritual or progressive (Jn. 15:1-8; Rom. 6:3-4; Gal. 2:20; Col. 3:1).

---

[80] Witsius, *The Economy of the Covenants*, 1:316.

[81] Adolf Deissmann attributes the neglect of union with Christ to a doctrinaire approach to Pauline studies that characterized nineteenth-century scholarship. He claims that Pauline scholars focused on the apostle's fight against the law, on justification, redemption, and "almost anything else," except union with Christ (*The Religion of Jesus and the Faith of Paul: The Selly Oak Lectures, 1923 on the Communion of Jesus with God and the Communion of Paul with Christ*, second ed. [New York: George H. Doran, 1926], 154, 202). Muller laments that in the recovery of union with Christ in studies of historical theology, emphasis is placed on Calvin to the downplaying of the theme in the writings of other Reformers and later Reformed theological writings. He aids the recovery by tracing the theme onwards from Calvin and other influences such as Pierre Viret, Peter Martyr Vermigli, and Wolfgang Musculus (*Calvin and the Reformed Tradition*, 202–41).

It is especially pneumatological union in its mystical or definitive facet that interests us here, for several reasons.

First, pneumatological union helps us understand the balance between the objective and subjective aspects of the gospel. That is to say, between what Christ has accomplished for his people once-for-all, and what we experience due to his accomplishment. We seek not to play down the work of Christ for us, but to play up the work of the Spirit in us. In so doing, we accord fresh justice to the theme of union with Christ and safeguard the benefits we receive in him.

When we understand the saving benefits of Christ to be grounded in our union with Christ, we nullify the charge that justification (notably the double imputation at its heart) is but a legal fiction and that adoption is, to quote Palmer's depiction of the charge, but a "paper-money adoption . . . want[ing] a silver or gold one."[82] We are, let us remember, justified *in Christ*, adopted *in him*, and, yes, sanctified *in him*, too. Writes Calvin:

> We do not contemplate him [Christ] outside ourselves from afar in order that his righteousness may be imputed to us, but because we put on Christ and are engrafted into his body—in short, because he deigns to make us one with him. For this reason we glory that we have fellowship of righteousness with him.[83]

Second, pneumatological union helps us to mediate today's division over the doctrine of justification. Whereas Wright prefers to deal with the charge of a legal fiction by redefining justification, those criticizing his approach too often overlook the need to rebalance the objective and subjective. They, thus, render ineffective their defense of justification.

More promising is Kevin Vanhoozer's interaction with Wright, for he understands how critical it is to respond to him on the basis of Scripture rather than of tradition. He distinguishes, accordingly,

---

[82] Palmer, *Scheeben's Doctrine of Divine Adoption*, 183.

[83] *Inst.* 3:11:10.

Wright's strengths (chiefly his affirmation of the Protestant principle of *sola Scriptura*) from his weaknesses (notably his denial of God's gracious justification of sinners by the merit of Christ).

Specifically, Vanhoozer sees in Michael Bird's idea of "incorporated righteousness" a way of mediating between two views of God's declaration in justifying sinners. In the one, the minimalist view and the one described as a legal fiction or a "conjuring trick with words," God solely declares that those resting in Christ are righteous. In the other, the maximalist view, the claim is made that something ontological or transformative occurs in the declaration. Emerging through the middle, the idea of incorporated righteousness seeks to uphold the classic emphasis in justification on the forensic (the imagery of the law court), but also, in adding the adjective *incorporated*, to uphold the believer's participation in Christ.[84]

Vanhoozer opines that the "incorporated righteousness" may not yet be the formula to succeed in procuring reconciliation within Protestantism, yet his pressing for the retrieval of union with Christ is significant. Not only does "in Christ" occur 150 times in Paul's corpus, it reminds us of Calvin's use of *unio cum Christo* to hold together the distinct but inseparable forensic (justification) and transformative (sanctification) elements of the gospel. Since justification and sanctification both flow from union with Christ, it is impossible to enjoy a oneness with the Savior without being both justified *and* sanctified. Writes Vanhoozer, "Calvin's 'double grace' of union with Christ approaches what I mean by 'incorporated righteousness.'" "By partaking of [Christ]," says Calvin, "we principally receive a double grace: namely, that being reconciled [justified] to God through Christ's

---

[84] Kevin J. Vanhoozer, "Wrighting the Wrongs of the Reformation? The State of the Union with Christ in St. Paul and Protestant Soteriology," Nicholas Perrin and Richard B. Hays, Eds., *Jesus, Paul, and the People of God: A Theological Dialogue with N. T. Wright* (Downers Grove, IL: IVP Academic, 2011), 239, 241, 243, 247–59 (especially 248–49, 254).

blamelessness, we may have in heaven instead of a Judge a gracious Father; and, secondly, that sanctified by Christ's Spirit we may cultivate blamelessness and purity of life."[85]

Given all this, we have no need to choose which to emphasize, union with Christ or justification. Both are critical to soteriology. Whereas the former constitutes the main holding walls, the latter speaks of vital features hanging from them.[86] "Justification," says Bird,

> cannot be played off against union with Christ, since justification transpires in Christ. To be sure union with Christ is not something that is entirely synonymous with justification. Yet neither is union with Christ an ancillary concept subsumed under justification or *vice versa*. Rather, union with Christ comprises Paul's prime way of talking about the reception of the believer's new status through incorporation into the risen Christ by faith.

Bird's view has historical antecedence: "The genuine opinion of the Reformed is this," to quote Witsius, "that faith justifies, as it is the bond of our strictest union with Christ, by which all things that are Christ's become also ours."[87]

Union with Christ safeguards, then, respective Protestant and Catholic/Orthodox concerns: the freeness of the grace of justification and the importance of renovation. The same faith that unites us to

---

[85] *Inst.* 3:11:1 [*CO* 2 (30): 533]; cf., *Inst.* 3:16:1 [*CO* 2 (30): 586] and Randall C. Zachman, (*The Assurance of Faith: Conscience in the Theology of Martin Luther and John Calvin* [Minneapolis: Fortress Press, 1993], 189; see also 11, 188, and 204).

[86] *Cf.* Calvin, *Inst.* 3:11:10 and 3:16:1. Nonetheless, the phrase "in Christ" is much more frequent in Paul than objective references to Christ being "for us" (see Ridderbos, *When the Time had Fully Come*, 44–60). Paul makes profuse use of the formulae "in Christ," "with Christ," "through Christ," "of Jesus Christ," "in the blood of Christ," "in the name of Christ," "Christ in me" (see Deissmann, *The Religion of Jesus and the Faith of Paul*, 162, 171–80).

[87] Michael F. Bird, "Incorporated righteousness: A Response to Recent Evangelical Discussion concerning the Imputation of Christ's Righteousness in Justification," *JETS* 47:2 (June 2004), 275; Witsius, *The Economy of the Covenants*, 1:415.

Christ also justifies us, and the union that promises us justification promises us sanctification. Thus, we are justified through faith alone (solafideanism), yet never by a faith that remains alone. We are saved, says Benjamin Warfield, not out of works, but unto them.[88]

Third, pneumatological union helps us to do justice to the relationship between justification and adoption, for both spring simultaneously from the believer's union with Christ. While justification remains, of course, indispensable to soteriology, in the new biblical dogmatic it overshadows neither union with Christ nor other models of the union. Due attention to union with Christ also overhauls the perception that justification is temporally or logically priority to adoption, free to absorb it (à la Turretin, Dabney, Wright, et al.), or to be subsumed under adoption (as per A. A. Hodge, Lloyd-Jones, and Garner).

As distinct but inseparable models, justification and adoption serve to highlight complementary aspects of our salvation. Justification addresses the retrospective facts of personal sin, divine condemnation, and the standing of the sinner. Adoption depicts our new standing, its privileges (assurance, liberty, the household, and the inheritance) and its responsibility (obedience). The one model is chiefly legal, the other primarily relational. Justification takes us deeper into the heart of the gospel, but adoption takes us to its heights.

Palmer's comparison of justification and adoption, although citing Webb's more propositional or Westminster mode of reference, is nevertheless apposite:

---

[88] B. B. Warfield uses the term in contradistinction from Ethicism (justification by works) ("The Alien Righteousness," *Faith and Life* first published, 1916 [Carlisle, PA: The Banner of Truth Trust, 1974], 324). Elsewhere, he states: "Justification by Faith . . . is not to be set in contradiction to justification by Works. It is set in contradiction only to justification by our own works. It is justification by Christ's Works." ("Justification by Faith, Out of Date" in *Selected Shorter Writings of Benjamin B. Warfield—I,* ed. John E. Meeter (Phillipsburg, NJ: P&R, 1970), 283).

> Justification is that act of grace whereby we sinful subjects of God's government are received into the number of, and given a right and title to, all the privileges of the kingdom of God. Adoption is that act of grace, whereby we fallen sinners are received into the number of, and are given all the rights and privileges of, the sons of God.[89]

James Buchanan focuses on how adoption moves us beyond the realm of justification, yet without jettisoning its crucial importance:

> This closer and more endearing relation to God, which is constituted by Adoption, is necessary, in addition to that which is included in our Justification, to complete the view of our Christian privileges, and to enhance our enjoyment of them, by raising us above "the spirit of bondage, which is unto fear," and cherishing "the spirit of adoption, whereby we cry, Abba, Father." It is necessary, also, to explain how the sins of believers are not visited with penal afflictions properly so called, but are nevertheless treated in the way of fatherly chastisement; and, still further, to show that the kingdom of heaven hereafter will not be bestowed as wages for work done, but as an "inheritance," freely bestowed on those, and those only, who are "joint-heirs with Christ."[90]

Fourth, pneumatological union leads us to probe further the connection between adoption and union with Christ. Throughout we have claimed that adoption, like justification and sanctification, is grounded in union with Christ, but there is a school of thought which implies that adoption is solely a metaphorical expression of pneumatological union and not rather or additionally a benefit of the union.

Intensifying the conundrum is the uncertainty as to why Calvin writes of the benefits of union with Christ in terms of a *duplex* rather than a *triplex gratia Dei*. The mystery is exacerbated by his couching of the double grace of justification and sanctification in filial or familial terms. Having pondered this elsewhere, I am of the view that the matter

---

[89] Palmer, *Scheeben's Doctrine of Divine Adoption*, 167.

[90] James Buchanan, *The Doctrine of Justification: An Outline of its History in the Church and of its Exposition from Scripture*. First published 1867. Facsimile reprint ed. (Carlisle, PA: The Banner of Truth Trust, 1991), 263–64.

either needs further study or that Calvin himself was uncertain. Notes John Leith, Calvin

> wrote his theology with great intensity and depth of feeling. His gifts for language and for logical, orderly thought gave his writings a 'finished' quality that belies the intensity and haste with which they were written. Yet students of Calvin's theology have detected a lack of precision in definition and a failure to work through some theological problems that would require later attention. Luther, Calvin, and most of the early reformers were first of all preachers. They were not academic theologians, and their work reflects the needs of the congregation, not the concerns of the scholar as such.

Calvin, then, is not that helpful in resolving why he wrote specifically of a *duplex gatia Dei*. This vindicates Wright's observation that there is no pure return to the Reformation. We must return, rather, to Scripture.[91]

The question as to whether adoption is a powerful expression of union with Christ and/or one of its benefits is not easy to answer. Clearly, adoption *is* a metaphorical expression of union with Christ. First, because there is no adoptive sonship outside of the Son. As we have seen, Paul's filial language is, in contrast to John's, intended to draw together the sons and the Son. When the Father places us in his household (Eph. 2:19), he does so only because of his *a priori* placement of us in the relation of sons. Second, it seems that whereas the union between Christ and his people functions as the bare concept, adoption colors the concept metaphorically. The language of union can only tell us *that* we are one with the Son of God. It is the garb of adoption that tells us *how*.

Since, then, adoption is fundamentally a metaphorical expression of union with Christ, why also refer to it as a benefit of the union?

---

[91] Tim J. R. Trumper, "An Historical Study of the Doctrine of Adoption in the Calvinistic Tradition," 135–37. John H. Leith, *Introduction to the Reformed Tradition: A Way of Being the Christian Community*, Revised ed. (Atlanta: John Knox Press, 1981), 116–17. It could be said that the WCF contains a *triplex gratia dei*: justification, adoption, and sanctification. Cf., Calvin's comments in *Inst.* 3:11:1 with WCF 11–13 and LC 69.

First, because the former view does not invalidate the latter. Note that the adoption texts speak to our union with the Son, but also to so much more beside. Writes Constantine Campbell:

> While adoption is no doubt an important concept in Paul's thought (see Rom. 8:15, 23; 9:4; Gal. 4:5; Eph. 1:5) and must be *conceptually* related to union with Christ, there is only one instance in which it is *explicitly* connected to the language of union—Ephesians 1:5, which states that adoption occurs *through* Christ (*dia 'Iēsou Christou*). This would suggest that adoption—like blessings, redemption, and forgiveness—is received *through* our union with Christ, but it is not what union with Christ *is*.[92]

Specifically, the adoption texts place the believer's immediate union with the Son in the broader salvation-historical context. Adoption, we have seen, has relevance to the entirety of the history of salvation, from the first things to the last things. Moreover, the adoption texts speak of both the adoptive act (the Father's placement of us in the Son) and the believer's adoptive state. There is in adoption, then, a spiritual largesse that cannot be adequately expressed by the immediacy of our union and communion with the Son. By the Father's placement of us in the Son (the adoptive act) we gain not only a relationship to the Son, but through the Son a relationship to the Father. Yet, by introducing us through the adoptive act into the adoptive state (the life of sonship), we receive all the privileges and obligations of the sons of God. This takes us far beyond the immediacy of the union and communion with Christ.

Suffice it to say, that such is the richness of adoption that we may refer to it as *both* a powerful metaphorical expression of union with Christ *and* as a benefit of union with Christ. In fact, we diminish adoption when we curtail its scope and ramifications to the immediacy of our union and communion with Christ. This we cannot do, for we

---

[92] Constantine R. Campbell, *Paul and Union with Christ: An Exegetical and Theological Study* (Grand Rapids: Zondervan, 2012), 407fn.

have no remit to crop the scope of adoption, either salvation-historically or spiritually.

4. The balancing of our view of salvation received.

In the space afforded in the new dogmatic for the full scope of adoption, there is both acknowledgment and rectification of the heavily westernized or individualized appropriation of salvation. I do not imply by this that classic systematics have no doctrine of the church. After all, the discussion of salvation came into its own during the Protestant Reformation precisely for her sake. The reformers sought to ensure that church members knew the answer to Job's question, "How can a man be in the right before God?" (Job 9:2), and debated vigorously issues related to the church, such as the marks or *signa* of the true church, her sacraments, and so forth.

Baptism is particularly significant, for it is the symbol of our entrance into the covenant community of God's people. It was viewed by Calvin as the *symbolum adoptionis*. The WLC (Ans. 165) later confirmed this view, stating that baptism is "a sign and seal of ingrafting into himself, of remission of sins by his blood, and regeneration by his Spirit; *of adoption*, and resurrection unto everlasting life" (italics inserted). By contrast, Calvin understood the Lord's Supper to depict the continuation of union with Christ.[93] He pictured it as a lavish banquet laid on by the Father for his children. By partaking in faith, God's sons remember the Lord, are raised to heaven to eat of Christ's flesh and to drink of his blood, and to receive thereby the grace that sustains their union with the Savior. In the words of the WCF, the Supper is for our "spiritual nourishment and growth in [Christ]" (29:1; cf., WLC 168). There, however, the cannibalistic overtones of Calvin's

---

[93] John Calvin, "Catechism of the Church in Geneva" (1545), in *Calvin's Selected Works*, vol. 2 (Grand Rapids: Baker Book House, 1983), 86, 92–93 [*CO* 6:116–17, 132]; Ronald S. Wallace, *Calvin's Doctrine of the Word and Sacrament* (Edinburgh: Scottish Academic Press, 1995), 150.

imagery are toned down: "Worthy receivers," it is said, eat both outwardly and inwardly, "really and indeed, yet not carnally nor corporally, but spiritually, receive and feed upon Christ crucified, and all benefits of his death" (WCF 29:7).

The two sacraments complement each other. While entrance into a relationship with God is immensely personal, the relationship brings the believer into communion not only with the Trinity but with the church, the household of God. As we might expect in this regard, more communal implications of adoption are found in Calvin than in Luther. Yet, the loss of adoption in the centuries subsequent to the Westminster Assembly led also to the loss within the Reformed tradition of the flavoring of the sacraments and of the church as a family banquet. Add to this loss the prevalence of Western individualism and we may readily understand how Protestant perceptions of the gospel became lopsidedly individualistic.

It is against this backdrop that Wright has attempted the creation of a more corporate definition of justification: "God's declaration that we are members of the covenant family." I reject this proposal because it is adoption that facilitates the balancing of the individual and communal implications of the gospel. Adoption rightly expounded grants Wright his wish list—the story of Israel, God's faithfulness to his covenant, and a more corporate understanding of the gospel. Yet it does so without shedding any of the Reformation's advances in understanding justification.

Metaphors (read models) like adoption, writes Heim, "are particularly well-suited to creating a particular ethos and identity for a community, especially when they are integrated into a community's distinctive vocabulary." She continues, "when a metaphor is used repeatedly to describe a shared experience of a community, or when it becomes part of a community's vocabulary, it exerts a subtle yet profound influence over the community's understanding of its identity."[94] Indeed, the adoption model was introduced into Christian thought precisely to demonstrate how God has brought Jews and Gentiles together as his sons under one roof. Our integration is, then, what distinguishes the household of God from the household of the living dead. It does so more than we realize and less so than we would wish. It is in practicing the gospel that we reach out most effectively to the world with its "broken families and disrupted relationships, [for the] masses seek for a sense of belonging and intimate, personal, and family relations."[95]

Adoption inspires, accordingly, a plethora of communal applications, but we limit ourselves to two of the more obvious.

First, the model reminds us that every son of God entering the household was once a slave. The form of enslavement may differ, but not the reality of it. Some receive the grace of adoption from very obvious enslavements, having been held hostage to today's vast array of idols such as sex, sport, celebrity culture, entertainment, secular rationalism, and religious tradition. Others are rescued by adoptive grace from "respectable" enslavements to gossip, slander, conceit, covetousness, jealousy, envy, and so forth. Both forms of enslavement lead to emptiness, isolation, shame, and marginalization.

By contrast, our redemption by the precious blood of Christ and our adoption by the grace of our heavenly *paterfamilias* introduces us to a household marked, ideally, by grace, love, inclusion, and fellowship. Within it the adopted enjoy equal standing. We live together on the same floor, simultaneously erstwhile slaves and coheirs with the Son. We are united in our shared experiences of slavery, our shared

---

[94] Erin Heim, "Light through a Prism: New Avenues of Inquiry for the Pauline Υἱοθεσία Metaphors," (Ph.D. Diss.: University of Otago, Dunedin, New Zealand, 2014), 88, 95.

[95] Douglas F. Kelly, "Adoption: An Underdeveloped Heritage of the Westminster Standards," *Reformed Theological Review* 52:3 (Sept.–Dec. 1993), 114; Errol Hulse, "Recovering the Doctrine of Adoption" (*Reformation Today* 105 [1988]), 14.

dependence on the Son's redemption, our shared receipt of the Father's adoption, and our shared experience of the Spirit's indwelling.

This backdrop to adoptive sonship calls for a widespread realignment of popular treatments of adoption. The notion of adoption from orphanhood conflates two separate ideas in Scripture. Simply put, orphanhood is not the condition or situation Paul's model of adoption addresses. Orphanhood neither figures in adoption nor does it convey the bondage, fear, and shame entailed in the idea of slavery. Thus, the mantra "We were orphans, but are now adopted sons of God!", while a nice thought, is, to be honest, eisegetical. It is a reading of the New Testament's filial imagery through the lens of the contemporary plight of orphans. Popular expositions of adoption need a greater exegetical acumen, the sort typified by the line of Placide Cappeau (1808–77), author of the Cantique de Noël ("O Holy Night"): "Chains shall He [Christ] break for the slave is our brother."

None of this, however, ought to be read as a denigration of orphan care. The Bible places much weight on orphan care. King David took solace in the thought that the Lord takes in those whom father and mother desert (Ps. 27:10). Jesus promised us that in returning to heaven he would not leave us as (spiritual) orphans (Jn. 14:18). His half brother James taught that religion which is pure and undefiled before God, the Father (καὶ πατρὶ), includes "visit[ing] orphans and widows in their affliction" (Jas. 1:27). The present infinitive of the verb ἐπισκέπτομαι (ἐπισκέπτεσθαι) could be read to understand James envisioning the adopting of orphans, since the verb includes "to select" among its range of meanings. More likely, though, James was more informally urging the church to watch out for orphans for their comfort and relief. The infinitive implies a continuous action and fits better than the definitive act of adopting (unless multiple adoptions are in view).

Today's adoption of orphans constitutes, then, an incidental application of Scripture rather than one that is demanded by the text. Certainly, orphan care is a nonnegotiable of pure religion, but the adoption of orphans is a matter of divine calling or liberty of conscience. After all, when God adopted us, he did so not because he had to, but because he was free to and had the ability to provide for all whom he adopted. If we compel Christians to adopt, we lose sight of the archetypal grace of God's adoption.

Second, the model addresses today's segregation. Although a "Hebrew of the Hebrews" by background and former religion, Paul understood that God was building a household in which there is neither Jew nor Greek, slave nor free, male nor female. All are one in Christ and are heirs together with him (Gal. 3:28-29; Rom. 8:17). This is why we read nothing in the New Testament of either the planting or acceptance of willfully segregated churches. Yet, the apostle also fought against a view of God's household in which Jewish believers would remain culturally dominant. The Judaizers, by contrast, were prepared to admit Gentiles into the covenant community so long as they became like Jews.

Today's "Judaizers" tend to be more moderate. They may not say that those of different ethnicities or economic strata have to be like them to be saved, yet they are well capable of resisting crosscultural outreach and of emitting unwelcoming vibes to those reached who wish to take their place in the church family. Where a monocultural dominance in church life is subtly safeguarded or blatantly insisted on, typically by prioritizing personal or cultural preferences over biblical principle, there the Judaizing spirit prevails and the implications of adoption are denied.

The retrieval of adoption offers the church, notably in America, and without any capitulation to the critical race theory, a wonderful opportunity to rethink its acceptance of segregation and monocultural dominance. Christ has brought us near to God and to one another by his shed blood. Having broken down the middle wall of partition separating Jews and Gentiles, he surely frowns on convenient claims that the church is unable to tackle incipient ethnic or economic snobbery. We begin to counter such thinking not by signing up to the critical race theory's increasingly obvious reverse form of racism, but by recognizing that believers are one household no matter our background, and that the free grace of adoption is a strong cohesive against Satan's endeavors to undermine the contrast between the households of the living lively and the living dead.

5. The balancing of our view of salvation lived.

The retrieval of adoption affords us, furthermore, the opportunity to balance the retrospective and prospective aspects of the gospel. This balance could have been recovered in the early nineteenth century had there been a more constructive response to McLeod Campbell's protest for paternal grace. Our forebears need not have capitulated to MacLeod Campbell's rejection of a penal view of atonement, or to his belief that assurance is of the essence of the faith, to rescue the balance of the retrospective (what we are saved *from*) and prospective aspects (what we are saved *to*, namely, a life of sonship) of the atonement.

How true it is that we see the faults of others better than our own. Even today, there are Reformed-orthodox denominations in which a majority of communicant members refrain from coming to the Lord's Table for want of personal assurance of faith. Supposedly a sign of humility, this act of omission denies the sufficiency of Christ's merit and is disobedient to his explicit command that believers partake of his supper. Yet, since the phenomenon is found in both continental Reformed and Presbyterian circles, it cannot be reliably attributed to the Westminster Standards. Nor should it be attributed to the doctrine of particular redemption.[96]

---

[96] I do not recognize the neoorthodox claim that Calvinists believing in particular redemption are forever asking themselves how they can know they are among the elect. Every Christian struggles with assurance at some point or in some way (otherwise we would be walking by sight rather than by faith). Nevertheless, God has given us a

The phenomenon is better explained by the ongoing want of attention to the prospective aspects of the gospel. This has been demonstrated rather poignantly by Jack Millers' late twentieth-century Sonship Discipleship Course. Note the parallels between the two protests:

- Both were reactions against the retrospective and juridical lopsidedness of Presbyterian theology.
- Both understood the significance of the familial or filial emphases of the New Testament for the countering of joylessness and doubt. "Our goals will be communicated," wrote the Millers, "through the vehicle of one very central and exciting biblical image which embodies all that we are and have in Christ as believers: that of adoption and our resulting "sonship."[97]
- Both were influenced by Luther's Commentary on Galatians. I suspect that neither John McLeod Campbell nor Miller expected to find much on sonship in the writings of Calvin.[98]
- Both protests were correct in principle, but aberrant in their detail.
- Both protests were opposed but failed to see the kernel of truth

---

primary basis of assurance in the person and work of Christ (as applied to us by the Spirit), and a secondary ground of assurance in the fruit of Christ-centered obedience.

[97] *Sonship: Discovering Liberty in the Gospel as Sons and Daughters of God* (Jenkintwon, PA: World Harvest Mission [now Serge], v.

[98] Douglas Kelly may well be alluding to Miller's want of attention to Calvin when commenting: "In this book [Rose Marie Miller, *From Fear to Freedom*] and in their teaching about Sonship, Jack and Rose Marie Miller are developing and applying the most authentic aspect of Calvin's theology concerning the Christian life: union with Christ as adopted sons and daughters." (Rose Marie Miller, *From Fear to Freedom: Living as Sons and Daughters of God* [Wheaton, IL: Harold Shaw Publishers, 1994], front pages).

they conveyed.[99]

As needed as were these protests, in neither Campbell nor Miller do we find a reliable exegeting of the distinctive structures of the various filial or familial models of the New Testament. Whereas Campbell says very little of adoption *in se*, Miller mentions it frequently but blurs the content of the model through the infusion of unwarranted references to orphanhood. Lesson one of *Sonship* begins, for instance, with three quotations from Galatians, and then adds:

> The theme of these Scriptures is this: You are no longer a slave, by the power of the Cross, which alone deserves glory, because it alone can change you from being a slave, or an orphan, into a son. The key question, in a practical way, from Galatians is: "What has happened to all your joy?" Galatians 4:15.

In our retrieving of adoption—not in reaction but on account of its intrinsic worth—we need to say something of the prospective life of sonship, notably its freedom. If we understand that freedom to be absolute, then it becomes indistinguishable from the anarchy that enslaves and from which we need to be redeemed. If, conversely, our freedom is negligible—does not Paul say that, as sons of God, we are as obedient slaves who must present our members to God as instruments for righteousness? (Rom. 6:13, 16)—then what is it in the life of adoptive sonship which brings us joy and peace?

Our freedom in Christ is neither absolutist nor negligible. It is real but structured. "Thanks be to God," writes Paul, "that you who were once slaves of sin, have become obedient from the heart to the standard of teaching to which you were committed" (Rom. 6:17). In other words, we are no longer condemned by the moral law, for Christ has suffered the due penalty of death in our place (justification). Nor are we bound by the ceremonial law, for Christ has fulfilled its purpose (adoption).

---

[99] For a fuller unpacking of these points, see Tim J. R. Trumper, *When History Teaches Us Nothing: The Recent Reformed Sonship Debate in Context* (Eugene, OR: Wipf and Stock, 2008), 33–53.

Nevertheless, the moral law shapes our liberty in Christ as the sons of God, for our freedom is *from* sin not *to* sin.

We navigate, then, between the antinomian who denies the law's role in structuring our liberty and the legalist who would destroy it. Christ is critical to this navigation. By his life he not only procured our righteousness and offered himself up for our redemption, he provided us with a wonderful example of how to live lives of gratitude as sons of the Father. He kept the law not by fixating on rules and regulations, but out of delight in pleasing his Father and in redeeming slaves. That is the spirit of our freedom. It is because we delight in our Father that we keep his law. Our obedience, then, is born of love and not of slavish fear. Love helps us to resolve the tension between the indicative ("I am an adopted son!") and the imperative ("I am to present myself to my Father as an obedient slave!").

In Romans 6:17, Paul thus reflects John's remark that God's "commandments are not burdensome" (1 Jn. 5:3). While we are not saved by emulating Christ's example, those redeemed by him certainly emulate his delight in obeying the Father. To quote Isaac Watts (1674–1748):

> My dear Redeemer and my Lord,
> I read my duty in Thy Word;
> But in Thy life the law appears
> Drawn out in living characters.

Stated in trinitarian terms, we love our Father, seeking to please him; our older brother, patterning our lives after his; and the Spirit, too, dancing to his tune.

In balancing the retrospective and prospective aspects of the gospel, we also balance the juridical and the familial. While God's sons and daughters are no longer under the condemnation or dominion of law (Rom. 6:14; 8:1), our Father guides us into holiness within the sphere and atmosphere of our Father-son relationship. Not now as Israel under the old covenant beset by all the minutia of ceremonial rules and regulations appropriate to a son underage, but as the mature new Israel, taught of the Father to regulate ourselves by the precepts of the Word and the prompting of the Spirit.

We have no need, then, of pitting love and law against each other, nor indeed the law and the Spirit of sonship. Since love and law are compatible within a domestic household, why are there those who think that they are contradictory in the household of God? We maintain, rather, that in the new covenant era the freedom of God's sons and daughters coincides with the ministry of the Spirit of adoption. Our liberty is sustained not by Satan who drives our flesh to sin, but by the Spirit who applies the Word to our lives. While we have sought, then, to go deeper into the theology of adoption, we seek to maintain the Puritan, Methodist, and Brethren emphasis on the Spirit of adoption.

How we need to be filled with the Spirit today! "What a change would come over the face of Christendom," A. B. Bruce surmised in 1894, "if the Spirit of adoption were poured out in abundant measure on all who bear the Christian name!"[100] While history indicates that such an outpouring is not dependent on the retrieval of adoption, a more mature understanding of the grace of adoption should certainly encourage prayer amid God's household for a greater measure of the Spirit of adoption, as was experienced in bygone revivals.

6. The balancing of our view of salvation consummated.

Ultimately, our hope is found not in the life of sonship in the here and now, nor in the revival of the household of God, but in the return of the Lord Jesus. Just as Christ came two millennia ago in "the fullness of time" (Gal. 4:4), so he shall return in "the fullness of time" {Eph. 1:10}. His second advent will fulfill the fullness of new covenant adoption, for it will occasion the redemption of our bodies (Rom. 8:23) and the publication across the cosmos of the news of our adoption.

---

[100] A. B. Bruce, *St. Paul's Conception of Christianity* (Edinburgh: T&T Clark, 1894), 203–4.

While the consummation of adoption contrasts markedly with the locating of the gospel by John Gill and Abraham Kuyper in eternity past,[101] it ought not to be thought to corroborate fully the NPP's locating of the gospel in eternity future. Just as we have cautioned against the "then" but "no moreness" of those preoccupied with Adam, so we must warn against a "not yet" but "not now" perspective that undermines our present possession of adoption. A true salvation-historical perspective does justice to the "then," the "now," and the "not yetness" of the gospel. The adopted who were chosen in Christ in eternity past, receive their adoption *in transitu* through faith in Christ, and shall go on to experience its consummation throughout eternity future (Rom. 8:18-23).

I make this point for several reasons. Notably, because the discussion of heaven typically falls short of the vision of Scripture. Listen to many a sermon, read many a book on heaven, and you might be forgiven for thinking that heaven in its intermediate state (the paradise into which believers enter through death, cf., Lk. 23:43) is the climactic *terminus ad quem* of New Testament hope. Thus, pastors kneel beside the emaciated bodies of their members, whether riddled with cancer, succumbing to heart disease, or just wrinkled with old age, and assure the dying, "Take heart! Soon you will be with Christ!" Now this is a wonderful truth, but it is a half-truth. The better half for sure, but so much less than what God has revealed. The redeemer of our souls, with whom we fellowship immediately upon death, is the one who is yet to come to redeem our bodies also.

When, conversely, pastors grasp the fullness of adoptive grace, they kneel at the bedside of the dying, assuring those in Christ that not only will they soon be in his presence, but that the Father who sent

---

[101] We touched on Gill's view in ch. 1. See Abraham Kuyper's *The Work of the Holy Spirit*, transl. Henri De Vries; originally published, 1900 (Chattanooga, TN: AMG, 1995), 389; cf., 390.

Christ to redeem their souls has promised to send him again to redeem their bodies from death. In the adoption they already possess, they have experienced the firstfruits of the Spirit. In its fulfillment, they will experience the full harvest of his ministry. That is what it will take to raise our bodies from the hold of death and of the grave.

It has always been the Father's end goal that we should live with Christ psychosomatically. Moreover, that we should live in the glorious freedom of our new wholeness, on a redeemed earth. Our hope, then, is as tangible as it is psychic, and is the fulfillment of the promise given to Abraham and received in Christ, that the adopted should be coheirs with him "of the world" (Rom. 4:13). Our inheritance is, accordingly, very literal. While we hear little in the church of the new earth as our inheritance, it is no less the teaching of Scripture for that. Yet, unlike any other inheritances we may receive, this inheritance is given to us by our Father who yet remains alive. The sharing of the inheritance is, accordingly, his delight. He has foreordained it and shall observe it eternally as the undying and undiminished fount of life and blessedness.

Our talk of heaven needs, then, to catch up with Scripture's more tangible and glorious depiction of heaven in its consummated state. Heaven in its final state is the grand and glorious fulfillment of the inheritance first promised to Abraham. As possessors of the inheritance, we shall eternally enjoy God and his presence, doing so on a new earth, and in possession of redeemed bodies.

Given this, we close our time together with an instance of how theology touches life, desiring not only to teach a doctrine of the consummation but to offer a glimpse into how it has touched my life. It was, after all, in a moment of crisis that I came to see how practical the hope of adoption can be.

Four months had passed in 1999 since arriving in America from my native United Kingdom. Unbeknownst to me, my father back in Wales was brought very rapidly to the brink of death. If he had not been at his hospital cancer checkup when a burning sensation surged through his head, he would have died. In the next moments, he found himself confessing his sins and praying for our family, expecting to be taken home within moments. As his life hung in the balance, the hospital staff rushed to him to perform a full resuscitation. He remained on death's door for an hour and a half, long enough for the family to gather at his hospital bed. Only late in the day, collecting a voicemail from my mother, did I learn of the emergency. I recall her words: "The next seventy-two hours are critical."

Lying in bed that night with my mind spinning, feeling helpless three-thousand miles from my family, it was the truth of bodily redemption which God used to flood my heart with peace and to grant me sweet rest that night. "If Dad dies before I awake," God helped me to reason, "I will see him again. Not ultimately in a celestial heaven, but gloriously and psychosomatically liberated on the new earth—no [pneumonia, as it turned out], no cancer, none of the humiliation and paraphernalia that goes with M.S., no inhaler for his asthma, no glasses, or hearing aids!"

Dad survived and so did that vision of the new earth, the inheritance of the family of God. Fifteen years later, reading the Scriptures to him as he lay dying of another cancer, Multiple Myeloma, the thought was still on my mind: "Dad, won't it be wonderful to receive your redeemed body!" I didn't need to press home his upcoming entrance into the presence of Christ—"'Christ Is All' Colossians 3:11" were the first words he chose for his funeral bulletin. But I was keen to assure him in his final days, after a quarter of a century of being homebound, as I am to comfort us in these final moments together, that our adoption by the Father is only consummated when our bodies, by the fullest fullness of the Spirit, are redeemed by the returning Son.

What a day that will be! Indeed, to quote a forged decretal of Pontianus, Bishop of the Roman Church (230–35), we "sigh[] after [and seek] the true fatherland."[102] It is our inheritance and eternal home—the gift of the Father's lavish grace in Christ. We are never to forget, though, that our chief and unending delight will ever be the Father, the Son, and the Holy Spirit. Whether or not, then, we get to see on this earth the retrieval of adoption—the doctrine fitting fully and snugly in a fresh biblical dogmatic—we are assured, through faith in Christ, that we shall get to see the consummation of adoption, both personally and communally as the household of God. We shall know it and feel it in our bodies as well as our souls.

How much more could be said! What better way to close our journey together than with the second-century *Gloria Patri*?

> Glory be to the Father,
> and to the Son,
> and to the Holy Ghost;
> as it was in the beginning,
> is now, and ever shall be,
> world without end.
> Amen, amen.

~~~~

---

[102] *A-N F* 8:622–23.

CLOSING HYMN

THE HOPE OF OUR ADOPTION
Mk. 14:36; Gal. 4:4-7; Eph. 2:1-5; Rom. 8:12-23.

1. We praise you God, in nature seen by all!
But, in your Word, re-vealed through Mark and Paul
—Christ, our brother, who's taught us to call:
Abba, Father! Abba, Father!

2. We praise you Christ, this evil sphere did brave,
Us to redeem, who badly do behave;
Children of wrath, who bound in sin did rave.
Blessèd Redeemer! Blessèd Redeemer!

3. Adopted now, by Father, God of love,
Placed in the Son, closer than hand in glove
The Spirit sheds abroad through Christ his love.
Wonderful Spirit! Wonderful Spirit!

4. Bondage now gone, no turning back to fear!
As sons we're free, as siblings drawn near,
From house of death for home of him so dear.
We're brothers and sisters! Brothers and sisters!

5. In the firstborn, we adopted have hope!
Through his raised life, we live rather than cope,
We're heirs with him, God's great estate to scope.
Come, then, Lord Jesus! Come, then, Lord Jesus!

6. On that great day, our bodies raised again,
No more sinning, no more pain!
Completely whole, on new earth to proclaim:
Father, Son, Spirit! Father, Son, Spirit!

Words: Tim J. R. Trumper, 2017
Tune: *Sine Nomine*, Ralph Vaughan Williams, 1906

The hymn was first sung at Little Farms Chapel (OPC), Coopersville, Michigan, during evening worship on February 6, 2022.

APPENDIX

SOCIO-THEOLOGICAL TENDENCIES
IN THE REFORMED TRADITION

REFORMED CONCERN ~	REVISIONIST REFORMED	CONSTRUCTIVE REFORMED	ORTHODOX REFORMED
A Classic Protestant Doctrine of Scripture: Holy Scripture is God's Word, divinely inspired and kept, infallible, possessing perfectly both divineness and humanness, being fully and finally authoritative for faith and conduct (see WCF I).	The revisionist Reformed have departed from classic Protestant doctrine, either by opting for neoorthodoxy (God's Word is in Scripture, but is errant) or, more radically, by becoming liberal (Scripture is a human document, in which the supernatural is explained away).	The constructive Reformed uphold the classic Protestant conviction that Scripture is God's Word, but point out that, as such, it possesses humanness as well as divineness. While the latter guides the interpretation of the former, the former, rightly handled, aids the defense of Scripture as God's infallible and fully authoritative Word.	The orthodox Reformed uphold the classic Protestant doctrine, but, going by Reformed systematics, so focus on its divineness (unity and doctrine) as to underplay its humanness (progressive revelation, genre, authorial diversity, and figures of speech).
Subordinate Standards:	The revisionist Reformed may formerly retain historic standards, but function with minimalist or broadly ecumenical standards.	The constructive Reformed sincerely adhere to the theology of Reformed standards, but advocate, where necessary, their reform (chiefly of their form and feel).	The orthodox Reformed sincerely adhere to the theology of the classic standards, satisfied with both their form and feel.

Confessional Subscription:	From a vague system subscription to no subscription at all.	Flexible-full subscription (leaving particulars to the judgment of a church judicatory).	Tending emotionaly toward "jot and tittle" subscription. Exceptions are discouraged.
Perception of the Relationship between Scripture and the historic Subordinate Standards:	A loose or selective affiliation.	The subordinate standards, understood to summarize biblical teaching, are nevertheless read through Scripture and are subject to biblical critique.	Subordinate standards, reflecting biblical teaching, may become a means of read-ing Scripture and are rarely critiqued.
Sample Voices: Voices tending toward the said categories. Clearly hybrid voices have been omitted.	John MacLeod Campbell, Karl Barth, Peter Forsyth, James and Thomas Torrance.	Johannes Cocceius, Geerhardus Vos, Herman Ridderbos, John Murray, Martyn Lloyd-Jones, R. B. Kuiper, Richard Gaffin, John Frame, Vern Poythress, Kevin Vanhoozer, A.T. B. McGowan.	Francis Turretin, Charles Hodge, R. L. Dabney, Louis Berkhof, Richard Muller, Morton Smith, Robert Godfrey, Joel Beeke, Darryl Hart.
Outlook on the tradition of Reformed theology:	Ranging from critically-sympathetic (neoorthodox) to outrightly critical (liberal).	Sympathetic-critical (in that order!). The constructive Reformed sense a call to enhance the inherited tradition of theology.	Uncritical. The orthodox Reformed sense a call to attract from outside the Reformed tradition.

Vision for the Future of the Reformed Tradition:	The revisionist Reformed focus more on broadly ecumenical relationships to the catholic church than on the recovery of classic Reformed doctrine and spirituality.	The constructive Reformed seek the renewal of Reformed orthodoxy via biblical creativity (methodological renewal, doctrinal enhancements), believing renewal to foster the best defense of and attraction to the Reformed faith.	The orthodox Reformed seek the consolidation of historic Reformed method and content, focusing on attracting newcomers to the Reformed faith from other Christian traditions.
Primary Challenges:	To retain any semblance of attachment to a Protestant doctrine of Scripture and to the historic Reformed faith.	To ensure that their sympathetic-critical outlook does not slide into one that is critical-sympathetic.	To resist equating history and tradition with Scripture, thus idolizing historic Reformed orthodoxy.
Locale:	Broad mainline denominations.	Individual advocates of biblical reform found chiefly in confessional, Presbyterian and continental-Reformed denominations.	Confessional Presbyterian and continental Reformed denominations, plus some independent Reformed congregations.

Nota bene: Drawn from trans-Atlantic observations over the last thirty years, the Appendix seeks not to magnify such variations in methods and attitudes, but to suggest how consensus around the exposition and retrieval of adoption can, with God's blessing, consolidate and enhance the espousal, promotion, and defense of Reformed orthodoxy. My desire, then, comports with Paul's, utilizing adoption to bring believers together, beginning with those of the Reformed tradition.

SELECT BIBLIOGRAPHY [1]

A

"A Reforming Catholic Confession" (www.reformingcatholicconfession.com/explanation/), accessed September 18, 2017.

Ames, William. *The Marrow of Theology*, transl. from the third Latin ed. (1629) by John Dykstra Eusden (Durham, North Carolina: The Labyrinth Press, 1968).

Ante-Nicene Fathers. Ten volumes, reprinted from the American edition (Christian Literature Publishing Company, 1885–87); fourth printing (Peabody, MA: Hendrickson, 2004).

Aquinas, Thomas. *Summa Contra Gentiles*, published in four books (five volumes), reprinted from *On the Truth of the Catholic Faith* (Hanover House, 1955); transl. Anton C. Pegis, James F. Anderson, Vernon J. Bourke, and Charles J. O'Neil (Notre Dame and London: University of Notre Dame Press, 1975).

_____ . *Summa Theologica*, Complete Edition in Five Volumes, transl. Fathers of the English Dominican Province; reprinted from the New York: Benziger Bros, 1948 (Allen, Texas: Christian Classics, 1981).

Arndt, William F. (Ed.). *A Greek-English Lexicon of the New Testament and other Early Christian Literature*, A translation and adaptation of Walter Bauer's Griechisch-Deutsches Wörterbuch zu den Schriften des Neuen Testaments und der übrigen urchristlichen Literatur, fourth revised and augmented edition, 1952 (Chicago: University of Chicago Press and Cambridge: Cambridge University Press, 1957).

Asselt, W. J. van (Ed., et al.). *Reformation and Scholasticism: An Ecumenical Enterprise*, (Grand Rapids: Baker Academic, 2001).

B

Barr, James. Abba' isn't 'Daddy,'" *Journal of Theological Studies* 39.1 (1988), 28–47.

Barrett, Michael P. V. *Complete in Him: A Guide to Understanding and Enjoying the Gospel* (Grand Rapids: Reformation Heritage Books, 2017).

---

[1] To aid the use of the Bibliography, note, first, that edited volumes are listed according to the (first) named editor. Second, in the cases of multi-authored volumes, the Bibliography lists only the volume and not the relevant chapters.

BIBLIOGRAPHY

Barth, Karl. *Church Dogmatics*, authorized English translation of *Die Kirchliche Dogmatik*, 1932–67 (Peabody, MA: Hendrickson, 2010).

Batteau, J. M. (Ed., et al.). *The Vitality of Reformed Theology: Proceedings of the International Theological Congress June 20–24th 1994, Noordwijkerhout, The Netherlands* (Kampen: Kok, 1994).

Bavinck, Herman. *Our Reasonable Faith: A Survey of Christian Doctrine*, transl. Henry Zylstra (Grand Rapids: Baker, 1977).

_____ . *Reformed Dogmatics*, in four vols. ed. by John Bolt and transl. from the *Gereformeerde Dogmatiek* by John Vriend, for the Dutch Reformed Translation Society (Grand Rapids: Baker Academic, 2003–8).

_____ . *The Doctrine of God*, transl., edited, and outlined by William Hendrickson; first edition, Eerdmans, 1951, reprinted (Edinburgh and Carlisle, PA: The Banner of Truth Trust, 1991).

Baxter, Richard. *The Saints' Everlasting Rest*, with an introductory essay by Thomas Erskine *Esq.*, 1824 (no other details are given).

Beker, Christiaan J. *The Apostle Paul: The Triumph of God in Light and Thought*, first published by Fortress Press, 1980 (Edinburgh: T&T Clark, 1989).

Beeke, Joel R. *Assurance of Faith: Calvin, English Puritanism, and the Dutch Second Reformation*, American University Studies (Series 7 Theology and Religion) vol. 89 (New York: Peter Lang, 1991).

_____ (Ed.) . *Calvin for Today* (Grand Rapids: Reformation Heritage Books, 2009).

_____. *Heirs with Christ: The Puritans on Adoption* (Grand Rapids: Reformation Heritage Books, 2008).

_____ (Ed.). *The Beauty and Glory of the Father* (Grand Rapids: Reformation Heritage Books, 2013).

Beeke, Joel R. and Jones, Mark. *A Puritan Theology: Doctrine for Life* (Grand Rapids: Reformation Heritage Books, 2012).

Beeke. Joel R. and Pederson, Randall J. *Meet the Puritans: With a Guide to Modern Reprints* (Grand Rapids: Reformation Heritage Books, 2006).

Berkhof, Louis. *A Summary of Christian Doctrine*, first published 1938 (Carlisle, PA: The Banner of Truth Trust, 1993).

_____. *Systematic Theology*, first British ed., 1958; reprint ed. (Carlisle, PA: The Banner of Truth Trust, 1974).

_____ . *The History of Christian Doctrines*, reprint ed. (Carlisle, PA: The Banner of Truth Trust, 1985).

Billings, J. Todd. *Union with Christ: Reframing Theology and Ministry for the Church* (Grand Rapids: Baker Academic, 2011).

Bird, Michael F. "Incorporated righteousness: A Response to Recent Evangelical Discussion concerning the Imputation of Christ's Righteousness in Justification," *JETS* 47:2 (June 2004), 253–75.

_____ . *Jesus The Eternal Son: Answering Adoptionist Christology* (Grand Rapids: Eerdmans, 2017).

Black, Max. *Models and Metaphors: Studies in Language and Philosophy* (Ithaca, NY, 1962).

Blaise, Albert. *Dictionnaire Latin-Français des Auteurs Chrétiens* (Paris: Librairie des Méridiens, 1954).

Blocher, Henri. "Biblical Metaphors and the Doctrine of the Atonement," *JETS* 47:4 (December 2004), 629–45.

Blunt, John H. (Ed.). *Dictionary of Doctrinal and Historical Theology*, second edition (London: Rivingtons, 1872).

Bobick, Michael W. *From Slavery to Sonship: A Biblical Psychology for Pastoral Counseling* (D. Min.: Westminster Theological Seminary, 1988).

Bonar, Horatius (Ed.). *Catechisms of the Scottish Reformation* (London: James Nisbet and Co., 1866).

Bonner, Gerald. "Augustine's Conception of Deification," *Journal of Theological Studies*, NS, 37 pt. 2 (Oct. 1986), 369–86.

Boyce, James Petigru. *Abstract of Systematic Theology*, reprint ed. (Lexington, Kentucky: publisher not given, 2012).

Boyd, Brady. *Sons and Daughters: Spiritual Orphans Finding Our Way Home* (Grand Rapids: Zondervan, 2012).

Brakel, Wilhelmus à. *The Christian's Reasonable Service in which Divine Truths concerning the Covenant of Grace are Expounded, Defended against Opposing Parties, and their Practice Advocated as well as the Administration of this Covenant in the Old and New Testaments*, in four vols., transl. Bartel Elshout based on the 3rd ed. of the original Dutch work entitled *Redelijke Godsdienst* published by D. Bolle, Rotterdam, The Netherlands (Ligonier, PA: Soli Deo Gloria Publications, 1993).

BIBLIOGRAPHY

Breckinridge, Robert J. *The Knowledge of God, Subjectively considered. Being the Second Part of Theology considered as a Science of Positive Truth, both Inductive and Deductive* (New York: Robert Carter & Brothers and Louisville: A Davidson, 1859).

Bruce, A. B. *St. Paul's Conception of Christianity* (Edinburgh: T&T Clark, 1894).

Buchanan, James. *The Doctrine of Justification: An Outline of its History in the Church and of its Exposition from Scripture*. First published 1867. Facsimile reprint ed. (Carlisle, PA: The Banner of Truth Trust, 1991).

Burke, Trevor J. "Adoption and the Spirit in Romans 8" *EQ* 70:4 (1998), 311–24.

_____ . *Adopted into God's Family: Exploring a Pauline Metaphor* (Downers Grove, IL: InterVarsity Press, 2006).

_____ . "Pauline Adoption: A Sociological Approach" *EQ* 73:2 (2001), 119–34.

_____ . "The Characteristics of Paul's Adoptive-Sonship (Huiothesia) Motif," *Irish Biblical Studies* 17, January 1995, 62–74.

_____ . *The Message of Sonship* (Downers Grove, IL: InterVarsity Press, 2011).

Buttrick, George A. *The Interpreter's Dictionary of the Bible: An Illustrated Encyclopedia* (New York: Abingdon Press, 1962).

Byrne, Brendan, *"Sons of God"—"Seed of Abraham": A Study of the Idea of the Sonship of God of All Christians in Paul against the Jewish Background* (Rome: Biblical Institue Press, 1979).

C

Caird, G. B. *The Language and Imagery of the Bible*, reprint ed. (Grand Rapids: Eerdmans, 1997).

Calvin, John. "Catechism of the Church in Geneva" (1545), in *Calvin's Selected Works*, vol. 2 (Grand Rapids: Baker Book House, 1983).

_____ . *Commentaries* in 22 vols. with various translators, originally printed for the Calvin Translation Society, reprinted (Grand Rapids: Baker Books, 2005).

_____ . *Commentary on the Prophecy of Isaiah*, vol. 4, transl. William Pringle (Edinburgh: The Calvin Translation Society, 1853).

_____ . *Institutes of the Christian Religion*, in 2 vols., ed. by John T. McNeill and transl. by Ford Lewis Battles (Philadelphia: The Westminster Press, 1960).

BIBLIOGRAPHY

_____ . *Calvin's Tracts and Treatises*, transl. Henry Beveridge. Historical Notes and Introduction to the current edition by T. F. Torrance (Edinburgh and London: Oliver and Boyd, 1958).

_____ . *Sermons on Galatians*, first published in 1563 (French) and 1574 (English), transl. by Kathy Childress (Edinburgh and Carlisle, PA: The Banner of Truth Trust, 1997).

_____ . *Sermons on the Epistles to Timothy & Titus*. Facsimile ed. of 1579. Reprint ed. (Carlisle, PA: The Banner of Truth Trust, 1983).

_____ . *The Acts of the Apostles 14–28*, transl. John W. Fraser, ed. David W. Torrance and Thomas F. Torrance (Edinburgh and London: Oliver and Boyd, 1966).

_____ . *The Gospel According to St. John 1–10*, Calvin's Commentaries, transl., T. H. L. Parker, ed. D. W. Torrance and T. F. Torrance, 1959 ed.; reprint ed. (Grand Rapids: Oliver and Boyd, 1979).

Cameron, Nigel M. De S. (Ed.). *The Challenge of Evangelical Theology: Essays in Approach and Method* (Edinburgh: Rutherford House Books, 1987).

_____ (Ed., et al.). *Pulpit and People: Essays in Honour of William Still* (Edinburgh: Rutherford House, 1986).

Campenhausen, Hans von. *The Fathers of the Church: The Fathers of the Greek Church* (Peabody, MA: Hendrickson Publishers, 1998).

Candlish, Robert S. *The Fatherhood of God: Being the First Course of the Cunningham Lectures*, 5th ed. (Edinburgh: Adam and Charles Black, 1869).

_____ . *The Fatherhood of God: Being the First Course of Cunningham Lectures Delivered before the New College, Edinburgh, in March 1864*. Supplementary volume to the 5th ed. (Edinburgh: Adam and Charles Black, 1870).

Catechesis Christiane Religionis in *The Heidelberg Catechism in German, Latin, and English with an Historical Introduction Prepared and Published by the Direction of the German Reformed Church in the United States of America*, Tercentenary edition (New York: Charles Scribner, 1863).

"Catholic Answers: To Explain and Defend the Faith" (forums.catholic. com/ showthread. php?t=15167, accessed March 15, 2014).

Childs, Brevard S. *Biblical Theology of the Old and New Testaments: Theological Reflection on the Christian Bible* (Minneapolis: Fortress, 1992).

Chrysides, George. "Meaning, Metaphor and Meta–Theology," *SJT* 38 (1985), 145–53.

Conn, Harvie M (Ed.). *Inerrancy and Hermeneutic: A Tradition, A Challenge, A Debate* (Grand Rapids: Baker, 1988).

Campbell, Constantine R. *Paul and Union with Christ: An Exegetical and Theological Study* (Grand Rapids: Zondervan, 2012).

Congregational Studies Conference Papers. *Eternal Light, Adoption and Livingstone.* (Evangelical Fellowship of Evangelical Churches, 1998).

Conn, Harvie M (Ed.). *Inerrancy and Hermeneutic: A Tradition, A Challenge, A Debate* (Grand Rapids: Baker Book House, 1988).

Cook, James I (Ed.). *Saved by Hope: Essays in Honor of Richard C. Oudersluys*, ed. James I. Cook (Grand Rapids: Eerdmans, 1978).

Cooper, John W. *Our Father in Heaven: Christian Faith and Inclusive Language for God* (Grand Rapids: Baker Books, 1998).

Crawford, Thomas J. *The Fatherhood of God considered in its general and special aspects and particularly in relation to the atonement with a review of recent speculations on the subject.* 2nd ed. revised and enlarged with a reply to the strictures of Dr Candlish (Edinburgh and London: William Blackwood and Sons, 1867).

Cruver, Dan (Ed.) *Reclaiming Adoption: Missional Living through the Rediscovery of Abba Father* (Adelphi, MD: Cruciform Press, 2011).

_____ . "The First Step in the Way Forward: A Response to David M. Molin's 'Of Orphans and Adoption,'" *Journal of Christian Legal Thought* 2:1 (Spring 2012), 11–14.

Cunningham, William. *The Reformers and Theology of the Reformation*, first published 1862 (Edinburgh: The Banner of Truth Trust, 1989).

D

D'Angelo, Mary Rose. "*Abba* and 'Father': Imperial Theology and the Jesus Traditions" *Journal of Biblical Literature* 111.4 (winter, 1992), 611–30.

Dabney, Robert L. *Systematic Theology.* First published 1871 (Edinburgh: The Banner of Truth Trust, 1985).

Dagg, John L. *A Manual of Theology*, first published 1857 (Harrisonburg, VA: Gano Books, 1982).

Darby, J. N. *Collected Writings*, 34 vols; ed. William Kelly (Lancing, Sussex: Kingston Bible Trust, 1964[?]–67).

Davis, Francis (Ed., *et al.*). *A Catholic Dictionary of Theology* (London, New York: Nelson, 1962).

Deissmann, Adolf, *The religion of Jesus and the Faith of Paul: The Selly Oak Lectures, 1923 on the Communion of Jesus with God and the Communion of Paul with Christ*, second ed. (New York: George H. Doran, 1926).

Demura, Alkira. "Two Commentaries on the Epistle to the Romans: Calvin and Oecolampadius" in *Calvinus Sincerioris religionis vindex: Calvin as Protector of the Purer Religion*, ed. Wilhelm H. Neuser and Brian G. Armstrong (Kirksville, MO: Sixteenth Century Journal Publishers, 1997).

Dewar, Daniel. *Elements of Systematic Divinity*, vol. 2 (Glasgow: Thomas Murray and Son, 1867).

Dick, John. *Lectures on Theology*, two volumes (Philadelphia: F. W. Greenough, 1838) (available at https://babel.hathitrust.org/cgi/pt?id =njp.32101063702 136&view=1up&seq=230, accessed April 28, 2021).

_____ . *Lectures on Theology*, 2 vols in 1 (New York: Robert Carter and brothers, 1851).

Dictionnaire de Spiritualité: Ascétique et Mystique Doctrine et Histoire (Paris : Beauchesne, 1967).

Die Bibel nach der Übersetzung Martin Luthers (Stutgart: Deutsche Bibelgesellschaft, 1984).

Die Religion in Geschichte und Gegenwart: Handwörterbuch für Theologie und Religionwissenschaft, Herausgegeben von Kurt Galling (Tübingen: J. C. B. Mohr [Paul Siebeck], 1957).

Duff, Robert. "Theologians of the Past—Francis Turretin," *Catholic Presbyterian* v (Jan.-Jun. 1881), 372–83.

E

Echevarria Jr., Miguel G. *The Future Inheritance of Land in the Pauline Epistles* (Eugene, Oregon: Pickwick Publications, 2019).

Elwell, Walter A. (Ed.). *Evangelical Dictionary of Theology* (Grand Rapids: Baker Book House, 1984).

Erskine, Thomas. *The Doctrine of Election and its Connection with the General Tenor of Christianity*, second ed. (Edinburgh: David Douglas, 1878).

_____ . *The Spiritual Order and other Papers Selected from the Manuscripts of the late Thomas Erskine* (Edinburgh: Edmonston and Douglas, 1871).

Evans, Eifion. *Daniel Rowland and the Great Evangelical Awakening in Wales* (Edinburgh: The Banner of Truth Trust, 1985).

Evans, G. R. (Ed.). *The Medieval Theologians: An Introduction to the Theology of the Medieval Period* (Malden, MA: Blackwell Publishing, 2001).

F

Fairbairn, Donald. *Life in the Trinity: An Introduction to Theology with the Help of the Church Fathers* (Downers Grove, IL: IVP Academic, 2009).

Ferguson, Sinclair B. *Children of the Living God* (Edinburgh and Carlisle, PA: The Banner of Truth Trust, 1989).

_____ . *John Owen on the Christian Life* (Edinburgh and Carlisle, PA: The Banner of Truth Trust, 1987).

_____ (Ed., et al.). *New Dictionary of Theology* (Leicester, England and Downers Grove, IL: Inter Varsity Press, 1988).

_____ . *The Christian Life: A Doctrinal Introduction*, first published 1981, reprint ed. (Edinburgh and Carlisle, PA: The Banner of Truth Trust, 2009).

_____ . *The Holy Spirit*. Contours of Christian Theology, ed. Gerald Bray (Leicester, England: Inter-Varsity Press, 1996).

Fesko, J. V. *The Theology of the Westminster Standards: Historical Contests and Theological Insights* (Wheaton, IL: Crossway, 2014).

Fisher, Jeff. "The Reformation of Adoption: Calvin and Oecolampadius on Roman 8," (drivegoogle.com/file/d/0B1uICU_BoP_bWXhv ZUFfYk NJbjA/ view, accessed on October 27, 2016).

_____ "The Reformation of Adoption: The Exegesis of John Calvin and Johannes Oecolampadius on the Doctrine from Romans 8," a paper delivered at the Midwest meeting of the ETS, March 11, 2016.

Frame, John M. "In Defense of Something Close to Biblicism," *Westminster Theological Journal* 59 (1997), 269–318.

_____ . Personal email to the author, May 2, 2003.

BIBLIOGRAPHY

_____ . "Reflections of a Lifetime Theologian," interviewed by Andrew Sandlin in *Christian Culture* (April–May 2008), 1–8.

_____ . *Salvation Belongs to the Lord: An Introduction to Systematic Theology* (Phillipsburg, NJ: P&R, 2006).

_____ . *The Doctrine of God.* A Theology of Lordship Series (Phillipsburg, NJ: P&R, 2002).

_____ . *The Doctrine of the Christian Life.* A Theology of Lordship Series (Phillipsburg, NJ: P&R, 2008).

_____ . *The Doctrine of the Knowledge of God.* A Theology of Lordship Series (Phillipsburg, NJ: P&R, 1987).

Friedrich, Gerhard (Ed.). *Theological Dictionary of the New Testament*, transl. and ed. G. W. Bromiley (Grand Rapids: Wm. B. Eerdmans, 1972).

G

Gaffin, Richard B. (Ed.). *Redemptive history and biblical interpretation: the shorter writings of Geerhardus Vos*, (Phillipsburg, NJ: P&R), 1980.

_____ . *Resurrection and Redemption: A Study in Paul's Soteriology*, 2nd ed. (Phillipsburg, NJ: P&R, 1987).

Galling, Kurt (Ed.). *Die Religion in Geschichte und Gegenwart: Handwörterbuch für Theologie und Religionswissenschaft.* Dritte Band (Tübingen: J. C. B. Mohr [Paul Siebeck], 1959).

Gamble, Richard C. (Ed.). *Articles on Calvin and Calvinism*, (New York & London: Garland Publishing Inc., 1992).

Garner, David B. *Sons in the Son: The Riches and Reach of Adoption in Christ* (Phillipsburg, NJ: P&R, 2016).

Gerrish, Brian A. *Grace and Gratitude: The Eucharistic Theology of John Calvin* (Edinburgh: T&T Clark, 1993).

_____ . *Saving and Secular Faith: An Invitation to Systematic Theology* (Minneapolis: Fortress, 1999).

Gill, John. *Body of Divinity* (reprinted from the London ed. of 1839; Atlanta, GA: Turner Lassetter, 1950).

Girardeau, John L. *Discussions of Theological Questions* (Harrisonburg, VA: Sprinkle Publications, 1986).

BIBLIOGRAPHY

_____ .*The Federal Theology: Its Import and its Regulative Influence* (J. Ligon Duncan III, Ed., with an introduction by W. Duncan Rankin. Greenville, SC, 1994).

Gnuse, Robert. *Heilsgeschichte as a Model for Biblical Theology: The Debate Concerning the Uniqueness and Significance of Israel"s Worldview.* College Theology Society Studies in Religion 4 (Lanham *et al.*: University Press of America, 1989).

Graham, Michael A. "Cheer Up! A Biographical Study of the Life and Ministry of C. John ("Jack") Miller: A Twentieth Century Pioneer of Grace (Ph.D., Diss.: Southeastern Baptist Theological Seminary, Wake Forest, North Carolina, May 2019).

_____. *Cheer Up! The Life and Ministry of Jack Miller* (Phillipsburg, NJ: P&R, 2021).

Griffith, Howard. "'The First Title of the Spirit': Adoption in Calvin's Soteriology" *EQ* 73:2 (2001), 135–53.

Grimm, Jacob (Ed., et al.). *Deutsches Wörterbuch* (Leipzig: S. Hirzel, 1854–1971).

Gunton, Colin E. *The Actuality of the Atonement: A Study of Metaphor, Rationality and the Christian Tradition* (Edinburgh: T&T Clark, 1988).

H

Hall, David W. (Ed., et al.). *A Theological Guide to Calvin's Institutes: Essays and Analysis,* The Calvin 500 Series (Phillipsburg, NJ: P&R, 2008).

_____ . *Tributes to John Calvin: A Celebration of His Quincentenary,* The Calvin 500 Series (Phillipsburg, NJ: P&R, 2010).

Harnack, Adolf von. *What is Christianity?* Transl. Thomas Bailey Saunders (New York and Evanston: Harper and Row, Publishers, 1957).

Harrington, Wilfrid J. *The Path of Biblical Theology* (Dublin: Gill and Macmillan, 1973).

Hawthorne, Gerald F (Ed., et al.). *Dictionary of Paul in His Letters* (Downers Grove, IL: IVP Academic, 1993).

Heim, Erin. "Light through a Prism: New Avenues of Inquiry for the Pauline Υἱοθεσσία Metaphors," (Ph.D. Diss.: University of Otago, Dunedin, New Zealand, 2014).

Hein, Rolland. *George MacDonald: Victorian Mythmaker* (Nashville, TN: Star Song, 1993).

Hendrickson, William. *The Gospel of Mark*, reprint ed. (Edinburgh and Carlisle, PA: The Banner of Truth Trust, 1987).

Hendry, George S. *The Westminster Confession for Today: A Contemporary Interpretation*. (Richmond, VA: SCM Press, 1960).

Heppe, Heinrich. *Reformed Dogmatics: Set out and Illustrated from the Sources*, transl. G. T. Thomson, reprint ed. (Grand Rapids: Baker Books, 1978).

Heron, Alasdair I (Ed.). *The Westminster Confession in the Church Today: Papers Prepared for the Church of Scotland Panel of Doctrine* (Edinburgh: The Saint Andrew Press, 1982).

Hester, James D. *Paul's Concept of the Inheritance: A Contribution to the Understanding of Heilsgeschichte*, SJT Occasional Papers, 14 (Edinburgh and London: Oliver and Boyd, 1968).

Hewitson, Ian. *Trust and Obey: Norman Shepherd and the Justification Controversy at Westminster Theological Seminary* (Minneapolis, MN: NextStep Resources, 2011).

Hodge, A. A. *Outlines of Theology* (New York: Robert Carter and Brothers, 1866).

Hodge, Charles. *Systematic Theology*, three vols. (London and Edinburgh: Thomas Nelson and Sons, 1871–80).

Hooker, Thomas. *The Christians Two Chiefe Lessons* (London: TB for P. Stephens and C. Meredith, 1640).

Horton, Michael S (Ed.). *A Confessing Theology for Postmodern Times* (Wheaton, IL: Crossway, 2000).

_____. "Law, Gospel, and Covenant: Reassessing Some Emerging Antitheses," *Westminster Theological Journal* 64:2 (Fall 2002), 279–87.

Houston, Thomas. *The Adoption of Sons, Its Nature, Spirit, Privileges and Effects: A Practical and Experimental Treatise* (Paisley, UK: Alex. Gardner, 1872).

_____ . *The Adoption of Sons, Its Nature, Spirit, Privileges and Effects: A Practical and Experimental Treatise* (Brighton, UK: Ettrick Press, 2021).

Hughes, John J. (Ed.). *Speaking the Truth in Love: The Theology of John M. Frame* (Phillipsburg, NJ: P&R, 2009).

Hulse, Errol. "Recovering the Doctrine of Adoption" (*Reformation Today* 105 (1988), 5–14.

BIBLIOGRAPHY

Hymns and Spiritual Songs for the Little Flock, selected 1856 (revised ed.; Kingston-on-Thames: Stow Hill Bible and Tract Depot, 1962).

J

Jeremias, Joachim. *Prayers of Jesus, SBT* II 6 (London: SCM, 1967), 11–65.

John Wesley's "Revision of the Shorter Catechism," The Banner of Truth Magazine 47 (March–April 1967).

Jüngel, Eberhard. *Gott als Geheimnis der Welt* (Tübingen: J. C. B. Mohr [Paul Siebeck], 1978).

_____. *Justification: The Heart of the Christian Faith, transl. by Jeffrey F. Cayzer and introduced by John Webster*, third edition (Edinburgh and New York: T&T Clark, 2001).

_____. *Theological Essays*, transl. with an introduction by J. B. Webster (Edinburgh: T&T Clark, 1989).

K

Kelly, Douglas F. "Adoption: An Underdeveloped Heritage of the Westminster Standards" *Reformed Theological Review* (Australia) 52 (1993), 110–20.

Kennedy, John. *Man's Relations to God: Traced in the Light of "the Present Truth,"* reprint of 1869 ed. (The James Begg Society, 1995).

Kim, Seyoon. *Paul and the New Perspective: Second Thoughts on the Origin of Paul"s Gospel* (Grand Rapids: Eerdmans, 2002).

King, Samuel A. "The Grace of Adoption" *Union Seminary Magazine* 22 (1910), 30–35.

Knox, John. *Works*, collected and edited by David Laing; first published, 1846–1864 (Edinburgh: James Thin, 1895).

Kuiper, R. B. *The Glorious Body of Christ: A Scriptural Appreciation of the One Holy Catholic Church*, first published by Eerdmans, 1966; reprint ed. (Edinburgh and Carlisle, PA: The Banner of Truth Trust, 2006).

Kuyper, Abraham. *The Work of the Holy Spirit*, originally published 1900; transl. Henri De Vries (Chattanooga, TN: AMG Publishers, 1995).

L

Lakoff, George and Johnson, Mark. *Metaphors We Live By* (Chicago: University of Chicago Press, 2003).

404

BIBLIOGRAPHY

Lampe, G. W. H. (Ed.). *A Patristic Greek Lexicon* (Oxford: The Clarendon Press, 1961).

Lane, Anthony S. *John Calvin: Student of the Church Fathers* (Grand Rapids: Baker Books, 1999).

Leith, John H. *Introduction to the Reformed Tradition: A Way of Being the Christian Community*, Revised ed. (Atlanta: John Knox Press, 1981).

Letters of the Rev. Samuel Rutherford, with an introductory essay by Thomas Erskine, Esq., third ed. (Glasgow: William Collins, 1830).

Letters of Thomas Erskine of Linlathen, two vols., ed. William Hanna (Edinburgh: David Douglas, 1877).

Lewis, Alan E. *Motherhood of God: A Report by a Study Group appointed by the Woman's Guild and the Panel on Doctrine on the invitation of the General Assembly of the Church of Scotland* (Edinburgh: St. Andrew Press, 1984).

Lidgett, J. Scott. *The Fatherhood of God in Christian Truth and Life* (Edinburgh: T&T Clark, 1902).

_____. *The Victorian Transformation of Theology: The Second Series of Maurice Lectures delivered at King's College, London, Lent Term, 1934* (London, Epworth Press,1934).

Lienhard, Marc. "Luther et Calvin: Commentateurs du notre Père," *Revue D'Histoire et de Philosphie Religieuses* 72 (1992/1), 73–88.

Lightfoot, J. B. *St. Paul's Epistle to the Galatians: A Revised Text with Introduction, Notes, and Dissertations* (London: MacMillan, 1892).

Lillback, Peter A. *The Practical Calvinist: An Introduction to the Presbyterian and Reformed Heritage (In Honor of Clair Davis' Thirty Years at Westminster Theological Seminary)*, (Fearn, Ross-shire: Mentor [Christian Focus Publications], 2002).

Lindsay, James. "The Development of Scotch Theology", *Princeton Theological Review* vol. 4 no. 3 (1906), 339–51.

Lloyd-Jones, Martyn. *Great Doctrines of the Bible*, three vols. *God The Holy Spirit* (Wheaton, IL: Crossway, 1996–98).

_____. (Ed.). *Puritan Papers: Volume 1, 1956–1959* (Phillipsburg, NJ: P&R, 2000).

BIBLIOGRAPHY

Loci Commvnes D. Petri Martyris Vermilii, florentini, Sacrarvm Literarvm in Schola Tigvrina (Londini: Excudebat Thomas Vautrollerius typographus, 1583).

The Common Places of the Most Famous and Renowmed [*sic?*] *Diuine Doctor Peter Martyr, diuided into foure principall parts: with a large addition of Manie Theological and Necessarie discourses, some never extant before*, transl. Anthonie Marten, 1583.

Locke, John. *The Reasonableness of Christianity as Delivered in the Scriptures*, Reprint from the 1794 ed. (Bristol: Thoemmes Press, 1997).

Logan, John B. "Thomas Erskine of Linlathen: Lay Theologian of the 'Inner Light'," *Scottish Journal of Theology* 37 (1984), 23–40.

Longenecker, Richard. *Galatians*, Word Biblical Commentary 41 (Dallas, TX: Thomas Nelson, 1990).

Luther, Martin. *Commentary on the Epistle to the Romans*, abridged transl. J. Theodore Mueller (Grand Rapids: Zondervan, 1960).

Luther, Martin. *Works*, fifty-five vols., eds. Jaroslav Pelikan and Helmut T. Lehmann (Saint Louis, MO: Concordia Publishing House, 1964).

Lyall, Francis. *Slaves, Citizens, Sons: Legal Metaphors in the Epistles* (Grand Rapids: Academie Books [Zondervan], 1984).

_____ . Francis Lyall, "Metaphors, Legal and Theological," *Scottish Bulletin of Evangelical Theology* 10 (1992), 94–112.

Lyons, H. P. C. "Adoption of sons," *A Catholic Dictionary of Theology* (New York: Nelson, 1962).

M

M'Neile, Hugh. *The Adoption and other Sermons* (London: James Nisbet and Co., 1864).

MacArthur, John. *Slave: The Hidden Truth About Your Identity in Christ* (Nashville, et al.: Thomas Nelson, 2010).

MacDonald, George. *Unspoken Sermons: Series I, II, and III* (Radford, VA: Wilder Publications, 2008).

MacDonald, James A. (Ed.). *Wesley's Revision of the Shorter Catechism* (Edinburgh: Geo. A. Martin, 1906).

BIBLIOGRAPHY

Macleod, Donald. *Behold Your God* (Fearn: Ross-shire: Christian Focus Publications, 1990).

_____ . *Christ Crucified: Understanding the Atonement* (Downers Grove, Illinois: IVP Academic, 2014).

_____. *Shared Life: The Trinity and the Fellowship of God's People* (London: Scripture Union, 1987).

Marcel, Pierre Ch. *The Biblical Doctrine of Infant Baptism: Sacrament of the Covenant of Grace*, transl. Philip Edgcumbe Hughes; first published 1953, reprinted (Cambridge, England: James Clarke, 1981).

Marchel, Witold. *Abba, Vater! Die Vaterbotschaft Des Neuen Testaments,* Die Welt der Bibel (Düsseldorf: Patmos-Verlag, 1963).

Martin, Hugh. "Candlish's Cunningham Lectures," *British and Foreign Evangelical Review* 14 (Oct. 1865), 720–87.

_____. *Christ's Presence in the Gospel History*, second ed. (Edinburgh: Maclaren, 1865).

_____. *The Atonement in its Relation to the Covenant, the Priesthood, the Intercession of our Lord* (Edinburgh: Knox Press, 1976).

Matthew, James. "The Doctrine of Sonship and the Sonship of Believers," *The Theological Review and Free Church College Quarterly* 2 (1886), 18–31.

Mawhinney, Allen. "Baptism, Servanthood, and Sonship," *Westminster Theological Journal* 49:1 (Spring 1987), 35–54.

_____. "God as Father: Two Popular Theories Reconsidered," *JETS* 31:2 (Jun. 1988), 181–89.

_____. "υἱοθεσία in the Pauline Epistles: Its background, Use and Implications" (Ph.D.: Baylor University, Waco, TX, 1983).

_____ . "The family of God: one model for the church of the 90's," Forty-fourth National Conference, Evangelical Theological Society, San Francisco, 1992.

McCaulley, Esau. *Sharing in the Son's Inheritance: Davidic Messianism and Paul's Worldwide Interpretation of the Abrahamic Land Promise in Galatians* (London, et al.: T&T Clark, 2019).

McFague, Sallie. *Metaphorical Theology: Models of God in Religious Language* (Philadelphia: Fortress, 1982).

_____. *Models of God: Theology for an Ecological, Nuclear Age* (London: SCM Press, 1987).

McGillis, Roderick. *George MacDonald: Literary Heritage and Heirs* (Wayne, PA: Zosima Press, 2008).

McGowan, A. T. B. (Ed.) *Always Reforming: Explorations in Systematic Theology*, (Downers Grove, IL: IVP Academic, 2006).

_____. *The Federal Theology of Thomas Boston*, Rutherford Studies in Historical Theology (Edinburgh: Rutherford House Books, 1997).

McGrath, Alister E. *C. S. Lewis: A Life* (Carol Stream, IL: Tyndale House Publisher, Inc., 2013).

_____. *Iustitia Dei: A History of the Christian Doctrine of Justification—From 1500 to the Present Day*, reprint ed. (Cambridge: Cambridge University Press, 1991).

McIntyre, John. *The Shape of Soteriology: Studies in the Doctrine of the Death of Christ* (Edinburgh: T&T Clark, 1992).

_____. *Theology After The Storm: Reflections on the Upheavals in Modern Theology and Culture*, ed. with a critical introduction by Gary D. Badcock (Grand Rapids: Eerdmans, 1996).

McKinlay, Edward. "The relation of incarnation to atonement in the Christology of R. S. Candlish and its contribution to the development of Scottish Theology" (Ph.D. Diss.: University of Edinburgh, 1966).

Miller, Rose Marie. *From Fear to Freedom: Living as Sons and Daughters of God* (Wheaton, IL: Harold Shaw Publishers, 1994).

Moltmann, Jürgen, *Experiences in Theology: Ways and Forms of Christian Theology*, transl. Margaret Kohl (Minneapolis: Fortress Press, 2000).

_____. *The Spirit of Life*: *A Universal Affirmation*, transl. Margaret Kohl (London: SCM Press, 1992).

Morris, Edward D. *Theology of the Westminster Symbols: A Commentary Historical, Doctrinal, Practical on the Confession of Faith and Catechisms and the Related Formularies of the Presbyterian Churches* (Columbus, OH: Champlin Press, 1900).

Morris, Leon. *The Cross in the New Testament*, Mount Radford Reprints, No. 19, originally published by Wm. B. Eerdmans, 1965 (Exeter: Paternoster Press, 1976).

Muller, Richard A. *After Calvin: Studies in the Development of a Theological Tradition*, Oxford Studies in Historical Theology (Oxford, New York, et al.: Oxford University Press, 2003).

_____. *Calvin and the Reformed Tradition: On the Work of Christ and the Order of Salvation* (Grand Rapids: Baker Academic, 2012).

Murray, Iain H. "The End of the Puritan Conference," banneroftruth.org/us/resources/articles/2010/the-end-of-the-puritan-conference/, accessed June 29, 2017.

John Murray, *Calvin on Scripture and Divine Sovereignty*. First published 1960 (Welwyn, Hertfordshire: Evangelical Press, 1979).

_____. *Collected Writings.* Four vols. (Edinburgh and Carlisle, PA: The Banner of Truth Trust, 1977).

_____. *Redemption: Accomplished and Applied*, reprint ed. (Edinburgh and Carlisle, PA: The Banner of Truth Trust, 1979).

N

Neuser, Wilhelm H. *Calvinus Sacrae Scripturae Professor*, International Congress on Calvin Research (Grand Rapids: Eerdmans, 1994).

New Catholic Encyclopaedia (New York, et al.: McGraw-Hill Book Company, 1967).

Nicene and Post-Nicene Fathers. First series, fourteen volumes (Augustine and Chrysostom), and second series, fourteen volumes (Peabody, MA: Hendrickson, 1996).

O

O'Donovan, Oliver. *On the 39 Articles: A Conversation with Tudor Christianity*, A Latimer Monograph (reprint ed.; Carlisle: The Paternoster Press, 1993).

P

Packer, James I. *Among God's Giants: The Puritan Vision of the Christian Life* (Eastbourne: Kingsway, 1991).

_____. *Knowing God*, first printed, 1973 (London *et al.*: Hodder and Stoughton, 1975).

Palmer, Benjamin Morgan. *The Threefold Fellowship and the Threefold Assurance: An Essay in Two Parts*, reprint ed. (Harrisonburg, VA: Sprinkle Publications, 1980).

Palmer, Edwin H. *Scheeben's Doctrine of Divine Adoption* (Kampen: J. H. Kok N.V., 1953).

Pannenberg, Wolfhart. *Systematic Theology*, three volumes, transl. Geoffrey W. Bromiley; reprint ed. (Grand Rapids: Eerdmans, 1998).

Parker, T. H. L. *Calvin: An Introduction to His Thought* (London: Geoffrey Chapman, 1995).

Patterson, Richard D. "Parental Love as a Metaphor for Divine–Human Love," *JETS* 46:2 (June 2003), 205–16.

Payton Jr, James. *Getting the Reformation Wrong: Correcting Some Misunderstandings* (Downers Grove, Illinois: IVP Academic, 2010).

Peppard, Michael. *The Son of God in the Roman World: Divine Sonship in its Social and Political Context* (Oxford: Oxford University Press, 2011).

Perrin, Nicholas (Ed., et al.). *Jesus, Paul, and the People of God: A Theological Dialogue with N. T. Wright* (Downers Grove, IL: IVP Academic, 2011).

Peterson, Robert A. "Towards a Systematic Theology of Adoption," *Presbyterion* 27/2 (Fall 2001), 120–31.

Pictet, Benedict. *Christian Theology*, transl. from the Latin by Frederick Reyroux (London: R. B. Seeley and W. Burnside, 1834).

Pipa, Jr., Joseph A. (Ed., et al.). *Sanctification: Growing in Grace* (Greenville, SC: Southern Presbyterian Press, 2001).

Piper, John. *The Future of Justification: A Response to N. T. Wright* (Wheaton, IL: Crossway Books, 2007).

Poythress, Vern S. *Symphonic Theology: The Validity of Multiple Perspectives in Theology* (Grand Rapids: Academie Books [Zondervan]), 1987.

Priebe, Barton D. *Adopted by God: Discover the Life-Transforming Joy of a Neglected Truth* (independently published, 2021).

_____. *Belonging to God's Family: Measuring the Effect of Sermons on Paul's Doctrine of Adoption in the Lives of Believers* (D.Min. diss.: Associated Canadian Theological Schools [Northwest Baptist Seminary and Trinity Western University], Langley, British Columbia, 2020).

BIBLIOGRAPHY

Puritan Sermons 1659–1689: Being the Morning Exercises at Cripplegate, St. Giles in the Fields, and in Southwark by Seventy-five Ministers of the Gospel, originally published London, 1660 (Wheaton, IL: Richard Own Roberts, Publishers, 1981).

Q

Quigley, Lynn (Ed.). *Reformed Theology in Contemporary Perspective (Westminster: Yesterday, Today—and Tomorrow?)*, Edinburgh Dogmatic Conference Papers (Edinburgh: Rutherford House, 2006).

R

Radoicich, Russell. "Adoption in the Pauline Epistles" (Crestwood, NY: St. Vladimir's Orthodox Theological Seminary, Crestwood, 1999).

Reformed Confessions of the 16th and 17th Centuries in English Translation, four vols., compiled with an Intro., James T. Dennison, Jr., (Grand Rapids: Reformation Heritage Books, 2008–14).

Reformed Theology in America, ed. David F. Wells, three vols.; first published in a single volume by Wm. B. Eerdmans, 1985 (Grand Rapids: Eerdmans, 1989).

Ridderbos, Herman N. *Paul: An Outline of His Theology*, transl. J. R. de Witt (London: SPCK, 1977).

———. *Redemptive History and the New Testament Scriptures* (formerly *The Authority of the New Testament Scriptures*), Biblical and Theological Studies, transl. H. De Jongste and revised by Richard B. Gaffin Jr.; first published 1963; second revised ed. (Phillipsburg, NJ: P&R, 1988).

———. *The Epistle of Paul to the Churches in Galatia*, reprint ed., transl. Henry Zylstra (Grand Rapids: Eerdmans, 1981).

———. *When the Time had Fully Come: Studies in New Testament Theology* (Jordan Station, Ontario: Paideia Press, 1982).

Rishmawy, Derek. "Retrieval—It's What All the Hip Reformed Catholic Kids Do," *Reformdish* (https://derekzrishmawy.com/tag/retrieval-theology/, accessed December 29, 2017).

Ritschl, Dietrich. "Hippolytus' Conception of Deification: Remarks on the Interpretation of Refutation X," *SJT* 12:4 (Dec. 1959), 388–99.

Ryken, Philip G. *The Message of Salvation: By God's Grace, for God's Glory*, Bible Speaks Today (Downers Grove, IL: InterVarsity Press, 2002).

S

Saint Anselm: Basic Writings, transl. S. N. Deane with an introduction by Charles Hartshorne, second ed. (La Salle, IL: Open Court, 1974).

Saito, Isomi. "Divine Adoption in the Confessions of the Reformation Period," (Ph.D. Diss.: Vrije Universitaet, Amsterdam, 2016).

Schaff, Philip. *History of the Christian Church*, eight vols., first published by Charles Scribner's Sons, 1882–1910 (Peabody, MA: Hendrickson Publishers, 2006).

_____. *The Creeds of Christendom: With a History and Critical Notes*, 3 vols., ed., P. Schaff, rev. D. S. Schaff. Sixth ed. (reprinted from the 1931 ed.; Grand Rapids: Baker Books, 1990).

Schillebeeckx, Edward. *Jesus: An Experiment in Christology*, transl. Hubert Hoskins, reprint ed. (New York: Vintage Books, 1981).

Schlatter, Adolf. *The Theology of the Apostles: The Development of New Testament Theology*, originally published as *Die Theologie der Apostel* (Stuttgart: Calwer Vereinbuchhandlung, 1922), transl. Andreas J. Köstenberger (Grand Rapids: Baker Books, 1999).

Schutter, David H. "Jonathan Edwards's Preaching of Romans 8: Presenting and Evaluating Two Previously Unpublished Sermons" (Th.M. thesis: Westminster Theological Seminary, 2017).

_____. Unpublished paper, "The Place of the Doctrine of Adoption in the Ministry of Jonathan Edwards" (Philadelphia, PA: Westminster Theological Seminary, 2012).

Scott, James M. *Adoption as Sons of God: An Exegetical Investigation into the Background of ΥΙΟΘΕΣΙΑ in the Pauline Corpus*, Wissentschaftliche Untersuchungen zum Neuen Testament ·2. Reihe (J. C. B. Mohr [Paul Siebeck]: Tübingen, 1992).

Selvaggio, Anthony T. (Ed.). *The Faith Once Delivered: Essays in Honor of Dr. Wayne R. Spear* (Phillipsburg, NJ: P&R, 2007).

Skilton, John H (Ed.) *The New Testament Student and Theology*, vol. 3 (Phillipsburg, NJ: P&R, 1976).

Smail, Thomas A. *The Forgotten Father*, reprint ed. (London, et al.: Hodder and Stoughton, 1990).

Smeaton, George. *Christ's Doctrine of the Atonement*, republished from the 1870 edition (Edinburgh and Carlisle, PA: The Banner of Truth Trust, 1991).

_____. *The Apostles' Doctrine of the Atonement*, republished from the 1870 edition (Edinburgh and Carlisle, PA: The Banner of Truth Trust, 1991).

Smith, Morton H. *Studies in Southern Presbyterian Theology*, first published 1962 (Phillipsburg, NJ: P&R, 1987).

Smolin, David. "Of Orphans and Adoption, Parents and the Poor, Exploitation and Rescue: A Scriptural and theological critique of the evangelical Christian adoption and orphan care movement," *Regent International Law Review* 8:2 [Spring 2012]), 267–324.

Sonship: Discovering Liberty in the Gospel as Sons and Daughters of God (Jenkintwon, PA: World Harvest Mission [now Serge]).

Soskice, Janet Martin. *Metaphor and Religious Language* (Oxford: Clarendon Press, 1985).

Spurgeon, Charles H. *Expository Encyclopedia: Sermons by Charles H. Spurgeon*, Volume 1 (Grand Rapids: Baker Book House, 1951).

Spykman, Gordon J, *Reformational Theology: A New Paradigm for Doing Dogmatics* (Grand Rapids: William B. Eerdmans, 1992).

Stevens, George Barker. *The Christian Doctrine of Salvation*, International Theological Library, first published 1905, reprint ed. (Edinburgh: T&T Clark, 1930).

Stevenson-Moessner, Jeanne. *The Spirit of Adoption: At Home in God's Family* (Louisville: Westminster John Knox Press, 2003).

Stolt, Brigit. "Martin Luther on God as a Father," *Lutheran Quarterly*, New Series, 8 (Spring 1994), 385–95.

Stoughton, John. *History of Religion in England, from the Opening of the Long Parliament to the End of the Eighteenth Century*, multivolumes, new and revised ed. (London: Hodder and Stoughton, 1881).

Stout, Harry S (Ed.). *The Jonathan Edwards Encyclopedia* (Grand Rapids: Eerdmans, 2017).

Stuhlmacher, Peter. *Revisiting Paul's Doctrine of Justification: A Challenge to the New Perspective,* with an essay by Donald A. Hagner (Downers Grove, IL: IVP Academic, 2001).

BIBLIOGRAPHY

_____. *Wie treibt man Biblische Theologie?* Biblisch-Theologische Studien 24 (Neukirchen–Vluyn, 1995).

T

The Complete Sermons of Martin Luther, seven vols., variously edited and translated (Grand Rapids: Baker, 2000).

The Complete Works of the Late Reverend Thomas Boston, Ettrick, Rev. Samuel McMillan, ed., reprinted ed. (Wheaton, IL: Richard Owen Roberts, Publishers, 1980).

The 400th Anniversary Edition of the Heidelberg Catechism (Cleveland, OH: United Church Press, 1962).

The Reformation of the Church: A Collection of Reformed and Puritan Documents on Church Issues, Selected with introductory notes by Iain H. Murray, reprint ed. (Edinburgh: The Banner of Truth Trust, 1987).

The Reformed Forum podcast. "Adoption: Accomplished and Applied," https://www.facebook.com/reformedforum/videos/270556298144566, accessed last on September 30, 2021).

The Systematic Theology of John Brown of Haddington (Fearn, Ross-shire, Scotland: Christian Focus Publications and Grand Rapids: Reformation Heritage Books, 2002).

The Works of the Rev. John Gambold, A.M., with an Introductory Essay by Thomas Erskine, Esq., Advocate (Glasgow: Chalmers and Collins, 1822).

The Works of John Owen, sixteen vols., ed. W. H. Goold; facsimile reprint ed. (Edinburgh and Carlisle, PA: The Banner of Truth Trust, 1965–68).

The Works of Thomas Goodwin, D.D., twelve vols. (Edinburgh and London: James Nichol and James Nesbit, 1861).

Theron, Daniel J. "'Adoption' in the Pauline Corpus," *Evangelical Quarterly* vol. 28 (1956), 6–14.

Thornwell Centennial Addresses (Spartanburg: Band & White), 1913.

Thornwell, James H. *Collected Writings*, four vols., first published 1875; facsimile reprint ed., (Edinburgh: The Banner of Truth Trust, 1986).

Toon, Peter. *Puritans and Calvinism* (Swengel, PA, 1973).

_____. *The Emergence of Hyper-Calvinism in English Nonconformity 1689–1765* (London: The Olive Tree, 1967).

Torrance, T. F. *Scottish Theology: From John Knox to John McLeod Campbell* (Edinburgh: T&T Clark, 1996).

_____. (Transl. and Ed.). *The School of Faith: The Catechisms of the Reformed Church* (London: James Clarke & Co., 1959).

Townsend, William J. *The Great Schoolmen of the Middle Ages: An Account of their Lives, and the Services they Rendered to the Church and the World* (London: Hodder and Stoughton, 1881).

Trumper, Tim J. R. "An Historical Study of the Doctrine of Adoption in the Calvinistic Tradition" (University of Edinburgh: Ph.D. Diss., 2001).

_____. "Covenant Theology and Constructive Calvinism," *Westminster Theological Journal* 64:2 (Fall 2002), 387–404.

_____. Review of David B. Garner, *Sons in the Son JETS* (vol. 62, no. 1, March 2019), 204–9.

_____. "The Metaphorical Import of Adoption: A Plea for Realisation I. The Adoption Metaphor in Biblical Usage" *SBET* 14 no. 2 (Autumn 1996), 129–45.

_____. "The Metaphorical Import of Adoption: A Plea for Realisation II. The Adoption Metaphor in Theological Usage" *SBET* 15 no. 2 (Autumn 1997), 98–115.

_____. "The Theological History of Adoption: I. An Account" *SBET* 20 no. 1 (Spring 2002), 4–28.

_____. "The Theological History of Adoption: II. A *Rationale*" *SBET* 20 no. 2 (Autumn 2002), 177–202.

_____. "A Fresh Exposition of Adoption: I. An Outline" *SBET* 23 no. 1 (Spring 2005), 60–80.

_____. "A Fresh Exposition of Adoption: II. Its Implications" *SBET* 23 no. 2 (Autumn 2005), 194–215.

_____. *When History Teaches Us Nothing: The Recent Reformed Sonship Debate in Context* (Eugene, OR: Wipf and Stock, 2008). [Now available in a second edition, 2022.]

Turretin, Francis. *The Institutes of Elenctic Theology*, three vols., transl. George. M. Giger and ed. James T. Dennison Jr. (Phillipsburg, NJ: P&R, 1992–97).

Twisselmann, Willi. *Die Gotteskindschaft der Christen nach dem Neuen Testament*, Beiträge zur Förderung christlicher Theologie 41 (Gütersloh: Verlag C. Bertelsmann, 1939).

V

VanDrunen, David (Ed.). *The Pattern of Sound Doctrine: Systematic Theology at the Westminster Seminaries* (*Essays in Honor of Robert B. Strimple*), (Phillipsburg, NJ: P&R, 2004).

Vanhoozer, Kevin J. *Is There Meaning in This Text? The Bible, the reader and the morality of literary knowledge* (Leicester, England: Apollos, 1998).

Vellanickal, Matthew. *The Divine Sonship of Christians in the Johannine Writings* (Rome: Biblical Institute Press, 1977).

Voigt, Andrew George. *Biblical Dogmatics* (Columbia, S.C.: Lutheran Board of Education, 1917).

Vos, Geerhardus. *Biblical Theology: Old and New Testaments* reprint ed. (Carlisle, PA: The Banner of Truth Trust, 1985).

_____. *Reformed Dogmatics*, five vols., first published in 1896 (hand-written) and printed in 1910; transl. and ed. Richard B. Gaffin Jr. et al. (Bellingham, Washington: Lexham Press, 2012–16).

_____. *The Pauline eschatology* (Grand Rapids: Baker Book House, 1979).

W

Walker, Williston (et al.). *A History of the Christian Church*, Fourth Ed. (Edinburgh: T&T Clark, 1985).

Wallace Jr., Dewey D. *Puritans and Predestination: Grace in English Protestant Theology 1525–1695* (Chapel Hill: The University of North Carolina Press, 1982).

Wallace, Ronald S. *Calvin's Doctrine of the Word and Sacrament* (Edinburgh: Scottish Academic Press, 1995).

Warfield, Benjamin B. *Faith and Life* first published 1916 (Edinburgh and Carlisle, PA: The Banner of Truth Trust, 1974).

_____. *Selected Shorter Writings*, two vols., ed. John E. Meeter (Phillipsburg, NJ: P&R, 1970).

Watson, Thomas. *A Body of Divinity*, first published in 1692; reprinted as a revised edition in limp format (Edinburgh and Carlisle, PA: The Banner of Truth Trust, 1983).

Webb, Robert A. *The Reformed Doctrine of Adoption* (Grand Rapids: Eerdmans, 1947).

Wendel, François. *Calvin* (London: Collins, 1963).

Westhead, Nigel. "Adoption in the Thought of John Calvin," *SBET* 13 (1995), 102–15.

Whaling, Thornton. "Adoption," *Princeton Theological Review* 21 (1923), 223–35.

White, John L. *The Apostle of God: Paul and the Promise of Abraham* (Peabody, MA: Hendrickson, 1999).

Widdicombe, Peter. *The Fatherhood of God from Origen to Athanasius*, Oxford Theological Monographs (Oxford: Clarendon Press, 1994).

Williams, David J. *Paul's Metaphors: Their Context and Character* (Peabody, MA: Hendrickson, 1999).

Wilson, William. *Memorials of Robert Smith Candlish, D.D.* (Edinburgh: Adam and Charles Black, 1880).

Wilterdink, Garret A.. *Tyrant or Father? A Study of Calvin's Doctrine of God*, two vols., Scholastic Monograph Series (Bristol, IN: Wyndham Hall Press, 1985).

Witsius, Herman. *The Economy of the Covenants Between God and Man: Comprehending a Complete Body of Divinity*, two vols., facsimile reprint of the London 1822 ed. (Kingsburg, CA: den Dulk Christian Foundation, 1990).

Wolfe, Judith (Ed., et al.). *C. S. Lewis and the Church: Essays in Honour of Walter Hooper* (London and New York: T&T Clark International, 2011).

Wright, C. J. H. *God's People in God's Land: Family, Land and Property in the Old Testament* (Exeter: The Paternoster Press, 1990).

Wright, N. T. *Justification: God's Plan and Paul's Vision* (Downers Grove, IL: IVP Academic, 2009).

_____. *Paul and the Faithfulness of God* (Minneapolis: Fortress, 2013).

_____. *The Climax of the Covenant, Christ and the Law in Pauline Theology*, reprint ed. (Edinburgh: T&T Clark, 1993).

_____ (et al.). *The Grace of God in the Gospel* (Edinburgh: The Banner of Truth Trust, 1971).

_____ (et al.). *The Great Acquittal: Justification by Faith and Current Christian Thought* (London: Collins, 1980).

BIBLIOGRAPHY

_____. *What Saint Paul Really Said: Was Paul of Tarsus the Real Founder of Christianity?* (Grand Rapids: Eerdmans, 1997).

Z

Zachman, Randall C. *The Assurance of Faith: Conscience in the Theology of Martin Luther and John Calvin* (Minneapolis: Fortress Press, 1993).

~~~~

NAME INDEX[1]

A

Achillas	12
Adams, Edward	279
Agricola, Rudolf	39
Akira Demura	44
Albert the Great	32
Alcuin	116
Alexander of Alexandria	11–13
Alexander of Cappadocia	11
Alexander of Hales	32
Alexander of Lycopolis	12
Alexander the Great	171
Ambrose of Milan	25, 37
Ames, William	60, 126fn., 178
Ammon-Zeus	171
Anselm	xv, 34–35, 118
Aphrahat	25fn.
Aquinas, Thomas	32, 34, 35–37, 39, 156, 196, 300
Archelaus	12
Aristotle	31, 35, 208, 225
Arius	12
Arminius, Jacobus	58
Arnzen, Chris	xxiii
Asselt, van	xxxi, 30–31fn., 38fn., 39fn., 112fn., 173fn., 179fn., 205, 307, 312fn., 313
Asterius Urbanus	17
Athanasius	8, 12, 19–21, 23
Athenagoras	10
Augustine	1, 27–28, 37, 44, 55–56, 64, 106, 120, 187fn., 200, 347

---

[1] Biblical names are deferred to the subject index and are found under *Biblical characters.*

H

W

~~~~

SUBJECT INDEX

A

SUBJECT INDEX

SUBJECT INDEX

~~~~

INTERTESTAMENTAL LITERATURE

APOCRYPHAL WRITINGS

Judith

WISDOM LITERATURE

Sirach

PSEUDEPIGRAPHAL WRITINGS

The Book of Wisdom

3 Maccabees

Joseph and Aseneth

APOCALYPTIC WORKS

Psalms of Solomon

~~~~

READER'S NOTES

READER'S NOTES

READER'S NOTES

READER'S NOTES

READER'S NOTES

READER'S NOTES

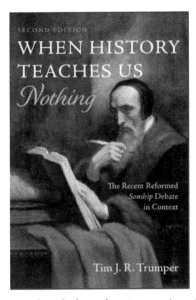

SECOND EDITION

WHEN HISTORY TEACHES US *Nothing*

The Recent Reformed *Sonship* Debate in Context

Tim J. R. Trumper

IF YOU LIKED
ADOPTION: A ROAD TO RETRIEVAL . . .

Much the buzz in confessional Presbyterian circles around the turn of the millennium, the debate concerned the discipleship course developed by practical theologian John C. ("Jack") Miller (1928–96) and his wife Rose Marie. Whereas some testified to God's use of *Sonship* in their spiritual rejuvenation, others questioned its Reformed credentials.

Setting the debate, in pioneering fashion, against the backdrop of the historical theology of adoption, Tim J. R. Trumper offers an assessment that is enlightening, evenhanded, and constructive. His fresh portrayal of the history of the Reformed tradition teaches the value of pausing before rushing to judgment. It reminds us that the meeting of spiritual needs requires more biblical exposition not less of it.

While addressing the points of debate, *When History Teaches Us Nothing* is, above all, a call to the church to recover the doctrine of adoption. Specifically, the study is a call to the Reformed community to revive her creative orthodoxy, to recapture Scripture's balance of the juridical and familial aspects of the faith, and to do so with grace.

"*When History Teaches Us Nothing* has been invaluable . . . a remarkable book"
D. Clair Davis, Professor Emeritus, Westminster Theological Seminary, PA.

"an irenic scholarly critique . . . "
Michael A. Graham, Author, *Cheer Up! The Life and Ministry of Jack Miller.*

"We are never too big to fail or too weak to prevail—this is the feeling that overwhelmed me as I read Dr. Trumper's remarkable analysis . . ."
Levente Horváth, Pastor, President of "Bonus Pastor" Reformed Rescue Mission, Romania.

Purchases can be made online from the publisher Wipf and Stock (https://wipfandstock.com/) and via Amazon outlets.

 PREACHING, TEACHING, AND PUBLISHING
CHRIST IN AND FOR THE GLOBAL CONTEXT
FOUNDED 2017

Our Mission

To equip, biblically, church leaders in their global context;
to motivate, evangelistically, international congregations in their local
communities;
and to testify, inspirationally, to the works of God across the world.

Our Work

From His Fullness operates on two main fronts—

- Offering affordable theological education and practical training to
  pastors, church leaders, and women's ministry leaders *in situ*, in areas
  of the world possessing significant need but few resources.
- Encouraging congregational outreach, especially in areas of the world
  where secularism has eroded the Judeo-Christian values of society and
  where the foundations need rebuilding. Specifically, we publish a free
  four-page, quarterly titled *The Way* currently available in English,
  Spanish, Italian, and French.

Our Vision

A global church with trained leaders and evangelistic congregations.

For further information, visit www.fromhisfullness.com. For *The Way* and/or
our newsletter, write to fromhisfullness@mail.com (not gmail!).

I praise God for establishing From His Fullness Ministries and for using the
mission around the world. I sincerely believe that God has much to deliver
to His people through From His Fullness Ministries. It is my prayer and
heart's desire that all individuals and organizations wanting to see the
growth and maturing of God's church around the globe will stand alongside
From His Fullness Ministries in whatever ways are possible so that this
ministry can proclaim unhindered the name of our Lord and Savior Jesus
Christ to those places least reached with the gospel.

Frew Tamrat, PhD., Principal, Evangelical Theological College,
Addis Ababa, Ethiopia.

~~~~

Printed in the USA
CPSIA information can be obtained
at www.ICGtesting.com
LVHW071416260124
769242LV00006B/3/J